MW00715046

PHILOSOPHICAL WRITINGS

OF

HENRY MORE

EDITED WITH INTRODUCTION AND NOTES BY

FLORA ISABEL MACKINNON, Ph.D.

ASSISTANT PROFESSOR OF PHILOSOPHY AND PSYCHOLOGY
IN WELLESLEY COLLEGE

The Wellesley Semi-Centennial Series

NEW YORK
OXFORD UNIVERSITY PRESS
AMERICAN BRANCH: 35 WEST 32ND STREET
LONDON, TORONTO, MELBOURNE & BOMBAY
1925

PREFACE

THE purpose of this volume is to rescue the name of Henry More from the list of those philosophers whom " everyone knows but no one reads." More's philosophical writings are overvoluminous, his thought is often obscure, burdened with the strange, confused, and uncritical learning of his time; but to leave him unread is to miss one of the finer spirits of English philosophy and to ignore an interesting link in the development of modern metaphysics. The attempt is here made to provide within readable compass such selections from the writings of More as shall make clear the distinctive character of his answers to the problems of truth and reality, and to suggest by introduction and notes something of the relation which his thought bears to that of other men and other times.

I gratefully acknowledge help of various kinds from sources too many to be told. The one debt which cannot be included in this general acknowledgment is my deep obligation to Professor Mary Whiton Calkins at whose suggestion the work was begun. Her counsel of wisdom and sensitive sympathy has lessened its faults and contributed largely to whatever it may have of value; to her unfailing encouragement is due in great measure its final completion and publication.

FLORA ISABEL MacKINNON

WELLESLEY, 1924.

iii

CONTENTS

INTRODUCTION

INTRODUCTION

I. BIOGRAPHICAL

A SCHOOLBOY musing wistfully on the decrees of God and the mysteries of predestination, a youth at Cambridge throwing aside his books of dialectic and dogma to seek the mystic way, an older man, eager in study and in friendship, treading his college cloister in the joy and peace of the heavenly vision: these successive phases characterize the life of Henry More, poet, philosopher, and mystic of seventeenth century England. Remote from his country and his time in that his interest lies in the quest for the eternal truths rather than in the particulars of contemporary life, he is yet so characteristically a child of his age that none of its many aspects quite fails of reflection in his thought.

The facts of More's life we learn partly from references in his own works and partly from the biography written by Richard Ward, rector of Ingoldsby and devoted friend of More from whom he held the living. Ward has been criticised as having " achieved the difficult feat of writing a biography without giving any information of its hero." [1] It is true he tells us very little, but this may be at least in part because the acts and events are so few. Through all the troublous times of the revolution More led a quiet scholar's life, saddened by the conflict but undisturbed by either party because he had accepted preferment from neither. " For some of the first fights in [the] war he continued (as he told a friend) more still and patient, hoping that at length some happy end might be put to them, . . . but things going on but worse and worse, upon the news of some sore battle his passive melancholiz'd spirit, able no longer to contain, sat it self down and with tears bewail'd the evils and miseries of his native country." [2] More's nearest rela-

[1] Rev. B. Street, Quoted by Alexander Grosart, in his Memorial Introduction, 9, to the *Poems of Henry More*.
[2] Ward, *Life of More*, p. 189.

tives were deep sufferers for the king and his own loyalty was unquestioned and unquestioning; but he felt that the dissensions were far worse than the errors of the Puritans and that the wounds and bitterness of the world could be healed only by the turning of men's minds to the love and truth of God.

Henry More was born October 12, 1614, in Grantham, Lincolnshire,[3] where Isaac Newton went to school.   His father, Alexander More, alderman and several times mayor of that town, was a strict Calvinist, though not a member of the Puritan party. With all his strictness of religion he had, however, no bigoted contempt for beauty, since his son says of him later that he had " from my childhood tuned mine ears to Spencers rhymes, entertaining us on winter nights, with that incomparable piece of his, the Fairy Queen, a poem as richly fraught with divine Morality as Phansy."[4]   At the time of More's entering college he seems to have become somewhat estranged from his father by his refusal of the Calvinist doctrine.   They were reconciled soon afterward, however, for Ward tells that his Father " coming into his Room, and seeing him there with his Books about him, and full well knowing the Tendencies of his Studies, was most highly affected with it; and in a Rapture said That he thought he spent his time in an Angelical way."[5]   More dedicated his *Philosophical Poems* to his father, wishing himself, he says, " a stranger to your blood that I might with better decorum set out the noblenesse of your spirit."

In the Preface to the Latin edition of his collected works More has given an account of his youth and early manhood which throws light on some of the forces influencing his spiritual development.[6]   " But for the better Understanding of all this, we are to take (saith he) our Rise a little higher and to premise some things which fell out in my Youth; if not also in my Childhood it self: To the end that it may more fully appear, that the things which I have written, are not any borrowed, or far-fetched Opinions, owing unto Education and the Reading of Books; but the proper Sentiments of my own Mind, drawn

[3] *Ibid.,* p. 22.
[4] *Philosophical Poems,* Dedication, To his Father.
[5] Ward, *op. cit.,* p. 60.
[6] The following quotations are from the translation in Ward, *op. cit.,* pp. 5–16.

and derived from my most intimate Nature; . . . I being bred up, to the almost 14th year of my Age, under Parents and a Master that were great Calvinists (but withal, very pious and good ones): At which time, by the order of my Parents, persuaded to it by my Uncle, I immediately went to Aeton School. . . . But neither there, nor yet anywhere else, could I ever swallow down that hard Doctrine concerning Fate. On the contrary, I remember . . . that I had such a deep aversion in my Temper to this Opinion, and so firm and unshaken a Persuasion of the Divine Justice and Goodness; that on a certain Day in a Ground belonging to Aeton College, where the Boys us'd to play and exercise themselves, musing concerning these Things with myself, and recalling to my mind this Doctrine of Calvin, I did thus seriously and deliberately conclude within myself, viz. If I am one of those that are predestinated unto Hell where all things are full of nothing but Cursing and Blasphemy, yet will I behave myself there patiently and submissively towards God; and if there be any one thing more than another, that is acceptable to him, that will I set myself to do with a sincere Heart, and to the utmost of my power: Being certainly persuaded, that if I thus demeaned myself, he would hardly keep me long in that Place. Which Meditation of mine, is as firmly fix'd in my Memory, and the very place where I stood, as if the Thing had been transacted but a Day or two ago." Emphasizing the dependence of his knowledge of God on " Nature herself " rather than on his training, More continues, " Endued as I was with these principles, . . . having spent about three years at Aeton, I went to Cambridge, recommended to the care of a person both learned and pious, and what I was not a little sollicitous about, not at all a Calvinist." This Mr. Chappell, More's tutor, was also the tutor of Milton who left Cambridge the year after More entered. Another connection with Milton is made by the fact that More also wrote verses mourning the death of Edward King, Milton's Lycidas.[7]

In these early years at Cambridge More was possessed, he recalls, of a " mighty and almost immoderate thirst after Knowledge, especially for that which was Natural; and above all others, that which was said to dive into the deepest Cause of

[7] *Philosophical Poems:* Occasional Poems, V, Memorial Introduction, p. xv.

Things, and Aristotle calls the first and highest Philosophy or
Wisdom. . . . Thus then persuaded and esteeming it what
was highly fit, I immerse myself over Head and Ears in the
study of Philosophy; promising a most wonderful Happiness to
myself in it. Aristotle therefore, Cardan, Julius Scaliger, and
other Philosophers of the greatest Note I very diligently peruse.
In which, the Truth is, though I met here and there with some
things wittily and acutely and sometimes also solidly spoken;
Yet the most seemed to me either so false or so uncertain, or
else so obvious and trivial, that I looked upon myself as having
plainly lost my time in the reading of such authors. And to
speak all in a word, Those almost whole Four Years which I
spent in Studies of this kind, as to what concern'd those Matters
which I chiefly desired to be satisfied about, . . . ended in
nothing, in a manner, but mere Scepticism. . . . And these things
happened to me before that I had taken any Degree in the
University. But after taking my Degree . . . it fell out truly
very happily for me, that I suffer'd so great a Disappointment
in my Studies. For it made me seriously at last begin to think
with myself; whether the Knowledge of things was really that
supreme Felicity of Man; . . . Or supposing it to be so, whether
it was to be acquir'd by such an Eagerness and Intentness in the
reading of Authors, and contemplating of Things, or by the
Purging of the Mind from all sorts of Vices whatsoever:
Especially having begun to read now the Platonic writers, Marsilius Ficinus, Plotinus himself, Mercurius Trismegistus; and
the Mystical Divines, among whom there was frequent mention
made of the Purification of the Soul, and of the Purgative
Course that is previous to the Illuminative; as if the Person
that expected to have his Mind illuminated of God, was to endeavor after the Highest Purity." Among all the writings of
the mystics the one which More found most to his mind was the
Theologia Germanica, " the golden little book," as Luther called
it. While deprecating the occasional melancholy mood of its
unknown author, More found its teachings the very expression
of his new convictions. " That which he doth so mightily in-
culcate," the merging of our own wills in the will of God, was,
More writes, " so Connatural, as it were, and agreeable to my
most inward Reason and Conscience that I could not of any-

thing whatsoever be more clearly or certainly convinced. . . .
But after that the Sense and Consciousness of this great and
plainly Divine Duty, was thus awakened in me: Good God!
what Struglings and Conflicts follow'd presently between this
Divine Principle and the Animal Nature! . . . And that in-
satiable Desire and Thirst of mine after the Knowledge of
things was almost wholly extinguish'd in me: as being sollicitous
now about nothing so much as a more full Union with this
Divine and Coelestial Principle, the inward flowing Wellspring
of Life Eternal: With the most fervent Prayers breathing often
unto God that he would be pleas'd throughly to set me free
from the dark Chains, and this so sordid captivity of my own
will.

" But here openly to declare the Thing as it was; When this
inordinate Desire after the Knowledge of things was thus allay'd
in me, and I aspir'd after nothing but this sole Purity and
Simplicity of Mind, there shone upon me daily a greater Assurance than ever I could have expected, even of those things which
before I had the greatest desire to know: Insomuch that within
a few years I was got into a most Joyous and Lucid state of
Mind."

Having attained to this vision and assurance, More spent his
time thenceforth in a certain quietude of mind, living as Fellow
and tutor at Christ's College, studying and writing, laboring to
share with others and to perfect in himself the peace that
possessed his spirit. From his own experience he could write
of the soul that " quit from the troubles and anxieties of this
present world, staies in it with Tranquillity and Content and at
last leaves it with joy." [8]

In appearance, according to the rector of Ingoldsby, More was
tall and thin, " of a serene and vivacious countenance," rather
pale complexion, but " clear and spiritous," his eye hazel, and
" vivid as an Eagle," his temper " sanguine yet with a due
quantity of Noble Melancholy." [9] The portrait by Loggan,
with its broad, high forehead, clearly marked lines, and firmly
curving lips, is that of a thinker and a dreamer, serene, but
neither cold nor unsympathetic. At Cambridge he was " a con-

[8] *Immortality of the Soul,* I, I, 4.
[9] Ward, *op. cit.,* pp. 228, 229.

stant Frequenter of the Publick Hall; except on Fridays which
being a Fish Day, and that a sort of Food which did not then
so well agree with him, he chose rather to Dine upon something
else in his chamber." In his hours of relaxation he was " fond
of playing at Bowles," and having some little skill in music, he
" play'd sometimes upon the Theorbo." When More was about
to be chosen Fellow of Christ's College, Ward recounts that
" they were afraid of him as a Melancholy Man, till some that
knew him . . . assured them of his being more than ordinarily
Pleasant as well as studious and serious, and that he was indeed,
in his way, one of the merriest Greeks they were acquainted
with." [10]

Though to a certain extent remote from the world in his long
quiet years at Cambridge, More was no solitary recluse, but
held warmly to many friends, both within and without the
University. Royalists, Puritans, philosophers, students, Quakers, men of the Church, and men of the world, all were greeted
in the same spirit in which he wrote to one friend, a Familist,
" For all your difference in Opinion, you should be exceeding
welcome to me, for that in you which is better than Opinion." [11]
Occasional visits to London, where he had a lodging in St.
Paul's Churchyard, and frequent guests at Cambridge kept
More in touch with the world outside the University. The diary
of his friend John Worthington gives illuminating glimpses of
the circle in which they moved and adds many concrete details
of More's life. " I should be glad," More writes to Worthington in one letter, " that your nephew's occasion or any other
might bring you to Cambridge. I have a cup of Norden's Ale
and a lesson of the lute to entertain you." [12] Among his close
friends were Lord and Lady Conway, at whose home at Ragley
More was a frequent visitor. Lady Conway, to whom the
Antidote against Atheism is dedicated, was the sister of one of
More's early pupils and became herself for a time one of his
most earnest students. She experimented with all the new
thought of the time, occultism, mystical theosophy, familism,
spiritism, and became a Quaker in spite of More's remon-

[10] *Ibid.*, pp. 54, 68, 94, 120.
[11] Letter IX, in Ward, *op. cit.* *Cf.* Epistle Dedicatory to *Antidote against
Atheism.*
[12] *Diary of John Worthington,* More to Worthington, May 19, 1671.

strances. It was at her desire that he wrote the *Conjectura Cabbalistica,* some portions of which she is said to have written herself.[13] At Ragley More met Franz Mercurious Van Helmont, son of the famous chemist, a man whose character seems to have been compounded of piety, sympathy and charlatanry, as his books are a mixture of erudition and the wildest speculation. Here came also Victor Greatrakes, a famous healer, dealing largely in superstitions and fake remedies, but combining in his mind and practice the curious lore of a vanishing day with hints of the methods of a newer time. A vivid impression of the household at Ragley is given in Joseph Shorthouse's *John Inglesant* in which More figures briefly. In dedicating his *Immortality of the Soul* to Lord Conway, More writes with appreciation of " those shady walks, those Hills and Woods " of Ragley, " where often, having lost the sight of the rest of the World, and the World of me, I found out in that hidden solitude, the choicest Theories in the following Discourse."

More carried on an extensive correspondence, both with his personal friends and with others in whom he found interests akin to his own. These included, among many, Descartes, Van Helmont, William Penn, John Norris, author of *The Ideal or Intelligible World,* William Coward, the skeptical London physician to whom More wrote the exposition of Cartesianism included in his collected works, Cudworth, Glanvil, and Baron Knorr, the compiler of the first Latin translation of the *Cabbala.* More's letters to Descartes reflect the early enthusiasm and the gradually growing opposition which characterized his attitude to the Cartesian philosophy. They are the object of severe censure in Baillet's *Life of Descartes,* in which More is accused of wilful and insincere inconstancy. The letters to Norris are those of an older student to a beginner in the way that he has travelled. Their tone of sympathetic encouragement roused Norris's sincere appreciation even while their content left his doubts still unresolved.[14]

[13] Worthington, *op. cit.,* Vol. II, Pt. i, p. 94.

[14] The correspondence with Descartes is published in volume V of the Adam and Tannery edition of Descartes's works, and, in part, in More's collected philosophical writings. The correspondence with Norris is included in Norris's *Theory and Regulation of Love.* For other letters see Ward, *op. cit.,* and Worthington's *Diary.*

While devotedly attached to the established Church of England, finding no cause for complaint either in its creed or in its
manner of worship, More yet formed one of that group of
Latitude-Men who upheld the beauty and power of toleration in
a day of religious conflict and fanaticism.   Partly from the influence of Whichcote and Smith, his friends and teachers, partly
from his own sense of the unimportance of many of the points
of bitterest controversy, More took little part in the doctrinal
disputations of his time.   He deplored the " unrighteousness
of Schisms and Sects amongst us," emphasized the value of
" Right Liberty of Conscience," and insisted that differences of
religious opinions matter little if men will but " serve God in
them in the simplicity and sincerity of their hearts." [15]   His
toleration, though unusually broad for his time, did not extend
to those whom he calls Enthusiasts or Familists, " that sweet
sect that have usurped to themselves the Title of the Family
of Love."   These, because of their denial of historic revelation
and their complete reliance upon individual intuition and emotion as a guide to truth, seemed to him to deny the possibility
of a reasonable religion and to expose Christianity to all the
scorn of its critics.   The Cambridge Platonists, as the " Latitude-Men " later came to be called, while admitting the reality
and value of inspiration, were distinguished from the Enthusiasts
and Quakers by their emphasis on the importance of reason in
religion.   This emphasis connects them with the deistic writers
of the period, from whom, however, they are clearly separated
by their belief in revelation, by the insistence that true knowledge comes only to the pure in heart, and by that sense of
immediate communion with God which is their inheritance from
the mystics of all ages.

In most of his interests More was associated with some or all
of this group of the Cambridge Platonists with whom his name
is always connected.   Held together by personal friendships, by
academic associations, by common philosophical interests, and
by their common opposition to dogmatism and intolerance, they
formed the center of a broad movement of philosophical religion in seventeenth century England.   More, in Tulloch's

[15] *Mystery of Godliness*, X, 1 and 2, To the Reader 13; *Cf. Philosophical
Poems*, Song of the Soul, To the Reader.

phrase, " at once the most typical and the most vital and interesting " [16] of them all, is to a certain extent differentiated from the others by the variety of his interests. Primarily, like Smith and Whichcote, a student of divinity, he was also interested in the new science of the time and was one of the early members of the Royal Society. With Cudworth he labored to establish religion and morality against the atheism and scepticism of Hobbes; with Gale he sought to prove the dependence of ancient philosophies on the Hebrew Scriptures; with Pordage he explored the literature of mysticism; with Glanvil he delved into the mysteries of haunted houses and familiar spirits. With all his devotion to ancient and modern learning, More never lost his keen sense for beauty, whether in nature or in the smoothly flowing rhythms of his favorite poets. To Virgil and Horace he refers again and again, and occasionally to the other Latin poets and to the Greek dramatists. His first publicly published work was in the form of philosophical poems, long, complex, and wearisome expositions of Platonic philosophy in Spenserian verse, relieved by gleams of simple sincere feeling and by occasional briefly expressive phrase. Always eager and interested, he never lost his enthusiasm for study or his zeal for writing. At the time of his death he was engaged, according to Ward, on a work called *Medela Mundi;* and a short time before he had written to a friend, " If it please God, that I live to finish the present task I am taken up with, it is likely enough I shall write such a practical treatise in English which I have long since called " The Safe Guide." [17]

More died September 1, 1687, and was buried in Christ's College chapel. The hope that he voiced for others had been fulfilled in himself, " Thy way shall be made so plain before thee, that thou shalt not err nor stumble, but arrive at last to the desired Scope of all thy Travels and Endeavors, to a firm peace and unfailing Righteousness and shall be fulfilled with all the fullness of God."

[16] *Rational Theology and Christian Philosophy,* II, 303.
[17] Ward, *op. cit.,* p. 212.

II. Critical and Historical

In many of our histories of philosophy Descartes is hailed as the originator of modern ways of thinking, the Father of Modern Philosophy. True as this estimate is in many respects, from another point of view Cartesianism is less the beginning of the new era than the culmination of the old. In the *Meditations* and the *Principles* Descartes gives definite form and clear statement to that division of the universe and of the life of man into two distinct parts which was implicit in much of preceding thought. Foreshadowed in the Platonic dialogues and in the Neo-Platonic writings, the dualism of matter and spirit is implied in most of the scholastic philosophy, growing out of the earlier logical distinction between matter and form, and needed only the application of the Cartesian method to bring it to clear formulation. The course of philosophy in the period immediately following the work of Descartes was in part a further working out of his ideas, but in large measure it consisted in a reaction against this sundering of reality, this unbridged chasm between body and mind.

In the main line of English philosophy of the seventeenth and eighteenth centuries this opposition to dualism appeared on the one hand in the materialism of Hobbes, and on the other in various forms of subjective idealism. In each case the demand for unity was met by the sacrifice of one of the factors of traditional dualism. In the same time of transition there were other attempts to overcome this opposition of matter and spirit. Though inadequate, often, and incomplete, these show the same groping after a unified conception of reality. Among them is the work of Henry More. In partly conscious antagonism to the prevailing method of analysis and division, More emphasizes the concrete unity of life and spirit. In clearly stated opposition to Hobbes he insists on the inadequacy and the danger of the materialistic theory. His opposition is not directed against the belief in the reality of matter so much as against the assertion of matter as the only reality, as containing in itself an adequate explanation of the world. But the philosophical connection of More, as that also of Cudworth, is rather with the development of vitalistic speculation than with either the idealism or the materialism of seventeenth century thought. The sense of the pervading life and activity of the universe, which goes back for its earliest expression to the animism of primitive belief, had been strongly felt by the nature-philosophers of the Renaissance. Their reaction against the barren categories of the peripatetic philosophy led them at once backward to the mystical thought of Alexandrian Platonism and forward into the new science of observation and experiment. Levying upon remote and noble sources, they endeavored to combine in one fabric of thought the cosmology of the *Timaeus,* the magical number-theories of the Pythagoreans, the vivid mysticism of Plotinus, and the ancient wisdom of Egypt. In the pantheistic mysticism of Giordano Bruno, the magico-medical theories of Paracelsus and Van Helmont, the mingled scepticism and superstition of Cornelius Agrippa, is shown in varying forms this sense of the unity of man with nature which was denied by the dualism of more orthodox writers. It is in this tradition, rather than in the epistemological development of English philosophy, that More's thought finds its place. Insisting on the continuity between man and nature, he likewise asserts the intimate connection between man and God. The soul is divine, bearing the image of God, " akin to the divine and immortal and ever-existent "; the reason of man is the " candle of the Lord " lighting the path to truth and righteousness. Though influenced by contemporary movements, and bound in many ways by the scholasticism which set the pattern of his thinking, More's spirit goes back to " the golden chain of the Platonic succession," to find there the true companions of its wanderings.

Since his interest lay rather in the spiritual significance of his doctrine than in its logical formulation, More has nowhere set it forth completely in systematic form, but its main outlines can be gathered from any one of his philosophical works. The various aspects of his thought are most clearly shown in the *Immortality of the Soul* and the *Antidote against Atheism,* although the *Divine Dialogues,* easier reading because less cumbered with learned digressions, is more generally known than either of the others. There are no signs of growth in More's thought, no increase in depth or lucidity, after the publication of the *Divine Dialogues* in 1668. The later philosophical writings are almost entirely amplifications of the doctrine of the earlier books, and questions of prophetical interpretation come to take an ever larger place in his work.

The unquestioned, uncriticised principle which underlies all More's philosophical thinking is that of the unity of reality. Anything which opposes this original affirmation is clearly unthinkable. Unrealized contradictions there may be, mysteries beyond human comprehension there certainly are, but the essential identity of faith and reason, the oneness of the world of nature and the world of truth, the thorough-going connection of reality and knowledge, though never clearly stated, are assumed in all More's doctrine, unquestioned even in his most skeptical moments, exercising over his thought all the power for good and ill that lies in assured but unanalyzed conviction. The effects of this fundamental insistence on unity are seen in all his writings, in his choice of guides for his thinking, and in the accepted maxims that are the basis of his philosophy. He had also a strong sense of fact, when not misled by enthusiasm, and held firmly that experience must be the test of truth. On both these grounds More felt Descartes's dualism to be an impossible conception. That clear-cut cleavage of reality into spirit and matter, so separated as to be incapable of reunion even in thought, he found opposed both by reason and by experience. He saw clearly and expressed effectively the fundamental difficulty of materialism, but, so far as is shown in his writings, never even considered the opposite method of idealism. More's way out of the dualistic dilemma was not that of denying the reality either of matter or of spirit, but consisted in bringing them closer together, denying the fissure between them by asserting that their likeness and their connection are far more fundamental than their differences. The exact line between soul and body in man, between spirit and matter in the universe, becomes in More's hands a wavy, misty, boundary, so that it is impossible to trace just where, for him, the one passes over into the other.

More emphasizes the difficulties inherent in identifying matter and extension, thus breaking completely with Descartes. His argument is often a mixture of emotion and assertion, set out

in all the panoply of logical form; his solution of the problem
of the relation between matter and spirit is inadequate and at
points ambiguous; but he had a clear sense of some impossibilities which must be avoided in any reasonable conception of
the universe. Although More never questions the real existence
of material substance, his treatment of it is confused and contradictory. The only clear and unambiguous difference between
material and spiritual substance in his discussion lies in the
assertion that two bodies cannot occupy the same space at the
same time, while spirits, being extended but " penetrable," are
not subject to this limitation. If one combines, as More apparently never thought of combining, this sole distinction between
matter and spirit with the argument in the *Enchiridion Meta-*
physicum that space itself is immaterial, may indeed be considered as a manifestation of the infinite spirit, the result is a
queer hybrid conception, in which matter, though independently
real, is dependent for meaning on its relation to spirit. More
himself insists that none of the objects or events in the world
can be explained in terms of matter alone. There are " no
purely mechanical phenomena in the universe." [18]

But, in truth, More has little interest, one way or the other,
in matter. His abiding concern is with the spirit itself. He
spends himself gallantly in defence of its reality, caring little,
it would seem, whether the spirit be that of man, of God, or of
a world-soul, if so be he may prove to all comers the futility
of trying to conceive of reality in purely material terms. It is
from the standpoint of this insistence on the reality of spirit,
of " that which a man knows himself to be," that one has the
clearest view both of the value of More's thinking and of his
relation to his contemporaries and successors. He lacks that
disinterested vision, that following of the argument whither-
soever it may lead, which is the mark of the great lover of
truth. He comes to test all arguments, judge all doctrines, less
by their inherent value than by their adaptation to this end of
upholding the assurance of spiritual reality. The theory of
knowledge contributes its doctrine of the activity of the mind
in thought and perception; physics and physiology are made
to build up the argument from design; experiment, reason, and

[18] *Divine Dialogues,* " To the Reader," X; *Cf.* Dialogue I, *passim.*

authority combine to show that the nature of the world, the nature of space, and the nature of consciousness, all are inexplicable save on the basis of the ultimate reality of spirit. In lesser points More is unbiased and open-minded, devoted to old truths, but without prejudice against new thoughts, tolerant of differences in philosophical thinking as of divergencies in religious creed. Even those conceptions which plainly oppose his previous convictions he would not absolutely refuse, having, as he says, " sworn more faithful friendship with Truth than with myself." [19] It is only when new thoughts seem to endanger the pre-eminence of spiritual reality in the universe that More is too far swayed by the importance of the issue to follow the narrow path of pure reason. His refusal to accept the mechanical explanations of natural phenomena which were gradually being worked out by the new science is argued with sincere conviction and great wealth of detail, but beneath the argument, moulding and directing it, lies the inner conviction that the mechanical explanation is necessarily inadequate since its truth would deny the spiritual meaning of reality.

More's treatment of the problem of evil is marked by the easy optimism of his time. His dismissal of " what the ignorant call evil in this universe " as being nothing more than " the shadowy stroakes in a fair picture, or the mournful notes in Musick, by which the beauty of the one is more lively and express and the melody of the other more pleasing and melting," is very like the evasion of the same difficulty by Leibniz and Berkeley.[20] More does, however, avoid the obvious fallacy of Berkeley's argument since he bases his assertion of the goodness of God less on the beneficence of nature than on the necessary inclusion of moral goodness in the conception of a perfect being.

Another result of the lack of clear discrimination in More's thinking is seen in his tendency to include both of two alternative solutions to a problem without showing the relation between them. In his explanation of bodily movements, for example, he holds both the mechanical principle of the animal spirits

[19] *Philosophical Poems*, Democritus Platonissans: " To the Reader."
[20] *Immortality of the Soul*, III, 15, 9; Berkeley, *Principles of Human Knowledge*, CLII and CLIII; Leibniz, *Theodicy*.

and the vitalistic conception of a " plastic soul "; in the doctrine of knowledge he interprets innate idea or common notion sometimes in the sense of mental activity and sometimes in the sense of an inborn principle, known without experience; in his opposition to the Cartesian identification of extension and matter he argues at one time that spirit as well as matter is extended in space, and at another that space itself is not real but " notional."

More's claim to a distinctive place in English philosophy does not rest either on the completeness or logical precision of his doctrine or on any direct contribution to that transition from dualism to idealism which is the outstanding philosophical movement of his time. The value of his thought is to be found, first, in its historical significance as carrying on the tradition of mystical and vitalistic speculation, and secondly, in the vigor and insight with which he suggests certain conceptions which did not attain clear formulation until a triumphing idealism revealed its own need of criticism and analysis. His insistence on the real unity of consciousness and his opposition to the " white paper " doctrine of mind form his connection with Kant and the Scottish philosophy; his assertion of activity as the fundamental character of reality connects him with Leibniz and with the personalists of a later day.

Freed from the defects with which his fears and enthusiasms burdened it, More's doctrine of spirit is noteworthy as an anticipatory reply to Hume's rejection of the self and as a foreshadowing of later conflicts between absolutism and pluralism. His use of the argument for the reality of spirit from the nature of " common percipiency," like Kant's doctrine of " the synthesis of apprehension," is an assertion of the unity of individual experience, in opposition to any attempt to substitute for that unity a mere succession of ideas. His whole argument against a materialistic interpretation of consciousness is based on this conviction that the soul or self cannot be resolved into a manifold of " shreds and rags of spirit," but has in itself a principle of unity and self-identity. In his criticism of Hobbes he gives new emphasis to the unity of self-consciousness by noting the " obscurity " which is caused by " talking of Faculties and Operations as separate from the Essence they belong to." [21] On

[21] *Immortality of the Soul*, II, III, 8.

the basis of this same assertion of the self-identity of the individual, More argues that the soul of the world cannot be considered as including human souls. Unconscious spirits, he holds, or those which are barely conscious, may perhaps be considered as forming parts of a greater spirit, but any degree of self-consciousness is irreconcilable with such a conception.

Another point at which More makes a definite contribution to philosophical theory is in his recognition of the activity of mind. In the doctrine of innate ideas to which More frequently recurs, as in the principle of the " notion " set forth by Richard Burthogge, his contemporary, is involved that conception of the mind's active contribution to the formation of its own object which finds fuller development in Kantian doctrine. For More the innate ideas, or common notions, are not a certain number of ideas implanted in the soul, but the " active sagacity " of the soul herself, the mind ordering and systematizing sense-impressions by means of its own original activity. The ideas of relation, of cause, of equality, difference, and the like, are not impressions on the soul from without, but neither are they completely independent of experience since they come to light only in application to experience. In actual argument, however, More occasionally betrays his own doctrine and ascribes to intuitive knowledge, not simply the forms of the mind's activity, but those principles of morality and religion which he feels to be necessarily true but is unable to justify. In such ways does his enthusiasm overpower his critical sense so that his insight into the nature of knowledge fails to develop into a real critique of reason.

More's doctrine of spirit is very like that of Leibniz in its recognition of the importance of individuality and in its emphasis on activity as the essential character of spiritual substance. He holds clearly and even vehemently that an individual soul can neither be divided into parts nor become part of another without loss of its own reality, but this individuality does not involve absolute separateness. His sense of the real unity of all things is too strong to admit of a cold and barren pluralism. Spirits, according to More, are distinct one from another, but not utterly separate; they are " penetrable," not cut off from each other but entering into the closest and most intimate relationship. He does not argue this penetrability of spirit, insisting that it is an " immediate attribute," and as such can only be accepted, not explained or demonstrated; but he leaves no doubt of the importance he attaches to this principle of union in an otherwise monadistic universe. More nowhere makes clear his conception of the relation between God and created spirits. From his acceptance of the Platonic analogy between the relation of the individual soul to its body and the relation of God to the whole physical universe, it would seem as if he might consider God as all-inclusive as well as all-creating. But the whole discussion of the different classes of spirits makes against the probability of this interpretation. Both More's emphasis on the reality of spirit and his assertion of direct interrelation between spirits may be considered to have their source in the mysticism which pervaded his thought and characterized his attitude toward reality. The accentuation of the inner life which plays so large a part in the mystic experience necessarily has as its theoretical counterpart the recognition of self-consciousness as the starting-point of philosophical theory. And the very conception of the goal of the mystic's endeavor as the attainment of real communion with God makes impossible the denial of the direct interrelation of spirits.

Through all More's writings can be traced the three main currents of varying admiration and criticism of Descartes, of opposition to Hobbes, and of devotion to Plato and the Platonists. " The Philosophy of that pleasant wit Renatus des Cartes," More describes at one time as " the most admirable that ever yet appeared in these European parts "; but at other times his distrust of the mechanistic aspects of Cartesianism causes him to write scornfully of his own previous admiration. More's whole attitude toward the Cartesian philosophy turns, in fact, on his conception of its bearing on the question of the reality of spirit. Agreeing enthusiastically with Descartes's doctrine of the independence of the soul from matter, he rejects absolutely the materialistic and mechanistic interpretation of the natural world which seemed to be the goal of Descartes's theories of physics.

For More, as for all his like-minded contemporaries, Hobbes

stands as the very embodiment of all that they most condemned and feared. Against him were raised all the voices of orthodox churchmen and moralists. His materialistic philosophy, the more to be dreaded because of its very clearness and plausibility, the more to be distrusted because of its outward conformity to established doctrine, provided at once a strong stimulus to the reassertion of the claims of the spirit and a definite point against which to direct the attack. More's attempts to show that natural facts cannot be mechanically explained are frequently weak and sophistical, but he states clearly the failure of the materialist to justify his initial assumption. The assertion that all that exists is matter is, More says, " mear precarious opinion," neither immediately known nor capable of proof.[22]

It is rather because of More's reverence for Plato than from clear understanding or following of Platonic doctrine that he is given the name of Platonist. There are reflections in his writings of the arguments of the *Theaetetus,* the *Parmenides,* and the *Phaedo,* and, most obviously, of the myth of the *Timaeus;* but of the characteristically Platonic method he shows little trace, and the Platonic doctrine of ideas appears only in so far as it influences his argument for the reality of spirit. More and Cudworth, Whichcote, Smith, and Worthington, and the other men more or less closely connected with their group at Cambridge, made common cause against whatever seemed to threaten the spiritual reality in the universe. For many of them the Platonic tradition seemed to offer a stronger bulwark against the attacks of atheism than any of the current philosophical conceptions. This common devotion to Plato was unmarred by any realization of the fact that their interpretation of their master is Neo-Platonic rather than purely Greek. Their Platonism is in large part that of Plotinus, of Marsilius Ficinus, or of the mediaeval mystics, but it is all attributed to Plato, of whom More writes, " I do with my pen, my mouth and from my heart praise that excellent philosophy of Plato's as the most consistent and coherent Metaphysical Hypothesis that has yet been found out by the wit of man."

In addition to these predominant elements, we find in More

---

[22] *Enchiridion Metaphysicum,* XXVIII, 20; *Immortality of the Soul,* I, IX and II, III.

nearly all of those many-motived tendencies that run through the thought of the seventeenth century. Like a gorgeous tapestry in which many-colored threads appear and disappear, obscuring the main design by the very luxuriance of their inter-weaving, More's thought takes up into itself these threads from the past without too close regard for their mutual harmony. Aristotle's logic filtered through the theology cf the Schoolmen, the mystic pantheism of Plotinus adapted by Augustine to the demands of Christianity, Jewish philosophy and mysticism, the allegorical interpretations of the Cabbalists, the symbolism of Gnostics and Rosicrucians, with its "shadowy attendants of magic and alchemy," all these thoughts and visions from the past ages of philosophy mingle almost unassimilated with the new science stimulated by Bacon and Descartes. The conflict between the old and the new, between authority and reason in religion, between rationalism and empiricism in philosophy, is reflected in More's writings less as conflict than as an attempt to incorporate into his thought all the elements that seem to him to have value either in themselves or for his main purpose. In his volumes, as the very type of the time in which he lived, the crudest superstitions of witchcraft and folklore appear side by side in apparent harmony and concord with clear thought, scientific deduction, and acute psychological observation. His work has for a later day the value of any sincere attempt to gain a vision of the truth. Besides this it has the interest which results from the very inclusiveness which mars its internal con-sistency. It is as a glass in which one may see the transition from mediaeval to modern philosophy, an unstable compound in which one can find by analysis the elements which have sur-vived through the changing thought of the centuries, and trace the beginning of new combinations, the formation of new con-ceptions never completely severed from the old.

This introduction to the selections from Henry More's writ-ings commits them to the reader with the concluding words from More's own foreword to one of his poems. " Reader, 'tis time now to leave thee to the perusall of my writings, which if they chance to please thee, I repent me not of my pains: if they chance not to please, that shall not displease me much, for I consider that I also with small content and pleasure have read the writings of other men."

An

ANTIDOTE
AGAINST
ATHEISM
o r,

An Appeal to the Natural Faculties of
the Mind of Man, Whether there
be not a GOD.

By *HENRY MORE*, D.D.

The *third Edition* corrected and enlarged:
with
AN APPENDIX
thereunto annexed.

Trismegist.
Ἡ μεγάλη νόσος τῆς ψυχῆς ἡ ἀθεότης.

Aristot.
Οἱ ἄνθρωποι πρὸς τὸ ἀληθὲς πεφύκασιν ἱκανῶς, καὶ τὰ πλείω τυγχάνουσι
τῆς ἀληθείας.

LONDON,
Printed by *James Flesher*, for *William Morden* Book-
seller in *Cambridge*.
MDCLXII.

AN
ANTIDOTE
AGAINST
ATHEISM

BOOK I.

CHAP. I.

1. *That the Pronenesse of these Ages of the World to winde themselves from under the awe of Superstition makes the attempt seasonable of endeavouring to steer them off from Atheisme.* 2. *That they that adhere to Religion in a mere superstitious and accustomary way, if that tye once fail, easily turn Atheists.* 3. *The usefulness of this present Treatise even to them that are seriously Religious.*

1. The grand Truth which we are now to be imployed about and to prove, is, *That there is a God:* And I made choice of this Subject as very seasonable for the Times we are in, and are coming on, wherein Divine Providence more universally loosening the minds of men from the awe and tyranny of mere accustomary Superstition, and permitting a freer perusal of matters of Religion than in former Ages, the Tempter would take advantage, where he may, to carry men captive out of one dark prison into another, out of *Superstition* into *Atheism* it self.

2. Which is a thing feasible enough for him to bring about in such men as have adhered to Religion in a mere externall way, either for fashion sake, or in blinde obedience to the Authority of a Church. For when this externall frame of Godliness shall break about their ears, they being really at the bottome devoid of the true fear and love of God, and destitute of a more free and unprejudic'd use of their Faculties, by reason of the sinfulness and corruption of their natures, it will be an easy thing to allure them to an assent to that which seems so

3

much for their present Interest; and so being imboldened by the tottering and falling of what they took for the chief Structure of Religion before, they will gladly in their conceit cast down also the very Object of that Religious Worship after it, and conclude that there is as well no God as no Religion; that is, they have a mind there should be none, that they may be free from all wringings of Conscience, trouble of correcting their Lives, and fear of being accountable before that great Tribunall.

3. Wherefore for the reclaiming of these, if it were possible, at least for the succouring and extricating of those in whom a greater measure of the love of God doth dwell, (who may probably by some darkening cloud of Melancholy, or some more then ordinary importunity of the Tempter, be dissettled and intangled in their thoughts concerning this weighty matter) I held it fit to bestow mine endeavours upon this so useful and seasonable enterprise, as to demonstrate *That there is a God.*

CHAP. II.

1. *That there is nothing so demonstrable, that the Mind of man can rationally conclude that it is impossible to be otherwise.* 2. *That the Soul of man may give full Assent to that which notwithstanding may possibly be otherwise, made good by severall Examples.* 3. *A like Example of Dissent.* 4. *The Reasons why he has so sedulously made good this point.* 5. *That the Atheist has no advantage from the Authour's free confession, that his Arguments are not so convictive but that they leave a possibilitiy of the thing being otherwise.*

1. But when I speak of demonstrating there is a God, I would not be suspected of so much vanity and ostentation, as to be thought I mean to bring no Arguments but such as are so convictive, that a mans Understanding shall be forced to confesse that it is impossible to be otherwise then I have concluded. For, for mine own part, I am prone to believe that there is nothing at all to be so demonstrated. For it is possible that *Mathematical evidence* it self may be but a constant undis-

coverable Delusion, which our nature is necessarily and perpetually obnoxious unto, and that either fatally or fortuitously
there has been in the world time out of minde such a Being
as we call *Man,* whose essentiall Property it is to be then most
of all mistaken, when he conceives a thing most evidently
true. (1)* And why may not this be as well as any thing else,
if you will have all things fatall or casuall without a God?
For there can be no curb to this wilde conceit, but by supposing that we our selves exist from some higher Principle that is
absolutely *Good* and *Wise,* which is all one as to acknowledge
That there is a God.

2. Wherefore when I say that I will demonstrate *That there
is a God,* I do not promise that I will alwayes produce such
Arguments, that the Reader shall acknowledge so strong, as
he shall be forced to confesse that it is utterly unpossible that
it should be otherwise: but they shall be such as shall deserve
full assent, and win *full assent* from any unprejudic'd mind.

For I conceive that we may give *full assent* to that which
notwithstanding may possibly be otherwise: which I shall illustrate by severall Examples. Suppose two men got to the top of
mount *Athos,* and there viewing a Stone in the form of an *Altar*
with *Ashes* on it, and the *footsteps of men* on those ashes, or
some *words,* if you will, as *Optimo Maximo,* or τῷ ἀγνώστῳ θεῷ,
or the like, written or scralled out upon the ashes; and one
of them should cry out, Assuredly here have been some men
here that have done this: but the other more nice than wise
should reply, Nay, it may possibly be otherwise; for this stone
may have naturally grown into this very shape, and the seeming
ashes may be no ashes, that is, no remainders of any fewell
burnt there, but some unexplicable and imperceptible motions
of the Airè, or other particles of this fluid Matter that is
active every where, have wrought some parts of the Matter
into the form and nature of ashes, and have fridg'd and play'd
about so, that they have also figured those intelligible Characters in the same. But would not any body deem it a piece of
weaknesse no less than dotage for the other man one whit to
recede from his former apprehension, but as fully as ever to

* This number and those of like form which follow refer to the editor's
notes, historical and bibliographical, in the Appendix, beginning on page 310.

agree with what he pronounced first, notwithstanding this bare possibility of being otherwise?

So of *Anchors* that have been digged up, either in plain fields or mountainous places, as also the *Roman Urnes* with ashes and inscriptions, as *Severianus, Ful. Linus,* and the like, or *Roman Coins* with the *effigies* and *names* of the *Caesars* on them, or that which is more ordinary, the *Sculls* of men in every Church-yard, with the right figure, and all those necessary perforations for the passing of the vessels, besides those conspicuous hollows for the eyes and rowes of teeth, the *Os Styloeides, Ethoeides,* and what not? if a man will say of them, that the Motion of the particles of the Matter, or some hidden Spermatick power has gendered these both *Anchors, Urnes, Coins,* and *Sculls* in the ground, he doth but pronounce that which humane Reason must admit as possible: Nor can any man ever so demonstrate that those *Coins, Anchors* and *Urnes* were once the Artifice of men, or that this or that *Scull* was once a part of a living man, that he shall force an acknowledgment that it is impossible that it should be otherwise. But yet I do not think that any man, without doing manifest violence to his Faculties, can at all suspend his assent, but freely and fully agree that this or that *Scull* was once part of a living man, and that these *Anchors, Urnes* and *Coins,* were certainly once made by humane artifice, notwithstanding the possibility of being otherwise.

3. And what I have said of *Assent* is also true in *Dissent.* For the Mind of man, not craz'd nor prejudic'd will fully and unreconcilably disagree, by its own naturall sagacity, where notwithstanding the thing that it doth thus resolvedly and undoubtingly reject, no wit of man can prove impossible to be true. As if we should make such a Fiction as this, that *Archimedes* (2) with the same individuall body that he had when the Souldiers slew him, is now safely intent upon his Geometricall Figures under ground, at the Center of the Earth, farre from the noise and din of this world, that might disturb his Meditations, or distract him in his curious delineations he makes with his Rod upon the dust; which no man living can prove impossible: Yet if any man does not as unreconcilably dissent from such a Fable as this as from any Falshood imagin-

able, assuredly that man is next door to madness or dotage, or does enormous violence to the free use of his Faculties.

Wherefore it is manifest that there may be a very firm and unwavering *Assent* or *Dissent,* whenas yet the thing we thus assent to may be possibly otherwise, or that which we thus dissent from cannot be proved impossible to be true.

4. Which point I have thus long and thus variously sported my self in, for making the better impression upon my Reader, it being of no small use and consequence, as well for the advertising of him that the Arguments which I shall produce, though I do not bestow that ostentative term of *Demonstration* upon them, yet they may be as effectual for winning *a firm and unshaken assent* as if they were in the strictest notion such; as also to re-minde him, that if they be so strong, and so patly fitted and sutable with the Faculties of mans Mind, that he has nothing to reply, but only that for all this it may possibly be otherwise, that he should give a free and full *Assent* to the Conclusion: and if he do not, that he is to suspect himself rather of some distemper, prejudice, or weakness, then the Arguments of want of strength.

5. But if the *Atheist* shall contrariwise pervert my candour and fair dealing, and phansie that he has got some advantage upon my free confession, that the Arguments that I shall use are not so convictive but that they leave a possibilty of the thing being otherwise; let him but compute his supposed gains, by adding the limitation of this possibility, (*viz.* that it is no more possible, then that the clearest *Mathematicall evidence* may be false, (which is impossible, if our Faculties be true) or in the second place, then that the *Roman Urnes* and *Coins* above mentioned may prove to be the works of Nature, not the Artifice of man; which our Faculties admit to be so little probable, that it is impossible for them not fully to assent to the contrary:) and when he has cast up his account, it will be evident that it can be nothing but his grosse ignorance in this kinde of Arithmetick that shall embolden him to write himself down gainer, and not me.

CHAP. III.

1. *That we are first to have a settled notion* What God is, *before we goe about to demonstrate* That he is.   2. *The Definition of God.*   3. *That there is an* Idea *of a Being absolutely perfect in our Minde, whether the* Atheist *will allow it to be the* Idea *of God or not.*   4. *That it is no prejudice to the Naturality of this* Idea, *that it may be framed from some occasions from without.*

1. And now having premised thus much, I shall come on nearer to my present designe. In prosecution whereof it will be requisite for me, first to define *What God is,* before I proceed to demonstration *That he is.* For it is obvious for Man's Reason to finde Arguments for the impossibility, possibility, probability, or necessity of the Existence of a thing, from the explication of the Essence thereof.

And now I am come hither, I demand of any *Atheist* that denies there is a God, or of any that doubts whether there be one or no, what *Idea* or *Notion* they frame of that they deny or doubt of. If they will prove nice and squeamish, and profess they can frame no *Notion* of any such thing, I would gladly ask them, why they will then deny or doubt of they know not what. For it is necessary that he that would rationally doubt or deny a thing, should have some settled *Notion* of the thing he doubts of or denies. But if they profess that this is the very ground of their denying or doubting whether there be a God, because they can frame no *Notion* of him; I shall forthwith take away that Allegation, by offering them such a *Notion* as is as proper to God, as any *Notion* is proper to any thing else in the world.

2. I define God therefore thus, *An Essence* or *Being fully and absolutely Perfect.* I say, *fully and absolutely Perfect,* in counterdistinction to such *Perfection* as is not *full* and *absolute,* but the Perfection of this or that *Species* or *Kind* of *finite Beings,* suppose of a Lion, Horse, or Tree. But to be *fully and absolutely Perfect* is to be at least as Perfect as the apprehension of a man can conceive without a contradiction: for what is

inconceivable or contradictious, is nothing at all to us, who are not now to wag one Atome beyond our Faculties; but what I have propounded is so far from being beyond our Faculties, that I dare appeal to any *Atheist,* that hath yet any command of Sense and Reason left in him, if it be not very easy and intelligible at the first sight, and that if there be a God, he is to be deemed of us such as this *Idea* or *Notion* sets forth.

3. But if he will sullenly deny that this is the proper Notion of God, let him enjoy his own humour; this yet remains undeniable, That there is in man an *Idea* of a *Being absolutely and fully Perfect,* which we frame out by attributing all conceivable *Perfection* to it whatsoever that implies no contradiction. And *this Notion* is naturall and essentiall to the Soul of man, & cannot be washt out, nor conveigh'd away by any force or trick of wit whatsoever, so long as the Mind of man is not craz'd but hath the ordinary use of her own Faculties.

4. Nor will that prove any thing to the purpose, whenas it shall be alleg'd that *this Notion* is not so connatural and essential to the Soul, because she framed it from some occasions from without. For all those undeniable Conclusions in Geometry which might be help'd and occasioned from something without, are so natural notwithstanding and Essentiall to the Soul, that you may as soon unsoul the Soul as divide her from perpetual assent to those Mathematical Truths, supposing no distemper nor violence offered to her Faculties. As for example, she cannot but acknowledge in her self the *several distinct Ideas of the five regular Bodies,* as also, *that it is impossible that there should be any more then five.* (3) And this *Idea* of *a Being absolutely Perfect* is as distinct and indeleble an *Idea* in the Soul, as the *Idea* of the *five Regular Bodies,* or any other *Idea* whatsoever.

It remains therefore undeniable, that there is an inseparable *Idea* of *a Being absolutely Perfect* ever residing, though not alwayes acting, in the Soul of man.

CHAP. IV.

1. *What Notions are more particularly comprised in the* Idea *of* a Being absolutely Perfect. 2. *That the difficulty of framing the conception of a thing ought to be no Argument against the Existence thereof; the nature of corporeall Matter being so perplex'd and intricate, which yet all men acknowledge to exist.* 3. *That the* Idea *of a* Spirit *is as easy a Notion as of any other Substance whatsoever. What powers and properties are contained in the Notion of a* Spirit. 4. *That* Eternity *and* Infinity, *if God were not, would be cast upon something else; so that* Atheism *cannot free the Mind from such Intricacies.* 5. Goodness, Knowledge *and* Power, *Notions of highest Perfection, and therefore necessarily included in the* Idea *of* a Being absolutely Perfect. 6. *As also* Necessity, *it sounding greater Perfection then* Contingency.

1. But now to lay out more particularly the *Perfections* comprehended in this Notion of *a Being absolutely and fully Perfect,* I think I may securely nominate these; *Self-subsistency, Immateriality, Infinity as well of Duration as Essence, Immensity of Goodnesse, Omnisciency, Omnipotency,* and *Necessity of Existence.* Let this therefore be the Description of *a Being absolutely Perfect,* That it is *a Spirit, Eternall, Infinite in Essence and Goodnesse, Omniscient, Omnipotent, and of it self necessarily existent.* All which *Attributes* being *Attributes* of the *highest Perfection* that falls under the apprehension of man, and having no discoverable imperfection interwoven with them, must of necessity be attributed to that which we conceive *absolutely and fully Perfect.* And if anyone will say that this is but to dress up a *Notion* out of my own fancy, which I would afterwards slily insinuate to be the Notion of a *God;* I answer, that no man can discourse and reason of any thing without recourse to settled Notions deciphered in his own Mind: and that such an Exception as this implies the most contradictious Absurdities imaginable, to wit, as if a man should reason from something that never entered into his Mind, or that is utterly

out of the ken of his own Faculties. But such groundless allegations as these discover nothing but an unwillingness to find themselves able to entertain any conception of God, and a heavy propension to sink down into an utter oblivion of him, and to become as stupid and senseless in Divine things as the very Beasts.

2. But others, it may be, will not look on this Notion as contemptible for the easy composure thereof out of familiar conceptions which the Mind of man ordinarily figures it self into, but reject it rather out of some unintelligible hard terms in it, such as *Spirit, Eternall,* and *Infinite;* for they do profess they can frame no Notion of *Spirit,* and that any thing should be *Eternall* or *Infinite* they do not know how to set their mind in a posture to apprehend, and therefore some would have no such thing as a *Spirit* in the world.

But if the difficulty of framing a conception of a thing must take away the Existence of the thing it self, there will be no such thing as a *Body* left in the world, and then will all be *Spirit,* or nothing. For who can frame so safe a notion of a *Body,* as to free himself from the intanglements that the *Extension* thereof will bring along with it? For this *extended Matter* consists of either indivisible points, or of particles divisible *in infinitum.* (4) Take which of these two you will, (and you can find no third) you will be wound into the most notorious Absurdities that may be. For if you say it consists of points, from this position I can necessarily demonstrate, that every *Spear* or *Spire-Steeple,* or what long body you will, is as thick as it is long; that the tallest *Cedar* is not so high as the lowest *Mushrome;* and that the *Moon* and the *Earth* are so near one another, that the thickness of your hand will not goe betwixt; that *Rounds* and *Squares* are all one Figure; that *Even* and *Odde Numbers* are Equall one with another; and that the clearest *Day* is as dark as the blackest *Night.* And if you make choice of the other Member of the Disjunction, your Fancy will be little better at ease; for nothing can be divisible into parts it has not: therefore if a *Body* be divisible into infinite parts, it has infinite extended parts: and if it has an infinite number of extended parts, it cannot be but a hard mysterie to the Imagination of Man, that infinite extended parts should not amount to one whole infinite Extension. And thus *a grain of Mustard-seed* would be as well infinitely extended as the whole Matter of the Universe, and a thousandth part of that grain as well as the grain it self. Which things are more unconceivable then any thing in the Notion of a *Spirit*. Therefore we are not scornfully and contemptuously to reject any Notion, for seeming at first to be clouded and obscured with some difficulties and intricacies of conception; sith that of whose being we seem most assured, is the most intangled and perplex'd in the conceiving, of any thing that can be propounded to the apprehension of a Man. But here you will reply, that our *Senses* are struck by so manifest impressions from the *Matter,* that though the *nature* of it be difficult to conceive, yet the *Existence* is palpable to us by what it acts upon us. Why then, all that I desire is this, that when you shall be re-minded of some *Actions* and *Operations* that arrive to the notice of your Sense or Understanding, which, unless we do violence to our Faculties, we can never attribute to *Matter* or *Body,* that then you would not be so nice and averse from the admitting of such a Substance as is called a *Spirit,* though you fancy some difficulty in the convincing thereof.

3. But for mine own part, I think the *nature* of a *Spirit* is as conceivable and easy to be defined as the nature of any thing else. For as for the very *Essence* or bare *Substance* of any thing whatsoever, he is a very Novice in speculation that does not acknowledge that utterly unknowable; but for the *Essentiall* and *Inseparable Properties,* they are as intelligible and explicable in a *Spirit* as in any other Subject whatever. As for example, I conceive the intire *Idea* of a *Spirit* in generall, or at least of all finite created and subordinate *Spirits,* to consist of these several powers or properties, viz. *Self-penetration, Self-motion, Self-contraction* and *Dilatation,* and *Indivisibility;* and these are those that I reckon more absolute: I will adde also what has relation to another, and that is the power of *Penetrating, Moving,* and *Altering the Matter.* These *Properties* and *Powers* put together make up the *Notion* and *Idea* of a *Spirit,* whereby it is plainly distinguished from a *Body,* whose parts cannot *penetrate* one another, is not *Self-moveable,* nor can *contract* nor *dilate* it self, is *divisible* and *separable* one part from another; but the parts of a *Spirit* can be no more separated,

though they be dilated, then you can cut off the *Rayes* of the *Sun* by a pair of Scissors made of pellucid *Crystall*. And this will serve for the settling of the *Notion* of a *Spirit;* the proof of its *Existence* belongs not unto this place. And out of this Description it is plain that a *Spirit* is a notion of more *Perfection* then a *Body,* and therefore the more fit to be an *Attribute* of what is *absolutely Perfect* then a *Body* is. (5)

4. But now for the other two hard terms of *Eternall* and *Infinite,* if any one would excuse himself from assenting to the *Notion* of a *God* by reason of the Incomprehensiblenesse of those *Attributes,* let him consider, that he shall whether he will or no be forced to acknowledge something *Eternall,* either *God* or the *World,* and the Intricacy is alike in either. (6) And though he would shuffle off the trouble of apprehending an *Infinite Deity,* yet he will never extricate himself out of the intanglements of an *Infinite Space;* which Notion will stick as closely to his Soul as her power of *Imagination.*

5. Now that *Goodnesse, Knowledge* and *Power,* which are the three following *Attributes,* are *Attributes* of *Perfection,* if a man consult his own Faculties, it will be undoubtedly concluded; and I know nothing else he can consult with. At least this will be returned as infallibly true, That a *Being absolutely Perfect* has these, or what supereminently contains these. (7) And that *Knowledge* or something like it is in God, is manifest, because without *Animadversion* in some sense or other it is impossible to be *Happy.* But that a *Being* should be *absolutely Perfect,* and yet not *Happy,* is as impossible. But *Knowledge* without *Goodness* is but dry *Subtilty* or mischievous Craft; and *Goodness* with *Knowledge* devoid of *Power* is but lame and ineffectuall. Wherefore whatever is *absolutely Perfect,* is *Infinitely* both *Good, Wise and Powerfull.*

6. And lastly, it is more *Perfection* that all this be *Stable, Immutable* and *Necessary,* then *Contingent* or *but Possible.* Therefore the *Idea* of a *Being absolutely Perfect* represents to our mindes, That that of which it is the *Idea* is *necessarily to exist:* and that which of its own nature doth *necessarily exist,* must never fail to be. And whether the Atheist will call this *absolute Perfect Being* God or not, it is all one; I list not to contend about words. But I think any man else at the first sight will say that we have found out the true *Idea* of *God.*

CHAP. V.

1. *What has occasioned sundry men to conceit that the Soul is* Abrasa Tabula. 2. *That the Mind of Man is not* Abrasa Tabula, *but has* actuall Knowledge *of her own, and in what sense she has so.* 3. *A further illustration of the truth thereof.*

1. And now we have found out this *Idea* of a *Being absolutely Perfect,* that the use which we shall hereafter make of it may take the better effect, it will not be amisse, by way of further preparation, briefly to touch upon that notable point in Philosophy, *Whether the Soul of man be* Abrasa Tabula, *a Table-book in which nothing is writ;* or *Whether she have some Innate Notions and Ideas in her self.* (8) For so it is, that she having taken first occasion of thinking from externall Objects, it hath so imposed upon some mens judgements, that they have conceited that the Soul has no Knowledge nor Notion, but what is in a *Passive* way impressed or delineated upon her from the Objects of *Sense;* they not warily enough distinguishing betwixt extrinsecall Occasions, and the adequate or principal Causes of things.

2. But the Mind of Man more free, and better exercised in the close observations of its own operations and nature, cannot but discover that there is an active and *actuall Knowledge* in a man, of which these outward Objects are rather the re-minders then the first begetters or implanters. And when I say *actuall Knowledge,* I do not mean that there is a certain number of *Ideas* flaring and shining to the *Animadversive Faculty,* like so many *Torches* or *Starres* in the *Firmament* to our outward Sight, or that there are any *Figures* that take their distinct places, and are legibly writ there like the *Red Letters* or *Astronomical Characters* in an *Almanack:* but I understand thereby an active sagacity in the Soul, or quick recollection, as it were, whereby some small businesses being hinted unto her, she runs out presently into a more clear and larger conception.

3. And I cannot better describe her condition then thus: Suppose a skilfull *Musician* fallen asleep in the field upon the grasse, during which time he shall not so much as dream any

thing concerning his Musicall faculty, so that in one sense there is no *actuall Skill* or Notion, nor representation of any thing musicall in him; but his friend sitting by him, that cannot sing at all himself, jogs him and awakes him, and desires him to sing this or the other Song, telling him two or three words of the beginning of the Song, whereupon he presently takes it out of his mouth, and sings the whole Song upon so slight and slender intimation: So the *Mind* of Man being jogg'd and awakened by the impulses of outward Objects, is stirred up into a more full and clear conception of what was but imperfectly hinted to her from externall occasions; and this Faculty I venture to call *actuall Knowledge,* in such a sense as the sleeping Musician's skill might be called *actuall Skill* when he thought nothing of it.

CHAP. VI.

1. *Sundry Instances arguing* actual Knowledge *in the Soul: as that she has a more accurate* Idea *of a* Circle *and* Triangle *then Matter can exhibite to her:* 2. *And that upon one single consideration she assures her self of the Universal Affection of a* Triangle. 3. *The same argued from the nature of Mathematical and Logical Notions, which come not in by the Senses, as being no Physical affections of the Matter;* 4. *Because they are produced without any Physical motion upon the Matter;* 5. *And that contrary kindes may be intirely in one and the same part of Matter at once.* 6. *That there are certain sure Complex Notions of the Mind for which she was not beholden to Sense.*

1. And that this is the condition of the Soul is discoverable by sundry observations. As for example, Exhibite to the Soul through the outward Senses the figure of a *Circle;* she acknowledgeth presently this to be one kind of *Figure,* and can adde forthwith, that if it be perfect, all the lines from some one point of it drawn to the *Perimeter* must be exactly *Equal.* In like manner shew her a *Triangle;* she will straightway pronounce, that if that be the right figure it makes toward, the

Angles must be closed in indivisible *points*. But this accuracy either in the *Circle* or the *Triangle* cannot be set out in any material Subject: therefore it remains that she hath a more full and exquisite knowledge of things in her self then the *Matter* can lay open before her.

2. Let us cast in a third Instance: Let some body now demonstrate this *Triangle* described in the *Matter* to have its three Angles equal to two right ones; Why yes, saith the Soul, this is true, and not only in this particular *Triangle,* but in all plain *Triangles* that can possibly be describ'd in the *Matter*. And thus, you see, the Soul sings out the whole Song upon the first hint, as knowing it very well before.

3. Besides this, there are a multitude of *Relative Notions* or *Ideas* in the Mind of Man, as well *Mathematical* as *Logical,* which if we prove cannot be the Impresses of any material Object from without, it will necessarily follow that they are from the Soul her self within, and are the natural furniture of humane Understanding. Such as are these, *Cause, Effect, Whole* and *Part, Like* and *Unlike,* and the rest. So *Equality* and *Inequality,* λόγος and ἀναλογία, *Proportion* and *Analogy, Symmetry* and *Asymmetry,* and such like: all which *Relative Ideas* I shall easily prove to be no material Impresses from without upon the Soul, but her own active conception proceeding from her self whilest she takes notice of *external Objects*. For that these *Ideas* can make no Impresses upon the outward Senses is plain from hence, because they are no *sensible* nor *Physical affections* of the *Matter*. And how can that that is no *Physical affection* of the *Matter,* affect our corporeal Organs of *Sense?*

But now that these *Relative Ideas,* whether *Logical* or *Mathematical,* be no *Physical affections* of the *Matter,* is manifest from these two Arguments. First, They may be produced when there has been no *Physical Motion* nor alteration in the Subject to which they belong, nay, indeed, when there hath been nothing at all done to the Subject to which they do accrue. As for example, suppose one side of a Room whitened, the other not touch'd or meddled with, this other has thus become unlike, and hath the Notion of *Dissimile* necessarily belonging to it, although there has nothing at all been done thereunto. So suppose two Pounds of *Lead,* which therefore are two *Equal* Pieces of that Metall; cut away half from one of them, the other Pound, nothing at all being done unto it, has lost its Notion of *Equal,* and hath acquired a new one of *Double* unto the other. Nor is it to any purpose to answer, That though there was nothing done to this Pound of *Lead,* yet there was to the other; for that does not at all enervate the Reason, but shews that the Notion of *Sub-double,* which accrued to that *Lead* which had half cut away, is but our *Mode* of conceiving, as well as the other, and not any *Physical affection* that strikes the corporeal Organs of the *Body,* as *Hot* and *Cold, Hard* and *Soft, White* and *Black,* and the like do. Wherefore the *Ideas* of *Equal* and *Unequal, Double* and *Sub-double, Like* and *Unlike,* with the rest, are no external Impresses upon the Senses, but the Souls own active manner of conceiving those things which are discovered by the outward Senses.

5. The Second Argument is, That one and the same part of the *Matter* is capable at one and the same time wholly and entirely of two contrary *Ideas* of this kind. As for example, any piece of Matter that is a *Middle proportional* betwixt two other pieces is *Double,* suppose, and *Sub-double,* or *Triple* and *Sub-Triple,* at once. Which is a manifest sign that these *Ideas* are no *affections* of the *Matter,* and therefore do not affect our Senses; else they would affect the Senses of *Beasts,* and they might also grow good Geometricians and Arithmeticians. And they not affecting our Senses, it is plain that we have some *Ideas* that we are not beholding to our Senses for, but are the mere exertions of the Mind occasionally awakened by the Appulses of the outward Objects; which the outward Senses do no more teach us, then he that awakened the *Musician* to sing taught him his skill.

6. And now in the third and last place it is manifest, besides these single *Ideas* I have proved to be in the Mind, that there are also severall *complex Notions* in the same, such as are these, *The Whole is bigger then the Part; If you take Equall from equall, the Remainders are Equall; Every Number is either Even or Odde;* which are true to the Soul at the very first proposal, as any one that is in his wits does plainly perceive.

CHAP. VII.

1. *The Mind of Man being not unfurnish'd of* Innate Truth, *that we are with confidence to attend to her naturall and unprejudic'd Dictates and Suggestions.* 2. *That some Notions and Truths are at least naturally and unavoidably assented unto by the Soul, whether she have of her self Actual Knowledge in her or not.* 3. *And that the Definition of a* Being absolutely Perfect *is such.* 4. *And that this* absolutely Perfect Being *is God, the* Creator *and* Contriver *of all things.* 5. *The certainty and settledness of this* Idea.

1. And now we see so evidently the Soul is not unfurnished for the dictating of Truth unto us, I demand of any man, why under a pretence that she having nothing of her own, but may be moulded into an assent to any thing, or that she does arbitrariously and fortuitously compose the severall Impresses she receives from without, he will be still so squeamish or timorous as to be afraid to close with his own Faculties, and receive the Naturall Emanations of his own Mind, as faithfull Guides.

2. But if this seem, though it be not, too subtile which I contend for, *viz.* That the Soul hath *actuall Knowledge in her self* in that sense which I explained; yet surely this at least will be confess'd to be true, That the nature of the Soul is such, that she will certainly and fully assent to some Conclusions, however she came to the knowledge of them, unless she doe manifest violence to her own Faculties. Which Truths must therefore be concluded not fortuitous or arbitrarious, but Natural to the Soul: such as I have already named, as, that *Every finite number is either even or odde; If you adde equal to equal, the wholes are equal:* and such as are not so simple as these, but yet stick as close to the Soul once apprehended, as, that *The three Angles in a Triangle are equal to two right ones; That there are just five regular Bodies, neither more nor less,* and the like, which we will pronounce necessarily true according to the light of Nature. (9)

3. Wherefore now to re-assume what we have for a while laid aside, the *Idea* of a *Being absolutely Perfect* above proposed; it being in such sort set forth that a man cannot rid his Minde of it, but he must needs acknowledge it to be indeed the *Idea* of such a *Being,* it will follow, that it is no *arbitrarious* nor fortuitous conceipt, but *necessary,* and therefore *natural* to the Soul at least, if not ever actually there.

Wherefore it is manifest, that we consulting with our own Natural light concerning the Notion of a *Being absolutely Perfect,* that this Oracle tells us, That it is *A Spiritual substance, Eternal, Infinite in Essence and Goodness, Omnipotent, Omniscient, and of it self necessarily existent.*

For this Answer is such, that if we understand the sense thereof, we cannot tell how to deny it, and therefore it is true according to the light of Nature.

4. But it is manifest that that which is *Self-subsistent, infinitely Good, Omniscient* and *Omnipotent,* is the *Root* and *Original* of all things. For *Omnipotency* signifies a power that can effect any thing that implies no contradiction to be effected; and *Creation* implies no contradiction: therefore this *perfect Being* can *create* all things. But if it found the *Matter* or other Substances existing aforehand of themselves, this *Omnipotency* and power of *Creation* will be in vain, nay, indeed, *a full Omnipotency* will not be in this absolute *Omnipotent;* which the free and unprejudic'd Faculties of the Minde of man do not admit of, but look upon as a Contradiction. Therefore the natural notion of a *Being absolutely Perfect,* implies that the same *Being* is *Lord and Maker of all things.* And according to Natural Light, that which is thus, is to be adored and worshipped of all that has the knowledge of it, with all humility and thankfulness: and what is this but to be acknowledged to be *God?*

5. Wherefore I conceive I have sufficiently demonstrated that the *Notion* or *Idea* of God is as *Natural, necessary* and *essential* to the Soul of Man, as any other *Notion* or *Idea* whatsoever, and is no more *arbitrarious* or *fictitious* then the Notion of a *Cube* or *Tetraedrum,* or any other of the *Regular Bodies* in Geometry: which are not devised at our own pleasure (for such Figments and *Chimaeras* are infinite,) but for these it is demon-

strable that there can be no more then Five of them; which shews that their Notion is necessary, not an arbitrarious compilement of what we please.

And thus having fully made good the Notion of God, *What he is,* I proceed now to the next Point, which is to prove *That he is.*

CHAP. VIII.

1. *That the very* Idea *of God implies his* necessary Existence. 2. *That his Existence is not* hypothetically *necessary, but* absolutely, *with the occasion noted of that slippery Evasion.* 3. *That to acknowledge God a Being* necessarily Existent *according to the true Notion of him, and yet to say he may not Exist, is a plain contradiction.* 4. *That* Necessity *is a Logical term, and implies an indissoluble connexion betwixt Subject and Praedicate, whence again this Axiome is necessarily and eternally true,* God doth exist. 5. *A further Demonstration of his Existence from the incompetibility of Contingency or Impossibiltiy to his Nature or* Idea. 6. *That necessary Self-existence belongs either to God, or to Matter, or to both.* 7. *The great Incongruities that follow the admission of the Self-existency of Matter.* 8. *An Answer to an Evasion.* 9. *That a number of Self-essentiated Deities plainly takes away the Being of the true God.* 10. *The onely undeniable Demonstration of the Unity of the God-head.* 11. *The absurdness in admitting actual Self-existence in the Matter, and denying it in God.* 12. *That this absurdity cannot be excused from the sensibleness of Matter, sith the Atheist himself is forced to admit such things as fall not under Sense.* 13. *That it is as foolish a thing to reject the Being of God because he does not immediately fall under the Senses, as it were to reject the Being of Matter because it is so incomprehensible to the Phansy.* 14. *The factious Humoursomeness of the Atheist in siding with some Faculties of the Soul, and rejecting the rest, though equally competent judges.*

1. And now verily casting my eyes upon the true *Idea* of God which we have found out, I seem to myself to have struck

further into this business then I was aware of. For if this *Idea*
or *Notion* of God be true, as I have undeniably proved, it is also
undeniably true That he doth exist: For this *Idea* of God being
no arbitrarious Figment taken up at pleasure, but the necessary
and natural Emanation of the Minde of Man, if it signifies to
us that the Notion and Nature of God implies in it *necessary*
Existence, as we have shewn it does, unless we will wink against
our own natural Light, we are without any further Scruple to
acknowledge *That God does exist.* (10)

2. Nor is it sufficient ground to diffide to the strength of this
Argument, because our Phansy can shuffle in this Abater, *viz.*
That indeed this *Idea* of God, supposing God did exist, shews
us that his Existence is necessary, but it does not shew us that
he doth necessarily exist. For he that answers thus, does not
observe out of what prejudice he is enabled to make this Answer,
which is this: He being accustomed to fancy the Nature or
Notion of every thing else without *Existence,* and so ever easily
separating *Essence* and *Existence* in them, here unawares he
takes the same liberty, and divides *Existence* from that *Essence*
to which *Existence* it self is essential. And that's the witty
Fallacy his unwariness has intangled him in.

3. Again, when as we contend that the true *Idea* of God
represents him as a *Being necessarily existent,* and therefore
that he does exist; and you to avoid the edge of the Argument
reply, If he did at all exist; by this answer you involve your
self in a manifest Contradiction. For first, you say with us,
That the Nature of God is such, that in its very Notion it
implies its *Necessary Existence;* and then again you unsay it,
by intimating that notwithstanding this true *Idea* and *Notion,*
God may not exist; and so acknowledge that what is *absolutely*
necessary according to the Free Emanation of our Faculties,
yet may be otherwise: Which is a palpable Contradiction as
much as respects us and our Faculties, and we have nothing
more inward and immediate then these to steer our selves by.

4. And to make this yet plainer at least, if not stronger; when
we say that the *Existence* of God is *Necessary,* we are to take
notice that *Necessity* is a *Logical Term,* and signifies so firm a
Connexion betwixt the *Subject* and *Praedicate* (as they call
them) that it is impossible that they should be dissevered, or

should not hold together; and therefore if they be affirm'd one
of the other, that they make *Axioma Necessarium,* an Axiome
that is Necessary, or eternally true. Wherefore there being a
Necessary Connexion betwixt *God* and *Existence,* this Axiome,
God does Exist, is an Axiome Necessarily and Eternally true.
Which we shall yet more clearly understand, if we compare
Necessity and *Contingency* together. For as *Contingency* signifies not onely the *Manner of Existence* in that which is *Contingent* according to its *Idea,* but does intimate also a *Possibility*
of *Actual Existence;* so (to make up the true and easie Analogy)
Necessity does not onely signifie the *Manner of Existence* in
that which is *Necessary* but also that it does *actually Exist,*
and *could never possibly do otherwise.* For ἀναγκαῖον εἶναι and
ἀδύνατον μὴ εἶναι, Necessity of being and Impossibility of Not being, are all one with *Aristotle* and the rest of the *Logicians.* But
the *Atheist* and the *Enthusiast* are usually such profess'd Enemies
against *Logick;* the one merely out of Dotage upon outward gross
Sense, the other in a dear regard to his stiffe and untamed Phansy,
that shop of Mysteries and fine things.

5. Thirdly, we may further adde, That whereas we must
needs attribute to the *Idea* of God either *Contingency, Impossibility,* or *Necessity of Actuall Existence,* (some one of these
belonging to every *Idea* imaginable) and that *Contingency* is
incompetible to an *Idea of a Being absolutely Perfect,* much
more *Impossibility,* the *Idea* of God being compiled of no
Notions but such as are *possible* according to the Light of
Nature, to which we now appeal; it remains therefore that
Necessity of Actuall Existence be unavoidably cast upon the
Idea of God, and that therefore God does *actually Exist.*

6. But fourthly and lastly, If this seem more subtile, though
it be no lesse true for it, I shall now propound that which is
so palpable, that it is impossible for any one that has the use
of his wits for to deny it. I say therefore, that either *God,*
or this *corporeall* and *sensible World* must of it self *necessarily
exist.* Or thus, Either *God,* or *Matter,* or *both,* do of themselves *necessarily Exist:* If *both,* we have what we would drive
at, the *Existency* of God.

7. But yet to acknowledge the *necessary Existence* of the
Matter of it self, is not so congruous and suteable to the Light

of Nature. For if any thing can exist *independently* of God, all things may: so that not onely the *Omnipotency* of God might be in vain, but beside, there would be a letting in from hence of all confusion and disorder imaginable; nay, of some grand Devil of equal Power and of as large Command as God himself; or, if you will, of six thousand Millions of such monstrous Gigantick Spirits, fraught with various and mischievous Passions, as well as armed with immense power, who in anger or humour appearing in huge shapes, might take the Planets up in their prodigious Clutches, and pelt one another with them as Boyes are wont to doe with snow-balls. And that this has not yet happened, will be resolved onely into this, that the humour has not yet taken them: but the frame of Nature and the generation of things would be still liable to this ruine and disorder. So dangerous a thing it is to slight the natural *dependencies* and *correspondencies* of our Innate *Ideas* and *Conceptions.*

8. Nor is there any Refuge in such a Reply as this, That the full and perfect Infinitude of the Power of God is able easily to overmaster these six thousand Millions of Monsters, and to stay their hands. For I say that six or fewer may equalize the Infinite Power of God. For if any thing may be *Self-essentiated* besides God, why may not a *Spirit* of just six times less power then God *exist of it self?* and then six such will equalize him, a seventh will will over-power him.

9. But such a rabble of *Self-essentiated* and *divided* Deities does not onely hazzard the pulling the world in pieces, but plainly takes away the Existence of the true God. For if there be any *Power* or *Perfection* whatsoever which has its original from any other then God, it manifestly demonstrates that God is not God, that is, not a *Being absolutely and fully Perfect,* because we see some Power in the world that is not his, that is, that is not from him. But what is fully and wholly from him is very truly and properly his, as the *thought* of my minde is rather my mind's then my thought's.

10. And this is the onely way that I know to demonstrate that it is impossible that there should be any more then *One* true God in the world: For if we did admit another beside him, this other must be also *Self-originated;* and so neither of them would be God. For the *Idea* of God swallows up into it self all

Power and *Perfection* conceivable, and therefore necessarily implies that whatever hath any Being derives it from him.

11. But if you say the *Matter* does only exist, and not *God*, then this *Matter* does *necessarily exist of it self,* and so we give that Attribute unto the *Matter* which our Natural Light taught us to be contain'd in the Essential conception of no other thing besides *God.* Wherefore to deny that of God which is so *necessarily* comprehended in the true *Idea* of him, and to acknowledge it in that in whose *Idea* it is not at all contain'd, (for *necessary Existence* is not contain'd in the *Idea* of any thing but of a *Being absolutely Perfect*) is to pronounce contrary to our Natural Light, and to doe manifest violence to our Faculties. (11)

12. Nor can this be excused by saying that the Corporeal *Matter* is palpable and *sensible* unto us, but *God* is not, and therefore we pronounce confidently that it is, though God be not; and also that it is *necessary* of it self, sith that which is without help of another, must necessarily be, and eternally.

For I demand of you then, sith you professe your selves to believe nothing but *Sense,* how could *Sense* ever help you to that Truth you acknowledged last, *viz. That that which exists without the help of another is necessary and eternall?* For *Necessity* and *Eternity* are no *sensible* Qualities, and therefore are not the Objects of any *Sense;* and I have already very plentifully proved, that there is other Knowledge and perception in the Soul besides that of *Sense.* Wherefore it is very unreasonable, whenas we have other Faculties of Knowledge besides the *Senses,* that we should consult with the *Senses* alone about matters of Knowledge, and exclude those Faculties that penetrate beyond *Sense.* A thing that the profess'd *Atheists* themselves will not doe when they are in the humor of Philosophising; for their Principle of *Atomes* is a business that does not fall under *Sense,* as *Lucretius* at large confesses. (12)

13. But now seeing it is so manifest that the Soul of man has other *Cognoscitive* Faculties besides that of *Sense,* (which I have clearly above demonstrated) it is as incongruous to deny there is a *God,* because *God* is not an Object fitted to the *Senses,* as it were to deny there is *Matter* or a *Body,* because

that *Body* or *Matter,* in the imaginative Notion thereof, lies so unevenly and troublesomly in our *Phansy* and *Reason.*

In the contemplation whereof our Understanding discovereth such contradictious incoherencies, that were it not that the Notion is sustain'd by the confident dictates of *Sense, Reason* appealing to those more crass Representations of *Phansy,* would by her shrewd *Dilemmas* be able to argue it quite out of the world. But our *Reason* being well aware that *corporeall Matter* is the proper Object of the *Sensitive* Faculty, she gives full belief to the information of *Sense* in her own sphear, slighting the puzling objections of perplexed *Phansy,* and freely admits the existence of *Matter,* notwithstanding the intanglements of *Imagination;* as she does also the existence of God, from the contemplation of his *Idea* in our Soul, notwithstanding the silence of the Senses therein.

14. For indeed it were an unexcusable piece of folly and madnesse in a man, whenas he has *Cognoscitive* Faculties reaching to the knowledge of God, and has a certain and unalterable *Idea* of God in his Soul, which he can by no device wipe out, as well as he has the knowledge of *Sense* that reaches to the discovery of the *Matter;* to give *necessary Self-existence* to the *Matter,* no Faculty at all informing him so; and to take *necessary Existence* from *God,* though the natural Notion of God in the Soul inform him to the contrary; and onely upon this pretence, because God does not immediately fall under the Knowledge of the *Senses:* thus partially siding with one kinde of Faculty onely of the Soul, and proscribing all the rest. Which is as humoursomely and foolishly done, as if a man should make a faction amongst the *Senses* themselves, and resolve to believe nothing to be but what he could see with his *Eyes,* and so confidently pronounce that there is no such thing as the Element of *Aire,* nor *Winds,* nor *Musick,* nor *Thunder.* And the reason, forsooth, must be, because he can *see* none of these things with his *Eyes,* and that's the sole *Sense* that he intends to believe.

CHAP. IX.

1. *The Existence of God argued from the Finall cause of the implantation of the* Idea *of God in the Soul.*   2. *An Evasion of the Argument, by supposing all things to be such as they are, by Chance.*   3. *That the Evasion is either impossible, or but barely possible, and therefore of no weight.*   4. *That we are not to attend to what is simply possible, but to what our Natural Faculties determine.*   5. *He urges therefore again the Final cause of the indeleble* Idea *or Image of God in the Soul, illustrating the force thereof from a Similitude.*   6. *That supposing God did exist, he would have dealt no otherwise with us for the making himself known unto us then we are* de facto *dealt with; which therefore again argues that He doth exist.*

1. And hitherto I have argued from the naturall *Notion* or *Idea* of God as it respects that of which it is the *Idea* or *Notion*. I shall now try what advantage may be made of it from the respect it bears unto our *Souls,* the *Subject* thereof, wherein it does reside.

I demand therefore, who put this Indeleble Character of God upon our Souls? why, and to what purpose is it there?

2. Nor do not think to shuffle me off by saying, We must take things as we finde them, and not inquire of the finall Cause of any thing: for things are necessarily as they are of themselves, whose guidance and contrivance is from no Principle of Wisdome or Counsel, but every Substance is now and ever was of what nature and capacity it is found, having its Originall from none other then it self; and all those changes and varieties we see in the World are but the result of an Eternal Scuffle of coordinate Causes, bearing up as well as they can, to continue themselves in the present state they ever are; and acting and being acted upon by others, these varieties of things appear in the world, but every particular Substance with the Essential Properties thereof is self-originated, and independent of any other.

3. For to this I answer, That the very best that can be made

of all this is but thus much, That it is merely and barely *possible,*
nay, if we consult our own Faculties, and the *Idea* of God,
utterly impossible: but admit it possible; this bare *possibility*
is so laxe, so weak and so undeterminate a consideration, that
it ought to have no power to move the Mind this way or that
way that has any tolerable use of her own Reason, more then
the faint breathings of the loose Aire have to shake a Mountain
of brasse. For if bare *possibility* may at all intangle our *assent*
or *dissent* in things, we cannot fully misbelieve the absurdest
Fable in *Æsop* or *Ovid,* or the most ridiculous Figments that can
be imagin'd; as suppose that *Ears of Corn in the field hear the*
whistling of the wind and chirping of the Birds: that the stones
in the street are grinded with pain when the Carts goe over
them: that the Heliotrope eyes the Sun, and really sees him,
as well as turns round about with him: that the Pulp of the
Wall-nut, as bearing the signature of the Brain, is indued with
Imagination and Reason. I say, no man can fully mis-believe
any of these fooleries, if bare *Possibility* may have the least
power of turning the Scales this way or that way. For none
of these, nor a thousand more such like as these, imply a perfect
and palpable Contradiction, and therefore will put in for their
right of being deemed *possible.*

4. But we are not to attend to what is simply *possible,* but
to what our *Natural Faculties* do direct and determine us to.
As for example, Suppose the question were, *Whether the stones*
in the street have sense or no; we are not to leave the point as
indifferent, or that may be held either way, because it is *possible,*
and implies no palpable Contradiction, that they may have
sense, and that a *painfull* sense too: but we are to consult with
our *Naturall Faculties,* and see whither they propend; and they
do plainly determinate the controversy, by telling us that what
has *sense* and is capable of *pain* ought to have also progressive
Motion, to be able to avoid what is hurtfull and painfull, and
we see it is so in all Beings that have any considerable share of
Sense. And *Aristotle* who was no doter on a *Deity,* yet frequently does assume this Principle, Ἡ φύσις οὐδὲν μάτην ποιεῖ,
That *Nature does nothing in vain.* (13) Which is either an
acknowledgment of a *God,* or an appeal to our own *Rationall*
Faculties; and I am indifferent which, for I have what I would

out of either; for if we appeal to the naturall suggestions of our own Faculties, they will assuredly tell us There is a God.

5. I therefore again demand, and I desire to be answered without prejudice, or any restraint laid upon our Naturall Faculties, To what purpose is this Indeleble *Image* or *Idea* of God in us, if there be no such thing as *God* existent in the World? or who seal'd so deep an impression of that Character upon our Minds?

If we were travelling in a desolate *Wilderness,* where we could discover neither Man nor House, and should meet with *Herds of Cattel* or *Flocks of Sheep* upon whose bodies there were branded certain *Marks* or *Letters,* we should without any hesitancy conclude that these have all been under the hand of some man or other that has set his name upon them And verily when we see writ in our Souls in such legible Characters the *Name,* or rather the *Nature* and *Idea,* of God, why should we be so slow and backward from making the like reasonable inference. Assuredly, he whose *Character* is signed upon our Souls has been here, and has thus marked us, that we and all may know to whom we belong, That *it is he that has made us, and not we our selves; that we are his people, and the sheep of his Pasture.* And it is evidently plain from the *Idea* of God, which includes *Omnipotency* in it, that we can be made from none other then he; as I have * before demonstrated. And therefore there was no better way then by sealing us with this *Image* to make us acknowledge our selves to be his, and to doe that Worship and Adoration to him that is due to our mighty *Maker* and *Creator,* that is, to our *God.*

Wherefore things complying thus naturally and easily together, according to the free Suggestions of our *Naturall Faculties,* it is as perverse and forced a businesse to suspend *assent,* as to doubt whether those *Roman Urnes* and *Coins* I spoke of, digg'd out of the Earth, be the works of Nature, or the Artifice of Men.

6. But if we cannot yet for all this give free assent to this Position, *That God does Exist,* let us at least have the Patience a while to suppose it. I demand therefore, supposing God did *Exist,* What can the Mind of Man imagine that this God should doe better or more effectuall for the making himself known to

* See the foregoing Chap. Sect. 7, 8, 9.

such a Creature as Man, indued with such and such Faculties, then we finde really already done? For God being a *Spirit* and *Infinite*, cannot ever make himself known Necessarily & Adequately by any appearance to our outward *Senses*. For if he should manifest himself in any outward figures or shapes, portending either love or wrath, terror or protection, our Faculties could not assure us that this were *God*, but some particular *Genius*, good or bad: and besides, such dazling and affrightfull externall forces are neither becoming the Divine Nature, nor suteable with the Condition of the Soul of Man, whose *better Faculties* and more free God meddles with, does not force nor amaze us by a more course and oppressing power upon our weak and brutish *Senses*. What remains therefore but that he should manifest himself to our *Inward Man?* And what way imaginable is more fit then the indeleble Impression of the *Idea* of himself, which is (not Divine life and sense, for that's an higher prize laid up for them that can win it, but) a naturall representation of the Godhead, and a Notion of his *Essence,* whereby the Soul of Man could no otherwise conceive of him then as an *Eternall Spirit, Infinite in Goodnesse, Omnipotent, Omniscient, and Necessarily of himself Existent?* But this, as I have fully proved, we finde *de facto* done in us. Wherefore we being every way dealt with as if there were a God *Existing,* and no *Faculty* discovering any thing to the contrary, what should hinder us from the concluding that he does really *Exist?*

CHAP. X.

1. *Several other Affections or Properties in the Soul of Man that argue the Being of God.* 2. *As Natural Conscience.* 3. *A pious Hope or Confidence of success in affairs upon dealing righteously with the World.* 4. *An Answer to an Objection, That some men are quite devoid of these Divine senses.* 5. *That the Universality of Religious Worship argues the Knowledge of the Existence of God to be from the Light of Nature.* 6. *An Answer to an Objection, viz. That this general acknowledgement of a God amongst the Nations may be but an Universal Tradition.* 7. *Another Objection*

answered, viz. *That what is universally received by all Nations may notwithstanding be false.* 8. *An Objection taken from the general falsness and perversness of the Religions of the Nations. The first Answer thereto by way of Apologie.* 9. *The second Answer, supposing the Religions of the Nations as depraved as you please.* 10. *A further Objection from the long continuance of those false Religions, and the hopelesness of ever getting out of them, with a brief Answer thereto.*

1. Hitherto we have argued for the Existency of the Godhead from the natural *Idea* of God, inseparably and immutably residing in the Soul of Man. There are also other Arguments may be drawn from what we may observe to stick very close to mans Nature; and such is *Natural remorse of Conscience,* and a fear and disturbance from the committing of such things as notwithstanding are not punishable by men, as also *a Natural hope* of being prosperous and successfull in doing those things which are conceived by us to be good and righteous; and lastly, *Religious Veneration,* or *Divine worship:* all which are fruits unforcedly and easily growing out of the Nature of man; and if we rightly know the meaning of them, they all intimate *That there is a God.*

2. And first, of *Natural Conscience* it is plain, that it is a Fear and Confusion of Minde arising from the presage of some mischief that may befall a man beside the ordinary course of Nature, or the usuall occurrences of affairs, because he has done thus or thus. Not that what is supernatural or absolutely extraordinary must needs fall upon him, but that at least the ordinary calamities and misfortunes which are in the world will be directed and levelled at him some time or other, because he hath done this or that Evil against his *Conscience.* And men do naturally in some heavy *Adversity,* mighty *Tempest* on the Sea, or dreadful *Thunder* on the Land (though these be but from Natural Causes) reflect upon themselves and their actions, and so are invaded with fear, or are unterrified, accordingly as they condemn or acquit themselves in their own *Consciences.* And from this supposal is that magnificent Expression of the *Poet* concerning the Just man,

Nec fulminantis magna Jovis manus,

That he is not afraid of the darting down of *Thunder* and *Lightning* from Heaven. (14)   But this *Fear*, that one should be struck rather then the rest, or at this time rather then another time, because a man has done thus or thus, is a natural acknowledgement that these things are guided and directed from some discerning Principle, which is all one as to confess *That there is a God*.   Nor is it material, that some alledge, that *Mariners* curse and swear the lowdest when the storm is the greatest; for it is because the usualness of such dangers hath made them lose the sense of the danger, not the sense of a *God*.

3. It is also very natural for a man that follows honestly the dictates of his own *Conscience*, to be full of *good Hopes*, and much at ease, and secure that all things at home and abroad will go successfully with him, though his actions or sincere motions of his Minde act nothing upon Nature or the course of the world to change them any way: wherefore it implies that there is a *Superintendent Principle* over Nature and the material frame of the world, that looks to it so, that nothing shall come to pass but what is consistent with the good and welfare of honest and conscientious men.   And if it does not happen to them according to their expectations in this world, it does naturally bring in a belief of a world to come.

4. Nor does it at all enervate the strength of this Argument, that some men have lost the sense and difference betwixt *Good* and *Evil*, if there be any so fully degenerate; but let us suppose it, this is a monster, and, I suspect, of his own making.   But this is no more prejudice to what I aim at, who argue from the *Natural constitution* of a Man the *Existency of a God*, then if, because *Democritus* put out his Eyes, some are born blind, others drink out their Eyes and cannot see, that therefore you should conclude that there is neither *Light* nor *Colours:* for if there were, then every one would see them; but *Democritus* and some others do not see them.   But the reason is plain, there hath been force done to their *Natural Faculties*, and they have put out their Sight.

Wherefore I conclude from *natural Conscience* in a man, that puts him upon *Hope* and *Fear* of *Good* and *Evil* from what he does or omits, though those actions and omissions doe nothing to the change of the course of Nature or the affairs of the

world, that there is an *Intelligent Principle* over universall
Nature that takes notice of the Actions of men, that is, that
there is a God; for else this *Natural Faculty* would be false and
vain.

5. Now for *Adoration* or *Religious Worship,* it is as universall
as mankind, there being no Nation under the cope of Heaven
that does not doe Divine worship to something or other, and in
it to God, as they conceive; wherefore according to the ordinary
natural light that is in all men, there is a God.

6. Nor can the force of this Argument be avoided, by saying
it is but an universall *Tradition* that has been time out of minde
spred among the Nations of the world: For if it were so (which
yet cannot at all be proved) in that it is universally received,
it is manifest that it is according to the *light of Nature* to
acknowledge there is a God; for that which all men admit as
true, though upon the proposall of another, is undoubtedly to
be termed true according to the *light of Nature.* As many
hundreds of *Geometrical Demonstrations,* that were first the
inventions of some one man, have passed undeniable through all
Ages and places for true according to the *light of Nature,* with
them that were but Learners, not Inventors of them. And it
is sufficient to make a thing true according to the *light of Nature,*
that no man upon a perception of what is propounded and the
Reasons of it (if it be not clear at the first sight, and need
Reasons to back it) will ever stick to acknowledge it for a
Truth. And therefore if there were any Nations that were
destitute of the knowledge of a *God,* as they may be, it is likely,
of the Rudiments of *Geometry;* so long as they will admit of
the knowledge of one as well as of the other, upon due and fit
proposal, the acknowledgement of a *God* is as well to be said
to be according to the *light of Nature,* as the knowledge of
Geometry which they thus receive.

7. But if it be here objected, That a thing may be universally
received of all Nations, and yet be so farre from being true
according to the *light of Nature,* that it is not true at all,
as for example, that the *Sun* moves about the *Earth,* and that the
Earth stands still as the fixed *Center* of the world, which the best
of Astronomers & the profoundest of Philosophers pronounce to
be false; I answer, that in some sense it does stand still, if you

understand by *motion* the translation of a Body out of the vicinity of other Bodies. But suppose it did not stand still, this comes not home to our Case; for this is but the just victory of *Reason* over the generall prejudice of *Sense;* and every one will acknowledge that *Reason* may correct the Impresses of *Sense,* otherwise we should, with * *Epicurus* and *Lucretius,* admit the Sun and Moon to be no wider then a Sieve, and the bodies of the Stars to be no bigger then the ordinary flame of a Candle. (15) Therefore you see here is a clashing of the Faculties one against another, and the stronger carries it. But there is no Faculty that can be pretended to clash with the judgment of Reason and naturall Sagacity, that so easily either concludes or presages that there is a God: wherefore that may well goe for a Truth according to the *light of Nature* that is universally receiv'd of men, be it by what Faculty it will they receive it, no other Faculty appearing that can evidence to the contrary. And such is the *universall acknowledgement* that *there is a God.*

8. Nor is it much more material to reply, That though there be indeed a *Religious Worship* exercised in all Nations upon the face of the Earth, yet they worship many of them but *stocks* and *stones,* or some particular piece of Nature, the *Sun, Moon,* or *Stars.* For I answer that, first, it is very hard to prove that they worship any Image or Statue without reference to some Spirit at least, if not to the Omnipotent God. So that we shall hence at least win thus much, That there are in the Universe some more subtile and Immaterial Substances that take notice of the affairs of men; and this is as ill to a slow Atheist as to believe that *there is a God.*

And for that *Adoration* some of them doe to the *Sun* and *Moon,* I cannot believe they doe it to them under the notion of mere *Inanimate Bodies,* but they take them to be the habitation of some *Intellectual Beings,* as the verse does plainly intimate to us, Ἥλιός θ'ὅς πάντ' ἐφορᾷ καὶ πάντ' ἐπακούει, (16) *The Sun that hears and sees all things:* and this is very near the true Notion of a *God.*

9. But be this *universal Religious Worship* what it will, as absurd as you please to fancy it, yet it will not fail to reach very far for the proving of a *Deity.* For there are no *natural*

* See Lucret. *de Natura Rerum* li. 5. and Diog. Laert. *Vita Epicur.*

Faculties in things that have not their. Object in the world; as
there is *meat* as well as *mouths, sounds* as well as *hearing,
colours* as well as *sight, dangers* as well as *fear,* and the like.
So there ought in like manner to be a *God* as well as a *natural
propension* in men to *Religious Worship, God* alone being the
proper *Object* thereof.

Nor does it abate the strength of the Argument, that this so
deeply-radicated Property of *Religion* in man that cannot be
lost does so ineptly and ridiculously display it self in Mankind.

For as the plying of a *Dog's* feet in his sleep, as if there were
some game before him, and the butting of a young *Lamb* before
he has yet either horns or enemies to encounter, would not be
in nature, were there not such a thing as a *Hare* to be coursed,
or an *horned Enemy* to be encountred with horns: so there
would not be so *universal* an exercise of *Religious Worship* in
the world, though it be done never so ineptly and foolishly, were
there not really a due *Object* of this *Worship,* and a capacity in
Man for the right performance thereof; which could not be
unless there were a *God.*

But the truth is, Man's Soul, in this drunken drowzy condition
she is in, has fallen asleep in the Body, and like one in a dream
talks to the bed-posts, embraces her pillow instead of her friend,
falls down before Statues in stead of adoring the Eternal and
Invisible God, prayes to stocks and stones in stead of speaking
to him that by his Word created all things.

10. I but you will reply, that a young *Lamb* has at length
both his weapon and *Enemy* to encounter, and the dreaming
Dog did once and may again pursue some real game; and so
he that talks in his sleep did once confer with men awake, and
may doe so once again: but whole Nations for many successions
of Ages have been very stupid Idolaters, and do so continue to
this day. But I answer, that this rather informs us of another
great Mystery, then at all enervates the present Argument, or
obscures the grand Truth we strive for. For this does plainly
insinuate thus much, That Mankind is in a laps'd condition,
like one fallen down in the fit of an *Epilepsie,* whose limbs by
force of the convulsion are moved very incomposedly and
ilfavour'dly; but we know that he that does for the present
move the members of his body so rudely and fortuitously, did

before command the use of his Muscles in a decent exercise of his progressive faculty, and that when the fit is over he will doe so again.

This therefore rather implies that these poor barbarous Souls had once the true knowledge of *God* and of his *Worship,* and by some hidden Providence may be recover'd into it again, then that this propension to *Religious Worship,* that so conspicuously appears in them, should be utterly in vain: as it would be both in them and in all men else, if there were no *God.*

CHAP. XI.

1. *A concerning Enquiry touching the Essence of the Soul of Man.*   2. *That the Soul is not a mere Modification of the Body, the Body being uncapable of such Operations as are usually attributed to the Soul, as* Spontaneous Motion, Animadversion, Memory, Reason.   3. *That the* Spirits *are uncapable of* Memory, *and consequently of* Reason, Animadversion, *and of* Moving of the Body.   4. *That the* Brain *cannot be the Principle of* spontaneous Motion, *having neither Muscles nor Sense.*   5. *That* Phansy, Reason *and* Animadversion *is seated neither in any Pore, nor any particular part of the* Brain, *nor is all the* Brain *figured into this or that Conception, nor every Particle thereof.*   6. *That the Figuration of one part of the* Brain *is not reflected to the rest, demonstrated from the Site of things.*   7. *That the* Brain *has no Sense, further demonstrated from Anatomical Experiments.*   8. *How ridiculously the Operations of the Soul are attributed to the* Conarion.   9. *The Conclusion, That the* Impetus *of Spontaneous Motion is neither from the* Animal spirits *nor the* Brain.   10. *That the Soul is not any Corporeal substance distinct from the Animal Spirits and the Body;*   11. *And therefore is a Substance Incorporeal.*   12. *The discovery of the Essence of the Soul, of what great usefulness for the easier conceiving the nature of God.*   13. *And how there may be an Eternal Mind that has both Understanding and power of Moving the Matter of the Universe.*

1. We have done with all those more obvious Faculties in the Soul of Man that naturally tend to the discovery of the Existence of a God. Let us briefly, before we loose from our selves and lanch out into the vast Ocean of the Externall *Phaenomena of Nature,* consider the Essence of the *Soul* her self, what it is, whether a mere *Modification* of the *Body,* or *Substance distinct* therefrom; and then whether *Corporeal* or *Incorporeal.* For upon the clearing of this point we may haply be convinced that there is a *Spiritual* Substance really distinct from the *Matter;* which who so does acknowledge, will be easilier induced to believe there is a God.

2. First therefore, if we say that the *Soul* is a mere *Modification* of the *Body,* the *Soul* then is but one universal Faculty of the *Body,* or a many Faculties put together, and those Operations which are usually attributed unto the *Soul,* must of necessity be attributed unto the *Body.* I demand therefore, to what in the *Body* will you attribute *Spontaneous Motion?* I understand thereby, A power in our selves of moving or holding still most of the parts of our Body, as our hand, suppose, or little finger. If you will say that it is nothing but the *immission* of the *Spirits* into such and such Muscles, I would gladly know what does *immit* these *Spirits,* and *direct* them so curiously. Is it *themselves,* or the *Brain,* or that particular piece of the *Brain* they call the *Conarion* or *Pinekernel?* (17) Whatever it be, that which does thus *immit* them and *direct* them must have *Animadversion,* and the same that has *Animadversion* has *Memory* also and *Reason.* Now I would know whether the *Spirits themselves* be capable of *Animadversion, Memory* and *Reason;* for it indeed seems altogether impossible. For these *Animal Spirits* are nothing else but matter very thin and liquid, whose nature consists in this, that all the particles of it be in Motion, and being loose from one another, fridge and play up and down according to the measure and manner of agitation in them.

3. I therefore now demand, which of the particles in these so many loosely moving one from another has *Animadversion* in it? If you say that they all put together have, I appeal to him that thus answers, how unlikely it is that that should have *Animadversion* that is so utterly uncapable of *Memory,* and conse-

quently of *Reason.* For it is as impossible to conceive *Memory* competible to such a Subject, as it is how to write Characters in the water or in the wind.

4. If you say the *Brain immits* and *directs* these *Spirits,* how can that so freely and spontaneously move it self or another that has no *Muscles?* Besides, *Anatomists* tell us, that though the *Brain* be the instrument of sense, yet it has no sense at all of it self; how then can that that has no sense direct thus spontaneously and arbitrariously the *Animal Spirits* into any part of the Body? an act that plainly requires determinate sense and perception. But let the Anatomists conclude what they will, I think I shall little less then demonstrate that *the Brains have no sense.* For the same thing in us that has *Sense* has likewise *Animadversion;* and that which has *Animadversion* in us, has also a Faculty of *free* and arbitrarious *Phansy* and of *Reason.*

5. Let us now consider the nature of the *Brain,* and see how competible those Operations and Powers are to such a Subject. Verily if we take a right view of this laxe pithe or marrow in a man's head, neither our Sense nor Understanding can discover any thing more in this substance that can pretend to such noble Operations as *free Imagination* and the sagacious collections of *Reason,* then we can discern in a Cake of Sewet or a Bowl of Curds. For this loose Pulp that is thus wrapt up within our *Cranium* is but a spongy and porous Body, and pervious not only to the Animal Spirits, but also to more grosse juice and Liquor; else it could not well be nourished, at least it could not be so soft and moistened by Drunkenness and excess, as to make the Understanding inept and sottish in its Operation.

Wherefore I now demand, in this soft substance which we call the *Brain,* whose *softness* implies that it is in some measure *liquid,* and *liquidity* implies a severall *Motion* of loosned parts, in what part or parcel thereof does *Phansy, Reason* and *Animadversion* lye? In this laxe consistence that lies like a Net all on heaps in the water, I demand in what knot, loop or interval thereof does this Faculty of *free Phansy* and *active Reason* reside? I believe you will be asham'd to assign me any one in particular.

And if you will say in *all together,* you must say that the whole *Brain* is figured into this or that representation, which would cancell *Memory,* and take away all capacity of there being any distinct Notes and places for the several *Species* of things there represented.

But if you will say there is in *every Part* of the *Brain* this power of *Animadversion* and *Phansy,* you are to remember that the Brain is in some measure a *liquid Body,* and we must enquire how these loose parts understand one anothers several *Animadversions* and *Notions:* And if they could (which is yet very inconceivable) yet if they could from hence doe any thing toward the *Immission* and *Direction* of the *Animal Spirits* into this or that part of the body, we must consider that they must doe it (upon the knowing one anothers minds,) as it were by a joynt contention of strength; as when many men at once, the word being given, lift or tug together for the moving of some so massie a body that the single strength of one could not deal with.   But this is to make the *several particles* of the *Brain* so many *individual persons;* a fitter object for Laughter then the least measure of Belief.

6. Besides, how come these *many Animadversions* to seem *but one* to us, our Mind being these, as is supposed?   Or rather why, if the figuration of one part of the *Brain* be communicated to all the rest, does not the same Object seem situated both behinde and before us, above and beneath, on the right hand and on the left, and every way as the Impress of the Object is reflected against all the parts of the *Brains?*   But there appearing to us *but one Animadversion,* as but *one site of things,* it is a sufficient Argument that there is *but one;* or if there be *many,* that they are not mutually communicated from the parts one to another, and that therefore there can be no such joynt endeavor toward one designe: whence it is manifest that the *Brains* cannot *immit* nor *direct* these *Animal Spirits* into what part of the Body they please.

7. Moreover, that the *Brain has no Sense,* and therefore cannot impress spontaneously any motion on the *Animal Spirits,* it is no slight Argument, in that some being dissected have been found *without Brains;* and *Fontanus* tells us of a Boy at *Amsterdam* that had nothing but limpid *water* in his head in stead of *Brains* (18); and the *Brains* generally are easily dissolvable into a *watery* consistence; which agrees with what I intimated before.

Now I appeal to any free Judge, how likely these *liquid* particles are to approve themselves of that nature and power as to be able, by erecting and knitting themselves together for a moment of time, to bear themselves so as with one joynt contention of strength to cause an arbitrarious ablegation of the *Spirits* into this or that determinate part of the Body. But the absurdity of this I have sufficiently insinuated already.

Lastly, the *Nerves,* I mean the marrow of them, which is of the selfsame substance with the *Brain,* have *no Sense,* as is demonstrable from a *Catalepsis* or *Catochus.* But I will not accumulate Arguments in a matter so palpable.

8. As for that little sprunt piece of the *Brain* which they call the *Conarion,* that this should be the very substance whose natural faculty it is to move it self, and by its motions and nods to determinate the course of the *Spirits* into this or that part of the Body, seems to me no less foolish and fabulous then the story of him that could change the wind as he pleased, by setting his cap on this or that side of his head.

If you heard but the magnificent stories that are told of this little lurking Mushrome, how it does not onely hear and see, but imagines, reasons, commands the whole fabrick of the body more dexterously then an *Indian* boy does an *Elephant,* what an acute *Logician,* subtle *Geometrician,* prudent *Statesman,* skilfull *Physican,* and profound *Philosopher* he is, and then afterward by dissection you discover this worker of Miracles to be nothing but a poor silly contemptible Knob or Protuberancy, consisting of a thin Membrane containing a little pulpous *Matter,* much of the same nature with the rest of the Brain;

Spectatum admissi risum teneatis amici? (19)

would you not sooner laugh at it then go about to confute it? And truly I may the better laugh at it now, having already confuted it in what I have afore argued concerning the rest of the *Brain.*

9. I shall therefore make bold to conclude, that the impress of *Spontaneous Motion* is neither from the *Animal spirits* nor from the *Brain,* and therefore that those Operations that are usually attributed unto the *Soul* are really incompetible to any part of the *Body;* and therefore that the *Soul* is not a mere *Modification* of the *Body,* but a *Substance distinct* therefrom.

10. Now we are to enquire whether this *Substance distinct* from what ordinarily we call the *Body*, be also it self a *Corporeal* Substance, or whether it be *Incorporeal*. If you say that it is a *Corporeal Substance*, you can understand no other then *Matter* more subtile and tenuious then the *Animal Spirits* themselves, mingled with them and dispersed through the vessels and porosities of the Body; for there can be no Penetration of Dimensions. But I need no new Arguments to confute this fond conceit, for what I said of the *Animal Spirits* before, is applicable with all ease and fitness to this present case. And let it be sufficient that I advertise you so much, and so be excused from the repeating of the same things over again.

11. It remains therefore that we conclude, That that which impresses *Spontaneous Motion* upon the *Body*, or more immediately upon the *Animal Spirits*, that which *imagines, remembers* and *reasons*, is an *Immaterial Substance distinct from the Body*, which uses the *Animal Spirits* and the *Brains* for instruments in such and such Operations. And thus we have found a *Spirit* in a proper Notion and signification that has apparently these Faculties in it, it can both *understand* and *move Corporeal Matter*.

12. And now the prize that we have wonne will prove for our design of very great Consequence: For it is obvious here to observe, that the Soul of man is as it were ἄγαλμα θεοῦ, a *compendious Statue of the Deity;* her substance is a *solid Effigies of God.* (20) And therefore as with ease we consider the Substance and Motion of the vast *Heavens* on a little *Sphere* or *Globe,* so we may with like facility contemplate the nature of the *Almighty* in this little *meddal of God,* the Soul of Man, enlarging to infinity what we observe in our selves when we transferre it unto God; as we do imagine those *Circles* which we view on the *Globe* to be vastly bigger while we fancy them as described in the *Heavens.*

13. Wherefore we being assured of this, That there is a *Spiritual* Substance in our selves in which both these Properties do reside, *viz.* of *Understanding,* and of *moving Corporeall Matter;* let us but enlarge our minds so as to conceive as well as we can of a *Spiritual* Substance that is able to *move and actuate all Matter* whatsoever never so farre extended, and after

what way and manner soever it please, and that it has not the *Knowledge* only of this or that *particular thing,* but a distinct and plenary *Cognoscence* of *all things;* and we have indeed a very competent apprehension of the Nature of the Eternall and Invisible God, who, like the Soul of Man, does not indeed fall under *Sense,* but does every where operate so, that his presence is easily to be gathered from what is discoverd by our outward Senses.

BOOK II.

CHAP. I.

1. *That the more general* Phaenomena *of External Nature argue the Being of a God.* 2. *That if Matter be self-moved, it cannot work it self into these* Phaenomena. 3. *Much less if it rest of it self.* 4. *That though it were partly self-moving, partly self-resting, yet it could not produce either Sun or Stars of that figure they are.* 5. *That the Laws of the Motion of the Earth are not casual or fortuitous.* 6. *That there is a Divine Providence that does at least approve, if not direct, all the Motions of the Matter; with a Reason why she permits the Effects of the mere Mechanical motion of the Matter to goe as far as they can.*

CHAP. II.

1. *The perpetual Parallelisme of the* Axis *of the Earth a manifest argument of Divine Providence.* 2. *The great Inconveniences, if the posture of this parallel* Axis *were Perpendicular to the Plane of the Ecliptick:* 3. *Or Co-incident with the said Plane.* 4. *The excellent advantages of that Inclining posture it hath, and what a manifest Demonstration it is of Providence.* 5. *The same Argument urged from the* Ptolemaical Hypothesis. 6. *A further consideration of the* Axis *of the Earth, and of the Moon's crossing the* Æquinoctial Line. 7. *A Demonstration from the* Phaenomenon *of* Gravity, *that there is a Principle distinct from* Matter. 8. *That neither the Aire, nor any more subtile Matter in the Aire, have any Knowledge or free Agency in them.* 9. *A notable Demonstration from the Sucker of the Aire-Pump's drawing up so great a weight, that there is a Substance distinct from* Matter *in the world.* 10. *That this* Phaenomenon *cannot be salv'd by the* Elastick *power*

42

of the Aire, demonstrated from the Phaenomenon *it self.*
11. *An Evasion produced and answered.*   12. *Another Evasion anticipated.*   13. *That this peremptory force of Nature against the first Lawes of Mechanical motion and against that of Gravity, is a palpable pledge, that where things fall out fitly, there is the same Immaterial Guide, though there be not the same sensibility of force on the Matter.*   14. *The ridiculous Sophistry of the Atheist, arguing from some petty effects of the mere Motion of Matter that there is no higher Principle, plainly discovered and justly derided.*   15. *Providence concluded from the Lawes of Day and Night, Winter and Summer, &c.*

CHAP. III.

1. *That there is nothing in Nature but what passes the approbation of a Knowing Principle.*   2. *The great Usefulness of Hills and Mountains.*   3. *The Condition of Man in order and respect to the rest of the Creation.*   4. *The designed Usefulness of Quarries of Stone, Timber-Wood, Metalls and Minerals.*   5. *How upon these depend the glory and magnificence both of Peace and Warre:*   6. *As also the defense of Men against Beasts.*

CHAP. IV.

1. *Distinction of* Land *and* Sea *not without a Providence.*   2. *As also the Consistence of the* Sea-Water *that it can bear Ships.*   3. *The great convenience and pleasure of Navigation.*   4. *The admirable train of fit Provisions in Nature for gratifying the Wit of man in so concerning a Curiosity.*

CHAP. V.

1. *That the* Form *and* Beauty, Seed *and* Signature *of* Plants *are Arguments of a* Providence.   2. *That though the mere motion of the Matter might produce certain Meteors, as*

Haile, Snow, Ice, *&c. yet it will not follow that the same is the adequate cause of* Animals *and* Plants. 3. *That it were no great botch nor gap in Nature, if some more rude* Phaenomena *were acknowledged the Results of the mere Mechanical Motion of Matter.* 4. *That the Forme and Beauty of Flowers and Plants are from an higher Principle.* 5. *That there is such a thing as Beauty, and that it is the Object of our Intellectual Faculties.* 6. *From whence it follows, that the beautiful Formes and Figures of Plants and Animals are from an Intellectual Principle.*

CHAP. VI.

1. Providence *argued from the* Seeds *of Plants.* 2. *An Objection answered concerning stinking Weeds and poisonous Plants.* 3. *The* Signature *of Plants an argument of* Providence. 4. *Certain Instances of Signatures.* 5. *An Answer to an Objection concerning such Signatures in Plants as cannot referre to Medicine.*

CHAP. VII.

1. *That the* Usefulness *of* Plants *argues a Providence, particularly those that afford Timber.* 2. *As also such Herbs and Plants as serve for* Physick *for* Men *and* Beasts. 3. *Of Plants fit for* Food. 4. *Of the* Colour *of Grass and Herbs, and of the* Fruits *of Trees.* 5. *The notable provision in Nature for* Husbandry *and* Tillage, *with the universal Usefulness of* Hemp *and* Flaxe. 6. *The marvellous Usefulness of the* Indian Nut-Tree.

CHAP. VIII.

1. *The designed Usefulness of* Animals *for Man, as in particular of the* Dog *and the* Sheep. 2. *As also of the* Oxe *and other Animals.* 3. *Of Mans subduing the Creatures to himself.* 4. *Of those that are as yet untamed.* 5. *The excellent Usefulness of the* Horse. 6. *The Usefulness of some Animals that are Enemies to such Animals as are hatefull or noisome to Man.*

CHAP. IX.

1. *The* Beauty *of several brute Animals.* 2. *The goodly Stateliness of the* Horse. 3. *That the Beauty of Animals argues their Creation from an Intellectual Principle.* 4. *The difference of* Sexes *a Demonstration of Providence.* 5. *That this difference is not by Chance.* 6. *An Objection answered concerning the* Eele. 7. *Another answered, taken from the consideration of the same careful provision of difference of Sexes in viler Animals.* 8. *Of* Fishes *and* Birds *being Oviporous.* 9. *Of Birds building their Nests and hatching their Eggs.* 10. *An Objection answered concerning the* Ostrich. 11. *That the Homogeneity of that Crystalline liquor which is the immediate Matter of the generation of Animals implies a Substance Immaterial or Incorporeal in Animals thus generated.* 12. *An Answer to an Elusion of the foregoing Argument.*

CHAP. X.

1. *That the* Fabrick *of the* Bodies *of Animals argues a Deity: as namely the number and situation of their* Eyes *and* Ears; 2. *As also of their* Legs. 3. *The* Armature *of Beasts, and their use thereof.* 4. *Of the general structure of* Birds *and* Fishes. 5. *The admirable Fabrick of the* Mole. 6. Cardan's *rapture upon the consideration thereof.* 7. *Of the* Hare *and* Grey-hound. 8. *Of the structure of the body of the* Camel.

CHAP. XI.

1. *Some general observables concerning Birds.* 2. *Of the* Cock. 3. *Of the* Turkey-Cock. 4. *Of the* Swan, Hern, *and other* Waterfowl. 5. *Of the* γαμψώνυχα *and* πληκτροφόρα, *and of the peculiarity of Sight in Birds of prey.* 6. *The Description of the* Bird of Paradise *according to* Cardan. 7. *The suffrages of* Scaliger, Hernandes *and* Nierembergius. 8. Aldro-

CHAP. XII.

BOOK III.

CHAP. I.

1. *That, good men not always faring best in this world, the great examples of Divine Vengeance upon wicked and blasphemous Persons are not so convincing to the obstinate* Atheist. 2. *The irreligious Jeers and Sacrileges of* Dionysius *of* Syracuse. 3. *The occasion of the Atheists incredulity in things supernatural or miraculous.* 4. *That there have been* true Miracles *in the world as well as false.* 5. *And what are the best and safest ways to distinguish them, that we may not be impos'd upon by History.*

CHAP. II.

1. *The Moving of a* Sieve *by a Charm,* Coskinomancy. 2. *A Magical Cure of an Horse.* 3. *The Charming of* Serpents. 4. *A strange Example of one* Death-strucken *as he walked the streets.* 5. *A story of a sudden Wind that had like to have thrown down the Gallows at the hanging of two Witches.*

CHAP. III.

1. *That* Winds *and* Tempests *are raised upon mere Ceremonies or forms of words.* 2. *The unreasonableness of* Wierus *his doubting of the Devils power over the* Meteors *of the Aire.* 3. *Examples of that power in* Rain *and* Thunder. 4. Margaret Warine *discharged upon an Oake at a Thunder-Clap.* 5. Amantius *and* Rotarius *cast headlong out of a cloud upon an house-top.* 6. *The Witch of* Constance *seen by the Shepherds to ride through the Aire.* 7. *That he might adde several other Instances from Eye-witnesses, of the strange Effects of invisible Daemons.* 8. *His compen-*

47

dious Rehearsal of the most remarkable exploits of the Devil of Mascon *in lieu thereof.* 9. *The Reasons of giving himself the trouble of this Rehearsal.*

CHAP. IV.

1. *The Supernatural Effects observed in the bewitched Children of M*ʳ Throgmorton *and M*ʳⁱˢ Muschamp. 2. *The general Remarkables in them both.* 3. *The possession of the Religious Virgins of* Werts, Hessimont, &c. 4. *The story of that famous Abbatess* Magdalena Crucia, *her useless and ludicrous Miracles.* 5. *That she was a Sorceress, and was thirty years married to the Devil.* 6. *That her story is neither any Figment of Priests, nor delusion of Melancholy.*

CHAP. V.

1. *Knives, Wood, Pieces of Iron, Balls of Haire in the body of* Ulricus Neusesser. 2. *The vomiting of Cloth stuck with Pins, Nails and Needles, as also Glass, Iron and Haire, by* Wierus *his Patients, and by a friend of* Cardan's. 3. *Wierus his Story of the thirty possessed Children of* Amsterdam. 4. *The Convictiveness of these Narrations.* 5. *Objections against their Convictiveness answered.* 6. *Of a Maid Daemoniack speaking* Greek; *and of the Miraculous binding of anothers hands by an invisible power.*

CHAP. VI.

1. *The Apparition* Eckerken. 2. *The Story of the* pyed Piper. 3. *A* Triton *or Sea-God seen on the banks of* Rubicon. 4. *Of the* Imps *of Witches, and whether those old women be guilty of so much dotage as the* Atheist *fancies them.* 5. *That such things pass betwixt them and their* Imps *as are impossible to be imputed to* Melancholy. 6. *The examination of* John Winnick *of* Molesworth. 7. *The reason of* Sealing Covenants *with the* Devil.

CHAP. VII.

1. *The Story of* Anne Bodenham, *a Witch who suffered at* Salisbury, Anno 1653.   *The Author's punctual Information concerning her.*   2. *The manner and circumstances of her first Conjuring up the Devil.*   3. *An Objection answered concerning the truth thereof.*   4. *The Objection more fully answered by a second Conjuration.*   5. *An Objection answer'd concerning this second Conjuraton, and still further cleared by the circumstances of a third.*   6. *The Witches fourth and last Conjuration, at which* Anne Styles *made a Contract with the Devil.*   7. *That these transactions could be no Dreams nor Fancies of* Anne Styles, *nor she knowingly forsworn in her avouching them upon Oath.*   8. *Which is further proved by the impartialness of her Confession.*   9, 10.   *By her Contract with the Devil, evidenced from the real effects thereof.*   11. *And by her behaviour at the Assizes when she gave evidence.*   12. *An answer to certain Objections.*   13. *Sundry Indications that* Anne Bodenham *was a Witch.*   14. *The Summary Conclusion, That the above related Conjurations are no Fictions of* Anne Styles, *but real Transactions by* Anne Bodenham.

CHAP. VIII.

1. *Two memorable Stories, with the credibility of them.*   2. *The first of a Shoemaker of* Breslaw, *who cut his own throat.*   3. *His appearing after death in his usual habit, and his vexatious haunting the whole Town.*   4. *That he being dug up after he had been eight moneths buried, his body was found intire and fresh, and his joynts limber and flexible.*   5. *That upon the burning thereof the Apparition ceased.*   6. *Which also hapned in a Maid of his, when she had vext and disturbed people for a whole moneth together.*   7. *That the Relator of the Story lived in the Town at what time these things fell out.*

CHAP. IX.

1. *The second Story of one* Cuntius, *whose first Pen-man not onely dwelt in the Town, but was a sad sufferer in the Tragedie.* 2. *The quality of* Cuntius, *his fatal blow by his Horse, and his desperate affliction of Mind.* 3. *Prodigies attending his death.* 4. *A* Spiritus Incubus *in the shape of him, with other disorders.* 5. *More hideous disorders, as also his appearing to a Gossip of his in behalf of his Child.* 6. *Several sad effects of his appearing upon several persons.* 7. *His miserable usage of the Parson of the Parish and his Family, who is the Pen-man of the Story.* 8. *A brief Rehearsal of many other mad Pranks of this Spectre.* 9. *A remarkable passage touching his Grave-stone.* 10. *The florid plight of* Cuntius *after he had been buried near half a year, his grasping of a Staff, and the motion of his Eyes and of his Blood.* 11. *The prodigious Weight of his body.* 12. *As also the Incombustibleness thereof.* 13. *How hard set the Atheist will be for a subterfuge against this Story.*

CHAP. X.

1. *The Nocturnal Conventicles of Witches ; two examples thereof out of* Paulus Grillandus. 2. *Of the Witch of* Lochiae, *with a reflexion on the unexceptionableness of these Instances for the proof of* spirits. 3. *The piping of* John *of* Hembach *to a Conventicle of Witches.* 4. *The dancing of Men, Women and cloven-footed Satyrs at Mid-day.* 5. John Michael's *dumb Musick on his crooked staff from the bough of an Oak at that Antick dancing.* 6. *The Impresse of a Circle with cloven feet in it on the ground where they danced.*

CHAP. XI.

1. *Of* Fairy-Circles.   2. *Questions propounded concerning Witches leaving their bodies, as also concerning their Transformation into bestial shapes.*   3. *That the Reasons of* Wierus *and* Remigius *against reall* Transformation *are but weak.*   4. *The Probabilities for, and the Manner of, reall* Transformation.   5. *An argumentation for their being out of their bodies in their Ecstacies.*   6. *That the Soul's leaving the Body thus is not* Death, *nor her return any proper* Miracle.   7. *That it is in some cases most easie and natural to acknowledge they do leave their bodies, with an instance out of* Wierus *that suits to that purpose.*   8. *The Author's Scepticism in the point, with a favourable interpretation of the proper extravagances of* Temper *in* Bodinus *and* Des-Cartes.

CHAP. XII.

1. *The* Coldness *of those* Bodies *that* Spirits appear in, *witnessed by the experience of* Cardan *and* Bourgotus.   2. *The natural reason of this* Coldness.   3. *That the Devil does really* lie *with Witches.*   4. *That the very Substance of Spirits is not* Fire.   5. *The Spectre at* Ephesus.   6. *Spirits* skirmishing *on the ground.*   7, 8. *Field*-fights *and* Sea-fights seen in *the* Aire.

CHAP. XIII.

1. *The main reason why* good Spirits *so seldome consociate with men.*   2. *What manner of Magick* Bodinus *his friend used to procure the more sensible assistance of a good* Genius.   3. *The manner of this* Genius *his sensible Converse.*   4. The *Religiousness of the Party, and the Character of his Temper.*   5. *His escapes from danger by advertisements of the good* Genius.   6. *The* Genius *his averseness from Vocall conversation with him.*   7. *His usefull Assistance by other Signs.*   8. *The manner of his appearing to him awake, and once in a Slumber.*

CHAP. XIV.

1. *Certain Enquiries upon the preceding Narration; as, What these* Guardian Genii *may be.* 2. *Whether* one *or* more *of them be allotted to every man, or to some none.* 3. *What may be the reason of Spirits so* seldome appearing; 4. *And whether they have any settled* shape *or no.* 5. *What their* manner *is of* assisting *men in either Devotion or Prophecy.* 6. *Whether every mans complexion is capable of the Society of a good* Genius. 7. *And lastly, Whether it be lawful to pray to God to send such a* Genius *or* Angel *to one, or no.* 8. *What the most effectual and divinest Magick.*

CHAP. XV.

1. *The* Structure of Mans body, *and* Apparitions, *the most convictive Arguments against the Atheist.* 2. *His first Evasion of the former of them, pretending it never was but there were men and women and other* Species *in the World.* 3. *The Author's answer to this pretension. First, That every man was mortall, and therefore was either created or rose out of the Earth.* 4. *Secondly, That even in infinite succession there is something First* ordine Naturae, *and that these First were either created or rose out of the Earth.* 5. *Thirdly, That if there were alwaies men in the world, and every man born of a woman, some was both Father and Son, Man and Babe at once.* 6. *That it is contrary to the Laws of mere blind Matter, that man in his adult perfections should exist therefrom at once.* 7. *The* Atheist's *second Evasion, That the* Species *of things arose from the multifarious attempts of the motion of the Matter; with a threefold Answer thereto.* 8. *An Evasion of the last Answer, touching the perpetual exactness in the fabrick of all living* Species; *with a threefold Answer also to that Evasion.* 9. *The further serviceableness of this Answer for the quite taking away the first Evasion of the Atheist.*

CHAP. XVI.

1. *The Atheists Evasions against* Apparitions: *as first, That they are mere Imaginations.* 2. *Then, That though they be Realities without, yet they are caused by the force of Imagination; with the confutation of these Conceits.* 3. *Their fond conceit, That the Skirmishings in the Aire are from the exuvious Effluxes of things; with a confutation thereof.* 4. *A copious confutation of their last subterfuge,* (viz. *That those Fightings are the Reflexions of Battels on the Earth) from the distance, and debility of Reflexion;* 5. *From the rude Politure of the Clouds;* 6. *From their inability of reflecting so much as the image of the starrs; which yet were a thing far easier; First, by reason of the undiminishableness of their magnitude.* 7. *Then from the purity of their light.* 8. *Thirdly, from the posture of our Eye in the shade of the Earth.* 9. *Lastly, from their dispersedness, ready from every part to be reflected if the Clouds had any such Reflexivity in them.* 10. *That if they have any such Reflexivity as to represent battels so exceding distant, it is by some supernatural Artifice.* 11. *That this Artifice has its limited laws.* 12. *Whence at least some of these Aereal battels cannot be Reflexions from the Earth.* 13. Machiavel's *opinion concerning these Fightings in the Aire.* 14. *Nothing so demonstrable in Philosophy as the being of a God.* 15. *That Pedantick affectation of Atheisme whence it probably arose.* 16. *The true causes of being really prone to Atheisme.* 17. *That men ought not to oppose their mere complexional humours against the Principles of Reason, and Testimonies of Nature and History. His Apology for being so copious in the reciting of Stories of Spirits.*

THE
IMMORTALITY
OF
THE SOUL,

So farre forth as it is demonstrable from
the Knowledge of NATURE and
the Light of REASON.

By *HENRY MORE*, D.D.

Fellow of *Christ's* College in *Cambridge*.

Pythag.

Πάντα τὸν ἀέρα ἔμπλεον εἶναι ψυχῶν, καὶ τούτοις δαίμονάς τε καὶ ἥρωας
νομίζεσθαι.

Cardanus.

*Quid jucundius quam scire quid simus, quid fuerimus, quid erimus;
atque cum his etiam divina atque suprema illa post obitum Mundíque
vicissitudines?*

LONDON,

Printed by *James Flesher*, for *William Morden* Book-
seller in *Cambridge.*
MDCLXII.

THE
IMMORTALITY
OF
THE SOUL.

CHAP. I.

1. *The Usefulness of the present Speculation for the understand-*
standing of Providence, and the management of our lives
for our greatest Happiness; 2. *For the moderate bearing the*
death and disasters of our Friends; 3. *For the begetting true*
Magnanimity in us, 4. *and Peace and Tranquillity of Mind.*
5. *That so weighty a Theory is not to be handled perfunc-*
torily.

1. Of all the Speculations the *Soul* of man can entertain her
self withall, there is none of greater moment, or of closer con-
cernment to her, then this of her own *Immortality,* and *Inde-*
pendence on this *Terrestriall Body.*   For hereby not onely the
intricacies and perplexities of *Providence* are made more easy
and smooth to her, and she becomes able, by unravelling this
clue from end to end, to pass and repass safe through this
Labyrinth, wherein many both anxious and careless Spirits have
lost themselves; but also (which touches her own interest more
particularly) being once raised into the knowledge and belief
of so weighty a Conclusion, she may view from this Prospect
the most certain and most compendious way to her own *Hap-*
piness; which is, the bearing a very moderate affection to whatever tempts her, during the time of this her Pilgrimage, and a
carefull preparing of her self for her future condition, by such
Noble actions and Heroicall qualifications of Mind as shall
render her most welcome to her own Countrey.

2. Which Belief and Purpose of hers will put her in an utter incapacity of either *envying* the *life* or *successes* of her most imbittered *Enemies,* or of *over-lamenting* the *death* or *misfortunes* of her dearest *Friends;* she having no Friends but such as are Friends to God and Vertue, and whose Afflictions will prove advantages for their future Felicity, and their departure hence a passage to present possession thereof.

3. Wherefore, being fully grounded and rooted in this so concerning a Perswasion, she is freed from all *poor* and *abject* thoughts and designs; and as little admires him that gets the most of this World, be it by Industry, Fortune or Policy, as a discreet and serious man does the spoils of School-boyes, it being very inconsiderable to him who got the victory at Cocks or Cob-nut, or whose bag returned home the fullest stuffed with Counters or Cherry-stones.

4. She has therefore no *aemulation,* unless it be of doing good, and of out-stripping, if it were possible, the noblest examples of either the present or past Ages; nor any *contest,* unless it be with her self, that she has made no greater proficiency towards the scope she aimes at: and aiming at nothing but what is not in the power of men to confer upon her, with courage she sets upon the main work; and being still more faithfull to her self, and to that Light that assists her, at last tasts the *first fruits* of her future *Harvest,* and does more then presage that *great Happiness* that is accrewing to her. And so quit from the troubles and anxieties of this present world, *staies* in it with *Tranquillity* and *Content,* and at last *leaves* it with *Joy.*

5. The Knowledge therefore and belief of the *Immortality of the Soul* being of so grand Importance, we are engaged more carefully and punctually to handle this so weighty a Theory: which will not be performed by multiplying of words, but by a more frugall use of them; letting nothing fall from our pen, but what makes closely to the matter, nor omitting any thing materiall for the evincing the truth thereof.

CHAP. II.

1. *That* the Soule's Immortality *is demonstrable, by the Authors method, to all but mere Scepticks.* 2. *An Illustration of his First Axiome.* 3. *A confirmation and example of the Second.* 4. *An explication of the Third.* 5. *An explication and proof of the Fourth.* 6. *A proof of the Fifth.* 7. *Of the Sixth.* 8. *An example of the Seventh.* 9. *A confirmation of the truth of the Eighth.* 10. *A demonstration and example of the Ninth.* 11. Penetrability *the immediate Property of Incorporeall Substance.* 12. *As also* Indiscerpibility. 13. *A proof and illustration of the Tenth Axiome.*

1. And to stop all Creep-holes, and leave no place for the subterfuges and evasions of confused and cavilling spirits, I shall prefix some few *Axiomes,* of that plainness and evidence, that no man in his wits but will be ashamed to deny them, if he will admit any thing at all to be true. But as for perfect *Scepticisme,* it is a disease incurable, and a thing rather to be pitied or laught at, then seriously opposed. For when a man is so fugitive and unsetled, that he will not stand to the verdict of his own Faculties, one can no more fasten any thing upon him, then he can write in the water, or tye knots of the wind. But for those that are not in such a strange despondency, but that they think they know something already and may learn more, I do not doubt, but by a reasonable recourse to these few Rules, with others I shall set down in their due place, that they will be perswaded, if not forced, to reckon this Truth, of *the Immortality of the Soul,* amongst such as must needs appear undeniable to those that have parts and leisure enough accurately to examine, and throughly to understand what I have here written for the demonstration thereof.

Axiome I.

What ever things are in themselves, they are nothing to us, but so far forth as they become known to our Faculties or Cognitive powers.

2. This *Axiome* is plain of it self, at the very first proposal. For as nothing, for example, can concern the *Visive* faculty, but so far forth as it is *visible;* so there is nothing that can challenge any stroke to so much as a touching, much less determining, our *Cognitive* powers in generall, but so far forth as it is *cognoscible.*

Axiome II.

Whatsoever is unknown to us, or is known but as merely possible, is not to move us or determine us any way, or make us undetermined; but we are to rest in the present light and plain determination of our owne Faculties.

3. This is an evident Consectary from the foregoing Axiome. For the Existence of that that is *merely possible* is utterly unknown to us to *be,* and therefore is to have no weight against any Conclusion, unless we will condemn ourselves to eternall *Scepticisme.** As for example, If after a man has argued for a *God* and *Providence,* from the wise contrivance in the frame of all the Bodies of Animals upon earth, one should reply, That there may be, for all this, Animals in *Saturn, Jupiter,* or some other of the Planets, of very inept fabricks; Horses, suppose, and other Creatures, with onely one Eye, and one Eare, (and that both on a side, the Eye placed also where the Eare should be,) and with onely three Leggs; Bulls and Rams with horns on their backs, and the like: Such allegations as these, according to this Axiome, are to be held of no force at all for the enervating the Conclusion.

* See *Antidote,* Book I, Ch. 2, and 9.

AXIOME III.

*All our Faculties have not a right of suffrage for determining of
Truth, but onely Common Notions, Externall Sense, and
evident and undeniable Deductions of Reason. (21)*

4. By *Common Notions* I understand whatever is *Noëmat-
ically* true, that is to say, true at first sight to all men in their
wits, upon a clear perception of the Terms, without any further
discourse or reasoning. (From *Externall Sense* I exclude not
Memory, as it is a faithfull Register thereof.) And by *undeniable Deduction of Reason,* I mean such a collection of one
Truth from another, that no man can discover any looseness or
disjoyntedness in the cohesion of the Argument.

AXIOME IV.

*What is not consonant to all or some of these, is mere Fancy,
and is of no moment for the evincing of Truth or False-
hood, by either it's Vigour or Perplexiveness.*

5. I say *mere Fancy,* in Counter-distinction to such Representations as, although they be not the pure Impresses of some
reall Object, yet are made by *Rationall deduction* from them,
or from *Common Notions,* or from both. Those Representations that are not framed upon such grounds, I call *mere
Fancies;* which are of no value at all in determining of Truth.
For if *Vigour of Fancy* will argue a thing true, then all the
dreams of mad-men must goe for Oracles: and if the *Perplexiveness of Imagination* may hinder assent, we must not
believe Mathematicall demonstration, and the 16th Proposition
of the 3d Book of *Euclide* will be confidently concluded to contain a contradiction.*

AXIOME V.

*Whatever is clear to any one of these Three Faculties, is to be
held undoubtedly true, the other having nothing to evidence
to the contrary.*

6. Or else a man shall not be assured of any sensible Object
that he meets with, nor can give firm assent to such Truths as

* See *Antidote,* Book I, Ch. 4, Sect. 2.

these, *It is impossible the same thing should be, and not be, at once; Whatever is, is either finite, or infinite;* and the like.

Axiome VI.

What is rejected by one, none of the other Faculties giving evidence for it, ought to goe for a Falsehood.

7. Or else a man may let pass such Impossibilities as these for Truth, or doubt whether they be not true or no, viz. *The part is greater then the whole; There is something that is neither finite nor infinite;* Socrates *is invisible;* and the like.

Axiome VII.

What is plainly and manifestly concluded, ought to be held undeniable, when no difficulties are alledged against it, but such as are acknowledged to be found in other Conclusions held by all men undeniably true.

8. As for example, suppose one should conclude, *That there may be Infinite Matter,* or, *That there is Infinite Space,* by very rationall arguments; and that it were objected onely, That then the *Tenth* part of that *Matter* would be Infinite; it being most certain That there is *Infinite Duration* of something or other in the world, and that the *Tenth* part of this *Duration* is Infinite; it is no enervating at all of the former Conclusion, it being incumbred with no greater incongruity then is acknowledged to consist with an undeniable Truth.

Axiome VIII.

The Subject, or naked Essence or Substance of a thing, is utterly unconceivable to any of our Faculties. (22)

9. For the evidencing of this Truth, there needs nothing more then a silent appeal to a mans owne Mind, if he do not find it so; and that if he take away all *Aptitudes, Operations, Properties* and *Modifications* from a *Subject,* that his conception thereof vanishes into nothing, but into the *Idea* of a mere *Undiversificated* Substance; so that one *Substance* is not then distinguishable from another, but onely from *Accidents* or *Modes,* to which properly belongs no subsistence.

AXIOME IX.

There are some Properties, Powers and Operations, immediately appertaining to a thing, of which no reasons can be given, nor ought to be demanded, nor the Way or Manner of the cohesion of the Attribute with the Subject can by any means be fancyed or imagined. (23)

10. The evidence of this Axiome appears from the former. For if the *naked substance* of a Thing be so utterly unconceivable there can be nothing deprehended there to be a connexion betwixt it and it's first Properties. Such is *Actual Divisibility* and *Impenetrability* in *Matter.* By *Actual Divisibility* I understand *Discerpibility,* gross tearing or cutting one part from another. These are *Immediate Properties of Matter;* but why they should be there, rather then in any other Subject, no man can pretend to give, or with any credit aske, the reason. For *Immediate Attributes* are indemonstrable, otherwise they would not be *Immediate.*

11. So the *Immediate Properties* of a *Spirit* or Immateriall Substance are *Penetrability* and *Indiscerpibility.* The necessary cohesion of which Attributes with the Subject is as little demonstrable as the former. For supposing that, which I cannot but assert, to be evidently true, That there is no Substance but it has in some sort or other the Three dimensions; This Substance, which we call *Matter,* might as well have been *penetrable* as *impenetrable,* and yet have been Substance: But now that it does so certainly and irresistibly keep one part of it self from *penetrating* another, it is so, we know not why. For there is no necessary connexion discernible betwixt *Substance* with *three dimensions,* and *Impenetrability.* For what some alledge, that it implies a contradiction, that *Extended* Substance should run one part into another; for so part of the *Extension,* and consequently of the *Substance,* would be lost; this, I say, (if nearly looked into) is of no force. For the *Substance* is no more lost in this case, then when a string is doubled and redoubled, or a piece of wax reduced from a long figure to a round: The dimension of *Longitude* is in some part lost, but without detriment to the *Substance* of the wax. In like manner when one part of an *Extended* Substance runs into another, something both of *Longi-*

tude, Latitude and *Profundity* may be lost, and yet all the
Substance there still; as well as *Longitude* lost in the other case
without any loss of the *Substance.* (24)

And as what was lost in *Longitude,* was gotten in *Latitude* or
Profundity before, so what is lost here in all or any two of the
dimensions, is kept safe in *Essential Spissitude:* For so I will
call this *Mode* or *Property of a Substance,* that is able to receive
one part of it self into another. Which *fourth Mode* is as easy
and familiar to my Understanding, as that of the *Three dimensions* to my Sense or Phansy. For I mean nothing else by
Spissitude, but the redoubling or contracting of Substance into
less space then it does sometimes occupy. And Analogous to
this is the lying of two Substances of several kinds in the same
place at once.

To both these may be applied the termes of *Reduplication*
and *Saturation:* The former, when Essence or Substance is but
once redoubled into it self or into another; the latter, when so
oft, that it will not easily admit anything more. And that more
Extensions then one may be commensurate, at the same time, to
the same Place, is plain in that *Motion* is coextended with the
Subject wherein it is, and both with *Space.* And *Motion* is not
nothing; wherefore two things may be commensurate to one
Space at once.

12. Now then *Extended Substance* (and all Substances are
extended) being of it self indifferent to *Penetrability* or *Impenetrability,* and we finding one kind of *Substance* so *impenetrable,* that one part will not enter at all into another, which
with as much reason we might expect to find so irresistibly
united one part with another that nothing in the world could
dissever them: (For this *Indiscerpibility* has as good a connexion
with Substance as *Impenetrability* has, they neither falling under
the cognoscence of Reason or Demonstration, but being *Immediate* Attributes of such a Subject. For a man can no more argue
from the *Extension* of Substance, that it is *Discerpible,* then
that it is *Penetrable;* there being as good a capacity in *Extension*
for *Penetration* as *Discerption*) I conceive, I say, from hence we
may as easily admit that *some Substance* may be of it self
Indiscerpible, as well as others *Impenetrable;* and that as there
is one kind of *Substance,* which of it's own nature is *Impene-*

trable and *Discerpible,* so there may be another *Indiscerpible* and *Penetrable.* Neither of which a man can give any other account of, then that they have the Immediate Properties of such a Subject.

AXIOME X.

The discovery of some Power, Property, or Operation, incompetible to one Subject, is an infallible argument of the Existence of some other, to which it must be competible. (25)

13. As when *Pythagoras* was spoken unto by the River *Nessus,* when he passed over it, and a Tree by the command of *Thespesion* the chief of the *Gymnosophists* saluted *Apollonius* in a distinct and articulate voice, but small as a womans; it is evident, I say, That there was something there that was neither *River* nor *Tree,* to which these salutations must be attributed, no *Tree* nor *River* having any Faculty of *Reason* nor *Speech.**

CHAP. III.

1. *The general Notions of* Body *and* Spirit.   2. *That the Notion of* Spirit *is altogether as intelligible as that of* Body.   3. *Whether there be any Substance of a* mixt *nature, betwixt* Body *and* Spirit.

1. The greatest and grossest Obstacle to the belief of *the Immortality of the Soul,* is that confident opinion in some, as if the very notion of *a Spirit* were a piece of Non-sense and perfect Incongruity in the conception thereof. Wherefore to proceed by degrees to our maine designe, and to lay our foundation low and sure, we will in the first place expose to view the genuine notion of *a Spirit,* in the *generall* acception thereof; and afterwards of *severall kinds* of *Spirits:* that it may appear to all, how unjust that cavill is against *Incorporeal Substances,* as if they were mere Impossibilities and contradictious Inconsistencies. I will define therefore *a Spirit* in generall thus, *A substance penetrable and indiscerpible.* The fitness of which Definition will be the better understood, if we divide *Substance* in

* Iamblich. *de vita Pythag. cap.* 18. Philostrat. *de vita Apollon. lib.* 6. (26)

generall into these first kindes, viz. *Body* and *Spirit,* and then define *Body* to be *A Substance impenetrable and discerpible.* Whence the contrary kind to this is fitly defined, *A Substance penetrable and indiscerpible.*

2. Now I appeal to any man that can set aside prejudice, and has the free use of his Faculties, whether every term in the Definition of a *Spirit* be not as intelligible and congruous to Reason, as in that of a *Body.* For the precise Notion of *Substance* is the same in both, in which, I conceive, is comprised *Extension* and *Activity* either connate or communicated. For *Matter* it self once moved can move other *Matter.* And it is as easy to understand what *Penetrable* is as *Impenetrable,* and what *Indiscerpible* as *Discerpible;* and *Penetrability* and *Indiscerpibility* being as *immediate* to *Spirit,* as *Impenetrablity* and *Discerpibility* to *Body,* there is as much reason to be given for the Attributes of the one as of the other, by Axiome 9. And *Substance* in its precise notion including no more of *Impenetrability* then *Indiscerpibilty,* we may as well wonder how one kind of Substance can so firmly and irresistibly keep out another Substance (as *Matter,* for example, does the parts of *Matter*) as that the parts of another Substance hold so fast together, that they are by no means *Discerpible,* as we have already intimated. And therefore this *holding out* in one being as difficult a business to conceive as the *holding together* in the other, this can be no prejudice to the notion of a *Spirit.* For there may be very fast union where we cannot at all imagine the cause thereof, as in such Bodies which are exceeding hard, where no man can fancy what holds the parts together so strongly; and there being no greater difficulty here, then that a man cannot imagine what holds the parts of a *Spirit* together, it will follow by Axiome 7. that the Notion of a *Spirit* is not to be excepted against as an incongruous notion, but is to be admitted for the notion of a thing that may really exist. (27)

3. It may be doubted, whether there may not be Essences of a *middle* condition betwixt these *Corporeal* and *Incorporeal* Substances we have described, and that of two sorts, The one *Impenetrable and Indiscerpible,* the other *Penetrable and Discerpible.* But concerning the first, if *Impenetrability* be understood in reference to *Matter,* it is plain there can be no such

Essence in the world; and if in reference to its own parts, though it may then look like a possible *Idea* in it self, yet there is no footsteps of the existence thereof in Nature, the Souls of men and Daemons implying contraction and dilatation in them.

As for the latter, it has no privilege for any thing more then *Matter* it self has, or some *Mode* of *Matter*. For it being *Discerpible*, it is plain it's union is by *Juxtaposition* of parts, and the more *penetrable*, the less likely to conveigh Sense and Motion to any distance. Besides the ridiculous sequel of this supposition, that will fill the Universe with an infinite number of shreds and rags of Souls and Spirits, never to be reduced again to any use or order. And lastly, the proper Notion of a Substance *Incorporeal* fully counter-distinct to a *Corporeal* Substance, necessarily including in it so strong and indissoluble union of parts, that it is utterly *Indiscerpible*, whenas yet for all that in this general notion thereof neither *Sense* nor *Cogitation* is implied, it is most rational to conceive, that that Substance wherein they are must assuredly be *Incorporeal* in the strictest signification; the nature of *Cogitation and communion of Sense* arguing a more perfect degree of union then is in mere *Indiscerpibility of parts.*

But all this Scrupulosity might have been saved; for I confidently promise my self, that there are none so perversely given to tergiversations and subterfuges, but that they will acknowledge, wherever I can prove that there is *a Substance distinct from Body or Matter,* that it is in the most full and proper sense *Incorporeal.*

CHAP. IV.

1. *That the Notions of the several kinds of* Immaterial Beings *have no Inconsistency nor Incongruity in them.* 2. *That the Nature of God is as intelligible as the Nature of any Being whatsoever.* 3. *The true Notion of his* Ubiquity, *and how intelligible it is.* 4. *Of the Union of the Divine Essence.* 5. *Of his Power of Creation.*

1. We have shewn that the Notion of a *Spirit* in general is not at all incongruous nor impossible: And it is as congruous,

consistent and intelligible in the *sundry kinds* thereof; as for example that of God, of Angels, of the Souls of Men and Brutes, and of the λόγοι σπερματικοί or *Seminal Forms* of things.

2. The Notion of God, though the knowledge thereof be much prejudiced by the confoundedness and stupidity of either superstitious or profane men, that please themselves in their large Rhetorications concerning the unconceivableness and utter incomprehensibleness of the Deity; the one by way of a devotional exaltation of the transcendency of his Nature, the other to make the belief of his Existence ridiculous, and craftily and perversely to intimate that there is no God at all, the very conception of him being made to appear nothing else but a bundle of inconsistencies and impossibilities: Nevertheless I shall not at all stick to affirm, that his *Idea* or Notion is as easy as any Notion else whatsoever, and that we may know as much of him as of any thing else in the world. For the *very Essence* or *naked Substance* of nothing can possibly be known, by Axiome 8. But for His *Attributes*, they are as conspicuous as the Attributes of any Subject or Substance whatever: From which a man may easily define Him thus; *God is a Spirit Eternal, Infinite in Essence and Goodness, Omniscient, Omnipotent, and of himself necessarily Existent.*

I appeal to any man, if every term in this Definition be not sufficiently intelligible. For as for *Spirit*, that has been already defined and explained. By *Eternal* I understand nothing here but Duration without end or beginning: by *Infiniteness of Essence*, that his Essence or Substance has no bounds, no more then his Duration: by *Infinite in Goodn*ess, such a benign Will in God as is carried out to boundless and innumerable benefactions: by *Omnisciency* and *Omnipotency*, the ability of knowing or doing any thing that can be conceived without a plain contradiction: by *Self-existency*, that he has his Being from none other: and by *necessary Existence*, that he cannot fail to be. What terms of any Definition are more plain then these of this? or what Subject can be more accurately defined then this is? For the naked Subject or Substance of any thing is no otherwise to be known then thus. And they that gape after any other Speculative knowledge of God then what is from his *Attributes* and *Operations*, they may have their heads and mouths filled with many hot scalding fancies and words, and run mad with the boisterousness of their own Imagination, but they will never hit upon any sober Truth.

3. Thus have I delivered a very explicite and intelligible Notion of *the Nature of God;* which I might also more compendiously define, *An Essence absolutely Perfect,* in which all the terms of the former Definition are comprehended, and more then I have named, or thought needful to name, much less to insist upon; as his *Power of Creation,* and his *Omnipresence* or *Ubiquity,* which are necessarily included in the *Idea* of *absolute Perfection.* The latter whereof some ancient Philosophers endeavoring to set out, have defined God to be *a Circle whose Center is every where and Circumference no where.* By which Description certainly nothing else can be meant, but that the Divine Essence is *every where present* with all those adorable Attributes of *Infinite* and *absolutely-Perfect Goodness, Knowledge and Power,* according to that sense in which I have explained them. Which *Ubiquity* or *Omnipresence* of God is every whit as intelligible as the overspreading of *Matter* into all places.

4. But if here any one demand, How the Parts, as I may so call them, of the Divine Amplitude hold together, that of *Matter* being so discerpible; it might be sufficient to re-mind him of what we have already spoken of the general Notion of a *Spirit.* But besides that, here may be also a peculiar rational account given thereof, it implying a contradiction, that an *Essence absolutely Perfect* should be either limited in presence, or change place in part or whole, they being both notorious Effects or Symptoms of Imperfection, which is inconsistent with the Nature of God. And no better nor more cogent reason can be given of any thing, then that it implies a contradiction to be otherwise.

5. That *Power* also *of creating things of nothing,* there is a very close connexion betwixt it and the *Idea* of *God,* or of *a Being absolutely Perfect.* For this Being would not be what it is conceived to be, if it were destitute of the *Power of Creation;* and therefore this Attribute has no less coherence with the Subject, then that it is a contradiction it should not be in it, as was observed of the foregoing Attribute of *Indiscerpibilty* in God. But to alledge that a man cannot imagine how God should

create something of nothing, or how the Divine Essence holds so closely and invincibly together, is to transgress against the 3, 4, and 5. Axiomes, and to appeal to a Faculty that has no right to determine the case.

CHAP. V.

1. *The Definition belonging to all* Finite *and* Created Spirits.
2. *Of* Indiscerpibilty, *a Symbolical representation thereof.*
3. *An Objection answered against that representation.*

1. We have done with the Notion of that *Infinite* and *Uncreated* Spirit we usually call *God:* we come now to those that are *Created* and *Finite,* as the *Spirits of Angels, Men* and *Brutes;* we will cast in the *Seminal Forms* also, or *Archei,* as the *Chymists* call them, though haply the world stands in * no need of them. The *Properties* of a *Spirit* as it is a Notion common to all these, I have already enumerated in my Antidote, *Self-motion, Self-penetration, Self-contraction* and *dilatation,* and *Indivisibility,* by which I mean *Indiscerpibility:* to which I added *Penetrating, Moving* and *Altering the Matter.** We may therefore define *This kind* of *Spirit* we speak of, to be *A substance Indiscerpible, that can move it self, that can penetrate, contract, and dilate it self, and can also penetrate, move, and alter the Matter.* We will now examine every term of this Definition, from whence it shall appear, that it is as congruous and intelligible, as those Definitions that are made of such things as all men without any scruple acknowledge to exist.

2. Of the *Indiscerpibilty* of a *Spirit* we have already given rational grounds to evince it not impossible, it being an *Immediate Attribute* thereof, as *Impenetrability* is of a *Body;* and as conceivable or imaginable, that one *Substance* of its own nature may invincibly *hold its parts together,* so that they cannot be disunited nor dissevered, as that another may *keep out* so stoutly and irresistibly another Substance from entring into the same space or place with it self. For this ἀντιτυπία or *Im-*

---

* See Book 3. Ch. 12, and 13.
* Book I. Ch. 4. sect. 3.

penetrabilty is not at all contained in the precise conception of
a *Substance as Substance* as I have already signified.

But besides that *Reason* may thus easily apprehend that it
may be so, I shall a little gratifie *Imagination,* and it may be
Reason too, in offering the *manner* how it is so, in this kind of
Spirit we now speak of. That ancient notion of *Light* and
Intentional species is so far from a plain impossibility, that it
has been heretofore generally, and is still by very many persons,
looked upon as a Truth, that is, That *Light* and *Colour* do ray
in such sort as they are described in the Peripatetical Philosophie. (28) Now it is observable in *Light,* that it is most vigorous
towards its fountain, and fainter by degrees.   But we will reduce
the matter to *one lucid point,* which, according to the acknowledged Principles of Opticks, will fill a distance of space with its
rays of light: Which *rayes* may indeed be reverberated back
towards their Centre by interposing some opake body, and so
this *Orbe of light* contracted; but, according to the *Aristotelean*
Hypothesis, it was alwayes accounted impossible that they should
be clipt off, or cut from this *lucid point,* and be kept apart by
themselves.* Those whom dry Reason will not satisfy, may, if
they please, entertain their Phansy with such a Representation
as this, which may a little ease the anxious importunity of their
Mind, when it too eagerly would comprehend the manner how
this *Spirit* we speak of may be said to be *Indiscerpible.* For
think of any *ray* of this *Orbe of light,* it does sufficiently set out
to the *Imagination* how *Extension* and *Indiscerpibilty* may consist together.

3. But if any object, That the *lucid Centre of this Orbe,* or
the *Primary Substance,* as I * elsewhere call it, is either *divisible*
or *absolutely indivisible;* and if it be *divisible,* that as concerning that *Inmost* of a *Spirit,* this Representation is not at all
serviceable to set off the nature thereof, by shewing how the
parts there may hold together so indiscerpibly; but if *absolutely
indivisible,* that it seems to be nothing: To this I answer, what
Scaliger somewhere has noted, *That what is infinitely great or
infinitely small, the Imagination of man is at a loss to conceive
it.* Which certainly is the ground of the perplexedness of that

---

* See further in my *Antidote,* Book I, Ch. 4. sect. 3.   Also the *Append.*
Chap. 3, *ad* 10.   * *Append.* C. 13. sect. 2.

Probleme concerning *Matter,* whether it consists of points, or onely of particles divisible *in infinitum.* (29)

But to come more closely to the business; I say that though we should acknowledg the *Inmost Centre of life,* or the very First point, as I may so call it, of the *Primary Substance* (for this *Primary Substance* is in some sort gradual) to be *purely indivisible,* it does not at all follow, no not according to *Imagination* it self, that it must be nothing. For let us imagine a perfect *Plane,* and on this *Plane* a perfect *Globe,* we cannot conceive but this *Globe* touches the *Plane,* and that in what we ordinarily call a *point,* else the one would not be a *Globe,* or the other not a *Plane.* Now it is impossible that one Body should touch another, and yet touch one another in nothing. This *inmost Centre* therefore *of life* is something, and something so full of essential vigour and virtue, that though gradually it diminish, yet can fill a certain Sphere of Space with its own presence and activity, as a spark of light illuminates the duskish aire.

Wherefore there being no greater perplexity nor subtilty in the consideration of this *Centre of Life* or *Inmost of a Spirit,* then there is in the *Atomes of Matter,* we may by Axiome 7. rightly conclude, That *Indiscerpibility* has nothing in the notion thereof, but what may well consist with the possibility of the existence of the Subject whereunto it belongs.

CHAP. VI.

1. *Axiomes that tend to the demonstrating how the Centre or First point of the* Primary Substance *of a* Spirit *may be* Indiscerpible. 2. *Several others that demonstrate how the* Secondary Substance *of a* Spirit *may be* Indiscerpible. 3. *An application of these Principles.* 4. *Of the union of the* Secondary Substance *considered transversely.* 5. *That the Notion of a* Spirit *has less difficulty then that of* Matter. 6. *An Answer to an Objection from the Rational faculty.* 7. *Answers to Objections suggested from Fancy.* 8. *A more compendious satisfaction concerning the Notion of a* Spirit.

1. And thus we have fairly well gratified the *Fancy* of the Curious concerning the *Extension* and *Indiscerpibilty* of a *Spirit;*

but we shall advance yet higher, and demonstrate the possibility of this Notion to the severest Reason, out of these following Principles.

AXIOME XI.

A Globe touches a Plane in something, though in the least that is conceivable to be reall.

AXIOME XII.

The least that is conceivable is so little, that it cannot be conceived to be discerpible into less.

AXIOME XIII.

As little as this is, the repetition of it will amount to considerable magnitudes.

As for example, if this Globe be drawn upon a Plane, it constitutes a *Line ;* and a *Cylinder* drawn upon a Plane, or this same *Line* described by the Globe multiplied into it self, constitutes a *superficies,* &c. This a man cannot deny, but the more he thinks of it, the more certainly true he will find it.

AXIOME XIV.

Magnitude cannot arise out of mere Non-Magnitudes.

For multiply *Nothing* ten thousand millions of times into nothing, the Product will be still *Nothing.* Besides, if that wherein the Globe touches a Plane were more then *Indiscerpible,* that is, *purely Indivisible,* it is manifest that a *Line* will consist of *Points* Mathematically so called, that is, *purely Indivisible ;* which is the grandest absurdity that can be admitted in Philosophy, and the most contradictious thing imaginable.

AXIOME XV.

The same thing by reason of its extreme littleness may be utterly Indiscerpible, though intellectually Divisible.

This plainly arises out of the foregoing Principles : For every Quantity is *intellectually* divisible ; but something Indiscerpible was afore demonstrated to be Quantity, and consequently divisible, otherwise Magnitude would consist of Mathematicall points. Thus have I found a possibility for the Notion of *the Center of a Spirit*, which is not a Mathematicall point, but Substance, in Magnitude so little, that it is *Indiscerpible;* but in virtue so great, that it can send forth out of it self so large a Sphere of *Secondary Substance,* as I may so call it, that it is able to actuate grand Proportions of *Matter,* this whole Sphere of life and activity being in the mean time utterly *Indiscerpible.*

2. This I have said, and shall now prove it by adding a few more Principles of that evidence, as the most rigorous Reason shall not be able to deny them.

AXIOME XVI.

An Emanative Cause is the Notion of a thing possible. (30)

By an *Emanative Cause* is understood such a Cause as merely by Being, no other activity or causality interposed, produces an Effect. That this is possible is manifest, it being demonstrable that there is *de facto* some such Cause in the world; because something must move it self. Now if there be no *Spirit, Matter* must of necessity move it self, where you cannot imagine any activity or causality, but the bare essence of the *Matter* from whence this motion comes. For if you would suppose some former motion that might be the cause of this, then we might with as good reason suppose some former to be the cause of that, and so *in infinitum.**

AXIOME XVII.

An Emanative Effect is coexistent with the very Substance of that which is said to be the Cause thereof.

This must needs be true, because that very Substance which is said to be the Cause, is the adequate and immediate Cause, and wants nothing to be adjoyned to its bare essence for the production of the Effect; and therefore by the same reason the Effect is at any time, it must be at all times, or so long as that Substance does exist.

* See *Append.* to the *Antidote,* chap. 13. sect. 4.

AXIOME XVIII.

*No Emanative Effect, that exceeds not the virtues and powers
of the Cause, can be said to be impossible to be produced
by it.*

This is so plain, that nothing need be added for either explanation or proof.

AXIOME XIX.

*There may be a Substance of that high Virtue and Excellency,
that it may produce another Substance by Emanative
casuality, provided that Substance produced be in due graduall proportions inferiour to that which causes it.*

This is plain out of the foregoing Principle. For there is
no contradiction nor impossibility of a Cause producing an Effect
less noble then it self, for thereby we are the better assured
that it does not exceed the capacity of its own powers: Nor is
there any incongruity, that one Substance should cause something else which we may in some sense call Substance, though
but *Secondary* or *Emanatory;* acknowledging the *Primary Substance* to be the more adequate Object of Divine Creation, but
the *Secondary* to be referrible also to the *Primary* or *Centrall*
Substance by way of causall relation. For suppose God
created the *Matter* with an immediate power of *moving it self,*
God indeed is the Prime Cause as well of the *Motion* as of the
Matter, and yet nevertheless the *Matter* is rightly said *to move
it self.* Finally, this *Secondary* or *Emanatory* Substance may
be rightly called *Substance,* because it is a Subject indued with
certain powers and activities, and that it does not inhere as an
Accident in any other Substance or Matter, but could maintain
its place, though all Matter or what other Substance soever
were removed out of that space it is extended through, provided
its *Primary Substance* be but safe.

3. From these four Principles I have here added, we may have
not an imaginative but rationall apprehension of that part of *a
Spirit* which we call the *Secondary Substance* thereof. Whose
Extension arising by graduall Emanation from the First and
Primest Essence, which we call the *Centre of the Spirit* (which
is no impossible supposition by the 16, 18, and 19. Axiomes) we
are led from hence to a necessary acknowledgment of perfect

Indiscerpibility of parts, though not intellectuall Indivisibility, by Axiome 17. For it implies a contradiction that an *Emanative* effect should be disjoyned from its originall.

4. Thus have I demonstrated how a *Spirit*, considering the lineaments of it (as I may so call them) from the Centre to the Circumference, is utterly *indiscerpible*. But now if any be so curious as to ask how the parts thereof hold together in a line drawn cross to these from the Centre, (for *Imagination*, it may be, will suggest they lye all loose;) I answer, that the conjecture of *Imagination* is here partly true and partly false, or is true or false as she shall be interpreted. For if she mean by loose, actually disunited, it is false and ridiculous: but if only so discerpible, that one part may be disunited from another, that may not only be true, but, upon supposition the essentiall rayes are not fully enough redoubled within, plainly necessary; otherwise a *Spirit* could not *contract* one part and extend another, which is yet an Hypothesis necessary to be admitted. Wherefore this Objection is so far from weaking the possibility of this Notion, that it gives occasion more fully to declare the exact concinnity thereof.

To be brief therefore, a *Spirit* from the Centre to the Circumference is utterly *indiscerpible*, but in lines cross to this it is closely coherent, but need not be indiscerpibly; which cohesion may consist in an immediate union of these parts, and transverse penetration and transcursion of *Secondary Substance* through this whole Sphere of life which we call a *Spirit*.

Nor need we wonder that so full an Orbe should swell out from so subtil and small a point as the *Centre of this Spirit* is supposed. Ἐι γὰρ καὶ τῷ ὄγκῳ μικρόν ἐστι, δυνάμει καὶ τιμιότητι πολὺ μᾶλλον ὑπερέχει πάντων, as *Aristotle* speaks of the Mind of Man. And besides, it is but what is seen in some sort to the very eye in light, how large a spheare of Aire a little spark will illuminate.*

5. This is the pure *Idea* of a *created Spirit* in general, concerning which if there be yet any cavil to be made, it can be none other then what is perfectly common to it and to *Matter*, that is, the unimaginableness of Points and smallest Particles, and how what is discerpible or divisible can at all hang together:

* *Ethic. ad Nicomach. lib. 10. cap. 7.*

˙but this not hindering *Matter* from actual existence, there is no reason that it should any way pretend to the inferring of the impossibility of the existence of a *Spirit,* by Axiome 7.

But the most lubricous supposition that we goe upon here, is not altogether so intricate as those difficulties in *Matter.* For if that be but granted, in which I find no absurdity, That a Particle of *Matter* may be so little that it is utterly uncapable of being made less, it is plain that one and the same thing, though intellectually divisible, may yet be really indiscerpible. And indeed it is not only possible, but it seems necessary that this should be true: For though we should acknowledge that *Matter* were discerpible *in infinitum,* yet supposing a Cause of Infinite distinct perception and as Infinite power, (and God is such) this Cause can reduce this capacity of infinite discerpibleness of *Matter* into act, that is to say, actually and at once discerp it or disjoyn it into so many particles as it is discerpible into. From whence it will follow, that one of these particles reduced to this perfect Parvitude is then utterly indiscerpible, and yet intellectually divisible, otherwise Magnitude would consist of mere points, which would imply a contradiction.

We have therefore plainly demonstrated by reason, that *Matter* consists of parts indiscerpible; and therefore there being no other Faculty to give suffrage against it, for neither Sense nor any Common Notion can contradict it, it remains by Axiome 5. that the Conclusion is true.

6. What some would object from Reason, that these *perfect Parvitudes* being acknowledged still intellectually divisible, must still have parts into which they are divisible, and therefore be still discerpible; To this it is answered, That *division into parts* does not imply any *discerpibility,* because the parts conceived in one of these *Minima Corporalia* (as I may so call them) are rather *essential* or *formal* parts then *integral,* and can no more actually be dissevered, then Sense and Reason from the Soul of a man. For it is of the very Essence of *Matter* to be *divisible,* but it is not at all included in the essence thereof to be *discerpible;* and therefore where *discerpibility* fails there is no necessity that *divisibility* should fail also. See the Preface, Sect. 3. (31)

7. As for the trouble of spurious suggestions or representa-

tions from the *Phansy,* as if these *perfect Parvitudes* were
Round bodies, and that therefore there would be *Triangular
intervalls betwixt,* void of Matter; they are of no moment in
this case, she alwayes representing a *Discerpible* magnitude in
stead of an *Indiscerpible* one. Wherefore she bringing in a false
evidence, her testimony is to be rejected; nay if she could perplex the cause far worse, she was not to be heard, by Axiome
the 4.

Wherefore *Phansy* being unable to exhibite the Object we
consider, in its due advantages, for ought we know these *perfect
Parvitudes* may lye so close together, that they have no
intervalls betwixt: nay it seems necessary to be so; For if there
were any such *intervalls,* they were capable of particles less
then these least of all; which is a contradiction in Reason, and
a thing utterly impossible.

But if we whould gratifie *Phansy* so far as to admit of these
intervalls, the greatest absurdity would be, that we must admit
an insensible *Vacuum,* which no Faculty will be able ever to
confute.   But it is most rationall to admit none, and more consonant to our determination concerning these *Minima Corporalia,*
as I call them, whose largeness is to be limited to the least real
touch of either a Globe on a Plane, or a Cone on a Plane, or a
Globe on a Globe: if you conceive any real touch less then
another, let that be the measure of these *Minute Realities* in
Matter. From whence it will follow, they must touch a whole
side at once, and therefore can never leave any empty *intervalls.*

Nor can we imagine any Angulosities or Round protuberancies
in a quantity infinitely little, more then we can in one infinitely
great, as I have already declared in my Preface. I must confess, a mans *Reason* in this speculation is mounted far beyond
his *Imagination;* but there being worse intricacies in Theories
acknowledged constantly to be true, it can be no prejudice to
the present Conclusion, by the 4, and 7. Axiomes.

8. Thus have we cleared up *a full and distinct Notion of a
Spirit,* with so unexceptionable accuracy, that no Reason can
pretend to assert it impossible nor unintelligible. But if the
Theory thereof may seem more operose and tedious to impatient
wits, and the punctuality of the Description the more hazardous

and incredible, as if it were beyond our Faculties to make so
precise a Conclusion in a Subject so obscure, they may ease
their Understanding, by contenting themselves with what we
have set down Chap. 2. Sect. 11, 12. and remember that that
Wisdome and Power that created all things, can make them of
what nature He pleases; and that if God will that there shall
be a Creature that is *penetrable and indiscerpible,* that it is
as easy a thing for him to make one so of its own nature, as one
impenetrable and discerpible, and indue it with what other
Properties he pleases, according to his own will and purpose:
which induments being immediately united with the Subject
they are in, Reason can make no further demand how they are
there, by the 9. Axiome.

CHAP. VII.

1. *Of the Self-motion of a Spirit.* 2. *Of Self-penetration.* 3. *Of
Self-contraction and dilatation.* 4. *The power of penetrating of* Matter. 5. *The power of moving,* 6. *And of altering the* Matter.

1. We have proved the *Indiscerpibility of a Spirit* as well in
Centre as *Circumference,* as well in the *Primary* as *Secondary*
Substance thereof, to be a very consistent and congruous Notion.
The next Property is *Self-motion,* which must of necessity be
an Attribute of something or other; For by *Self-motion* I understand nothing else but *Self-activity,* which must appertain to a
Subject active of it self.   Now what is simply active of it self, can
no more cease to be active then to Be; which is a sign that *Matter*
is not active of it self, because it is reducible to Rest: Which is
an Argument not only that *Self-activity* belongs to *a Spirit,* but
that there is such a thing as *a Spirit* in the world, from which
activity is communicated to *Matter.*   And indeed if *Matter* as
Matter had motion, nothing would hold together; but Flints,
Adamant, Brass, Iron, yea this whole Earth would suddenly
melt into a thinner Substance then the subtile Aire, or rather it
never had been condensated together to this consistency we finde
it.   But this is to anticipate my future purpose of proving
That there are Spirits existing in the world: It had been sufficient
here to have asserted, That *Self-motion* or *Self-activity* is as

conceivable to appertain to *Spirit* as to *Body,* which is plain at first sight to any man that appeals to his own Faculties. Nor is it at all to be scrupled at, that any thing should be allowed *to move it self;* because our Adversaries, that say there is nothing but *Matter* in the world, must of necessity (as I have intimated already) confess that *this Matter moves it self,* though it be very incongruous so to affirm.

2. The congruity and possibilty of *Self-penetration* in a *created Spirit* is to be conceived, partly from the limitableness of the Subject, and partly from the foregoing Attributes of *Indiscerpibilty* and *Self-motion.* For *Self-penetration* cannot belong to God, because it is impossible any thing should belong to him that implies imperfection, and *Self-penetration* cannot be without the lessening of the presence of that which does penetrate it self, or the implication that some parts of that Essence are not so well as they may be; which is a contradiction in a Being which is *absolutely Perfect.* From the Attributes of *Indiscerpibility* and *Self-motion* (to which you may adde *Penetrability* from the general notion of a *Spirit*) it is plain that such a *Spirit* as we define, having the power of Motion upon the whole extent of its essence, may also determine this Motion according to the Property of its own nature: and therefore if it determine the motion of the exteriour parts inward, they will return inward towards the Centre of essential power; which they may easily doe without resistance, the whole Subject being *penetrable,* and without damage, it being also *indiscerpible.*

3. From this *Self-penetration* we do not only easily, but necessarily, understand *Self-contraction* and *dilatation* to arise. For this *Self-moving Substance,* which we call a *Spirit,* cannot penetrate it self, but it must needs therewith contract it self; nor restore it self again to its former state, but it does thereby dilate it self: so that we need not at all insist upon these Termes.

4. That power which a *Spirit* has to *penetrate Matter* we may easily understand if we consider a *Spirit* only as a Substance, whose immediate property is *Activity.* For then it is not harder to imagine this Active Substance to pervade this or the other part of *Matter,* then it is to conceive the pervading or disspreading of motion it self therein.

5. The greatest difficulty is to fancy how this *Spirit,* being so

Incorporeal, can be able to move the *Matter,* though it be in it. For it seems so subtle, that it will pass through, leaving no more footsteps of its being there, then the Lightening does in the Scabbard, though it may haply melt the Sword, because it there findes resistance. But a *Spirit* can find no resistance any where, the closest *Matter* being easily penetrable and pervious to an *Incorporeal* Substance. The ground of this difficulty is founded upon the unconceivableness of any *Union* that can be betwixt the *Matter,* and a Substance that can so *easily pass through it.* For if we could but once imagine an *Union* betwixt *Matter* and a *Spirit,* the activity then of the *Spirit* would certainly have influence upon *Matter,* either for *begetting,* or *increasing,* or *directing* the *motion* therof.

But notwithstanding the *Penetrability* and easy passage of a *Spirit* through *Matter,* there is yet for all that a capacity of a strong union betwixt them, and every whit as conceivable as betwixt the parts of *Matter* themselves. For what glue or Cement holds the parts of hard matter in stones and metalls together, or, if you will, of what is absolutely hard, that has no pores or particles, but is one continued and perfectly homogeneous body, not only to Sense, but according to the exact *Idea* of Reason? what Cement holds together the parts of such a body as this? Certainly nothing but *immediate Union and Rest.* Now for *Union,* there is no comparison betwixt that of *Matter* with *Matter,* and this of *Spirit* with *Matter.* For the first is only superficiall; in this latter the very inward parts are united point to point throughout. Nor is there any feare it will not take hold, because it has a capacity of passing through. For in this absolutely solid hard Body, which let be A, in which let us conceive some inward superficies, suppose E A C, this superficies is so smooth as nothing can be conceived smoother: why does not therefore the upper E D C slide upon the neather part E F C upon the least motion imaginable, especially E F C being supposed to be held fast whilst the other is thrust against? This facilty therefore

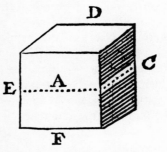

of one Body passing upon another without any sticking, seeming as necessary to our Phansy as a *Spirit's* passing through all Bodies without taking hold of them, it is plain by Axiome 7. That a firm union of *Spirit* and *Matter* is very possible, through we cannot conceive the manner thereof.

And as for *Rest*, it is competible also to this conjunction of *Matter* with *Spirit*, as well as of *Matter* with *Matter*. For suppose the whole body A moved with like swiftness in every part, the parts of A then are according to that sense of *Rest*, by which they would explain the adhesion of the parts of *Matter* one with another, truly quiescent. So say I that in the *Union* of *Matter* and *Spirit*, the parts of the *Matter* receiving from the *Spirit* just such a velocity of motion as the *Spirit* exerts, and no more, they both rest in firm *Union* one with another. That which comes to pass even then when there is far less immediate *Union* then we speak of. For if we do but lay a Book on our Hand, provided our Hand be not moved with a swifter motion then it communicates to the Book, nor the Book be pusht on faster then the swiftness of our Hand; the Book and our Hand will most certainly retain their Union and goe together. So naturall and easy is it to conceive how *a Spirit* may move *a Body* without any more perplexity or contradiction then is found in the *Union* and *Motion* of the parts of *Matter* it self. See the Appendix to my Antidote.*

6. The last Terme I put in the Definition of a *Spirit* is, *the power of altering the Matter;* which will necessarily follow from its *power of moving it* or *directing its motion.* For *Alteration* is nothing else but the varying of either the Figures, or postures, or the degrees of motion in the particles; all which are nothing else but the results of *Local motion.* Thus have we cleared the *intelligibility* and *possibility* of all the Terms that belong to the Notion of *a created* Spirit in general, at least of such as may be rationally conceived to be the causes of any visible *Phaenomena* in the world: We will now descend to the defining of the chief *Species* thereof.

* Chap. 3. sect. 7, and 8.

CHAP. VIII.

1. *Four main* Species *of Spirits.*   2. *How they are to be defined.*
3. *The definition of a Seminal Form;*   4. *Of the Soul of a
Brute;*   5. *Of the Soul of a Man.*   6. *The difference betwixt the Soul of an Angel and an Humane Soul.*   7. *The
definition of an Angelical Soul.*   8. *Of the Platonical* Νόες
and Ἑνάδες.   9. *That* Des-Cartes *his Demonstration of
the Existence of the Humane Soul does at least conclude
the possibility of a Spirit.*

1. We have enumerated *Four kinds of Spirits,* viz. *The* λόγοι
σπερματικοὶ or *Seminal Forms, the Souls of Brutes, the
Humane Soul, and that Soul or Spirit which actuates or informs
the vehicles of Angels:* For I look upon *Angels* to be as truly
a compound Being, consisting of Soul and Body, as that of Men
& Brutes.   Their Existence we shall not now goe about to prove,
for that belongs to another place.   My present design is onely
to expound or define the notion of these things, so far forth as
is needful for the evincing that they are the *Ideas* or Notions
of things which imply no contradiction or impossibility in their
conception; which will be very easy for us to perform: the chief
difficulty lying in that *more General notion* of a *Spirit,* which we
have so fully explained in the foregoing Chapters.

2. Now this *General notion* can be contracted into *Kindes,* by
no other *Differences* then such as may be called peculiar Powers
or Properties belonging to one *Spirit* and excluded from another,
by the 8. Axiome.   From whence it will follow, that if we
describe these *several kindes of Spirits* by *immediate* and *intrin-
secal* Properties, we have given as good Definitions of them as
any one can give of any thing in the world.

3. We will begin with what is most simple, the *Seminal Forms*
of things which, for the present, deciding nothing of their existence, according to their ἰδέα *possibilis,* we define thus; *A
Seminal Form is a created Spirit organizing duly-prepared
Matter into life and vegetation proper to this or the other kind
of Plant.*   It is beyond my imagination what can be excepted
against this Description, it containing nothing but what is very

coherent and intelligible. For in that it is a *Spirit,* it can *move Matter* intrinsecally, or at least *direct the motion* thereof: But in that it is not an *Omnipotent* Spirit, but *Finite* and Created, its power may well be restrained to *duly-prepared Matter* both for vital union and motion; He that has made *these Particular Spirits,* varying their Faculties of Vital union according to the diversity of the preparation of *Matter,* and so limiting the whole comprehension of them all, that none of them may be able to be vitally joyned with any *Matter* whatever: And the same first Cause of all things that gives them a power of uniting with & moving of *matter duly prepared;* may also set such laws to this motion, that when it lights on matter fit for it, it will produce such and such a Plant, that is to say, it will shape the matter into such Figure, Colour and other properties, as we discover in them by our Senses.

4. This is the First degree of *Particular Life* in the world,* if there be any purely of this degree Particular. But now, as *Aristotle* has somewhere noted, the Essences of things are like Numbers, whose *Species* are changed by adding or taking away an Unite: adde therefore another *Intrinsecall power* to this of *Vegetation,* viz. *Sensation,* and it becomes *the Soul of a Beast.* For in truth the bare Substance it self is not to be computed in explicite knowledg, it being utterly in it self unconceivable, and therefore we will onely reckon upon the Powers. *A Subject therefore from whence is both Vegetation and Sensation is the general notion of the Soul of a Brute.* Which is distributed into a number of kindes, the effect of every *Intrinsecall power* being discernible in the constant shape and properties of every distinct kind of Brute Creatures.

5. If we adde to *Vegetation* and *Sensation Reason* properly so called, we have then a settled notion of the *Soul of Man;* which we may more compleatly describe thus: *A created Spirit indued with Sense and Reason, and a power of organizing terrestrial Matter into humane shape by vital union therewith.*

6. And herein alone, I conceive, does the *Spirit* or *Soul* of an *Angel* (for I take the boldness to call that *Soul,* whatever it is, that has a power of vitally actuating the *Matter*) differ from the *Soul* of a *Man,* in that the Soul of an *Angel* may vitally

* See Book 3. ch. 12, & 13.

actuate an *Aerial* or *Æthereal* Body, but cannot be born into this world in a *Terrestrial* one.

7. To make an end therefore of our Definitions: an *Angelical Soul* is very intelligibly described thus; *A created Spirit indued with Reason, Sensation, and a power of being vitally united with and actuating of a Body of Aire or Æther onely.* Which power over an *Aereal* or *Æthereal* Body is very easily to be understood out of that *general notion of a Spirit* in the foregoing Chapters. For it being there made good, that union with *Matter* is not incompetible to a *Spirit,* and consequently nor moving of it, nor that kind of motion in a Spirit which we call *Contraction* and *Dilatation;* these Powers, if carefully considered, will necessarily infer the possibility of the Actuation and Union of an *Angelical Soul* with an Æthereal or Aiery Body.

8. The *Platonists* write of other Orders of *Spirits* or *Immaterial Substances,* as the Nóες and 'Ενάδες. (32) But there being more Subtilty then either usefulness or assurance in such like Speculations, I shall pass them over at this time; having already, I think, irrefutably made good, That there is no incongruity nor incompossibility comprised in the Notion of *Spirit* or *Incorporeal Substance.*

9. But there is yet another way of inferring the same, and it is the Argument of *Des-Cartes,* whereby he would conclude that there is *de facto* a *Substance in us distinct from Matter,* viz. our own *Mind.* For every Real Affection or Property being the *Mode* of some Substance or other, and *real Modes* being unconceivable without their *Subject,* he inferres that, seeing we can doubt whether there be any such thing as *Body* in the world (by which doubting we seclude *Cogitation* from *Body*) there must be some other Substance distinct from the *Body,* to which *Cogitation* belongs. (33)

But I must confess this Argument will not reach home to *Des-Cartes* his purpose, who would prove in Man a *Substance distinct from his Body.* For being there may be *Modes* common to more Subjects then one, and this of *Cogitation* may be pretended to be such as is compatible as well to Substance *Corporeal* as *Incorporeal,* it may be conceived apart from either, though not from both. And therefore his Argument does not prove That that in us which does *think* or *perceive* is a Substance dis-

tinct from our Body, but onely That there may be such a
Substance, which has the power of *thinking* or *perceiving,* which
yet is not a *Body.* For it being impossible that there should
be any *real Mode* which is in no Subject, and we clearly conceiving *Cogitation* independent for existence on *Corporeal* Substance; it is necessary, That there may be some other Substance
on which it may depend; which must needs be a Substance
Incorporeal.

CHAP. IX.

1. *That it is of no small consequence to have proved the* Possibility *of the Existence of a Spirit.* 2. *The necessity of
   examining of Mr.* Hobbs *his Reasons to the contrary.* 3.
   The first Excerption out of Mr. Hobbs. 4. *The second Excerption.* 5. *The third.* 6. *The fourth.* 7. *The fifth.* 8.
   The sixth. 9. *The seventh.* 10. *The eighth and last Excerption.*

1. I have been, I believe, to admiration curious and sollicitous
to make good, That the Existence of a *Spirit* or *Incorporeal Substance* is possible. But there is no reason any one should wonder
that I have spent so much pains to make so small and inconsiderable a progresse, as to bring the thing onely to a *bare
possibility.* For though I may seem to have gained little to my
self, yet I have thereby given a very signal overthrow to the
adverse party, whose strongest hold seems to be an unshaken
confidence, That the very Notion of a *Spirit* or *Substance Immaterial* is a perfect Incompossibility and pure Non-sense. From
whence are insinuated no better Consequences then these: That
it is impossible that there should be any God, or Soul, or Angel,
Good or Bad; or any Immortality or Life to come. That there
is no Religion, no Piety nor Impiety, no Vertue nor Vice, Justice
nor Injustice, but what it pleases him that has the longest Sword
to call so. That there is no Freedome of Will, nor consequently
any Rational remorse of Conscience in any Being whatsoever,
but that all that is, is nothing but *Matter* and *corporeal Motion;*
and that therefore every trace of mans life is as *necessary* as the
tracts of Lightning and the fallings of Thunder; the blind

impetus of the *Matter* breaking through or being stopt every where, with as certain and determinate *necessity* as the course of a Torrent after mighty storms and showers of Rain.

2. And verily considering of what exceeding great consequence it is to root out this sullen conceit that some have taken up concerning *Incorporeal Substance,* as if it bore a contradiction in the very termes, I think I shall be wanting to so weighty a Cause, if I shall content my self with a bare recitation of the Reasons whereby I prove it possible, and not produce their Arguments that seem most able to maintain the contrary.   And truly I do not remember that I ever met with any one yet that may justly be suspected to be more able to make good this Province then our Countreyman Mr. *Hobbs,* whose inexuperable confidence of the truth of the Conclusion may well assure any man that duely considers the excellency of his natural Wit and Parts, that he has made choice of the most Demonstrative Arguments that humane Invention can search out for the eviction thereof.

3. And that I may not incurre the suspicion of mistaking his Assertion, or of misrepresenting the force of his Reasons, I shall here punctually set them down in the same words I find them in his own Writings, that any man may judge if I doe him any wrong.   The first place I shall take notice of is in his * *Leviathan, The Word* Body *in the most general acceptation signifies that which filleth or occupieth some certain room or imagined place; and dependeth not on the Imagination, but is a real part of that we call the Universe.   For the Universe being the Aggregate of all* Bodies, *there is no real part thereof that is not also* Body; *nor any thing properly a* Body, *that is not also part of* (*that Aggregate of all* Bodies) *the Universe.   The same also, because Bodies are subject to change, that is to say, to variety of appearance to the sense of living Creatures, is called* Substance, *that is to say, subject to various Accidents; as sometimes to be moved, sometimes to stand still, and to seem to our Senses sometimes Hot, sometimes Cold, sometimes of one Colour, Smell, Tast, or Sound, sometimes of another.   And this diversity of seeming, (produced by the diversity of the operation of Bodies on the Organs of our Sense) we attribute to alterations of the*

* Chap. 34.

Bodies that operate, and call them Accidents *of those Bodies. And according to this acception of the word,* Substance *and* Body *signifie the same thing; and therefore* Substance Incorporeal *are words which when they are joyned together destroy one another, as if a man should say an* Incorporeal Body.

Hobbes on dreams

4. The second place is in his * *Physicks. But it is here to be observed that certain Dreams, especially such as some men have when they are betwixt sleeping and waking, and such as happen to those that have no knowledge of the nature of Dreams, and are withall superstitious, were not heretofore nor are now accounted Dreams. For the Apparitions men thought they saw, and the voices they thought they heard in sleep, were not believed to be Phantasmes, but things subsisting of themselves, and Objects without those that Dreamed. For to some men, as well sleeping as waking, but especially to guilty men, and in the night, and in hallowed places, Fear alone, helped a little with the stories of such Apparitions, hath raised in their mindes terrible Phantasmes, which have been and are still deceitfully received for things really true, under the names of Ghosts and Incorporeal Substances.*

dreams are "onely phantasmes of the mind that imagines them"

5. We will adde a third out of the same Book.* *For seeing Ghosts, sensible species, a shadow, light, colour, sound, space, &c. appear to us no less sleeping then waking, they cannot be things without us, but onely Phantasmes of the mind that imagines them.*

6. And a fourth out of his Humane Nature.* *But Spirits supernatural commonly signifie some Substance without dimension, which two words do flatly contradict one another. And Artic. 5. Nor I think is that word Incorporeal at all in the Bible, but it is said of the Spirit, that it abideth in men, sometimes that it dwelleth in them, sometimes that it cometh on them, that it descendeth, and goeth, and cometh, and that Spirits are Angels, that is to say, Messengers; all which words do imply Locality, and locality is Dimension, and whatsoever hath dimension is Body, be it never so subtile.*

spirits are angels, i.e. messengers

7. The fifth Excerption shall be again out of his Leviathan.* *And for the Matter or Substance of the Invisible agents so*

* Part 4. Chap. 25. Article 9.   * Chap. 11. Article 4.
* Part I. Chap. 5. Article 4.   * *Leviathan,* chap. 12.

fancyed, they could not by natural cogitation fall upon any other conceit, but that it was the same with that of the Soul of Man, and that the Soul of Man was of the same Substance with that which appeareth in a Dream to one that sleepeth, or in a Looking-glass to one that is awake: Which, men not knowing that such Apparitions are nothing else but creatures of the Fancy, think to be real and external Substances, and therefore call them Ghosts, as the Latines called them Imagines *and* Umbrae; *and thought them Spirits, that is, thin aerial bodies; and those invisible Agents, which they feared, to be like them, save that they appear and vanish when they please. But the opinion that such Spirits were Incorporeal or Immaterial could never enter into the mind of any man by nature; because, though men may put together words of contradictory significa-tion, as* Spirit *and* Incorporeal, *yet they can never have the imagination of any thing answering to them.*

We will help out this further from what he also writes in his Humane Nature.* *To know that a Spirit is, that is to say, to have natural evidence of the same, it is impossible. For all evi-dence is conception, and all conception is imagination, and pro-ceedeth from Sense; and Spirits we suppose to be those Sub-stances which work not upon the Sense, and therefore are not conceptible.*

8. The sixth, out of Chap. 45. where he writes thus:* *This nature of Sight having never been discovered by the ancient pretenders to Natural knowledge, much less by those that con-sider not things so remote (as that Knowledge is) from their present use; it was hard for men to conceive of those Images in the Fancy and in the Sense, otherwise then of things really without us. Which some (because they vanish away they know not whither nor how) will have to be absolutely Incorporeal, that is to say, Immaterial, or Forms without Matter, Colour and Figure, without any coloured or figured body, and that they can put on aiery bodies, (as a garment) to make them visible when they will to our bodily eyes; and others say, are Bodies and living Creatures, but made of Aire, or other more subtile and aethereal matter, which is then, when they will be seen, con-densed. But both of them agree on one general appellation of*

---

* Chap. 11. Article 5.   * *Leviathan*, chap. 45.

both the apparitions of a dream and the soul of man are " creatures of the Fancy ".

Sense
↓
imagination
↓
conception
↓

them, Daemons. *As if the dead of whom they dreamed were not the Inhabitants of their own Brain, but of the Aire, or of Heaven or Hell, not Phantasmes, but Ghosts; with just as much reason as if one should say he saw his own Ghost in a Looking-glass, or the Ghosts of the stars in a River, or call the ordinary Apparition of the Sun of the quantity of about a foot, the Daemon or Ghost of that great Sun that enlightneth the whole visible world.*

the ghosts are nothing but the "Inhabitants of their own Being"

9. The seventh is out of the next Chapter of the same book.* Where he again taking to task that *Jargon,* as he calls it, of *Abstract Essences* and *Substantial Formes,* writes thus: *The World (I mean not the Earth onely, but the Universe, that is, the whole mass of all things that are) is Corporeal, that is to say, Body, and hath the Dimensions of Magnitude, namely Length, Breadth and Depth; also every part of Body is likewise Body, and hath the like dimensions; and consequently every part of the Universe is Body, and that which is not Body is no part of the Universe: And because the Universe is all, that which is no part of it is nothing, and consequently no where.*

those Jargons about "Abstract Essences" and "Substantial Forms"

10. The eighth and last we have a little after in the same Chapter, which runs thus; *Being once fallen into this errour of Separated Essences, they are thereby necessarily involved in many other absurdities that follow it. For seeing they will have these Forms to be real, they are obliged to assign them some place. But because they hold them Incorporeal without all dimension of Quantity, and all men know that Place is Dimension, and not to be filled but by that which is corporeal, they are driven to uphold their credit with a distinction, that they are not indeed any where* Circumscriptive, *but* Definitivé. *Which termes, being mere words, and in this occasion insignificant, pass onely in Latine, that the vanity of them might be concealed. For the Circumscription of a thing is nothing else but the determination or defining of its place, and so both the termes of distinction are the same. And in particular of the essence of a man, which they say is his Soul, they affirm it to be all of it in his little finger, and all of it in every other part (how small soever) of his Body, and yet no more Soul in the whole Body then in any one of these parts. Can any man think that God*

* *Leviathan* chap. 46.

*is served with such Absurdities?   And yet all this is necessary
to believe to those that will believe the existence of an Incorporeal Soul separated from the Body.*

CHAP. X.

1. *An Answer to the first Excerption.   2. To the second.   3. An
Answer to the third.   4. To the fourth Excerption.   5. An
Answer to the fifth.   6. To the sixth.   7. To the seventh.
8. An Answer to the eighth and last.   9. A brief Recapitulation of what has been said hitherto.*

1. We have set down the chiefest passages in the Writings of
Mr. *Hobbs,* that confident Exploder of *Immaterial Substances*
out of the world.   It remains now that we examine them, and
see whether the force of his Arguments bears any proportion to
the firmness of his belief, or rather mis-belief, concerning these
things.   To strip therefore the first Excerption of that long *Am-
bages* of words, and to reduce it to a more plain and compendious
forme of reasoning, the force of his Argument lies thus: *That
seeing every thing in the Universe is* Body (*the Universe being
nothing else but an Aggregate of Bodies*) Body *and* Substance *are
but names of one and the same thing; it being called* Body *as it
fills a place, and* Substance *as it is the Subject of Several Alterations and Accidents.   Wherefore* Body *and* Substance *being
all one,* Incorporeal Substance *is no better sense then an Incorporeal* Body, *which is a contradiction in the very termes.*   But
it is plain to all the world that this is not to prove, but to suppose
what is to be proved, That the Universe is nothing else but an
Aggregate of Bodies: When he has proved that, we will acknowledge the sequel; till then, he has proved nothing, and therefore
this first argumentation must pass for nought.

2. Let us examine the strength of the second, which certainly
must be this, if any at all; *That which has its originall merely
from Dreams, Fears and Superstitious Fancies, has no reall
existence in the world: But Incorporeal Substances have no other
Original.*   The Proposition is a Truth indubitable, but the Assumption is as weak as the other is strong; whether you under-

[margin annotations:]

" that confident Exploder of Immaterial Substances "

Hobbes
body = substance

Incorporeal substances have their "Original" only in dreams, Fears, and fancies

stand it of the real Original of these Substances, or of the Principles of our knowledge That they are.   And be their Original what it will, it is nothing to us, but so far forth as it is cognoscible to us, by Axiome first.   And therefore when he sayes, they have no other Original then that of our own Phansy, he must be understood to affirme that there is no other Principle of the knowledge of their Existence then that we vainly imagine them to be; which is grossly false.

For it is not the *Dreams* and *Fears* of Melancholick and Superstitious persons, from which Philosophers and Christians have argued the Existence of *Spirits* and *Immaterial Substances*; but from the evidence of * Externall Objects of Sense, that is, the ordinary *Phaenomena* of *Nature*, in which there is discoverable so profound Wisdome and Counsell, that they could not but conclude that the Order of things in the world was from a higher Principle then the blind motions and jumblings of *Matter* and *mere Corporeal* Beings.

To which you may adde what usually they call * *Apparitions*, which are so far from being merely the *Dreams* and *Fancies* of the Superstitious, that they are acknowledged by such as cannot but be deemed by most men over-Atheistical, I mean *Pomponatius* and *Cardan*, nay by *Vaninus* himself, though so devoted to Atheisme, that out of a perfect mad zeale to that despicable cause he died for it. (34)   I omit to name the *Operations of the * Soul*, which ever appeared to the wisest of all Ages of such a transcendent condition, that they could not judge them to spring from so contemptible a Principle as *bare Body* or *Matter*.   Wherefore to decline all these, and to make representation onely of *Dreams* and *Fancies* to be the occasions of the world's concluding that there are *Incorporeal Substances*, is to fancy his Reader a mere fool, and publickly to profess that he has a mind to impose upon him.

3. The third argumentation is this: *That which appears to us as well sleeping as waking, is nothing without us: But Ghosts, that is Immaterial Substances, appear to us as well sleeping as waking.*   This is the weakest Argument that has been yet pro-

* See my *Antidote* against *Atheism*, the whole second Book.
* See my *Antidote*, the whole third Book.
* *Antid*. Book I. chap. 11.

duced: for both the Proposition and Assumption are false. For if the Proposition were true, the Sun, Moon, Stars, Clouds, Rivers, Meadows, Men, Women, and other living creatures were nothing without us: For all these appear to us as well when we are *sleeping* as *waking*. But *Incorporeal Substances* do not appear to us as well *sleeping* as *waking*. For the Notion of an *Incorporeal Substance* is so subtile and refined, that it leaving little or no impression on the *Phansy*, its representation is merely supported by the free power of *Reason,* which seldome exercises it self in *sleep,* unless upon easy imaginable Phantasmes.

4. The force of the fourth Argument is briefly this: *Every Substance has dimensions; but a Spirit has no dimensions.* Here I confidently deny the Assumption. For it is not the Characteristicall of *a Body* to have *dimensions,* but to be *Impenetrable.* All Substance has *Dimensions,* that is, Length, Breadth, and Depth: but all has not *Impenetrability.* See my Letters to Monsieur *Des-Cartes,* besides what I have here writ in this * present Treatise. (35)

5. In the Excerptions belonging to the fifth place these Arguments are comprised.   1. *That we have no principle of knowledge of any Immaterial Being, but such as a Dream or a Looking-Glasse furnisheth us withall.*   2. *That the word* Spirit *or Incorporeal implies a contradiction, and cannot be conceived to be sense by a natural Understanding.*   3. *That nothing is conceived by the Understanding but what comes in at the Senses, and therefore Spirits not acting upon the Senses must remain unknown and unconceivable.*

We have already answered to the first in what we have returned to his second Argument in the second Excerption.

To the second I answer, That *Spirit* or *Incorporeal* implies no contradiction, there being nothing understood thereby but *Extended Substance* with *Activity* and *Indiscerpability,* leaving out *Impenetrability:* Which I have above demonstrated to be the Notion of *a thing possible,* and need not repeat what I have already written.

To the third I answer, That *Spirits* do act really upon the *Senses,* by acting upon *Matter* that affects the *Senses;* and some of these Operations being such, that they cannot be rationally

* Book I. ch. 2. & 3.

[margin note: knowledge of an Immaterial Being is only furnished by dreams and looking-glasses]

attributed to the *Matter* alone, *Reason* by the information of the *Senses* concludes, that there is some other more noble principle distinct from the *Matter*. And as for that part of the Argument that asserts that there is nothing in the Understanding but what comes in at the Senses, I * have, and shall again in its * due place demonstrate it to be very gross Errour.

More But in the mean time I conclude, that the Substance of every thing being utterly unconceivable, by Axiome 8. and it being onely the *Immediate Properties* by which a man conceives every thing, and the Properties of *Penetrability* and *Indiscerpibility* being as easy to conceive, as of *Discerpibility* and *Impenetrability,* and the power of communicating of motion to *Matter* as easy as the *Matter's* reception of it, and the Union of *Matter* with *Spirit,* as of *Matter* with *Matter;* it plainly follows, that the Notion of a *Spirit* is as naturally conceivable as the Notion of a *Body.*

6. In this sixth Excerption he is very copious in jearing and making ridiculous the opinion of *Ghosts* and *Daemons;* but the strength of his Argument, if it have any, is this, viz. *If there be any such things as Ghosts or Daemons, then they are (according to them that hold this opinion) either those Images reflected from water or Looking-glasses, cloathing themselves in aiery garments, and so wandring up & down; or else they are living Creatures made of nothing but Aire or some more subtile and Æthereal Matter.* One might well be amazed to observe such slight and vain arguing come from so grave a Philosopher, were not a man well aware that his peculiar eminency, as himself somewhere professes, lies in *Politicks,* to which the humours and Bravadoes of Eloquence, especially amongst the simple, is a very effectuall and serviceable instrument. And certainly such Rhetorications as this cannot be intended for any but such as are of the very weakest capacity.

Those two groundless conceits that he would obtrude upon the sober Assertors of *Spirits* and *Daemons* belong not to them, but are the genuine issue of his own Brain. For, for the former of them, it is most justly adjudged to him, as the first Author thereof; it being a Rarity, which neither my self nor (I dare say) any else ever met with out of Mr *Hobbs* his Writings. And the latter

* *Antidote,* Book I. ch. 6. *Append.* ch. 2. sect. 4, 5, 6, &c.
* Book 2. ch. 2. sect. 9, 10, 11.

he does not onely not goe about to confute here, but makes a
shew of allowing it, for fear he should seem to deny Scripture,
in Chap. 34. of his *Leviathan*. But those that assert the Existence of *Spirits*, will not stand to Mr *Hobbs* his choice for defining of them, but will make use of their own Reason and Judgment for the settling of so concerning a Notion.

7. In this seventh Excerption is contained the same Argument
that was found in the first; but to deal fairly and candidly, I
must confess it is better back'd then before. For there he supposes, but does not prove, the chief ground of his Argument; but
here he offers at a proof of it, couched, as I conceive, in these
words [*and hath the dimensions of Magnitude, namely Length,
Breadth and Depth*] for hence he would infer that the whole Universe is *Corporeal*, that is to say, every thing in the Universe,
because there is nothing but has *Length, Breadth* and *Depth*.
This therefore is the very last ground his Argument is to be
resolved into. But how weak it is I have already intimated,
it being not *Trinal Dimension*, but *Impenetrability*, that constitutes a *Body*.

8. This last Excerption seems more considerable then any of
the former, or all of them put together: but when the force of
the Arguments therein contained is duly weighed, they will be
found of as little efficacy to make good the Conclusion as the
rest. The first Argument runs thus; *Whatsoever is real, must
have some place: But Spirits can have no place.* But this is
very easily answered. For if nothing else be understood by *Place*,
but *Imaginary Space*, Spirits and Bodies may be in the same *Imaginary Space*, and so the Assumption is false. But if by *Place*
be meant the *concave Superficies of one Body immediately en-
vironing another Body*, so that it be conceived to be of the very
Formality of a *Place*, immediately to environ the *corporeal*
Superficies of that Substance which is said to be placed; then it
is impossible that a *Spirit* should be properly said to be in a
Place, and so the Proposition will be false. Wherefore there
being these two acceptions of *Place*, that Distinction of being
there *Circumscriptivè* and *Definitivè* is an allowable Distinction,
and the terms may not signify one and the same thing. But if
we will with Mr. *Hobbs* (and I know no great hurt if we should
doe so) confine the Notion of *Place* to *Imaginary Space*, this

distinction of the Schools will be needless here, and we may, without any more adoe, assert, That *Spirits* are as truly in place as *Bodies*.

His second Argument is drawn from that Scholastick Riddle, which I must confess seems to verge too near to profound Nonsense, That the Soul of man is *tota in toto* and *tota in qualibet parte corporis*. This mad Jingle it seems has so frighted Mr *Hobbs* sometime or other, that he never since could endure to come near the Notion of a *Spirit* again, not so much as to consider whether it were a mere Bug-bear, or some real Being. But if Passion had not surprised his better Faculties, he might have found a true settled meaning thereof, and yet secluded these wilde intricacies that the heedless Schools seem to have charged it with: For the *Immediate Properties* of a *Spirit* are very well intelligible without these Ænigmatical flourishes, viz. That it is a *Substance Penetrable and Indiscerpible*, as I have already shewn at large.

Nor is that Scholastick Ænigme necessary to be believed by all those that would believe in the Existence of an *Incorporeal* Soul; nor do I believe Mr *Hobbs* his interpretation of this Riddle to be so necessary. And it had been but fair play to have been assured that the Schools held such a perfect contradiction, before he pronounced the belief thereof necessary to all those that would hold the Soul of Man *an Immaterial Substance, separable from the Body*. I suppose they may mean nothing by it, but what *Plato* did by his making the Soul to consist ἐκ μεριστῆς καὶ ἀμερίστου οὐσίας nor *Plato* any thing more by that *divisible* and *indivisible Substance,* then an Essence that is intellectually divisible, but really indiscerpible. (36)

9. We have now firmly made good, that the Notion of *a Spirit* implies no contradiction nor incompossibility of it; but is the Notion or *Idea* of a thing that may possibly be. Which I have done so punctually and particularly, that I have cleared every *Species* of *Substances Incorporeal* from the imputation of either obscurity or inconsistency. And that I might not seem to take advantage in pleading their cause in the absence of the adverse party, I have brought in the most able Advocate and the most assured that I have hitherto ever met withall; and dare now appeal to any indifferent Judge, whether I have not demonstrated

all his Allegations to be weak and inconclusive.   Wherefore having so clearly evinced the *possibility* of the Existence of a Spirit, we shall now make a step further, and prove That it is not onely a thing *possible,* but that it is *really* and *actually* in Nature.

CHAP. XI.

1. *Three grounds to prove the Existence of an* Immaterial Substance, *whereof the first is fetch'd from the Nature of God.* 2. *The second from the* Phaenomenon *of Motion in the World.* 3. *That the Matter is not Self-moveable.* 4. *An Objection that the Matter may be part Self-moved, part not.* 5. *The first Answer to the Objection.* 6. *The second Answer.* 7. *Other Evasions answered.* 8. *The last Evasion of all answered.* 9. *The Conclusion, That no Matter is Self-moved, but that a certain quantity of motion was impressed upon it at its first Creation by God.*

1. There be Three main Grounds from whence a man may be assured of *the Existence of Spiritual* or *Immaterial Substance.* The one is the consideration of the transcendent excellency of the Nature of God; who being, according to the true *Idea* of him, *an Essence absolutely Perfect,* cannot possibly be *Body,* and consequently must be something *Incorporeal:* and seeing that there is no contradiction in the Notion of a *Spirit in general* nor in any of *those kinds of Spirits* which we have defined, (where the Notion of God was set down amongst the rest) and that in the very Notion of him there is contained the reason of his Existence, as you may see at large in my * *Antidote;* certainly if we find any thing at all to *be,* we may safely conclude that He *is* much more.   For there is nothing besides Him of which one can give a reason why it is, unless we suppose him to be the Author of it.   Wherefore though God be neither *Visible* nor *Tangible,* yet his very *Idea* representing to our Intellectual Faculties the necessary reason of his Existence, we are, by Axiome 5. (though we had no other Argument drawn from our Senses) confidently to conclude That He is.

* Book I. chap. 7, 8.

2. The second ground is the ordinary *Phaenomena* of Nature, the most general whereof is *Motion*. Now it seems to me demonstrable from hence, That there is some Being in the World distinct from *Matter*. For *Matter* being of one simple homogeneal nature, and not distinguishable by specificall differences, as the Schools speak, it must have every where the very same Essentiall properties; and therefore of it self it must all of it be either without motion, or else be self-moving, and that in such or such a tenor, or measure of motion; there being no reason imaginable, why one part of the *Matter* should move of it self lesse then another; and therefore if there be any such thing, it can onely arise from externall impediment.

3. Now I say, if *Matter* be utterly devoid of motion in it self, it is plain it has its motion from some other Substance, which is necessarily a Substance that is not *Matter*, that is to say, a *Substance Incorporeal*. But if it be moved of it self, in such or such a measure, the effect here being an *Emanative effect*, cannot possibly fail to be wherever *Matter* is, by Axiome 17. especially if there be no external impediment: And there is no impediment at all, but that the Terrestrial parts might regain an activity very nigh equal to the Æthereal, or rather never have lost it. For if the Planets had but a common *Dividend* of all the motion which themselves and the Sun and Stars, and all the Æthereal matter possess, (the matter of the Planets being so little in comparison of that of the Sun, Stars, and *Æther*) the proportion of motion that will fall due to them would be exceeding much above what they have. For it would be as if four or five poor men in a very rich and populous City should, by giving up that estate they have, in a levelling way, get equal share with all the rest. Wherefore every Planet could not faile of melting it self into little less finer Substance then the purest *Æther*. But they not doing so, it is a signe they have not that Motion nor Agitation of themselves, and therefore rest content with what has extrinsecally accrued to them, be it less or more.

4. But the pugnacious, to evade the stroke of our *Dilemma*, will make any bold shift; and though they affront their own Faculties in saying so, yet they will say, and must say, That part of the *Matter* is self-moving, part without motion of it self.

5. But to this I answer, That first, this Evasion of theirs is not so agreeable to Experience; but, so far as either our Sense or Reason can reach, there is the *same Matter* every where. For consider the *subtilest parts of Matter* discoverable here below, those which for their Subtilty are invisible, and for their Activity wonderfull, I mean those particles that cause that vehement agitation we feel in *Winds:* They in time lose their motion, become of a visible vaporous consistency, and turn to Clouds, then to Snow or Rain, after haply to Ice it self; but then in process of time, first melted into Water, then exhaled into Vapours, after more fiercely agitated, do become *Wind* again. And that we may not think that this Reciprocation into *Motion* and *Rest* belongs onely to *Terrestrial* particles; that the *Heavens* themselves be of the same Matter, is apparent from the Ejections of *Comets* into our *Vortex,* and the perpetuall rising of those Spots and Scum upon the Face of the Sun.

6. But secondly, to return what is still more pungent. This *Matter* that is *Self-moved,* in the impressing of Motion upon other *Matter,* either looses of its own motion, or retains it still entire. If the first, it may be despoiled of all its motion; and so that whose immediate nature is to *move,* shall *rest,* the entire cause of its motion still remaining, viz. it self: which is a plain contradiction by Axiome 17. If the second, no meaner an inconvenience then this will follow, That the whole world had been turned into pure *Æther* by this time, if not into a perfect flame, or at least will be in the conclusion, to the utter destruction of all corporeal Consistencies. For, that these *Self-moving parts of Matter* are of a considerable copiousness, the event does testify, they having melted almost all the world already into *Suns, Stars* and *Æther,* nothing remaining but *Planets* and *Comets* to be dissolved: Which all put together scarce beare so great a proportion to the rest of the Matter of the Universe, as an ordinary grain of sand to the whole ball of the Earth. Wherefore so potent a Principle of Motion still adding new motion to *Matter,* and no motion once communicated being lost, (for according to the laws of Motion, no Body loses any more motion then it communicates to another) it plainly follows, that either the World had been utterly burnt up ere now, or will be at least in an infinite less time then it has existed, nay, I may

say absolutely, in a very little time, and will never return to any frame of things again; which though it possibly may be, yet none but a mad-man will assert, by Axiome 2. And that it has not yet been since the first *Epoches* of History, seems a Demonstration that this second Hypothesis is false.

7. There is yet another Evasion or two, which when they are answered there will be no Scruple remaining, touching this point. The first is, That the *Matter* is all of it homogeneall, of the like nature every where, and that it is the common Property of it all to be of it self indifferent to *Motion* or *Rest;* and therefore, that it is no wonder that some of it *moves,* and other some of it *rests,* or *moves less* then other some. To which I answer, That *this Indifferency* of the *Matter* to *Motion* or *Rest* may be understood two wayes: Either *privatively,* that is to say, That it has not any real or active propension to *Rest* more then to *Motion,* or *vice versâ,* but is merely passive and susceptive of what *Motion* or *Fixation* some other Agent confers upon it, and keeps that modification exactly and perpetually, till again some other Agent change it; (in which sense I allow the Assertion to be true, but it makes nothing against us, but for us, it plainly implying That there is an *Incorporeal Substance* distinct from the *Matter,* from whence the *Matter* both is and must be moved.) Or else, *this Indifferency* is to be understood *positively,* that is to say, That the *Matter* has a real and active propension as well to *Motion* as to *Rest,* so that it *moveth* it self and *fixeth* it self from its own immediate nature. From whence there are but these two Absurdities that follow: the first, That two absolutely contrary properties are *immediately* seated in one simple Subject; then which nothing can seem more harsh and unhandsome to our Logical faculties; unless the second, which is, That *Motion* and *Rest* being thus *Emanative* effects of this one simple Subject, the *Matter* will both *move* and *rest at once;* or, if they do not understand by *Rest,* Fixation, but a mere absence of motion, That it will both move and not move at once. For what is *immediate* to any Subject, will not cease to be, the Subject not being destroyed, by Axiome 17.

Nor will they much help themselves by fancying that *Matter* necessarily exerting both these *immediate* powers or properties at once of *Motion* and *Rest,* moves her self to such a measure and no swifter. For this position is but coincident with the second member of the *Dilemma*, Sect. 3. of this Chapter; and therefore the same Argument will serve for both places.

The other Evasion is, by supposing part of the *Matter* to be *Self-moving*, and part of it *Self-resting*, in a positive sense, or *Self-fixing*: Which is particularly directed against what we have argued Sect. 6. For thus they would avoid that hasty and universal Conflagration there inferred. But that this Supposition is false, is manifest from Experience. For if there be any such *Self-fixing* parts of *Matter*, they are certainly in Gold and Lead and such like Metalls; but it is plain that they are not there. For what is *Self-fixing*, will immediately be reduced to *Rest*, so soon as external violence is taken off, by Axiome 17. Whence it will follow, that though these *Self-fixing parts of Matter* may be carried by other Matter while they are made fast to it, yet left free they will suddainly *rest*, they having the *immediate* cause of *Fixation* in themselves. Nor can any one distrust that the change will be so suddain, if he consider how suddainly an external force puts *Matter* upon motion. But a Bullet of gold or lead put thus upon motion, swift or slow, does not suddainly reduce it self to *rest*. Whence it plainly appears that this other Evasion contradicts Experience, and therefore has no force against our former Arguments.

8. The utmost Evasion the Wit of man can possibly excogitate is that Figment of a certain *Divine Matter* dispersed in the World, which some conceit the onely *Numen* thereof, whose motions they make not *necessary*, but *voluntary;* whereby they would decline that exorbitant inconvenience mentioned in the sixth Section of this Chapter. But the opinion to me seems very harsh and prodigious for these reasons following.

First, they seem very absurd in imagining this to be the *Numen* of the World or God himself, it being so inconsistent with *Personality* and the *Unity* of the Godhead to be made up of an Infinite number of interspersed *Atoms* amidst the Matter of the World: For this cannot be *one* God in any sense; nor a single *Divine* Atome an Entire Deity. From whence it would follow that there is no God at all.

And then in the second place, They acknowledging this *Divine Matter* to be *Matter*, acknowledge therewith *Impenetrability* and *Juxta-position* of parts, diversity also of *figure*, and, where there are no pores at all, absolute *Solidity* and *Hardness*. Whence it is manifest that whatsoever Reasonings are strong against *Ordinary Matter* for making it uncapable of *Perception* and *free Action,* from the *Nature* and *Idea* thereof, they are as strong against this, on which they have conferred the title of *Divine.*

And thirdly and lastly, That there is no such *Divine Matter* interspersed amongst the *subtile Matter* of the World, that can act freely and knowingly, *Effects* also and *Experiments* plainly declare, as I have abundantly noted in my * *Antidote against Atheism.* (37)

9. Wherefore it is most rational to conclude, That no *Matter* whatsoever of its own Nature has any active Principle of *Motion,* though it be receptive thereof; but that when God created it, he superadded an impress of *Motion* upon it, such a measure and proportion to all of it, which remains still muchwhat the same for quantity in the whole, though the parts of *Matter* in their various occursion of one to another have not alwaies the same proportion of it. Nor is there any more necessity that God should reiterate this impress of *Motion* on the *Matter* created, then that he should perpetually create the *Matter.* Neither does his conservation of this quantity of Motion any thing more imply either a repetition or an augmentation of it, then the conservation of the *Matter* does the superaddition of new *Matter* thereunto. Indeed he need but conserve the *Matter,* and the *Matter* thus conserved will faithfully retain, one part with another, the whole summe of Motion first communicated to it, some small moments excepted, which are not worth the mentioning in this place.

CHAP. XII.

1. *That the Order and Nature of things in the Universe argue an* Essence Spiritual *or* Incorporeal. 2. *The Evasion of this Argument.* 3. *A preparation out of Mr* Hobbs *to answer the Evasion.* 4. *The first Answer.* 5. *The second Answer.* 6. *Mr* Hobbs *his mistake, of making the Ignorance of Second Causes the onely Seed of Religion.*

1. We have discovered out of the simple *Phaenomenon* of *Motion,* the necessity of the Existence of some *Incorporeal*

* See Book 2. ch 2. sect. 8.

Essence distinct from the Matter: But there is a further assurance of this Truth, from the consideration of the Order and admirable Effect of this Motion in the world. Suppose *Matter* could move it self, would mere *Matter,* with Self-motion, amount to that admirable wise contrivance of things which we see in the World? Can a blind *impetus* produce such Effects, with that accuracy and constancy, that, the more wise a man is, the more he will be assured *That no Wisdome can adde, take away, or alter any thing in the works of Nature, whereby they may be bettered?* How can that therefore that has not so much as *Sense,* arise to the Effects of the highest pitch of *Reason* or *Intellect?* But of this I have spoke so fully and convincingly in the second Book of my *Antidote,* that it will be but a needless repetition to proceed any further on this Subject. (38)

2. All the Evasion that I can imagine our Adversaries may use here, will be this: That *Matter* is capable of *Sense,* and the finest and most subtile of the most refined Sense, and consequently of *Imagination* too, yea haply of *Reason* and *Understanding.* For *Sense* being nothing else, as some conceit, but *Motion,* or rather *Re-action of a Body pressed upon by another Body,* it will follow that all the *Matter* in the World has in some manner or other the power of *Sensation.*

3. Let us see now what this Position will amount to. Those that make *Motion* and *Sensation* thus really the same, they must of necessity acknowledge, That no longer *Motion,* no longer *Sensation,* (as Mr *Hobbs* has ingenuously confessed in his * *Elements* of Philosophy:) And that every *Motion* or *Re-action* must be a new Sensation, as well as every ceasing of Re-action a ceasing of Sensation.

4. Now let us give these busie active *particles* of the *Matter* that play up and down every where the advantage of *Sense,* and let us see if all their heads laid together can contrive the *Anatomical* fabrick of any Creature that lives. Assuredly when all is summ'd up that can be imagined, they will fall short of their account. For I demand, Has every one of these particles that must have an hand in the framing of the Body of an Animal, the whole design of the work by the impress of some *Phantasm* upon it, or, as they have several offices, so have they several

* Chap. 25.

parts of the design? If the first, it being most certain, even according to their opinion whom we oppose, that there can be no *knowledge* nor *perception* in the *Matter,* but what arises out of the *Re-action* of one part against another, how is it conceivable that any one particle of *Matter* or many together (there not existing yet in Nature any Animal) can have the *Idea* impressed of that Creature they are to frame? Or if one or some few particles have the sense of one part of the Animal (they seeming more capable of this, the parts being far more simple then the whole *Compages* and contrivement) and other some few of other parts, how can they confer notes? by what language or speech can they communicate their counsel one to another? Wherefore that they should mutually serve one another in such a design, is more impossible then that so many men blind and dumb from their nativity should joyn their forces and wits together to build a Castle, or carve a Statue of such a Creature as none of them knew any more of in several then some one of the smallest parts thereof, but not the relation it bore to the whole.

5. Besides this, *Sense* being really the same with *Corporeal Motion,* it must change upon new impresses of Motion; so that if a particle by Sense were carried in this line, it meeting with a counterbuffe in the way, must have quite another Impress and Sense, and so forget what it was going about, and divert its course another way. Nay though it scaped free, *Sense* being *Re-action,* when that which it bears against is removed, Sense must needs cease, and perfect Oblivion succeed. For it is not with these particles as with the Spring of a Watch or a bent Cross-bow, that they should for a considerable time retain the same *Re-action,* and so consequently the same Sense. And lastly, if they could, it is still nothing to the purpose; for let their Sense be what it will, their motion is necessary, it being merely corporeal, and therefore the result of their motion cannot be from any kind of knowledge. For the corporeal motion is first, and is only felt, not directed by feeling. And therefore whether the *Matter* have any Sense or no, what is made out of it is nothing but what results from the wild jumblings and knockings of one part thereof against another, without any purpose, counsel or direction. Wherefore the ordinary *Phaenomena* of Nature being

guided according to the most Exquisite Wisdome imaginable, it is plain that they are not the Effects of the mere motion of *Matter,* but of some *Immaterial* Principle, by Axiome 10.

6. And therefore *the Ignorance of Second Causes* is not so rightly said to be the *Seed of Religion,* (as Mr *Hobbs* would have it) as of *Irreligion* and *Atheism.* (39)   For if we did more punctually and particularly search into their natures, we should clearly discern their insufficiency for such effects as we discover to be in the world.   But when we have looked so closely and carefully into the nature of *Corporeal Beings,* and can finde no Causality in them proportionable to these Effects we speak of, still to implead our selves rather of Ignorance, then the *Matter* and *Corporeal motion* of Insufficiency, is to hold an opinion upon humour, and to transgress against our first and second Axiomes.

CHAP. XIII.

1. *The last proof of* Incorporeal Substances, *from* Apparitions.
2. *The first Evasion of the force of such Arguings.* 3. *An Answer to that Evasion.* 4. *The second Evasion.* 5. *The first kind of the second Evasion.* 6. *A description out of* Virgil *of that Genius that suggests the dictates of the* Epicurean *Philosophy.* 7. *The more full and refined sense of that Philosophy now-a-dayes.* 8. *The great efficacy of the Stars (which they suppose to consist of nothing but Motion and Matter) for production of all manner of Creatures in the World.*

1. The Third and last ground which I would make use of, for evincing the Existence of *Incorporeal Substances,* is such extraordinary Effects as we cannot well imagine any natural, but must needs conceive some free or spontaneous Agent to be the Cause thereof, whenas yet it is clear that they are from neither Man nor Beast.   Such are speakings, knockings, opening of doors when they were fast shut, sudden lights in the midst of a room floating in the aire, and then passing and vanishing; nay, shapes of Men and severall sorts of Brutes, that after speech and converse have suddainly disappeared.   These and many such like extraordinary Effects (which, if you please, you may call by

one generall terme of *Apparitions)* seem to me to be an undeniable Argument, that there be such things as *Spirits* or *Incorporeal
Substances* in the world; and I have demonstrated the sequel
to be necessary in the last Chapter of the *Appendix to my
Treatise against Atheism;* and in the third Book of that Treatise
have produced so many and so unexceptionable Stories concerning *Apparitions,* that I hold it superfluous to adde any thing
here of that kind, taking far more pleasure in exercising of my
Reason then in registring of History. Besides that I have made
so carefull choice there already, that I cannot hope to cull out
any that may prove more pertinent or convictive; I having penn'd
down none but such as I had compared with those severe lawes
I set my self in the first Chapter of that third Book, to prevent
all tergiversations & evasions of gain-sayers.

2. But, partly out of my own observation, and partly by information from others, I am well assured there are but two
wayes whereby they escape the force of such evident Narrations.
The first is a firm perswasion that the very *Notion of a Spirit* or
Immaterial Substance is an *Impossibility* or *Contradiction* in the
very termes. And therefore such stories implying that which
they are confident is *impossible,* the Narration at the very first
hearing must needs be judged to be false; and therefore they
think it more reasonable to conclude all those that profess they
have seen such or such things to be mad-men or cheats, then to
give credit to what implies a *Contradiction.*

3. But this Evasion I have quite taken away, by so clearly
demonstrating that the *Notion of a Spirit* implies no more *contradiction* then the *Notion of Matter;* and that its *Attributes*
are as conceivable as the Attributes of *Matter:* so that I hope
this creephole is stopt forever.

4. The second Evasion is not properly an Evasion of the
truth of these stories concerning *Apparitions,* but of our deduction therefrom. For they willingly admit of these *Apparitions*
and *Prodigies* recorded in History, but they deny that they are
any Arguments of a truly *Spiritual* and *Incorporeal Substance*
distinct from the *Matter* thus changed into this or that shape,
that can walk and speak, &c. but that they are special Effects
of the influence of the Heavenly Bodies upon this region of
Generation and Corruption.

5. And these that answer thus are of two sorts. The one have great affinity with *Aristotle* and *Avenroes,* who look not upon the Heavenly Bodies as mere Corporeal Substances, but as actuated with Intelligencies, which are Essences separate and Immaterial. But this Supposition hurts not us at all in our present design; they granting that which I am arguing for, viz. a *Substance Incorporeal.* The use of this perverse Hypothesis is only to shuffle off all Arguments that are drawn from *Apparitions,* to prove that the Souls of men subsist after death, or that there are any such things as *Daemons* or *Genii* of a nature permament and immortal. But I look upon this Supposition as confutable enough, were it worth the while to encounter it. (40)

That of the *Sadducees* is far more firm, they supposing their ἀπόῤῥοιαι to be nothing else but the efficacy of the presence of God altering *Matter* into this or the other Apparition or Manifestation; as if there were but one Soul in all things, and God were that Soul variously working in the Matter. But this I have already confuted in my Philosophicall Poems, and shall again in this present Treatise.* (41)

6. The other *Influenciaries* hold the same power of the Heavens as these; though they do not suppose so high a Principle in them, yet they think it sufficient for the salving of all Sublunary *Phaenomena,* as well ordinary as extraordinary. Truly it is a very venerable *Secret,* and not to be uttered or communicated but by some old *Silenus* lying in his obscure Grot or Cave, nor that neither but upon due circumstances, and in a right humour, when one may find him with his veins swell'd out with wine, and his Garland faln off from his head through his heedless drousiness: Then if some young *Chromis* and *Mnasylus,* especially assisted by a fair and forward *Ægle,* that by way of a love-frolic will leave the tracts of her fingers in the blood of Mulberies on the temples and forehead of this aged Satyre, while he sleeps dog-sleep, and will not seem to see, for fear he forfeit the pleasure of his feelings; then, I say, if these young lads importune him enough, he will again sing that old song of the *Epicurean* Philosophy in an higher strain then ever, which I profess I should abhor to recite, were it not to confute; it is so monstrous and impious. But because no sore can be cured that

* Book 3. ch. 16.

is concealed, I must bring this *Hypothesis* into view also, which the Poet has briefly comprised in this summary.

> *Namque canebat, uti magnum per inane coacta*
> *Semina terrarumque animaeque marisque fuissent,*
> *Et liquidi simul ignis; ut his exordia primis*
> *Omnia, & ipse tener mundi concreverit orbis.*
>
> Virgil. *Eclog* 6.

Contemporary
Epicurean
doctrine

7. The fuller and more refined sense whereof now-a-daies is this; That *Matter* and *Motion* are the Principles of all things whatsoever; and that by *Motion* some *Atomes* or particles are more subtile then others, and of more nimbleness and activity. That motion of one Body against another does every where necessarily produce Sense, *Sense* being nothing else but the *Reaction* of parts of the *Matter*. That the *subtiler* the *Matter* is, the *Sense* is more subtile. That the *subtilest Matter* of all is that which constitutes the *Sun* and *Stars,* from whence they must needs have the purest and *subtilest Sense.* That what has the most perfect *Sense,* has the most perfect *Imagination* and *Memory,* because *Memory* and *Imagination* are but the same with

Hobbes

Sense in reality, the latter being but certain *Modes* of the former. That what has the *perfectest Imagination,* has the *highest Reason* and *Providence; Providence* and *Reason* being nothing else but an exacter train of Phantasmes, Sensations or Imaginations. Wherefore the *Sun* and the *Stars* are the *most Intellectual Beings* in the world, and in them is that *Knowledge, Counsel* and *Wisdome* by which all Sublunary things are framed and governed.

8. These by their severall impresses and impregnations have filled the whole Earth with vital Motion, raising innumerable sorts of Flowers, Herbs and Trees out of the ground. These have also generated the several Kinds of living Creatures. These have filled the Seas with Fishes, the Fields with Beasts, and the Aire with Fowles; the Terrestrial matter being as easily formed into the living shapes of these several *Animals* by the powerful impress of the *Imagination* of the Sun and Stars, as the *Embryo* in the womb is marked by the strong fancy of his Mother that bears him. And therefore these *Celestial powers* being able to frame living shapes of Earthly matter by the impress of their *Imagina-*

tion, it will be more easy for them to change the vaporous Aire into like transfigurations.

So that admitting all these Stories of *Apparitions* to be true that are recorded in Writers, it is no Argument of the Existence of any *Incorporeal* Principle in the world. For the piercing Foresight of these glorious Bodies, the *Sun* and *Stars,* is able to raise what *Apparitions* or *Prodigies* they please, to usher in the *Births* or fore-signify the *Deaths* of the most considerable persons that appear in the world; of which * *Pomponatius* himself does acknowledge that there are many true examples both in *Greek* and *Latine* History. This is the *deepest Secret* that old *Silenus* could ever sing to ensnare the ears of deceivable Youth. And it is indeed φρικτὸν μυστήριον, in the very worst sense, *Horrendum mysterium,* a very dreadful and dangerous Mystery, saving that there is no small hope that it may not prove true. Let us therefore now examine it.

CHAP. XIV.

1. *That Splendor of the Celestial Bodies proves no Fore-sight nor Soveraignty that they have over us.* 2. *That the Stars can have no knowledge of us, Mathematically demonstrated.* 3. *The same Conclusion again demonstrated more familiarly.* 4. *That the Stars cannot communicate Thoughts, neither with the Sun nor with one another.* 5. *That the Sun has no knowledge of our affairs.* 6. *Principles laid down for the inferring that Conclusion.* 7. *A demonstration that he cannot see us.* 8. *That he can have no other kind of knowledge of us, nor of the frame of any Animal on Earth.* 9. *That though the Sun had the knowledge of the right frame of an Animal, he could not transmit it into Terrestrial matter.* 10. *An Answer to that Instance of the Signature of the* Foetus. 11, 12. *Further Answers thereto.* 13. *A short Increpation of the confident Exploders of* Incorporeal Substance *out of the world.*

1. That the Light is a very glorious thing, and the lustre of the *Stars* very lovely to look upon, and that the Body of the

* *De Immortalitate Animae, cap.* 14.

Sun is so full of splendour and Majesty, that without flattery we may profess our selves constrained to look aside, as not being able to bear the brightness of his aspect; all this must be acknowledged for Truth: but that these are so many *Eyes* of Heaven to watch over the Earth, so many kind and careful *Spectators* & *Intermedlers* also in humane affairs, as that phansiful Chymist * *Paracelsus* conceits, who writeth that not onely Princes and Nobles, or men of great and singular worth, but even almost every one, near his death has some prognostick sign or other (as knockings in the house, the dances of dead men, and the like) from these compassionate Fore-seers of his approaching Fate; this I must confess I am not so paganly Superstitious as to believe one syllable of; but think it may be demonstrated to be a mere fancy, especially upon this present Hypothesis, That the *Sun* and *Stars* have no immaterial Being residing in them, but are mere *Matter* consisting of the subtilest Particles and most vehemently agitated. For them we cannot but be assured that there is nothing in them more Divine then what is seen in other things that shine in the dark, suppose rotten wood, glo-worms, or the flame of a rush-candle.

2. This at least we will demonstrate, That let the *Sun* and *Stars* have what knowledge they will of other things, they have just none at all of us, nor of our affairs; which will quite take away this last Evasion. That the *Stars* can have no knowledge of us is exceeding evident: For whenas the *Magnus Orbis* of the Earth is but as a Point compared with the distance thereof to a fixed Star, that is to say, whenas that Angle which we may imagine to be drawn from a Star, and to be subtended by the Diameter of the *Magnus Orbis,* is to Sense no Angle at all, but as a mere Line; how little then is the Earth it self? and how utterly invisible to any *Star,* whenas her Diameter is above 1100. times less then that of her *Magnus Orbis?* From whence it is clear that it is perfectly impossible that the *Stars,* though they were endued with sight, could so much as see the *Earth* it self, (much less the inhabitants thereof) to be *Spectators* and *Intermedlers* in their affaires for good or evil; and there being no higher Principle to inspire them with the knowledge of these things, it is evident that they remain utterly ignorant of them.

* See *Enthusiasm. Triumphat.* sect. 45. (42)

3. Or if this Demonstration (though undeniably true in it self) be not so intelligible to every one, we may adde what is more easy and familiar, viz. That the *Stars* being lucid Bodies, and those of the first magnitude near an hundred times bigger then the Earth, and yet appearing so small things to us, hence any one may collect, that the opake Earth will either be quite invisible to the *Stars*, or else at least appear so little, that it will be impossible that they should see any distinct Countries, much less Cities, Houses, or Inhabitants.

4. Wherefore we have plainly swept away this numerous Company of the celestial Senators from having any thing to doe to consult about, or any way to oversee the affairs of Mankind; and therefore let them seem to wink and twinkle as cogitabundly as they will, we may rest in assurance that they have no plot concerning us, either for good or evill, as having no knowledge of us. Nor if they had, could they *communicate their thoughts* to that great deemed Soveraign of the world, the *Sun;* they being ever as invisible to him, as they are to us in the daytime. For it is nothing but his light that hinders us from seeing so feeble Objects, and this hinderance consisteth in nothing else but this, That that motion which by his Rayes is caused in the Organ is so fierce and violent, that the gentle vibration of the light of the *Stars* cannot master it, nor indeed bear any considerable proportion to it: What then can it do in reference to the very Body of the *Sun* himself, the matter whereof has the most furious motion of any thing in the world?

5. There is nothing now therefore left, but the *Sun* alone, that can possibly be conceived to have any knowledge of, or any superintendency over our terrestrial affairs. And how uncapable he is also of this office, I hold it no difficult thing to demonstrate. Whence it will plainly appear, that those *Apparitions* that are seen, whether in the Aire or on Earth (which are rightly looked upon as an Argument of Providence and Existence of some *Incorporeal Essence* in the world) cannot be attributed to the power and prevision of the *Sun,* supposing him purely corporeal.

6. For it is a thing agreed upon by all sides, That *mere Matter* has no *connate Ideas* in it of such things as we see in the world; but that upon *Re-action* of one part moved by another arises a

kind of *Sense,* or *Perception.* Which opinion as it is most
rational in it self to conceive (supposing *Matter* has any sense
in it at all) so it is most consonant to experience, we seeing
plainly that *Sense* is ever caused by some outward corporeal
motion upon our Organs, which are also corporeal. For that
Light is from a corporeal motion, is plain from the reflexion of
the rayes thereof; and no Sound is heard but from the motion
of the Aire or some other intermediate Body; no Voice but there
is first a moving of the Tongue; no Musick but there must
either be the blowing of wind or the striking upon strings, or
something Analogical to these; and so in the other Senses.

Wherefore if there be nothing but *Body* in the world, it is
evident that *Sense* arises merely from the *motion* of one part of
Matter against another, and that *Motion* is ever first, and *Perception* follows, and that therefore *Perception* must necessarily
follow the laws of *Motion,* and that no *Percipient* can have any
thing more to conceive then what is conveighed by Corporeal
motion. Now from these Principles it will be easy to prove
that, though we should acknowledge a power of *Perception* in
the *Sun,* yet it will not amount to any ability of his being either
a *Spectator* or *Governor* of our affairs here on Earth.

7. According to the Computation of *Astronomers,* even of those
that speak more modestly, the *Sun* is bigger then the *Earth* above
an hundred and fifty times. But how little he appears to us
every eye is able to judge. How little then must the *Earth*
appear to him? If he see her at all, he will be so far from
being able to take notice of any Persons or Families, that he
cannot have any distinct discerning of Streets, nor Cities, no
not of Fields, nor Countries; but whole Regions, though of very
great Extent, will vanish here, as *Alcibiades* his Patrimony in that
Map of the World *Socrates* shewed him, to repress the pride of
the young Heire. (43) The *Earth* must appear *considerably* less
to him then the *Moon* does to us, because the *Sun* appears to us
less then the *Moon.* It were easy to demonstrate that her *discus*
would appear to the *Sun* near thirty, nay sixty times less then
the Moon does to us, according to *Lansbergius* his computation. (44)

Now consider how little we can discern in that broader Object
of sight, the *Moon,* when she is the nighest, notwithstanding we

be placed in the dark, under the shadow of the *Earth,* whereby our sight is more passive and impressible. How little then must the fiery eye of that *Cyclops* the *Sun,* which is all Flame and Light, discern in this lesser Object the *Earth,* his vigour and motion being so vehemently strong and unyielding? What effect it will have upon him, we may in some sort judge by our selves: For though our Organ be but moved or agitated with the reflexion of his Rayes, we hardly see the *Moon* when she is above the Horizon by day: What impress then can our *Earth,* a less Object to him then the *Moon* is to us, make upon the *Sun,* whose Body is so furiously hot, that he is as boiling Fire, if a man may so speak, and the Spots about him are, as it were, the scum of this fuming Cauldron?

Besides that our *Atmosphere* is so thick a covering over us at that distance, that there can be the appearance of nothing but a white mist enveloping all and shining like a bright cloud; in which the rayes of the *Sun* will be so lost, that they can never return any distinct representation of things unto him. Wherefore it is as evident to *Reason* that he cannot see us, as it is to *Sense* that we see him; and therefore he can be no *Overseer* nor *Intermedler* in our actions.

8. But perhaps you will reply That though the *Sun* cannot see the *Earth,* yet he may have a *Sense* and *Perception* in himself (for he is a fine glittering thing, and some strange matter must be presumed of him) that may amount to a wonderful large sphere of *Understanding, Fore-knowledge* and *Power.* But this is a mere fancyful surmise, and such as cannot be made good by any of our Faculties: Nay the quite contrary is demonstrable by such Principles as are already agreed upon. For there are no *connate Ideas* in the *Matter,* and therefore out of the collision and agitation of these *Solar* particles, we cannot rationally expect any other effect in the *Sun,* then such as we experiment in the percussion of our own eyes, out of which ordinarily follows the sense of a confused light or flame. If the *Sun* therefore has any sense of himself, it must be only the perception of a very vigorous *Light* or *Fire,* which being still one and the same representation, it is a question whether he has a sense of it or no, any more then we have of our bones, which we perceive not by reason of our accustomary and uninterrupted

sense of them, as Mr *Hobbs* ingeniously conjectures in a like supposition. (45)

But if you will say that there is a perception of the jogging or justling, or of whatever touch or rubbing of one *Solar* particle against another, the body of the *Sun* being so exceeding liquid, and consequently the particles thereof never resting, but playing and moving this way and that way; yet they hitting and fridging so fortuitously one against another, the perceptions that arise from hence must be so various and fortuitous, so quick and short, so inconsistent, flitting and unpermanent, that if any man were in such a condition as the *Sun* necessarily is, according to this Hypothesis, he would both be, and appear to all the world to be, stark mad; he would be so off and on, and so unsettled, and doe, and think, and speak all things with such ungovernable rashness and temerity.

In brief, that the *Sun* by this tumultous agitation of his *fiery Atoms* should hit upon any rational contrivance or right *Idea* of any of these living Creatures we see here on Earth, is utterly as hard to conceive, as that the Terrestrial particles themselves should justle together into such contrivances and formes, which is that which I have * already sufficiently confuted.

9. And if the Sun could light on any such true frame or forme of any Animal, or the due rudiments or contrivance thereof, it is yet unconceivable how he should conveigh it into this Region of Generation here on *Earth,* partly by reason of the *Earth's* Distance and Invisibleness, and partly because the deepest Principle of all being but mere Motion, without any superior power to govern it, this *Imagination* of the *Sun* working on the *Earth* can be but a simple *Rectilinear* impress, which can never arise to such an inward solid organization of parts in living Creatures, nor hold together these *Spectres* or *Apparitions* in the Aire, in any more certain form then the smoak of chimnies or the fume of Tobacco.

10. Nor is that Instance of the power of the Mother's fancy on the *Foetus* in the womb, any more then a mere flourish; for the disparity is so great, that the Argument proves just nothing: For whereas the Mother has an Explicite *Idea* of the *Foetus* and every part thereof, the *Sun* and *Stars* have no distinct *Idea* at all

* Chap. 12. sect. 4, 5.

of the parts of the *Earth;* nay I dare say that what we have already intimated will amount to a Demonstration, That though they had *Sense,* yet they do not so much as *know* whether this Earth we live on be *in rerum Naturâ* or no.

11. Again, the *Mark* that is impressed on the *Foetus,* the Mother has a clear and vivid conception of; but the curious contrivance in the *Idea* of Animals, I have shewn how incompetible it is to the fortuitous justling of the fiery particles of either *Sun* or *Stars.*

12. Thirdly, the *Impress* on the *Foetus* is very simple and slight, and seldome so curious as the ordinary impresses of Seals upon Wax, which are but the modifications of the surface therof; but this supposed Impress of the *Imagination* of the *Sun* and *Stars* is more then a solid Statue, or the most curious *Automaton* that ever was invented by the wit of man; and therefore impossible to proceed from a mere *Rectilinear* impress upon the Æther down to the *Earth* from the *Imagination* of the *Sun,* no not if he were supposed to be actuated with an *Intelligent* Soul, if the *Earth* and all the space betwixt her and him were devoid thereof. Nor do I conceive, though it be an infinitely more slight business, that the direction of the *Signature* of the *Foetus* upon such a part were to be performed by the *Fancy* of the Mother, notwithstanding the advantage of the organization of her body, were not both her self and the *Foetus* animated *Creatures.*

13. Wherefore we have demonstrated beyond all Evasion, from the *Phaenomena* of the Universe, That of necessity there must be such a thing in the world as *Incorporeal Substance;* let inconsiderable Philosophasters hoot at it, and deride it as much as their Follies please.

THE

IMMORTALITY

OF

THE SOUL.

THE SECOND BOOK.

CHAP. I.

1. An addition of more Axiomes for the demonstrating that there is a Spirit *or* Immaterial Substance *in Man. 2. The Truth of the first of these Axiomes confirmed from the testimony of Mr* Hobbs, *as well as demonstrated in the Preface. 3, 4. That Demonstration further cleared and evinced by answering a certain Evasion. 5. The proof of the second Axiome. 6. The proof of the third. 7. The confirmation of the fourth from the testimony of Mr* Hobbs, *as also from Reason. 8. An explication and proof of the fifth. 9. A further Proof of the Truth thereof. 10. An Answer to an Evasion. 11. Another Evasion answered. 12. A further management of this first Answer thereto. 13. A second Answer. 14. A third Answer, wherein is mainly contained a confirmation of the first Answer to the second Evasion. 15. The plainness of the sixth Axiome. 16. The proof of the seventh.*

1. Having cleared the way thus far as to prove That there is *no Contradiction* nor Inconsistency in the *Notion of a Spirit,* but that it *may Exist* in Nature, nay that *de facto* there are *Incorporeal Substances* really Existent in the world; we shall now drive more home to our main design, and demonstrate *That there is such an Immaterial Substance in Man,* which, from the power it is conceived to have in actuating and guiding the *Body,* is usually called *the Soule.* This Truth we shall make good first in a more *general* way, but not a whit the lesse stringent, by evincing That *such Faculties* or *Operations* as we are conscious

of in our selves, are utterly incompetible to *Matter* considered *at large* without any *particular* organization. And then afterwards we shall more punctually consider the *Body of man,* and every possible fitness in the structure thereof that is worth taking notice of for the performance of *these Operations* we ordinarily find in our selves. And that this may be done more plainly and convincingly, we will here adde to the number of our Axiomes these that follow.

Axiome XX.

Motion *or* Re-action *of one part of the* Matter *against another, or at least a due continuance thereof, is really one and the same with* Sense *and* Perception, *if there be any* Sense *or* Perception *in* Matter.

2. This Axiome, as it is plain enough of it self (supposing there were nothing but *Body* in the world) so has it the suffrage of our most confident and potent adversary Mr. *Hobbs* in his * Elements of Philosophy. Whose judgment I make much of in such cases as these, being perswaded as well out of Reason as Charity, that he seeing so little into the nature *of Spirits,* that defect is compensated with an extraordinary Quicksightedness in discerning of the best and most warrantable wayes of salving all *Phaenomena* from the ordinary allowed properties of *Matter.*

Axiome XXI.

So far as this continued Re-action *reaches, so far reaches* Sense *or* Perception, *and no farther.*

Axiome XXII.

That diversity there is of Sense *or* Perception *does necessarily arise from the diversity of the Magnitude, Figure, Position, Vigour and Direction of* Motion *in parts of the* Matter.

* Chap. 25. Artic. 2. (46)

Axiome XXIII.

Matter *in all the variety of those* Perceptions *it is sensible of, has none but such as are impressed by Corporeal Motions, that is to say, that are* Perceptions *of some Actions or modificated Impressions of parts of* Matter *bearing one against another.*

7. To this Truth Mr. *Hobbs* sets his seal with all willingness imaginable, or rather eagerness, as also his Followers, they stoutly contending that we have not the *perception* of any thing but the Phantasms of material Objects, and of sensible words or Marks, which we make to stand for such and such Objects.

.   .   .   .

Axiome XXIV.

The distinct Impression of any considerable extent of variegated Matter *cannot be received by a mere point of* Matter.

8. By *a mere point of Matter* I do not mean a mere Mathematical point, but a *perfect Parvitude,* or the *least Reality* of Matter (concerning which I have spoke already.) * Which being the least quantity that *discerpible Matter* can consist of, no particle of *Matter* can touch it less then it self. This *Parvitude* therefore that is so little that it has properly no integral parts, really distinguishable, how can it possibly be a Subject distinctly receptive of the view, haply, of half an Horizon at once? which sight is caused by real and distinct motion from real distinct parts of the Object that is seen. But this *perfect Parvitude* being the minutest quantity that *Matter* is divisible into, no more then one *real* line of motion can be directed upon it, the rest will goe beside. To which you may adde that if this so *perfect Parvitude* were distinctly perceptive of variegated Objects, it were a miracle if it could not perceive the particles of the *Aire* and of the Atmosphere, the *Globuli* of light, and subtilest contexture of the parts of Opake bodies.

9. Again, this Object we speak of may be so variegated, I mean with such colours, that it may imply a contradiction, that

* Book I. ch. 6.

one and the same particle of *Matter* (suppose some very small round one, that shall be the Cuspe of the visual Pyramide or Cone) should receive them all at once; the opposite kindes of those colours being uncommunicable to this round particle otherwise then by contrariety of Motions, or by *Rest* and *Motion*, which are as contrary; as is manifest out of that excellent Theoreme concerning *Colours* in *Des-Cartes* his * *Meteors*, which if it were possible to be false, yet it is most certainly true, that seeing *Motion* is the cause of *Sight*, the contrariety of Objects for Colour must arise out of the contrary modifications of Motion in this particle we speak of, that immediately communicates the *Object* to the *Sentient*: which contrariety of Motion at the same time and within the same surface of the adequate place of a Body is utterly incompetible thereto.

Axiome XXV.

Whatever impression or parts of any impression are not received by this perfect Parvitude *or* Real point *of Matter, are not at all perceived by it.*

Axiome XXVI.

Whatever Sense *or* Motion *there is now in* Matter, *it is a necessary impression from some other part of* Matter, *and does necessarily continue till some part or other of* Matter *has justled it out.*

* Cap. 8. Artic. 4, 5, 6, 7, 8.

CHAP. II.

1. *That if* Matter *be capable of* Sense, Inanimate things *are so too: And of Mr* Hobbs his wavering in that point. 2. *An Enumeration of several Faculties in us that* Matter *is utterly uncapable of.* 3. *That* Matter *in no kind of Temperature is capable of* Sense. 4. *That no one point of* Matter *can be the Common* Sensorium. 5. *Nor a multitude of such Points receiving singly the entire image of the Object.* 6. *Nor yet receiving part part, and the whole the whole.* 7. *That* Memory *is incompetible to* Matter. 8. *That the* Matter *is uncapable of the notes of some circumstances of the Object which we remembred.* 9. *That* Matter *cannot be the Seat of second Notions.* 10. *Mr* Hobbs *his Evasion of the foregoing Demonstration clearly confuted.* 11. *That the Freedome of our Will evinces that there is a Substance in us distinct from* Matter. 12. *That Mr* Hobbs *therefore acknowledges all our actions necessary.*

1. We have now made our addition of such Axiomes as are most useful for our present purpose. Let us therefore, according to the order we propounded, before we consider *the fabrick and organization of the Body,* see if *such Operations* as we find in our selves be competible to *Matter* looked upon in a more *general* manner. That *Matter* from its own nature is uncapable of *Sense,* plainly appears from Axiome 20, and 21. For *Motion* and *Sense* being really one and the same thing, it will necessarily follow, that wherever there is *Motion,* especially any considerable duration thereof, there must be *Sense* and *Perception:* Which is contrary to what we find in a *Catochus,* and experience daily in dead Carkasses; in both which, though there be *Re-action,* yet there is no *Sense.* (47)

In brief, if any *Matter* have *Sense,* it will follow that upon *Re-action* all shall have the like, and that a Bell while it is ringing, and a Bow while it is bent, and every Jack-in-a-box that School-boyes play with, while it is held in by the cover pressing against it, shall be living Animals, or Sensitive Creatures. A thing so foolish and frivolous, that the mere recital

matter is Uhcapable of Sense

of the opinion may well be thought confutation enough with the sober.

And indeed Mr. *Hobbs* himself, though he resolve *Sense* merely into *Re-action of Matter*,* yet is ashamed of these odd consequences thereof, and is very loth to be reckoned in the company of those Philosophers, (though, as he saies, learned men) who have maintained That *all Bodies are endued with Sense,* and yet he can hardly abstain from saying that they are; onely he is more shie of allowing them *Memory,* which yet they will have whether he will or no, if he give them *Sense.* As for Example, in the ringing of a Bell, from every stroke there continues a *tremor* in the Bell, which decaying, must (according to his * Philosophie) be *Imagination,* and referring to the stroke past must be *Memory;* and if a stroke overtake it within the compass of this *Memory,* what hinders but *Discrimination* or *Judgment* may follow? But the Conclusion is consonant enough to this absurd Principle, *That there is nothing but* Matter *in the Universe, and that it is capable of perception.*

2. But we will not content our selves onely with the discovery of this one ugly inconvenience of this bold assertion, but shall further endeavour to shew that the Hypothesis is false, and that *Matter* is utterly *uncapable of such operations as we find in our selves,* and that therefore there is *Something in us Immaterial* or *Incorporeal.* For we find in our selves, that one and the same thing both *heares,* and *sees,* and *tasts,* and, to be short, *perceives* all the variety of Objects that Nature manifests unto us. Wherefore *Sense* being nothing but the impress of corporeal motion from Objects without, that part of *Matter* which must be the common *Sensorium,* must of necessity receive all that diversity of impulsions from Objects; it must likewise *Imagine, Remember, Reason,* and be the fountain of *Spontaneous Motion,* as also the Seat of what the Greeks call the τὸ αὐτεξούσιον or *liberty of Will:* Which supposition we shall finde involved in unextricable difficulties.

3. For first, we cannot conceive of any *Portion* of *Matter* but it is either *Hard* or *Soft.* As for that which is *Hard,* all men leave it out as utterly unlike to be endued with such Cognitive faculties as we are conscious to our selves of. That which is

* See his *Elements* of *Philosophy,* chap. 25. Artic. 5.
* Chap. 25. Artic. 7, 8.

Soft will prove either *opake, pellucid,* or *lucid.* If *opake,* it cannot *see,* the exterior superficies being a bar to the inward part. If *pellucid,* as *Aire* and *Water,* then indeed it will admit inwardly these *Particles* and that *Motion* which are the conveighers of the Sense, and distinction of *Colours;* and *Sound* also will penetrate. But this *Matter* being *heterogeneall,* that is to say, consisting of parts of a different nature and office, the *Aire,* suppose, being proper for *Sound,* and those *Round particles* which *Cartesius* describes for *Colour* and *Light;* the perception of these Objects will be differently lodged: but there is some one thing in us that perceives both. Lastly, if *lucid,* there would be much-what the same inconvenience that there is in the *opake,* for its own fieriness would fend off the gentle touch of external impresses; or if it be so mild and thin that it is in some measure *diaphanous,* the inconveniences will again recurre that were found in the *pellucid.* (48)

And in brief, any *liquid Matter* has such variety of particles in it, that if the Whole, as it must, (being the common *Sensorium*) be affected with any impress from without, the parts thereof must be variously affected, so that no Object will seem *homogeneall,* as appears from Axiome 22. Which Truth I shall further illustrate by a homely, but very significant, representation. Suppose we should put Feathers, Bullets and Spur-rowels in a Box, where they shall lye intermixedly, but close, one with another: upon any jog this Box receives, supposing all the stuffage thereof has *Sense,* it is evident that the several things therein must be differently affected, and therefore if the common *Sensorium* were such, there would seem no homogeneall Object in the world. Or at least these several particles shall be the several *Receptives* of the several motions of the same kinde from without, as the Aire of Sounds, the *Cartesian Globuli* of Light and Colours. But what receives all these, and so can judge of them all, we are again at a loss for, as before: unless we imagine it some very fine and *subtile* Matter, so *light* and *thin,* that it feels not it self, but so *yielding* and *passive,* that it easily feels the several assaults and impresses of other Bodies upon it, or in it; which yet would imply, that *this Matter* alone were *Sensitive,* and the others not; and so it would be granted, that not all Matter (no not so much as in *Fluid* Bodies) has *Sense.*

Such a tempered *Matter* as this is analogous to the *Animal Spirits* in Man, which, if *Matter* could be the *Soul*, were the very *Soul* of the *Body*, and *Common percipient* of all Motions from within or without, by reason of the tenuity, passivity and near homogeneity, and * (it may be) imperceptibility of any change or alteration from the playing together of its own tenuious and light particles; and therefore very fit to receive all manner of impresses from others. Whence we may rationally conclude, That some such *subtile Matter* as this is either the *Soul*, or her *immediate Instrument* for all manner of perceptions. The *latter* whereof I shall prove to be true in its due place. That the *former* part is false I shall now demonstrate, by proving more stringently, That no *Matter* whatsoever is capable of such *Sense* and *Perception* as we are conscious to our selves of.

4. For concerning that part of *Matter* which is the Common *Sensorium*, I demand whether some one point of it receive the whole image of the Object, or whether it is wholly received into every point of it, or finally whether the whole *Sensorium* receive the whole image by expanded parts, this part of the *Sensorium* this part of the image, and that part that. If the first, seeing that in us which *perceives* the external Object *moves* also the Body, it will follow, That one little point of *Matter* will give local motion to what is innumerable millions of times bigger then it self; of which there cannot be found nor imagined any example in Nature.

5. If the second, this difficulty presents it self, which also reflects upon the former Position, How so small a point as we speak of should receive the images of so vast, or so various Objects at once, without Obliteration or Confusion; a thing impossible as is manifest from Axiome 24. And therefore not receiving them, cannot perceive them, by Axiome 25. But if every point or particle of this *Matter* could receive the whole image, which of these innumerable particles, that receive the Image entirely, may be deemed *I my self* that perceive this Image? But if I be all those Points, it will come to pass, especially in a small Object, and very near at hand, that the line of impulse coming to divers and distant Points, will seem to come as from several

* But why it may not be, something is suggested in the foregoing chapter, sect. 3.

places, and so one Object will necessarily seem a Cluster of
Objects. And if I be but one of these Points, what becomes of
the rest? or *who* are they?

6. There remains therefore onely the third way, which is that
the parts of the image of the Object be received by the parts of
this portion of *Matter* which is supposed the common *Sensorium.*
But this does perfectly contradict experience; for we finde our
selves to perceive the whole Object, when in this case nothing
could perceive the whole, every part onely perceiving its part;
and therefore there would be nothing that can judge of the whole.
No more then three men, if they were imagined to sing a song
of three parts, and none of them should heare any part but his
own, could judge of the Harmony of the whole.

7. As concerning the *Seat of Imagination* and *Memory,* especially *Memory,* what kinde of *Matter* can be found fit for this
function? If it be *Fluid,* the images of Objects will be prone to
vanish suddainly, as also to be perverted or turned contrary
wayes.

.   .   .   .

If it be *Hard,* it will soon be composed to *Rest,* as in a Bell whose
tremor is gone in a little time; but we *remember* things some
years together, though we never think of them till the end of
that term. If *Viscid,* there is the like inconvenience, nay it is
the unfittest of all for either receiving of *Motion* or continuing
it, and therefore unlikely to be the *Seat* of either *Fancy* or
Memory. For if *Motion* or *Re-action* and *Sense,* whether internal
or external, be all one, *Motion* ceasing *Memory* must needs cease,
by Axiome 21. Nor can it any more *remember* when it is again
moved in the same manner, then a Stone or a piece of Lead that
was flung up into the Aire, can become more light or more prone
to flie upwards when they have once ceased from Motion; for
they are both exquisitely as if they had never been moved.

8. Lastly, we remember some things of which there can be no
Signatures in *Matter* to represent them, as for example, *Wideness*
and *Distance.*

.   .   .   .

9. Those that are commonly called by the name of *Secundae
Notiones,* and are not any sensible Objects themselves, nor the

Phantasmes of any sensible Objects, but onely our manner of conceiving them, or reasoning about them, in which number are comprehended all *Logical* and *Mathematical termes;* these, I say, never came in at the *Senses,* they being no impresses of corporeal motion, which excite in us, as in Doggs and other Brutes, the sense onely of Sounds, of Colours, of Hot, of Cold, and the like. Now *Matter* being affected by no perception but of corporeal impression, by the bearing of one Body against another; it is plain from Axiome 23. that these *Second Notions,* or *Mathematical* and *Logical* conceptions, cannot be seated in *Matter,* and therefore must be in some other Substance distinct from it, by Axiome 10. (49)

10. Here Mr. *Hobbs,* to avoid the force of this Demonstration, has found out a marvellous witty invention to befool his followers withall, making them believe that there is no such thing as these *Secundae Notiones,* distinct from the *Names* or *Words* whereby they are said to be signified; and that there is no perception in us, but of such *Phantasmes* as are impressed from external Objects, such as are common to Us and Beasts: and as for the *Names* which we give to these, or the *Phantasmes* of them, that there is the same reason of them as of other *Marks, Letters,* or *Characters;* all which coming in at the *Senses,* he would beare them in hand that it is a plain case, that we have the perception of nothing but what is impressed from corporeal Objects. But how ridiculous an Evasion this is, may be easily discovered, if we consider, that if these *Mathematical* and *Logical Notions* we speak of be nothing but *Names,* Logical and Mathematical Truths will not be the same in all Nations, because they have not the same *names.* For Example, *Similitudo* and ὁμοιότης, ἀναλογία and *Proportio,* λόγος and *Ratio,* these *names* are utterly different, the *Greek* from the *Latine;* yet the *Greeks, Latines,* nor any Nation else, do vary in their conceptions couched under these different *names:* Wherefore it is plain, that there is a *setled Notion* distinct from these *Words* and *Names,* as well as from those corporeal *Phantasmes* impressed from the Object; which was the thing to be demonstrated.

11. Lastly, we are conscious to our selves of that Faculty which the Greeks call αὐτεξούσιον, or *a Power in our selves,* notwithstanding any outward assaults or importunate tempta-

tions, *to cleave to that which is vertuous and honest, or to yield to pleasures or other vile advantages.*   That we have this *Liberty* and freedome in our selves, and that we refuse the good, and chuse the evil, when we might have done otherwise; that natural Sense of *Remorse of Conscience* is an evident and undeniable witness of.   For when a man has done amiss, the pain, grief, or indignation that he raises in himself, or at least feels raised in him, is of another kind from what we find from misfortunes or affronts we could not avoid.   And that which pinches us and vexes us so severely, is the sense that we have brought such an evil upon our selves, when it was in our power to have avoided it.   Now if there be no *Sense* nor *Perception* in us but what arises from the *Re-action of Matter* one part against another; whatever Representation of things, whatever Deliberation or Determination we fall upon, it will by Axiome 26, be *purely* necessary, there being upon this Hypothesis no more *Freedome* while we deliberate or conclude, then there is in a pair of scales, which rests as *necessarily* at last as it moved before.   Wherefore it is manifest that this Faculty we call *Free-will* is not found in *Matter,* but in some other Substance, by Axiome 10.

12. Mr *Hobbs* therefore, to give him his due, consonantly enough to his own principles, does very peremptorily affirm *That all our actions are necessary.*   But I having proved the contrary by that Faculty which we may call *Internal Sense* or *Common Notion,* found in all men that have not done violence to their own Nature; unless by some other approved Faculty he can discover the contrary, my Conclusion must stand for an undoubted Truth, by Axiome 5.

.   .   .   .

CHAP. III.

1. *Mr* Hobbs *his Arguments whereby he would prove all our actions necessitated.   His first Argument.*   2. *His second Argument.*   3. *His third Argument.*   4. *His fourth Argument.*   5. *What must be the meaning of these words,* Nothing taketh beginning from it self, *in the first Argument of Mr* Hobbs.   6. *A fuller and more determinate explication*

of the foregoing words, whose sense is evidently convinced to be, That no Essence of it self can vary its modification. 7. *That this is onely said by Mr* Hobbs, *not proved, and a full confutation of his Assertion.* 8. *Mr* Hobbs *imposed upon by his own Sophistry.* 9. *That one part of this first Argument of his is groundless, the other sophistical.* 10. *The plain proposall of his Argument, whence appeares more fully the weakness and sophistry thereof.* 11. *An Answer to his second Argument.* 12. *An Answer to the third.* 13. *An Answer to a difficulty concerning the Truth and False-hood of future Propositions.* 14. *An Answer to Mr* Hobbs *his fourth Argument, which, though slighted by himself, is the strongest of them all.* 15. *The difficulty of reconciling Free-will with Divine Prescience and Prophecies.* 16. *That the Faculty of Free-will is seldome put in use.* 17. *That the use of it is properly in Moral conflict.* 18. *That the Soul is not invincible there neither.* 19. *That Divine decrees either finde fit Instruments or make them.* 20. *That the more exact we make Divine Prescience, even to the com-prehension of anything that implies no contradiction in it self to be comprehended, the more clear it is that mans Will may be sometimes free.* 21. *Which is sufficient to make good my last Argument against Mr* Hobbs.

· · · · · · ·

CHAP. IV.

1. *An Enumeration of sundry Opinions concerning the Seat of Common Sense.* 2. *Upon supposition that we are nothing but mere Matter, That the whole Body cannot be the Com-mon* Sensorium; 3. *Nor the Orifice of the Stomack;* 4. *Nor the Heart;* 5. *Nor the Brain;* 6. *Nor the Mem-branes;* 7. *Nor the* Septum lucidum; 8. *Nor* Regius *his small and perfectly-solid Particle.* 9. *The probability of the* Conarion *being the common Seat of Sense.*

1. I have plainly proved, that neither those more Pure and Intellectual faculties of *Will* and *Reason,* nor yet those less pure

of *Memory* and *Imagination,* are competible to *mere Bodies.* Of which we may be the more secure, I having so convincingly demonstrated, That not so much as that which we call * *External Sense* is competible to the same: all which Truths I have concluded concerning *Matter generally considered.*

But because there may be a suspicion in some, which are overcredulous concerning *the powers of Body,* that *Organization* may doe strange feats (which Surmise notwithstanding is as fond as if they should imagine, that though neither Silver, nor Steel, nor Iron, nor Lute-strings, have any Sense apart, yet being put together in such a manner and formed as will (suppose) make a compleat *Watch,* they may have *Sense;* that is to say, that a Watch may be a living creature, though the several parts have neither *Life* nor *Sense;*) I shall for their sakes goe more *particularly* to work, and recite every Opinion that I could ever meet with by converse with either men or books concerning *the Seat of the Common Sense,* and after trie whether any of these Hypotheses can possibly be admitted for Truth, upon supposition that we consist of nothing but *mere modified and organized Matter.*

I shall first recite the Opinions, and then examine the possibility of each in particular, which in brief are these. 1. That the whole Body is the Seat of Common Sense. 2. That the Orifice of the Stomack. 3. The Heart. 4. The Brain. 5. The Membranes. 6. The *Septum lucidum.* 7. Some very small and perfectly-solid particle in the Body. 8. The *Conarion.* 9. The concurse of the Nerves about the fourth ventricle of the Brain. 10. The Spirits in that fourth ventricle. (50)

2. That the first Opinion is false is manifest from hence, That, upon supposition we are nothing but *mere Matter,* if we grant the *whole Body* to be one common *Sensorium,* perceptive of all Objects, *Motion* which is impressed upon the Eye or Eare, must be transmitted into all the parts of the Body. For *Sense* is really the same with *communication of Motion,* by Axiome 20. And the variety of Sense arising from the modification of Motion, which must needs be variously modified by the different temper of the parts of the Body, by Axiome 22. it plainly follows that the Eye must be otherwise affected by the motion of Light, then

---

* See chap. I. sect. 8, 9, 10, 11, 12, 13, 14, and chap. 2. sect. 3, 4, 5, 6.

the other parts to which this motion is transmitted. Wherefore if it be the *whole Body* that perceives, it will perceive the Object in every part thereof several wayes modified at once; which is against all Experience. It will also appear in all likelihood in several places at once, by reason of the many windings and turnings that must happen to the transmission of this *Motion,* which are likely to be as so many Refractions or Reflexions.

3. That *the Orifice of the Stomack* cannot be *the seat of Common Sense,* is apparent from hence, That that which is the common *Sentient* does not only *perceive* all Objects, but has the power of *moving* the Body. Now besides that there is no organization in the mouth of the Stomack that can elude the strength of our Arguments laid down in the foregoing Chapters, which took away all capacity from *Matter* of having any *perception* at all in it, there is no Mechanical reason imaginable to be found in the Body, whereby it will appear possible, that supposing the mouth of the Stomack were the *common Percipient* of all Objects, it could be able to *move* the rest of the members of the Body, as we finde something in us does. This is so palpably plain, that it is needless to spend any more words upon it.

4. The same may be said concerning *the Heart.* For who can imagine that, if the *Heart* were that *common Percipient,* there is any such Mechanical connexion betwixt it and all the parts of the Body, that it may, by such or such a perception, command the motion of the Foot or little Finger? Besides that it seems wholly imployed in the performance of its *Systole* and *Diastole,* which causes such a great difference of the situation of the *Heart* by turns, that if it were that Seat in which the sense of all Objects centre, we should not be able to see things steddily or fix our sight in the same place.

5. How uncapable the *Brain* is of being so active a Principle of *Motion* as we find in our selves, the *viscidity* thereof does plainly indicate. Besides that Physicians have discovered by experience, that *the Brain* is so far from being the *common Seat* of all senses, that it has in it none at all. And the *Arabians,* that say it has, have distinguished it into such severall offices of *Imagination, Memory, Common Sense,* &c. that we are still at a loss for some one part of *Matter* that is to be the *Common*

Percipient of all these.   But I have so clearly demonstrated the impossibility of the *Brain's* being able to perform those functions that appertain truly to what ordinarily men call the *Soul*, in my *Antidote against Atheism,** that it is enough to refer the Reader thither.

6. As for the *Membranes,* whether we would fancy them *all* the *Seat of Common Sense,* or *some one* Membrane, or *part* thereof; the like difficulties will occur as have been mentioned already.   For if *all the Membranes,* the difference and situation of them will vary the aspect and sight of the Object, so that the same things will appear to us in several hues and several places at once, as is easily demonstrated from Axiome 22.   If *some one Membrane,* or *part* thereof, it will be impossible to excogitate any Mechanical reason, how this *one* particular Membrane, or any *part* thereof, can be able so strongly and determinately to *move* upon occasion every part of the Body.

7. And therefore for this very cause cannot the *Septum lucidum* be the *Common Percipient* in us, because it is utterly unimaginable how it should have the power of so stoutly and distinctly *moving* our exterior parts and limbs.

8. As for that new and marvelous Invention of *Henricus Regius,** That it may be *a certain perfectly-solid, but very small, particle of Matter in the Body, that is the seat of common perception;* besides that it is as boldly asserted, that such an *hard* particle should have *Sense* in it, as that the filings of Iron and Steel should; it cannot be the spring of *Motion:* For how should so small an Atome *move* the whole Body, but by moving it self? But it being more subtile then the point of any needle, when it puts it self upon motion, especially such strong thrustings as we sometimes use, it must needs passe through the Body and leave it.

9. The most pure Mechanical Invention is that of the use of the *Conarion,* proposed by * *Des-Cartes;* which, considered with some other organizations of the Body, bids the fairest of any thing I have met withall, or ever hope to meet withall, for the

---

* See Book I. ch. 11. sect. 5, 6, 7.
* *Philosoph. Natural. lib.* 5. *cap.* I.
* *Dioptr. cap.* 5. *Artic.* 13. and *De Passion. Part.* I. *Artic.* 11, 12, 13, 14, 15, 16.

resolution of the Passions and Properties of living Creatures into mere *Corporeal* motion. And therefore it is requisite to insist a little upon the explication thereof, that we may the more punctually confute them that would abuse his Mechanical contrivances to the exclusion of all Principles but *Corporeal,* in either Man or Beast.

CHAP. V.

1. *How Perception of external Objects, Spontaneous Motion, Memory and Imagination, are pretended to be performed by the* Conarion, *Spirits and Muscles, without a Soul.* 2. *That the* Conarion, *devoid of a Soul, cannot be the* Common Percipient, *demonstrated out of* Des-Cartes *himself.* 3. *That the* Conarion, *with the Spirits and Organization of the Parts of the Body, is not a sufficient Principle of Spontaneous motion, without a Soul.* 4. *A description of the use of the* Valvulae *in the Nerves of the Muscles for spontaneous motion.* 5. *The insufficiency of this contrivance for that purpose.* 6. *A further demonstration of the insufficiency thereof, from whence is clearly evinced that Brutes have Souls.* 7. *That Memory cannot be salved the way above described;* 8. *Nor Imagination.* 9. *A Distribution out of* Des-Cartes *of the Functions in us, some appertaining to the Body, and others to the Soul.* 10. *The Author's Observations thereupon.*

1. The sum of this Abuse must in brief be this, That the *Glandula Pinealis* is the *common Sentient* or *Percipient of all Objects;* and without a *Soul,* by virtue of the *Spirits* and *Organization* of the Body, may doe all those feats that we ordinarily conceive to be performed by *Soul* and *Body* joyned together.* For it being *one,* whenas the rest of the Organs of Sense are *double,* and so handsomely seated as to communicate with the *Spirits* as well of the posteriour as anteriour Cavities of the *Brain;* by their help all the motions of the *Nerves* (as well of those that transmit the sense of *outward* Objects, as of them that

---

* *Cartes. De Passion. Part.* I, *Artic.* 32.

serve for the *inward* affections of the Body, such as Hunger, Thirst and the like) are easily conveighed unto it: and so being variously moved, it does variously determine the course of the *Spirits* into such and such *Muscles,* whereby it *moves* the Body.

Moreover that the transmission of Motion from the Object, through the *Nerves,* into the inward concavities of the *Brain,* and so to the *Conarion,* opens such and such Pores of the *Brain,* in such and such order or manner, which remain as tracts or footsteps of the presence of these Objects after they are removed. Which tracts, or signatures, consist mainly in this, that the *Spirits* will have an easier passage through these Pores then other parts of the *Brain.* And hence arises *Memory,* when the *Spirits* be determined, by the inclining of the *Conarion,* to that part of the *Brain* where these tracts are found, they moving then the *Conarion* as when the Object was present, though not so strongly.*

From the hitting of the *Spirits* into such like tracts, is also the nature of *Imagination* to be explained; in which there is little difference from *Memory,* saving that the reflexion upon time as past, when we saw or perceived such or such a thing, is quite left out. But these are not all the operations we are conscious to our selves of, and yet more then can be made out by this Hypothesis, That *Perception of Objects, Spontaneous Motion, Memory* and *Imagination,* may be all performed by virtue of this *Glandula,* the Animal Spirits, and mere Organization of the Body; as we shall plainly find, though but upon an easy examination.

2. For that the *Conarion,* devoid of a Soul, has no *perception* of any one Object, is demonstrable from the very description *Cartesius* makes of the transmission of the image, suppose through the Eye to the Brain, and so to the *Conarion.* For it is apparent from what he sets down in his *Treatise of the Passions of the Soul,** that the Image that is propagated from the Object to the *Conarion,* is impressed thereupon in some latitude of space. Whence it is manifest that the *Conarion* does not, nor can perceive the whole Object, though severall parts may be acknowledged to have the *perception* of the several parts therof. But something in us *perceives* the whole, which therefore cannot

* *Des-Cart. De Pass. Part.* I, *Artic.* 21.   * *Part.* I. *Art.* 35.

be the *Conarion*.* And that we do not perceive the external
Object *double,* is not so much because the Image is united in
the Organ of *Common Sense,* as that the lines come so from the
Object to both Eyes, that it is felt in one place; otherwise if the
Object be very near, and the direction of our eyes be not fitted
to that nearness, it will seem *double* however.   Which is a
Demonstration that a man may see with both Eyes at once; and
for my own part, I'm sure that I see better at distance, when
I use both, then when one.

3. As for *Spontaneous Motion,* that the *Conarion* cannot be a
sufficient Principle thereof, with the *Spirits* and *organization* of
other parts of the Body* though we should admit it a fit seat
of *Common Sense,* will easily appear, if we consider, that so weak
and so small a thing as that *Glandula* is, seems utterly unable to
determine the *Spirits* with that force and violence we find they
are determined in *running, striking, thrusting* and the like; and
that it is evident, that sometimes scarce the thousandth part of
the *Conarion* shall be director of this force; viz. when the Object
of Sight, suppose, is as little as a pin's point, or when a man is
prick'd with a needle, these receptions must be as little in the
Glandula as in the exteriour Sense.

But suppose the whole *Conarion* alwaies did act in the *deter-*
mining the motion of the *Spirits* into this or that *Muscle;* it is
impossible that such *fluid Matter* as these *Spirits* are, that upon
the noddings of the *Conarion* forward may easily recede back,
should ever determine their course with that force and strength
they are determined.

.   .   .   .

8. Lastly, for those imaginations or representations that are
of no one Object that we ever see, but made up of several that
have taken their distinct places in the *Brain,* some (suppose)
before and others behinde, how can the *Conarion* joyn these
together, and in such a posture of conjunction as it pleases?   Or
rather in one and the same Object, suppose this Man or that
House, which we see in a right posture, and has left such a
signature or figure in the *Brain* as is fit to represent it so,* how

* See   Book 2. ch. 2. sect. 6.
* See the *Appendix* to my *Antidote* chap. 10. sect. 6.
* See *Cartes. De Passion.* Part. I. Artic. 43.

can the *Conarion* invert the posture of the image, and make it represent the House and Man with the heels upwards? Besides the difficulty of representing the *Distance* of an Object, or the *Breadth* thereof, concerning which we have spoken * already. It is impossible the *Conarion,* if it be *mere Matter,* should perform any such operations as these. For it must raise motions in it self, such as are not necessarily conveighed by any corporeal impress of another Body, which is plainly against Axiome 26.

.   .   .   .

CHAP. VI.

1. *That no part of the Spinal Marrow can be the Common* Sensorium *without a Soul in the Body.* 2. *That the Animal Spirits are more likely to be that* Common Percipient. 3. *But yet it is demonstrable that they are not:* 4. *As not being so much as capable of Sensation;* 5. *Nor of directing Motion into the Muscles;* 6. *Much less of Imagination and rational Invention;* 7. *Nor of Memory.* 8. *An Answer to an Evasion.* 9. *The Author's reason, why he has confuted so particularly all the suppositions of the Seat of* Common Sense, *when few of them have been asserted with the exclusion of the Soul.*

1. There remain now onely Two Opinions to be examined: the one, *That place of the Spinal Marrow where* Anatomists conceive there *is the nearest concurse of all the Nerves of the Body;* the other, *the Animal Spirits in the fourth Ventricle of* the Brain. As for the former, viz. That part of the Spinal *Marrow where the concurse of the Nerves is conceived to be,* as I have answered in like case, so I say again, that besides that I have already demonstrated, that *Matter* is uncapable of *Sense,* and that there is no modification thereof in the *Spinal Marrow,* that will make it more likely to be indued with that Faculty then the pith of Elder or a mess of Curds; we are also to take notice, that it is utterly inept for *Motion,* nor is it conceivable how that part of it, or any other that is assigned to

* Chap. 2. sect. 8.

this office of being the *Common Percipient* in us of all Thoughts and Objects, (which must also have the power of *moving* our members) can, having so little agitation in it self, (as appearing nothing but a kind of soft Pap or Pulp) so nimbly and strongly *move* the parts of our Body.

2. In this regard the *Animal Spirits* seem much more likely to perform that office; and those, the importunity of whose gross fancies constrains them to make the Soul *Corporeal,* do nevertheless usually pitch upon some *subtile thin Matter* to constitute her nature or Essence: And therefore they imagine her to be either *Aire, Fire, Light,* or some such like Body; with which the *Animal Spirits* have no small affinity.

3. But this opinion, though it may seem plausible at first sight, yet the difficulties it is involved in are insuperable. For it is manifest, that all the Arguments that were brought * before will recur with full force in this place. For there is no *Matter* that is so perfectly *liquid* as the *Animal Spirits,* but consists of particles onely contiguous one to another, and actually upon Motion playing and turning one by another as busy as Atomes in the Sun. Now therefore, let us consider whether that Treasury of pure *Animal Spirits* contained in *the fourth Ventricle* be able to sustain so noble an office as to be the *common Percipient* in our Body, which, as I have often repeated, is so complex a Function, that it does not onely contain the *Perception of external Objects,* but *Motion, Imagination, Reason* and *Memory.*

4. Now at the very first dash, the transmission of the image of the Object into this crowd of particles cannot but hit variously upon them, and therefore they will have several *Perceptions* amongst them, some haply perceiving part of the Object, others all, others more then all, others also perceiving of it in one place, and others in another. But the *Percipient in us* representing no such confusion or disorder in our beholding of Objects, it is plain that it is not the *Animal Spirits* that is it.

5. Again, That which is so confounded a *Percipient,* how can it be a right Principle of *directing Motion* into the *Muscles?* For besides what disorder may happen in this function upon the distracted representation of present Objects, the power of

* Chap. 2. sect. 3, 4, 5, 6, 7, &c.

thinking, excogitating, and *deliberating,* being in these *Animal Spirits* also, (and they having no means of *communicating* one with another, but justling one against another; which is as much to the purpose, as if men should knock heads to communicate to each other their conceits of Wit,) it must needs follow that they will have their *perceptions, inventions,* and *deliberations* apart; which when they put in Execution, must cause a marvelous confusion in the Body, some of them commanding the parts this way, others driving them another way: or if their factions have many divisions and subdivisions, every one will be so weak, that none of them will be able to command it any way.   But we find no such strugling or countermands of any thing in us, that would act our Body one way when we would another; as if when one was a going to write

Μῆνιν ἄειδε, θεά ——

something stronger in him, whose conceits he is *not privy* to, should get the use of his hand, and in stead of that write down

Arma virúmque cano ——

And the like may be said of any other *Spontaneous Motion,* which being so constantly within our deliberation or command as it is, it is a sufficient Argument to prove that it is not such a lubricous Substance as the *Animal Spirits,* nor so disunited; but something more *perfectly One* and *Indivisible,* that is the Cause thereof.

6. We need not instance any further concerning the power of *Invention* and *Reason,* how every particle of these *Animal Spirits* has a liberty to *think* by it self, and *consult* with it self, as well as to *play* by it self, and how there is no possible means of *communicating* their Thoughts one to another, unless it should be, as I have said, by hitting one against another: but that can onely communicate *Motion,* not their determinate *Thought;* unless that these particles were conceived to figure themselves into the shape of those things they think of, which is impossible by Axiome 26.   And suppose it were possible one particle should shape it self, for example, into a *George on Horse-back* with a Lance in his hand, and another into an *Inchanted Castle;* this *George on Horse-back* must run against

the *Castle,* to make the *Castle* receive his impress and similitude. But what then? Truly the encounter will be very un-
fortunate: For S. *George* indeed may easily break his Lance,
but it is impossible that he should by justling against the
Particle in the form of a *Castle* conveigh the entire shape of
himself and his Horse thereby, such as we find our selves able
to imagine of a man on horse-back. Which is a Truth demonstrable as any Theorem in Mathematicks, but so plain at first
sight, that I need not use the curiosity of a longer Demonstration
to make it more firm.

Nor is there any colourable Evasion by venturing upon a new
way, as if this particle having transformed it self into a *Castle,*
and that into an *Horseman,* all the others then would see them
both and they one another. For by *what light,* and *how little*
would they appear, and in *what different places,* according to the
different posture of the particles of the *Animal Spirits,* and with
what *different faces,* some seeing one side, others another?

But besides this there is a further difficulty, that if such
Sensible representations as these could be conveighed from one
particle to another by corporeal encounters and justlings, or by
that other way after alledged; *Logical* and *Mathematical Notions*
can not. So that some of the *Animal Spirits* may think of one
Demonstration in *Mathematicks,* or of part of that Demonstration, and others of another: insomuch that if a *Mathematician* be to write, while he would write one thing upon the
determination of these *Animal Spirits,* others may get his hand
to make use of for the writing something else, to whose Thoughts
and Counsel he was not at all privy; nor can tell any thing,
till those other *Animal Spirits* have writ it down. Which Absurdities are so mad and extravagant, that a man would scarce
defile his pen by recording them, were it not to awaken those
that dote so much on *the power of Matter* (as to think it of it
self sufficient for all *Phaenomena* in the world) into due shame
and abhorrence of their foolish Principle.

7. The last Faculty I will consider is *Memory,* which is also
necessarily joyned with the rest in the *Common Percipient;*
of which not onely the fluidity of parts, but also their *dissipa-
bility,* makes the *Animal Spirits* utterly uncapable. For certainly, the *Spirits* by reason of their *Subtilty* and *Activity* are

very *dissipable*, and in all likelihood remain not the same for the space of a week together; and yet things that one has not thought of for many years, will come as freshly into a mans mind as if they were transacted but yesterday.

8. The onely Evasion they can excogitate here is this, That as there is a continual supply of *Spirits* by degrees, so, as they come in, they are *seasoned, fermented* and *tinctured* with the same *Notions, Perceptions* and *Propensions* that the *Spirits* they find there have. These are fine words, but signifie nothing but this, that the *Spirits* there present in the Brain communicate the *Notions* and *Perceptions* they have to these new-comers; which is that which I have already proved impossible in the foregoing Sections. And therefore it is impossible that the *Animal Spirits* should be that *Common Percipient* that *hears, sees, moves, remembers, understands,* and does other functions of life that we perceive performed in us or by us.

9. We have now particularly evinced, that neither the *whole Body*, nor any of those *parts* that have been pitched upon, if we exclude the presence of a *Soul* or *Immaterial Substance*, can be the *Seat of Common Sense*. In which I would not be so under-stood, as if it implied that there are none of these parts, but some or other have affirmed might be the *common Sensorium*, though we had no Soul: But because they have been stood upon, all of them, by some or other to be the Seat of *Common Sense*, supposing a *Soul* in the Body, that there might no imagi-nable doubt or scruple be left behind, I have taken the pains thus punctually and particularly to prove, that none of them can be the place of *Common Sense* without one.

And thus I have perfectly finished my main design, which was to demonstrate *That there is a Soul or Incorporeal Sub-stance residing in us, distinct from the Body.* But I shall not content my self here, but for a more full discovery of her *Nature* and *Faculties*, I shall advance further, and search out her *chief Seat in the Body,* where and from whence she exercises her most noble Functions, and after enquire whether she be *confined* to that part thereof alone, or whether she be *spred* through all our members; and lastly consider after what manner she *sees, feels, hears, imagines, remembers, reasons,* and *moves the Body.* For beside that I shall make some good use of these discoveries for further purpose, it is also in it self very pleasant to have in readiness a rational and coherent account, and a determinate apprehension of things of this nature.

CHAP.   VII.

1. *His Enquiry after the Seat of Common Sense, upon supposition there is a Soul in the Body.* 2. *That there is some particular Part in the Body that is the seat of Common Sense.* 3. *A general division of their Opinions concerning the place of Common Sense.* 4. *That of those that place it out of the Head there are two sorts.* 5. *The Invalidity of* Helmont's *reasons whereby he would prove the Orifice of the Stomack to be the principal Seat of the Soul.* 6. *An Answer to* Helmont's *stories for that purpose.* 7. *A further confutation out of his own concessions.* 8. *Mr.* Hobbs *his Opinion confuted, that makes the Heart the Seat of Common Sense.* 9. *A further confutation thereof from Experience.* 10. *That the Common Sense is seated somewhere in the Head.* 11. *A caution for the choice of the particular place thereof.* 12. *That the whole Brain is not it;* 13. *Nor* Regius *his small solid Particle;* 14. *Nor any external Membrane of the Brain, nor the* Septum Lucidum. 15. *The three most likely places.* 16. *Objections against* Cartesius *his Opinion concerning the* Conarion *answered.* 17. *That the* Conarion *is not the Seat of Common Sense;* 18. *Nor that part of the Spinal Marrow where the Nerves are conceived to concure, but the Spirits in the fourth Ventricle of the Brain.*

10. And that no man hereafter may make any other unhappy choice in the parts of the Body, we shall now propose such Reasons as we hope will plainly prove, That the common *Sensorium* must needs be in the *Head;* or indeed rather repeat them: For some of those whereby we proved that the *Heart* is not the Seat of *Common Sense,* will plainly evince that the *Head* is. As that out of *Laurentius,** that a *Nerve* being tied, *Sense* and

* *Histor. Anatom. lib. 4. quaest. 7.* (51)

Motion will be preserved from the Ligature up towards the *Head*, but downwards they will be lost. As also that experiment of a *Frog*, whose brain if you pierce will presently be devoid of *Sense* and *Motion,* though all the Entrals being taken out it will skip up and down, and exercise its Senses as before. Which is a plain evidence that *Motion* and *Sense* is derived from the *Head;* and there is now no pretence to trace any *Motion* into a farther fountain, the *Heart,* (from whence the *Nerves* were conceived to branch by *Aristotle,* and from whence certainly the *Veins* and *Arteries* do, as appears by every Anatomie) being so justly discharged from that office.

To which it may suffice to adde the consideration of those Diseases that seize upon all the Animal functions at once, such as are the *Lethargie, Apoplexie, Epilepsie,* and the like, the causes of which Physicians find in the *Head,* and accordingly apply remedies. Which is a plain detection that the Seat of the Soul, as much as concerns the Animal Faculties, is chiefly in the *Head.* The same may be said of *Phrensy* and *Melancholy,* and such like distempers, that deprave a mans *Imagination* and *Judgment;* Physicians alwaies conclude something amiss within the *Cranium.*

Lastly, if it were nothing but the near attendance of the outward Senses on the *Soul,* or her *discerning Faculty,* being so fitly placed about her in the *Head;* this, unless there were some considerable Argument to the contrary, should be sufficient to determine any one that is unprejudiced, to conclude that the Seat of *Common Sense, Understanding,* and *command* of *Motion,* is there also.

11. But now the greatest difficulty will be to define *In what part thereof it is to be placed.* In which, unless we will goe over-boldly and carelessly to work, we are to have a regard to Mechanical congruities, and not pitch upon any thing that, by the advantage of this Supposal, *That there is a Soul in man,* may goe for possible; but to chuse what is most handsome and convenient.

.   .   .   .

12. That the *whole Brain* is not the Seat of *Common Sense,* appears from the wounds and cuts it may receive without the

destruction of that Faculty; for they will not take away *Sense* and *Motion*, unless they pierce so deep as to reach the *Ventricles of the Brain*, as *Galen* has observed. (52)

13. Nor is it in *Regius* his *small solid particle*. For besides that it is not likely the *Centre of Perception* is so minute, it is very incongruous to place it in a Body so perfectly *solid*, more *hard* then Marble or Iron. But this Invention being but a late freak of his petulant fancy, that has an ambition to make a blunder and confusion of all *Des-Cartes* his Metaphysical Speculations, (and therefore found out this rare quirk of wit to shew, how though the *Soul* were nothing but *Matter*, yet it might be *incorruptible* and *immortal*) it was not worth the while to take notice of it here in this Hypothesis, which we have demonstrated to be true, viz. *That there is a Soul in the Body, whose nature is Immaterial or Incorporeal.*

14. Nor are the *Membranes in the Head* the common *Sensorium;* neither those that envelop the *Brain*, (for they would be able then to see the light through the hole the *Trepan* makes, though the party *Trepan'd* winked with his eyes; to say nothing of the conveyance of the *Nerves*, the Organs of external Sense, that carry beyond these exteriour Membranes, and therefore point to a place more inward, that must be the *Recipient* of all their impresses) nor any *Internal membrane*, as that which bids fairest for it, the *Septum Lucidum*, as being in the midst of the upper Ventricle.

15. The most likely place is some one of those that the three last Opinions point at, viz. either the *Conarion*, or the *Concurse of the Nerves in the fourth Ventricle*, or *the Animal Spirits there*.

16. The first is *Des-Cartes* Opinion, and not rashly to be refused, neither do I find any Arguments hitherto that are valid enough to deface it. . . .

17. But though these Arguments do not sufficiently confute the Opinion, yet I am not so wedded to it, but I can think something more unexceptionable may be found out, especially it being so much to be suspected that all Animals have not this Conarion; . . .

18. Wherefore that Opinion of the forecited Author * who

* *Adenograph.* Cap. 23.

places the Seat of *Common Sense* in that part of the *Spinal Marrow* where the *Nerves* are suspected to meet, as it is more plain and simple, so it is more irrefutable, supposing that the Soul's *Centre of perception* (whereby she does not onely apprehend all the Objects of the external Senses, but does *imagine, reason,* and *freely command* and *determine* the *Spirits* into what part of the Body she pleases) could be conveniently seated in such dull pasty Matter as the *Pith of the Brain* is; a thing, I must needs confess, that pleases not my Palate at all, and therefore I will also take leave of this Opinion too, and adventure to pronounce, *That the chief Seat of the Soul, where she perceives all Objects, where she imagines, reasons, and invents, and from whence she commands all the parts of the Body, is those purer Animal Spirits in the fourth Ventricle of the Brain.*

CHAP. VIII.

1. *The first reason of his Opinion, the convenient Situation of these Spirits.* 2. *The second, that the Spirits are the immediate Instrument of the Soul in all her functions.* 3. *The proof of the second Reason from the general Authority of Philosophers, and particularly of* Hippocrates; 4. *From our Sympathizing with the changes of the Aire;* 5. *From the celerity of Motion and Cogitation;* 6. *From what is observed generally in the Generation of things;* 7. *From* Regius *his experiment of a Snail in a glass;* 8. *From the running round of Images in a Vertigo;* 9. *From the constitution of the Eye, and motion of the Spirits there;* 10. *From the dependency of the actions of the Soul upon the Body, whether in Meditation or corporeal Motion;* 11. *From the recovery of Motion and Sense into a stupefied part;* 12. *And lastly, from what is observed in swooning fits, of paleness and sharpness of visage, &c.* 13. *The inference from all this, That the Spirits in the fourth Ventricle are the Seat of Common Sense, and that the main use of the Brain and Nerves is to preserve the Spirits.*

1. That which makes me embrace this Opinion rather then any other is this; That, first, this situation of the common *Sensorium*

betwixt the *Head* and the trunk of *the Body* is the most exactly convenient to receive the impresses of Objects from both, as also to impart Motion to the Muscles in both the *Head* and in the *Body*. In which I look upon it as equall with the last Opinion, and superiour to all them that went before. For whatever may be objected, is already answered in what I have said to the last Objection against *Des-cartes*.

2. But now in the second place, (wherein this Opinion of mine has a notorious advantage above all else that I know) It is most reasonable that that Matter which is the *immediate Instrument* of all the Animal functions of the Soul, should be the chiefest Seat from whence and where she exercises these functions, and if there be any place where there is a freer plenty of the purest sort of this Matter, that her *peculiar residence* should be there. Now the *immediate Instrument* of the functions of the Soul is that *thinner Matter* which they ordinarily call *Animal Spirits,* which are to be found in their greatest purity and plenty in the *fourth Ventricle of the Brain.* From whence it must follow that that precious and choice part of the Soul which we call *the Centre of perception* is to be placed in that Ventricle, not in any pith of the Brain thereabout, but in the midst of these Spirits themselves; for that is the most natural situation for the commanding them into the parts of the *Head* and *Body;* besides a more delicate and subtile use of them at home, in pursuing various imaginations and inventions.

5. The strange *Agility* also of *Motions* and *Cogitations* that we find in our selves, has forced the most sluggish witts, even such as have been so gross as to deem the Soul *Corporeal,* yet to chuse the freest, subtilest & most active Matter to compound her of, that their imaginations could excogitate. And *Lucretius,** the most confident of the *Epicurean* Sect, thinks he has hit the naile on the head in his choice;

> *Nunc igitur quoniam est animi natura reperta*
> *Mobilis egregiè, per quam constare necesse est*
> *Corporibus parvis & laevibus atque rotundis:*

* *De Natura Rerum, lib.* 3.

whose Testimony I account the better in this case, by how much the more crass Philosopher he is, the necessity of the tenuity of particles that are to pervade the Body of a Man being convinced hence to be so plain, that the dimmest eyes can easily discover it.

10. To which we may adde that in those *more noble* operations of the Mind, when she *meditates* and excogitates various Theorems, that either she uses some part of the Body as an Instrument then, or acts freely and independently of the Body. That the latter is false is manifest from hence, that then the change of Air, or Distemper and Diseasedness, could not prejudice her in her *Inventive* and *purely Intellectual* Operations; but it is manifest that they doe, and that a mans Mind is much more cloudy one time then another, and in one Country then another, whence is that proverbial Verse,

Boeotûm crasso jurares aëre natum. (53)

If she uses any part of the Body, it must be either these *Animal Spirits,* or the *Brain.* That it is not the *Brain,* the very consistency thereof so clammy and sluggish is an evident demonstration.

Which will still have the more force, if we consider what is most certainly true, That the Soul has not any *power,* or else exceedingly little, *of moving Matter;* but her peculiar priviledge is of *determining Matter in Motion;* which the more subtile and agitated it is, the more easily by reason of its own mobility is it determined by her. For if it were an immediate faculty of the Soul *to contribute Motion* to any Matter, I do not understand how that faculty never failing nor diminishing no more then the Soul it self can fail or diminish, that we should ever be weary of motion.

13. I have proved that the *Animal Spirits* are the Soul's immediate organ for *Sense* and *Motion.* If therefore there be any place where these *Spirits* are in the fittest plenty and purity, and in the most convenient situation for Animal functions; that in all reason must be concluded the chief seat and Acropolis of the Soul. Now the *Spirits* in the *middle ventricle of the Brain* are

not so indifferently situated for both the *Body* and the *Head*, as those in the *fourth* are; nor so pure. The upper Ventricles, being two, are not so fit for this office, that is so very much one and singular. Besides that the sensiferous impresses of motion through the eyes play under them; to say nothing how the *Spirits* here are less defecate also then in the *fourth* Ventricle.

Wherefore there being *sufficient plenty,* and *greatest purity,* and *fittest situation of the Spirits in this fourth Ventricle,* it is manifest that in these is placed the *Centre of Perception,* and that they are the *common Sensorium* of the Soul: And that as the *Heart* pumps out *Blood* perpetually to supply the whole Body with nourishment, to keep up the bulk of this Edifice for the Soul to dwell in, and also, from the more subtile and agile parts thereof, to replenish the *Brain* and *Nerves* with *Spirits,* (which are the immediate Instrument of the Soul for *Sense* and *Motion;*) So likewise is it plain that the main use of the *Brain* and *Nerves* is to keep these *subtile Spirits* from over-speedy dissipation; and that the *Brain* with its Caverns is but one great round *Nerve;* as the *Nerves* with their invisible porosities are but so many smaller productions or slenderer prolongations of the *Brain:* And so all together are but one continued Receptacle or Case of that immediate Instrument of the sensiferous motions of the Soul, the *Animal Spirits,* wherein also lies her hidden Vehicle of Life in this mortal body.

CHAP. IX.

1. *Several Objections against* Animal Spirits. 2. *An Answer to the first Objection touching the Porosity of the Nerves.* 3. *To the second and third, from the Extravasation of the Spirits and pituitous Excrements found in the Brain.* 4. *To the fourth, fetcht from the incredible swiftness of motion in the Spirits.* 5. *To the last, from Ligation.* 6. *Undeniable Demonstrations that there are* Animal *Spirits in the Ventricles of the Brain.*

CHAP. X.

1. We are now at leisure to resume the two remaining Enquiries; the former whereof is, whether the Soul be so in this
fourth Ventricle, that it is essentially no where else in the Body,
or whether it be spread out into all the Members. *Regius* * would
coup it up in the *Conarion,* which he believes to be the Common
Sensorium, and so by consequence it should be confined to the
fourth Ventricle, and not expatiate at all thence, supposing that
the Seat of *Common Sense.* The reason of this conceit of his
is this, That whatever is in the rest of the Body, may come to
pass by powers merely *Mechanical;* wherein he does very super-
stitiously tread in the footsteps of his Master *Des-Cartes.* But
for my own part, I cannot but dissent, I finding in neither any
sufficient grounds of so novel an opinion, but rather apparent
reasons to the contrary.

2. As first, the *Frame of the Body,* of which I think most
reasonable to conclude the *Soul* her self to be the more particular
Architect (for I will not wholly reject *Plotinus* his opinion);
and that the *Plastick power* resides in her, as also in the Souls
of Brute animals, as very learned and worthy Writers have
determined. That the *Fabrick of the Body* is out of the concurse of *Atomes,* is a mere precarious Opinion, without any
ground or reason. For *Sense* does not discover any such thing,
the first rudiments of life being out of some *liquid homogeneal*

* *Philos. Natural.* lib. 5. cap. I.

Matter; and it is against * *Reason,* that the tumbling of *Atomes* or corporeal particles should produce such exquisite frames of creatures, wherein the acutest wit is not able to find any thing inept, but all done exquisitely well every where, where the foulness and coursness of *Matter* has not been in fault.

That God is not the *immediate Maker* of these *Bodies,* the particular miscarriages demonstrate. For there is no Matter so perverse and stubborn but his *Omnipotency* could tame; whence there would be no Defects nor Monstrosities in the generation of Animals.

Nor is it so congruous to admit that the *Plastick* faculty of the *Soul of the World* is the *sole* contriver of these Fabricks of particular Creatures, (though I will not deny but she may give some rude * preparative strokes towards Efformation;) but that in every *particular* World, such as Man is especially, his own Soul is the peculiar and most perfective Architect thereof, as the Soul of the World is of it. For this *vital* Fabrication is not as in *artificial* Architecture, when an external person acts upon Matter; but implies a more particular and near union with that Matter it thus intrinsecally shapes out and organizes. And what ought to have a more particular and close union with our Bodies then our Souls themselves?

My opinion is therefore, That the Soul, which is a *Spirit,* and therefore *contractible* and *dilatable,* begins within less compass at first in Organizing the fitly-prepared Matter, and so bears it self on in the same tenour of work till the Body has attained its full growth; and that the Soul *dilates* it self in the dilating of the Body, and so possesses it through all the members thereof.

3. The congruity of this Truth will further discover it self, if we consider the nature of the Faculties of the Soul (of which you may read more fully in *Enthusiasmus Triumphatus* *) in what a *natural graduality* they arise till they come to the *most free* of all. The *deepest* or *lowest* is this *Plastick power* we have already spoke of, in virtue whereof is continued that perpetual

---

* See my *Antidote,* Book 2. chap. 12. sect. 2, 3, 4, &c.

* *Plotinus* calls them προϋπογροφὴν, and προδρόμους ἐλλάμψεις εἰς ὕλην *Ennead.* 6. *lib.* 7. *cap.* 7.

* *Enthus. Triump,* sect. 3, 4, 5. (54)

Systole and *Diastole* of the *Heart,* as I am more prone to think then that it is merely Mechanical, as also that *Respiration* that is performed without the command of our Will: For the *Libration* or *Reciprocation* of the *Spirits* in the *Tensility* of the *Muscles* would not be so perpetual, but cease in a small time, did not some more mystical Principle then what is merely Mechanical give Assistance; as any one may understand by observing the insufficiency of those devices that *Henricus Regius* * propounds for adequate causes of such motions in the Body. These I look upon as the *First Faculties* of the Soul, which may be bounded by this general character, That the exercise of them does not at all imply so much as our *Perception.*

4. Next to these is the *Sensation of any external Object,* such as *Hearing, Seeing, Feeling,* &c. All which include *Perception* in an unresistible necessity thereof, the Object being present before us, and no external Obstacle interposing.

5. *Imagination* is more *free,* we being able to avoid its representation for the most part, without any external help; but it is a degree on this side *Will* and *Reason,* by which we correct and silence unallowable fancies. Thus we see how the *Faculties* of the Soul rise *by Degrees;* which makes it still the more easy and credible, that the *lowest* of all is competible to her as well as the *highest.*

6. Moreover, *Passions* and *Sympathies,* in my judgment, are more easily to be resolved into this Hypothesis of the Soul's pervading the *whole Body,* then in restraining its essential presence to *one part* thereof.* For to believe that such an horrible Object, as, suppose, a Bear or Tiger, by transmission of Motion from it through the Eyes of an Animal to the *Conarion,* shall so reflect thence, as to determine the Spirits into such Nerves as will streighten the Orifice of the Heart, and lessen the Pulse, and cause all other symptomes of *Fear;* seems to me little better then a mere piece of *Mechanical Credulity.*

.   .   .   .

8. But we have yet a more clear discovery, that our Soul *is not confined to any one part* of the Head, but possesses the

* *Philos. Natural. lib. 4. cap.* 16.
* *See Des-Cartes De Passionibus, Part. I. Artic.* 36. (55).

whole Body, from the *Perception of Pain* in the parts thereof:
For it is plainly impossible that so high a torture as is felt
but in the pricking of a Pin, can be communicated to the *Centre
of Perception* upon a mere Mechanical account. For whether
the *immediate Instrument of Sense* be the *Pith of the Nerves,*
as *Des-Cartes* would have it, or whether it be the *Spirits* as is
most true; it is ridiculous to think, that by the forcible parting
of what was joyned together at ease (when this case is not
communicated to either the *Spirits,* or *Pith of the Nerves,* from
the place of the Puncture, to the very seat of Common Sense)
the Soul there seated should feel so smart a torture, unless that
her very Essence did reach to the part where the *pain* is felt to
be. For then the reason of this is plain, that it is the *Unity of
Soul* possessing the whole Body, and the *Continuity of Spirits*
that is the cause thereof.

.   .   .   .   .   .

CHAP. XI.

1. *That neither the Soul without the Spirits, nor the Spirits
without the presence of the Soul in the Organ, are sufficient Causes of* Sensation. 2. *A brief declaration how* Sensation *is made.* 3. *How Imagination.* 4. *Of* Reason *and*
Memory, *and whether there be any Marks in the Brain.*
5. *That the Spirits are the immediate Instrument of the
Soul in* Memory *also; and how* Memory *arises;* 6. *As also*
Forgetfulness. 7. *How* Spontaneous Motion *is performed.*
8. *How we walk, sing, and play, though thinking of something else.* 9. *That though the Spirits be not alike fine
every where, yet the* Sensiferous Impression *will pass to
the* Common Sensorium. 10. *That there is an* Heterogeneity *in the very Soul her self; and what it is in her
we call the* Root, *the* Centre, *and the* Eye; *and what the*
Rayes *and* Branches. 11. *That the sober and allowable
Distribution of her into Parts, is into* Perceptive *and*
Plastick.

CHAP. XII.

1. *An Answer to an Objection, That our Arguments will as well prove the Immortality of the Souls of Brutes as of Men.* 2. *Another Objection inferring the Praeexistence of Brutes Souls, and consequently of ours.* 3. *The first Answer to the Objection.* 4. *The second Answer consisting of four parts.* 5. *First, That the Hypothesis of* Praeexistence *is more agreeable to Reason then any other Hypothesis.* 6. *And not onely so, but that it is very solid in it self.* 7. *That the Wisdome and Goodness of God argue the truth thereof.* 8. *As also the face of Providence in the World.* 9. *The second part of the second Answer, That the* Praeexistence *of the Soul has the suffrage of all Philosophers in all Ages, that held it* Incorporeal. 10. *That the* Gymnosophists *of* Ægypt, *the* Indian Brachmans, *the* Persian Magi, *and all the learned of the* Jews *were of this Opinion.* 11. *A Catalogue of particular famous persons that held the same.* 12. *That* Aristotle *was also of the same mind.* 13. *Another more clear place in* Aristotle *to this purpose, with* Sennertus *his Interpretation.* 14. *An Answer to an Evasion of that Interpretation.* 15. *The last and clearest place of all out of* Aristotle's *Writings.*

CHAP. XIII.

1. *The third part of the second Answer, That the forgetting of the former state is no good Argument against the* Soule's Praeexistence. 2. *What are the chief causes of Forgetfulness.* 3. *That they all conspire, and that in the highest degree, to destroy the memory of the other state.* 4. *That mischances and Diseases have quite taken away the Memory of things here in this life.* 5. *That it is impossible for the Soul to remember her former condition without a Miracle.* 6. *The fourth part of the second Answer, That the Entrance of a Praeexistent Soul into a Body is as intelligible as either Creation or Traduction.*

CHAP. XIV.

1. *The knowledge of the difference of* Vehicles, *and the Soul's Union with them, necessary for the understanding how she enters into this Earthly Body.* 2. *That though the Name of* Vehicle *be not in* Aristotle, *yet the Thing is there.* 3. *A clearing of* Aristotle's *notion of the Vehicle, out of the Philosophy of* Des-Cartes. 4. *A full interpretation of his Text.* 5. *That* Aristotle *makes onely two Vehicles,* Terrestrial *and* Æthereal; *which is more then sufficient to prove the Soul's Oblivion of her former state.* 6. *That the ordinary Vehicle of the Soul after death is* Aire. 7. *The duration of the Soul in her several Vehicles.* 8. *That the Union of the Soul with her Vehicle does not consist in* Mechanical *Congruity, but* Vital. 9. *In what* Vital congruity *of the Matter consists.* 10. *In what* Vital congruity *of the Soul consists, and how it changing, the Soul may be free from her Aiery Vehicle, without violent precipitation out of it.* 11. *Of the manner of the Descent of Souls into Earthly Bodies.* 12. *That there is so little Absurdity in the* Praeexistence of Souls, *that the concession thereof can be but a very small prejudice to our Demonstrations of her Immortality.*

CHAP. XV.

1. *What is meant by the* Separation o, *the Soul, with a confutation of* Regius, *who would stop her in the dead Corps.* 2. *An Answer to those that profess themselves puzled how the Soul can get out of the Body.* 3. *That there is a threefold* Vital Congruity *to be found in three several Subjects.* 4. *That this triple Congruity is also competible to one Subject, viz. the Soul of Man.* 5. *That upon this Hypothesis it is very intelligible how the Soul may leave the Body.* 6. *That her Union with the* Aereal Vehicle *may be very suddain, and as it were in a moment.* 7. *That the*

*Soul is actually separate from the Body, is to be proved
either by* History *or* Reason. *Examples of the former kinde
out of* Pliny, Herodotus, Ficinus. 8. *Whether the Ecstasie
of Witches prove an actual separation of the Soul from the
Body.* 9. *That this real separation of the Soul in Ecstasie
is very possible.* 10. *How the Soul may be loosned and
leave the Body, and yet return thither again.* 11. *That
though Reason and Will cannot in this life release the Soul
from the Body, yet Passion may; and yet so that she may
return again.* 12. *The peculiar power of Desire for this
purpose.* 13. *Of* Cardan's *Ecstasies, and the Ointment of*
Witches, *and what truth there may be in their confessions.*

1. Concerning the *actual and local Separation of the Soul from
the Body,* it is manifest that it is to be understood of this
Terrestrial Body. For to be in such a separate state, as to be
where no *Body* or *Matter* is, is to be out of the World: the
whole Universe being so thick set with *Matter* or *Body,* that
there is not to be found the least vacuity therein. The question
therefore is only, whether upon death the Soul can pass from
the Corps into some other place. *Henricus Regius* * seems to
arrest her there by that *general law of Nature,* termed the *Law
of Immutabilty;* whereby every thing is to continue in the same
condition it once is in, till something else change it. But the
application of this law is very grossly injust in this case. For,
as I have above intimated, the Union of the Soul with the Body
is upon certain terms; neither is every piece of Matter fit for
every Soul to unite with, as *Aristotle* of old has very solidly
concluded. Wherefore that condition of the Matter being not
kept, the Soul is no longer engaged to the Body. What he here
says for the justifying of himself, is so arbitrarious, so childish
and ridiculous, that, according to the merit thereof, I shall
utterly neglect it, and pass it by, not vouchsafing of it any
Answer.

2. Others are much puzled in their imagination, how the Soul
can get out of the Body, being imprisoned and lockt up in so
close a Castle. But these seem to forget both the *Nature of the
Soul,* with the *tenuity of her Vehicle,* and also the *Anatomy of the*

* *Philosoph. Natural. lib. 5. cap.* I. *pag.* 351, 352.

Body. For considering *the nature of the Soul* her self, and of *Matter* which is alike penetrable every where, the Soul can pass through solid Iron and Marble as well as through the soft Air and Æther; so that the thickness of the Body is no impediment to her. Besides, her *Astral* Vehicle is of that tenuity, that it self can as easily pass the smallest pores of the Body as the Light does Glass, or the Lightning the Scabbard of a Sword without tearing or scorching of it. And lastly, whether we look upon that principal seat of the *Plastick* power of the *Heart,* or that of *Perception,* the *Brain;* when a man dies, the Soul may collect her self, and the small residue of Spirits (that may haply serve her in the inchoation of her new Vehicle) either into the Heart, whence is an easy passage into the Lungs, and so out at the Mouth; or else into the Head, out of which there are more doors open then I will stand to number. These things are very easily imaginable, though as invisible as the Air, in whose element they are transacted.

3. But that they may still be more perfectly understood, I shall resume again the consideration of that Faculty in the *Plastick* part of the Soul, which we call *Vital Congruity.* Which, according to the number of Vehicles, we will define to be three-fold, *Terrestrial, Aereal,* and *Æthereal* or *Celestial.* That these *Vital Congruities* are found, some in some kinde of Spirits and others in othersome, is very plain. For that the *Terrestrial* is in the Soul of Brutes and in our own is without controversie; as also that the *Aereal* in that kinde of Beings which the Ancients called Δαίμονες and lastly, that the *Heavenly* and *Æthereal* in those Spirits that Antiquity more properly called Θεοί, as being Inhabitants of the Heavens. For that there are such *Aereal* and *Æthereal Beings* that are analogous to *Terrestrial* Animals, if we compare the nature of God with the *Phaenomena* of the world, it cannot prove less then a Demonstration.

For this Earth that is replenisht with living Creatures, nay put in all the Planets too that are in the world, and fancy them inhabited, they all joyned together bear not so great a pro-portion to the rest of the liquid Matter of the Universe (that is in a nearer capacity of being the Vehicle of Life) as a single Cumin-seed to the Globe of the Earth. But how ridiculous a thing would it be, that all the Earth beside being neglected, onely one piece thereof, no better then the rest, nor bigger then the smallest seed, should be inhabited? The same may be said also of the compass of the Aire; and therefore it is necessary to enlarge their Territories, and confidently to pronounce there are *Æthereal Animals,* as well as *Terrestrial* and *Aereal.*

4. It is plain therefore that these three *Congruities* are to be found in several Subjects; but that which makes most to our purpose, is to finde them in one, and that in the Soul of Man. And there will be an easy intimation thereof, if we consider the vast difference of those Faculties that we are sure are in her *Perceptive* part, and how they occasionally emerge, and how upon the laying asleep of one, others will spring up. Neither can there be any greater difference betwixt the highest and lowest of these *Vital congruities* in the *Plastick* part, then there is betwixt the highest and lowest of those Faculties that result from the *Perceptive.* For some Perceptions are the very same with those of *Beasts;* others little inferiour to those that belong to *Angels,* as we ordinarily call them; some perfectly brutish, others purely divine: why therefore may there not reside so great a Latitude of capacities in the *Plastick* part of the Soul, as that she may have in her all those three *Vital Congruities,* whereby she may be able livingly to unite as well with the *Celestial* and *Aereal Body* as with this *Terrestrial* one? Nay, our nature being so free and multifarious as it is, it would seem a reproach to Providence, to deny this capacity of living in these several Vehicles; because that *Divine Nemesis* which is supposed to rule the world would seem defective without this contrivance.

But without controversy, Eternal Wisdome and Justice has forecast that which is the best: and, unless we will say nothing at all, we having nothing to judge by but our own Faculties, we must say that the Forecast is according to what we, upon our most accurate search, do conceive to be the best. For there being no Envy in the Deity, as *Plato* somewhere has noted, it is not to be thought but that He has framed our Faculties so, that when we have rightly prepared our selves for the use of them, they will have a right correspondency with those things that are offered to them to contemplate in the world.

And truly if we had here time to consider, I do not doubt but it might be made to appear a very rational thing, that there should be such an *Amphibion* as the Soul of man, that had a capacity (as some Creatures have to live either in the Water or on the Earth) to change her Element, and after her abode here in this *Terrestrial Vehicle* amongst Men and Beasts, to ascend into the company of the *Aereal Genii,* in a Vehicle answerable to their nature.

5. Supposing then this triple capacity of *Vital Congruity* in the Soul of Man, the manner how she may leave this Body is very intelligible. For the Bodies fitness of temper to retain the Soul being lost in Death, the lower *Vital Congruity* in the Soul looseth its Object, and consequently its Operation. And therefore as the letting goe one thought in the *Perceptive part* of the Soul is the bringing up another; so the ceasing of one *Vital Congruity* is the wakening of another, if there be an Object, or Subject, ready to entertain it; as certainly there is, partly in the Body, but mainly without it.

6. And being once recovered into this vast Ocean of *Life,* and *sensible Spirit of the world,* so full of enlivening Balsame; it will be no wonder if the Soul suddainly regain the use of her *Perceptive* faculty, being, as it were in a moment, regenerate into a natural power of Life and Motion, by so happy a concurse of rightly-prepared Matter for her *Plastick* part vitally to unite withall.

7. How the Soul *may* live and act separate from the Body, may be easily understood out of what has been spoken. But that she does so *de facto,* there are but two waies to prove it; the one by the testimony of *History,* the other by *Reason.*

CHAP. XVI.

1. *That Souls departed communicate Dreams.* 2. *Examples of Apparitions of Souls deceased.* 3. *Of Apparitions in fields where pitcht Battels have been fought; as also of those in Churchyards, and other vaporous places.* 4. *That the Spissitude of the Air may well contribute to the easiness of the appearing of* Ghosts *and* Spectres. 5. *A further proof thereof from sundry Examples.* 6. *Of* Marsilius Ficinus *his appearing after death.* 7. *With what sort of people such Examples as these avail little.* 8. *Reasons to perswade the unprejudiced that ordinarily those Apparitions that bear the shape and person of the deceased, are indeed the Souls of them.*

    •   •   •   •   •   •   •   •   •

7. The Examples I have produced of the *appearing* of the Souls of men after death, considering how clearly I have demonstrated the *separability* of them from the Body, and their capacity of Vital Union with an *Aiery Vehicle*, cannot but have their due weight of Argument with them that are unprejudiced.

    •   •   •   •   •   •   •   •

8. But *Misconceit* and *Prejudice,* though it may hinder the force of an Argument with those that are in that manner *entangled,* yet *Reason* cannot but take place with them that are *free.* To whom I dare appeal whether (considering the *Aëreal Vehicles* of Souls which are common to them with other *Genii,* so that whatever they are fancied to doe in their stead, they may perform themselves; as also how congruous it is, that those persons that are most concerned, when it is in their power, should act in their own affairs, as in detecting the Murtherer, in disposing their estate, in rebuking injurious Executors, in visiting and counselling their Wives and Children, in forewarning them of such and such courses, with other matters of like sort; to which you may adde the profession of the Spirit thus appearing, of being the Soul of such an one, as also the similitude of person; and that all this adoe is in things very just and

serious, unfit for a Devil with that care and kindness to promote, and as unfit for a good *Genius,* it being below so noble a nature to tell a Lie, especially when the affair may be as effectually transacted without it;) I say, I dare appeal to any one, whether all these things put together and rightly weighed, the violence of prejudice not pulling down the balance, it will not be certainly carried for the present Cause; and whether any indifferent Judge ought not to conclude, if these Stories that are so frequent every where and in all Ages concerning the Ghosts of men appearing be but true, that it is true also that they are their Ghosts, and that therefore the Souls of men subsist and act after they have left these Earthly Bodies.

CHAP. XVII.

1. *The preeminence of Arguments drawn from Reason above those from Story.* 2. *The first step toward a Demonstration of Reason that a Soul acts out of her Body, for that she is an* Immaterial Substance *separable there-from.* 3. *The second, That the* immediate Instruments *for Sense, Motion, and Organization of the Body, are certain* subtile *and* tenuious Spirits. 4. *A comparison betwixt the* Soul *in* the Body *and the* Aëreal Genii. 5. *Of the nature of* Daemons *from the account of* Marcus *the Eremite, and how the Soul is presently such, having once left this Body.* 6. *An Objection concerning the Souls of Brutes: to which is answered, First, by way of concession;* 7. *Secondly, by confuting the Arguments for the former concession.* 8. *That there is no rational doubt at all of the Humane Soul acting after Death.* 9. *A further Argument of her activity out of this Body, from her conflicts with it while she is in it.* 10. *As also from the general hope and belief of all Nations, that they shall live after death.*

1. But we proceed now to what is less subject to the evasions and misinterpretations of either the *Profane* or *Superstitious.* For none but such as will profess themselves mere Brutes can

cast off the Decrees and Conclusions of Philosophy and Reason; though they think that in things of this nature they may, with a great deal of applause and credit, refuse the testimony of other mens Senses, if not of their own: all *Apparitions* being with them nothing but the strong surprisals of *Melancholy* and *Imagination*. But they cannot with that ease nor credit silence the Deductions of Reason, by saying it is but a *Fallacy*, unlesse they can shew the Sophisme; which they cannot doe, where it is not.

2. To carry on therefore our present Argument in a rational way, and by degrees; we are first to consider, That (according as already has been clearly * demonstrated) there is a Substance in us which is ordinarily called *the Soul*, really distinct from the Body, (for otherwise how can it be a Substance?) And therefore it is really and locally separable from the Body. Which is a very considerable step towards what we aim at.

3. In the next place we are to take notice, That the *immediate Instrument* of the Soul are those tenuious and Aëreal particles which they ordinarily call the * *Spirits;* that these are they by which the Soul hears, sees, feels, imagines, remembers, reasons, and by moving which, or at least directing their motion, she moves likewise the Body; and by using them, or some subtile Matter like them, she either compleats, or at least contributes to the Bodie's Organization. For that the Soul should be the *Vital Architect* of her own house, that close connexion and sure possession she is to have of it, distinct and secure from the invasion of any other particular Soul, seems no slight Argument. And yet that while she is exercising that Faculty she may have a more then ordinary Union or Implication with the *Spirit of Nature*, or the *Soul of the World*, so far forth as it is *Plastick*, seems not unreasonable: and therefore is asserted by *Plotinus;* & may justly be suspected to be true, if we attend to the prodigious effects of the Mother's Imagination derived upon the Infant, which sometimes are so very great, that, unless she raised the *Spirit of Nature* into consent, they might well seem to exceed the power of any Cause. I shall abstain from producing any Examples till the proper place: in the mean time I hope I may be excused from any rashness in this assignation of the Cause of those many and various Signatures found in Nature, so plainly

* Chap. 2, 4, 5, 6.   * Chap. 8, 9.

pointing at such a Principle in the World as I have intimated *
before.

4. But to return, and cast our eye upon the Subject in hand.
It appears from the two precedent Conclusions, That the Soul
considered as invested immediately with this *tenuious Matter* we
speak of, which is her inward Vehicle, has very little more
difference from the *Aëreal Genii,* then a man in a Prison from
one that is free. The one can onely see, and suck air through
the Grates of the Prison, and must be annoyed with all the stench
and unwholesome fumes of that sad habitation; whenas the other
may walk and take the fresh air, where he finds it most com-
modious and agreeable.

This difference there is betwixt the *Genii* and an *incorporated
Soul.* The *Soul,* as a man faln into a deep pit, (who can have
no better Water, nor Air, nor no longer enjoyment of the Sun,
and his chearful light and warmth, then the measure and quality
of the pit will permit him) so she once immured in the Body
cannot enjoy any better Spirits (in which all her life and comfort
consists) then the constitution of the Body after such circuits
of concoction can administer to her. But those *Genii* of the
Aire, who possess their Vehicles upon no such hard terms, if themselves be not in fault, may by the power of their minds accommodate themselves with more pure and impolluted Matter, and such
as will more easily conspire with the noblest and divinest functions of their Spirit.

In brief, therefore, if we consider things aright, we cannot
abstain from strongly surmising, that there is no more difference
betwixt a Soul and an aëreal *Genius,* then there is betwixt a
Sword in the scabbard and one out of it: and that a Soul is but
a *Genius* in the Body, and a *Genius* a Soul out of the Body; as
the Ancients also have defined, giving the same name, as well
as nature, promiscuously to them both, by calling them both
Δαίμονες, as I have elsewhere noted.*

10. Adde unto all this, that *the Immortality of the Soul* is the
common, and therefore natural, hope and expectation of all
Nations; there being very few so barbarous as not to hold it for
a Truth: though, it may be, as in other things, they may be

* Chap. 10. sect. 7.   * Chap. 8. sect. 13.

something ridiculous in the manner of expressing themselves about it; as that they shall retire after Death to such a Grove or Wood, or beyond such a Hill, or unto such an Island, such as was Δρόμος 'Αχιλλέως, the Island where *Achilles* his Ghost was conceived to wander, or the *Insulae Fortunate,* the noted *Elysium* of the Ancients.   And yet, it may be, if we should tell these of the *Coelum Empyreum,* and compute the height of it, and distance from the Earth, and how many solid Orbs must be glided through before a Soul can come thither; these simple Barbarians would think as odly of the *Scholastick* Opinion as we do of theirs: and it may be some more judicious and sagacious Wit will laugh at us both alike.

It is sufficient, that in the main all Nations in a manner are agreed that there is an *Immortality* to be *expected,* as well as that there is a *Deity* to be *worshipped;* though ignorance of circumstances makes Religion vary, even to Monstrosity, in many parts of the world.   But both Religion, and the belief of the Reward of it, which is a blessed state after Death, being so generally acknowledged by all the Inhabitants of the Earth; it is a plain Argument that it is true according to the Light of Nature.   And not onely because they believe so, but because they do so seriously either desire it, or are so horribly afraid of it, if they offend much against their Consciences: which Properties would not be in men so universally, if there were no Objects in Nature answering to these Faculties, as I have elsewhere argued in the like case.*

CHAP. XVIII.

1. *That the* Faculties *of our* Souls, *and the nature of the imme-diate Instrument of them, the* Spirits, *do so nearly symbolize with those of* Daemons, *that it seems reasonable, if God did not on purpose hinder it, that they would not fail to act out of this earthly Body.* 2. *Or if they would, his Power and Wisdome could easily implant in their essence a double or triple* Vital Congruity, *to make all sure.* 3. *A further dem-*

* *Antidote,* Book I. ch. 10. sect. 9.

onstration of the present Truth from the Veracity of God.   4.
An Answer to an Objection against the foregoing Argument.
5. *Another demonstration from his Justice.*   6. *An Answer to
an Objection.*   7. *An Answer to another Objection.*   8. *Another Argument from the Justice of God.*   9. *An Objection
answered.*   10. *An invincible Demonstration of the Soul's
Immortality from the Divine Goodness.*   11. *A more particular enforcement of that Argument, and who they are
upon whom it will work least.*   12. *That the Noblest and
most Vertuous Spirit is the most assurable of the Soul's
Immortality.*

IMMORTALITY
OF
THE SOUL.

THE THIRD BOOK.

CHAP. I.

1. *Why the Author treats of the state of the Soul after Death, and in what Method.* 2. *Arguments to prove that the Soul is ever united vitally with some Matter or other.* 3. *Further Reasons to evince the same.* 4. *That the Soul is capable of an* Aiery *and* Æthereal *Body, as well as a* Terrestrial. 5. *That she ordinarily passes out of an* Earthly *into an* Aëreal *Vehicle first.* 6. *That in her* Aiery *Vehicle she is capable of* Sense, Pleasure, *and* Pain. 7. *That the main power of the Soul over her* Aëreal *Vehicle is the direction of Motion in the particles thereof.* 8. *That she may also adde or diminish Motion in her* Æthereal. 9. *How the purity of the Vehicle confers to the quickness of Sense and Knowledge.* 10. *Of the Soul's power of changing the temper of her* Aëreal *Vehicle;* 11. *As also the shape thereof.* 12. *The plainness of the last Axiome.*

1. We have, I hope, with undeniable evidence demonstrated *the Immortality of the Soul* to such as neither by their slowness of parts, nor any prejudice of Immortality, are made incompetent Judges of the truth of Demonstrations of this kind: so that I have already perfected my main Design. But my own curiosity, and the desire of gratifying others who love to entertain themselves with Speculations of this nature, do call me out something further; if the very Dignity of the present Matter I am upon doth not justly require me, as will be best seen after the finishing thereof: which is *concerning the State of the Soul after Death.* Wherein though I may not haply be able to fix

my foot so firmly as in the foregoing part of this Treatise, yet
I will assert nothing but what shall be reasonable, though not
demonstrable, and far preponderating to whatever shall be
alledged to the contrary, and in such clear order and Method,
that if what I write be not worthy to convince, it shall not
be able to deceive or entangle by perplexedness and obscurity;
and therefore I shall offer to view at once the main Principles
upon which I shall build the residue of my Discourse.

Axiome XXVII.

The Soul *separate from this* Terrestrial *Body is not released
from all* Vital Union *with* Matter.

Axiome XXVIII.

There is a Triple Vital Congruity *in the Soul, namely,* Æthereal,
Aëreal, *and* Terrestrial.

Axiome XXIX.

*According to the usual custome of Nature, the Soul awakes
orderly into these* Vital Congruities, *not passing from one
Extreme to another without any stay in the middle.*

Axiome XXX.

The Soul in her Aëreal *Vehicle is capable of* Sense *properly so
called, and consequently of* Pleasure *and* Pain.

Axiome XXXI.

*The Soul can neither impart to nor take away from the Matter
of her* Vehicle of Aire *any considerable degree of Motion,
but yet can direct the particles moved which way she pleases
by the* Imperium *of her Will.*

Axiome XXXII.

*Though the Soul can neither confer nor take away any con-
siderable degree of Motion from the Matter of her Aiery*

Vehicle, yet nothing hinders but that she may doe both in her Æthereal.

. . . .

AXIOME XXXIII.

The purer the Vehicle is, the more quick and perfect are the Perceptive Faculties of the Soul.

. . . .

AXIOME XXXIV.

The Soul has a marvellous power of not onely changing the temper of her Aiery Vehicle, but also of the external shape thereof.

. . . .

AXIOME XXXV.

It is rational to think, that as some Faculties are laid asleep in Death or after Death, so others may awake that are more sutable for that state.

. . . .

AXIOME XXXVI.

Whether the Vital Congruity of the Soul expire, as whose period being quite unwound, or that of the Matter be defaced by any essential Dis-harmony, Vital Union immediately ceases.

CHAP. II.

1. *Of the Dimensions of the Soul considered barely in her self.* 2. *Of the Figure of the Soul's Dimensions.* 3. *Of the Heterogeneity of her Essence.* 4. *That there is an Heterogeneity in her Plastick part distinct from the Perceptive.* 5. *Of the acting of this Plastick part in her framing of the Vehicle.* 6. *The excellency of Des-Cartes his Philosophy.* 7. *That the Vehicles of Ghosts have as much of solid corporeal Substance in them as the Bodies of Men.* 8. *The folly of the contrary Opinion evinced.* 9. *The advantage of the Soul, for matter of Body, in the other state, above this.*

CHAP. III.

1. *That the natural abode of the Soul after death is the* Air. 2. *That she cannot quit the* Aëreal *Regions till the* Æthereal *Congruity of life be awakened in her.* 3. *That all Souls are not in the same Region of the Aire.* 4. Cardan's *conceit of placing all* Daemons *in the upper Region.* 5. *The use of this conceit for the shewing the reason of their seldome appearing.* 6. *That this* Phaenomenon *is salved by a more rational Hypothesis.* 7. *A further confutation of* Cardan's *Opinion.* 8. *More tending to the same scope.* 9. *The original of* Cardan's *errour concerning the remote operations of* Daemons. 10. *An Objection how* Daemons *and Souls separate can be in this lower Region, where Winds and Tempests are so frequent.* 11. *A preparation to an Answer from the consideration of the nature of the Winds.* 12. *Particular Answers to the Objection.* 13. *A further Answer from the nature of the* Statick Faculty *of the Soul.* 14. *Another from the suddain power of actuating her Vehicle.* 15. *What incommodations she suffers from haile, rain, &c.*

CHAP. IV.

1. *That the Soul once having quitted this Earthly Body becomes a* Daemon. 2. *Of the* External Senses *of the Soul separate, their number and limits in the Vehicle.* 3. *Of* Sight *in a Vehicle organized and unorganized.* 4. *How* Daemons *and separate Souls hear and see at a vast Distance: and whence it is that though they may so easily hear or see us, we may neither see nor hear them.* 5. *That they have* Hearing *as well as* Sight. 6. *Of the* Touch, Smell, Tast, *and* Nourishment *of* Daemons. 7. *The external employment that the* Genii *and Souls deceased may have out of the Body.* 8. *That the actions of Separate Souls, in reference to us, are most-what conformable to their life here on Earth.* 9. *What their Entertainments are in reference to themselves.* 10. *The distinction of Orders of* Daemons *from the places they most frequent.*

CHAP. V.

CHAP. VI.

CHAP. VII.

1. *Three Notable Examples of* Signatures, *rejected by* Fienus: 2. *And yet so farre allowed for possible, as will fit our design.* 3. *That* Helmont's *Cherry and* Licetus *his Crab-fish are shrewd arguments that the Soul of the World has to doe with all Efformations of both Animals and Plants.* 4. *An Example of a most exact and lively Signature out of* Kircher: 5. *With his judgment thereupon.* 6. *Another Example out of him of a Child with gray hairs.* 7. *An application of what has been said hitherto, concerning the* Signatures *of the* Foetus, *to the transfiguration of the Aiery Vehicles of* Separate Souls *and* Daemons. 8. *Of their personal transformation visible to us.*

CHAP. VIII.

1. *That the Better sort of* Genii *converse in Humane shape, the Baser sometimes in Bestial.* 2. *How they are disposed to turn themselves into several Bestial forms.* 3. *Of* Psellus *his* αὐγαὶ πυρώδεις, *or Igneous splendours of* Daemons, *how they are made.* 4. *That the external Beauty of the* Genii *is according to the degree of the inward Vertue of their Minds.* 5. *That their Aëreal form need not be purely transparent, but more finely opake, and coloured.* 6. *That there is a distinction of Masculine and Feminine beauty in their personal figurations.*

CHAP. IX.

1. *A general account of the mutual entertains of the* Genii *in the other World.* 2. *Of their Philosophical and Political Conferences.* 3. *Of their Religious Exercises.* 4. *Of the innocent Pastimes and Recreations of the Better sort of them.* 5. *A confirmation thereof from the Conventicles of* Witches. 6. *Whether the purer* Daemons *have their times of repast or no.* 7. *Whence the Bad* Genii *have their food.* 8. *Of the food and feastings of the Better sort of* Genii.

CHAP. X.

1. *How hard it is to define any thing concerning the* Aëreal *or* Æthereal Elysiums. 2. *That there is Political Order and Laws amongst these* Aiery Daemons. 3. *That this Chain of Government reaches down from the highest Æthereal Powers through the* Aëreal *to the very* Inhabitants *of the* Earth. 4. *The great security we live in thereby.* 5. *How easily detectible and punishable wicked Spirits are by those of their own Tribe.* 6. *Other reasons of the security we find our selves in from the gross infestations of evil Spirits.* 7. *What kind of punishments the* Aëreal Officers *inflict upon their Malefactours.*

CHAP. XI.

1. *Three things to be considered before we come to the* Moral *condition of the Soul after Death: namely, her Memory of transactions in this Life.* 2. *The peculiar feature and individual Character of her* Aëreal Vehicle. 3. *The Retainment of the same Name.* 4. *How her ill deportment here lays the train of her Misery hereafter.* 5. *The unspeakable torments of Conscience worse then Death, and not to be avoided by dying.* 6. *Of the hideous tortures of external sense on them whose searedness of Conscience may seem to make them uncapable of her Lashes.* 7. *Of the state of the Souls of the more innocent and conscientious* Pagans. 8. *Of the natural accruments of* After-happiness *to the morally good in this life.* 9. *How the Soul enjoys her actings or sufferings in* this Life *for an indispensable Cause, when she has passed to the* other. 10. *That the reason is proportionably the same in things of less consequence.* 11. *What mischief men may create to themselves in the other world by their zealous mistakes in this.* 12. *That though there were no Memory after Death, yet the manner of our Life here may sow the seeds of the Soul's future happiness or misery.*

CHAP. XII.

1. *What* The Spirit of Nature *is.*　2. *Experiments that argue its real Existence; such as that of two Strings tuned Unisons.* 3. Sympathetick *Cures and Tortures.*　4. *The* Sympathy *betwixt the* Earthly *and* Astral *Body.*　5. *Monstrous Births.* 6. *The attraction of the Loadstone and Roundness of the Sun and Stars.*

1. We had now quite finished our Discourse, did I not think it convenient to answer a double Expectation of the Reader. The one is touching *The Spirit of Nature,* the other the producing of *Objections* that may be made against our concluded Assertion of the Soul's Immortality. For as for the former, I can easily imagine he may well desire a more punctual account of that Principle I have had so often recourse to, then I have hitherto given, and will think it fit that I should somewhere more fully explain what I mean by the terms, and shew him my strongest grounds why I conceive there is any such Being in the World. To hold him therefore no longer in suspense, I shall doe both in this place. *The Spirit of Nature* therefore, according to that notion I have of it, *is, A substance incorporeal, but without Sense and Animadversion, pervading the whole Matter of the Universe, and exercising a Plastical power therein according to the sundry predispositions and occasions in the parts it works upon, raising such* Phaenomena *in the World, by directing the parts of the Matter and their Motion, as cannot be resolved into mere Mechanical powers.* This rude Description may serve to convey to any one a conception determinate enough of the nature of the thing. And that it is not a mere Notion, but a real Being, besides what I have occasionally hinted already (and shall here again confirm by new instances) there are several other Considerations may perswade us. (56)

2. The first whereof shall be concerning those Experiments of *Sympathetick* Pains, Asswagements and Cures; of which there are many Examples, approved by the most scrupulous Pretenders to sobriety and judgment, and of all which I cannot forbear to pronounce, that I suspect them tò come to pass by some such power as makes Strings that be tuned *Unisons,* (though on

several Instruments) the one being touched, the other to tremble and move very sensibly, and to cast off a straw or pin or any such small thing laid upon it. Which cannot be resolved into any *Mechanical* Principle, though some have ingeniously gone about it. For before they attempted to shew the reason, why that String that is not *Unison* to that which is struck should not leap and move, as it doth that is, they should have demonstrated, that by the mere *Vibration of the Aire* that which is *Unison* can be so moved; for if it could, these *Vibrations* would not faile to move other Bodies more movable by farre then the String it self that is thus moved. As for example, if one hung loose near the string that is struck a small thred of silk or an hair with some light thing at the end of it, they must needs receive those reciprocal Vibrations that are communicated to the *Unison* string at a far greater distance, if the mere motion of the material Aire caused the subsultation of the string tuned *Unison:* Which yet is contrary to experience.

Besides that, if it were the mere *Vibration of the Aire* that caused this *tremor* in the *Unison* string, the effect would not be considerable, unless both the strings lay well-nigh in the same Plane, and that the Vibration of the string that is struck be made in that Plane they both lie in. But let the string be struck so as to cut the Plane perpendicularly by its tremulous excursions, or let both the strings be in two several Planes at a good distance above one another, the event is much-what the same, though the Aire cannot rationally be conceived to *vibrate* backwards and forwards, otherwise then well-nigh in the very Planes wherein the strings are moved.

All which things do clearly shew, that pure *Corporeal* causes cannot produce this effect: and that therefore we must suppose, that *both* the strings are united with some one *Incorporeal* Being, which has a different *Unity* and *Activity* from *Matter,* but yet a *Sympathy* therewith; which affecting this *Immaterial* Being, makes it affect the Matter in the same manner in another place, where it does symbolize with that other in some predisposition or qualification, as these two strings do in being tuned *Unisons* to one another: and this, without sending any particles to the Matter it does thus act upon; as my thought of moving of my Toe being represented within my Brain, by the power of my

Soul I can, without sending Spirits into my Toe, but onely by making use of them that are there, move my Toe as I please, by reason of that *Unity* and *Activity* that is peculiar to my Soul as a Spiritual substance that pervades my whole Body. Whence I would conclude also, that there is some such Principle as we call *The Spirit of Nature,* or *the inferiour Soul of the World,* into which such *Phaenomena* as these are to be resolved.

.   .   .   .

6. *The Attraction of the Load-stone* seems to have some affinity with these instances of *Sympathy.* This mystery *Des-Cartes* has explained with admirable artifice as to the immediate Corporeal causes thereof, to wit, those wreathed particles which he makes to pass certain screw-pores in the *Load-stone* and *Iron.* (57) But how the efformation of these particles is above the reach of the mere Mechanical powers in *Matter,* as also the exquisite direction of their motion, whereby they make their peculiar *Vortex* he describes about the Earth from Pole to Pole, and thread an incrustated Star, passing in a right line in so long a journey as the Diameter thereof without being swung to the sides; how these things, I say, are beyond the powers of *Matter,* I have fully enough declared and proved in a large Letter of mine to *V. C.** and therefore that I may not *actum agere,* shall forbear speaking any farther thereof in this place. To which you may adde, That mere corporeal motion in Matter, without any other guide, would never so much as produce a *round Sun* or *Star,* of which figure notwithstanding *Des-Cartes* acknowledges them to be. But my reasons why it cannot be effected by the simple *Mechanical* powers of *Matter,* I have particularly set down in my Letters to that excellent Philosopher.*

CHAP. XIII.

1. *That the Descent of heavy Bodies argues the existence of* The Spirit of Nature, *because else they would either hang in the Aire as they are placed,* 2. *Or would be diverted from a perpendicular as they fall near a Plate of Metall set slooping.* 3. *That the endeavour of the Æther or Aire*

* *Epist. ad* V.C. sect. 5. (58)   * *Epist.* 3. *ad* R. Cartes.

from the Centre to the Circumference is not the Cause of Gravity, against Mr. Hobbs. 4. A full confutation of Mr. Hobbs his Opinion. 5. An ocular Demonstration of the absurd consequence thereof. 6. An absolute Demonstration that Gravity cannot be the effect of mere Mechanical powers. 7. The Latitude of the operations of The Spirit of Nature, how large and where bounded. 8. The reason of its name. 9. Of Instinct, whether it be, and what it is. 10. The grand office of the Spirit of Nature in transmitting Souls into rightly-prepared Matter.

1. And a farther confirmation that I am not mistaken therein, is what we daily here experience upon Earth, which is *the descending of heavy Bodies,* as we call them. Concerning the motion whereof I agree with *Des-Cartes* * in the assignation of the immediate corporeal cause, to wit, the *Æthereal* matter, which is so plentifully in the Air over it is in grosser Bodies; but withall do vehemently surmise, that there must be some *Immaterial* cause, such as we call *The Spirit of Nature* or *Inferiour Soul of the World,* that must direct the motions of the *Æthereal* particles to act upon these grosser Bodies to drive them towards the Earth. For that surplusage of Agitation of the *globular* particles of the *Æther* above what they spend in turning the Earth about, is carried every way indifferently, according to his own concession; by which motion the drops of liquors are formed into *round* figures, as he ingeniously concludes. From whence it is apparent, that a bullet of iron, silver or gold placed in the Aire is equally assaulted on all sides by the occursion of these *Æthereal* particles, and therefore will be moved no more downwards then upwards, but hang *in aequilibrio,* as a piece of Cork rests on the water, where there is neither winde nor stream, but is equally plaied against by the particles of water on all sides.

·   ·   ·   ·   ·   ·   ·   ·

6. Adde unto all this, that if the motion of gross Bodies were according to mere Mechanical laws, a Bullet, suppose of Lead or Gold, cast up into the Aire, would never descend again, but would

---

* Cartes. *Princip. Philos. Part* 4. *Artic.* 15, 16, 18, 19, 20.

persist in a rectilinear motion. For it being far more solid then so much Aire and Æther put together as would fill its place, and being moved with no less swiftness then that wherewith the Earth is carried about in twenty four hours, it must needs break out in a straight line through the thin Aire, and never return again to the Earth, but get away as a *Comet* does out of a *Vortex.* And that *de facto* a Cannon-Bullet has been shot so high that it never fell back again upon the ground, *Des-Cartes* does admit of as a true experiment. Of which, for my own part, I can imagine no other unexceptionable reason, but that at a certain distance *The Spirit of Nature* in some regards leaves the motion of *Matter* to the pure laws of Mechanicks, but within other bounds checks it, whence it is that the Water does not swill out of the Moon.

7. Now if the pure Mechanick powers in *Matter* and Corporeal motion will not amount to so simple a *Phaenomena* as the falling of a stone to the Earth, how shall we hope they will be the adequate cause of sundry sorts of *Plants* and other things, that have farre more artifice and curiosity then the direct descent of a stone to the ground?

. . . .

CHAP. XIV.

CHAP. XV.

1. *An Answer to the experiment of the* Scolopendra *cut into pieces:* 2. *And to the flying of an headless Eagle over a barn, as also to that of the Malefactour's head biting a Dog by the eare.* 3. *A superaddition of a difficulty concerning Monsters born with two or more Heads and but one Body and Heart.* 4. *A solution of the difficulty.* 5. *An answer touching the seldome appearing of the Souls of the deceased:* 6. *As also concerning the fear of Death;* 7. *And a down-bearing sense that sometimes so forcibly obtrudes upon us the belief of the Soul's Mortality.* 8. *Of the Tragical Pompe and dreadful Preludes of Death, with some corroborative Considerations against such sad spectacles.* 9. *That there is nothing really sad and miserable in the Universe, unless to the wicked and impious.*

CHAP. XVI.

1. *That that which we properly* are *is both* Sensitive *and* Intellectual. 2. *What is the true Notion of* a Soul being One. 3. *That if there be* but One Soul *in the world, it is both* Rational *and* Sensitive. 4. *The most favourable representations of their Opinion that hold* but One. 5. *A Confutation of the foregoing representation.* 6. *A Reply to the Confutation.* 7. *An Answer to the Reply.* 8. *That the Soul of Man is not properly any Ray either of God or the Soul of the World.* 9. *And yet if she were so, it would be no prejudice to her Immortality: whence the folly of* Pomponatius *is noted.* 10. *A further animadversion upon* Pomponatius *his folly, in admitting a certain number of remote* Intelligencies, *and denying* Particular Immaterial Substances *in* Men *and* Brutes.

1. As for the last Objection, or rather Subterfuge, of such as have no minde to finde their Souls immortal, pretending indeed they have none distinct from that *one Universal Soul* of the

World, whereby notwithstanding they acknowledge that the Operations we are conscious to ourselves of, of Reason and other Faculties, cannot be without one; we shall easily discover either the falsness or unserviceableness of this conceit for their design, who would so fain slink out of Being after the mad freaks they have played in this Life. For it is manifestly true, that a Man is most properly that, whatever it is, that *animadverts* in him; for that is such an operation that no Being but himself can doe it for him. And that which *animadverts* in us, does not onely perceive and take notice of its *Intellectual* and *Rational* operations, but of all the *Sensations* whatsoever that we are conscious of, whether they terminate in our Body or on some outward Object. From whence it is plain, that *That which we are* is both *Sensitive* and *Intellectual*.

2. Now if we rightly consider what is comprehended in the true and usual Notion of the *Unity* of a Soul, it is very manifest that it mainly consists in this, that the *Animadversive* thereof is *but one,* and that there is no *Sensation* nor *Perceptio*n of any kind in the Soul, but what is communicated to and perceived by the whole *Animadversive*.

3. Which things being premised, it necessarily follows, that if there be *but one Soul* in the World, that Soul is both *Rational* and *Sensitive,* and that there cannot be any Pain, Pleasure or Speculation, in *one* mans Soul, but the same would be in *all ;* nay that a man cannot lash a Dog, or spur a Horse, but himself would feel the smart of it : which is flatly against all experience, and therefore palpably false. Of this wilde Supposition I have spoken so fully in my *Poems,* that I need adde nothing here in this place, having sufficiently confuted it there. (59)

4. But not to cut them so very short, let us imagine the most favourable contrivance of their Opinion we can, and conceit that though this *Soul of the World* be of it self every where alike, and that the *Animadversive* faculty is in it all in like vigour; yet it being engaged in severally-tempered Bodies, *Animadversion* is confin'd to that part of Matter onely which it actuates; and is stupid and unsensible of all other operations, whether Sensitive or Intellectual, that are transacted by her without, in other persons : a thing very hard to conceive, and quite repugnant to the Idea of the *Unity* of a Soul, not to be conscious to her self of

her own perceptions. But let it pass for a possibility, and let us suppose that one part of the *Soul of the World* informs one man, and another another, or at least some vital Ray there; yet notwithstanding, this opinion will be incumbred with very harsh difficulties.

For if several parts of the *Soul of the World* inform several parts of the Matter, when a man changes his place, he either tears one part of the *Soul of the World* from another, or else changes Souls every step; and therefore it is a wonder that he changes not his Wits too, and loses his Memory. Unless they will say that every part of the *Soul of the World,* upon the application of a new Body, acts just so in it as that part acted which it left, if there be no change or alteration thereof: whence every part of the *Soul of the World* will have the self-same Thoughts, Errours, Truths, Remembrances, Pains, Pleasures, that the part had the body newly left. So that a man shall always fancy it is himself, wherever he goes, though this self be nothing but the *Soul of the World* acting in such a particular Body, and retaining and renewing to her self the Memory of all Accidents, Impressions, Motions and Cogitations, she had the perception of in this particular piece of organized Matter. This is the most advantageous representation of this Opinion that can possibly be excogitated. But I leave it to those that love to amuse themselves in such Mysteries, to try if they can make any good sense of it.

5. And he that can fancy it as a thing possible, I would demand of him, upon this supposition, who *himself* is; and he cannot deny but that he is a Being *Perceptive* and *Animadversive,* which the *Body* is not, and therefore that himself is not the *Body;* wherefore he is that in him which is properly called *Soul:* But not its *Operations,* for the former reason; because they perceive nothing, but the Soul perceives them in exerting them: nor the *Faculties,* for they perceive not one anothers Operations; but that which is a mans *Self* perceives them all: Wherefore he must say he is the *Soul;* and there being but one Soul in the World, he must be forc'd to vaunt himself to be the *Soul of the World.* But this boasting must suddainly fall again, if he but consider that the *Soul of the World* will be every mans personal *Ipseity* as well as his; whence every *one* man will be *all* men, and *all*

men but *one* Individual man: which is a perfect contradition to all the Laws of *Metaphysicks* and *Logick.*

6. But re-minded of these inconveniences, he will pronounce more cautiously, and affirm that he is not the *Soul of the World* at large, but onely so far forth as she expedites or exerts herself into the Sense and Remembrance of all those Notions or Impresses that happen to her wherever she is joyned with his Body; but that so soon as this Body of his is dissipated and dissolved, that she will no longer raise any such determinate Thoughts or Senses that refer to that Union; and that so the Memory of such Actions, Notions and Impressions, that were held together in relation to a particular Body, being lost, and laid aside upon the failing of the Body to which they did refer, this *Ipseity* or *Personality,* which consisted mainly in this, does necessarily perish in death.

This certainly is that (if they know their own meaning) which many Libertines would have, who are afraid to meet themselves in the other World, for fear they should quarrel with themselves there for their transactions in this. And it is the handsomest Hypothesis that they can frame in favour of themselves, and far beyond that dull conceit, *That there is nothing but mere Matter in the World;* which is infinitely more liable to confutation.

7. And yet this is too scant a covering to shelter them and secure them from the sad after-claps they may justly suspect in the other life. For first, it is necessary for them to confess that they have in this life as particular and proper sense of Torment, of Pleasure, of Peace, and Pangs of Conscience, and of other impressions, as if they had an individual Soul of their own distinct from that of the World, and from every ones else; and that if there be any *Daemons* or *Genii,** as certainly there are, that it is so with them too. We have also demonstrated, that all *Sense* and *Perception* is immediately excited in the Soul by the * Spirits; wherefore with what confidence can they promise themselves that the death of this earthly Body will quite obliterate all the tracts of their Being here on earth? whenas the subtiler ruines thereof, in all likelihood, may determine the

* *Antidote,* Book 3. ch. 3, 4, 5, 6, 7, 8, 9, 10, &c.
* Book 2. chap. 8, 9.

Thoughts of the *Soul of the World* to the same tenour as before, and draw from her the memory of all the Transactions of this life, and make her exercise her judgment upon them, and cause her to contrive the most vital exhalations of the Terrestrial Body into an Aëreal Vehicle, of like nature with the ferment of these material rudiments of life, saved out of the ruines of death.

For any slight touch is enough to engage her to perfect the whole Scene; and so a man shall be represented to himself and others in the other state whether he will or no, and have as distinct a personal *Ipseity* there as he had in this life. Whence it is plain, that this false *Hypothesis, That we are nothing but the Soul of the World acting in our Bodies,* will not serve their turns at all that would have it so; nor secure them from future danger, though it were admitted to be true. But I have demonstrated it false already, from the Notion of the *Unity* of a Soul.

Of the truth of which Demonstration we shal be the better assured, if we consider that the subtile Elements, which are the immediate conveyors of *Perceptions* in our Souls, are continued throughout in the *Soul of the World,* and insinuate into all living Creatures. So that the *Soul of the World* will be necessarily informed in every one, what she thinks or feels every where, if she be the onely Soul that actuates every Animal upon Earth. Whence the Sun, Stars and Planets would appear to us in that bigness they really are of, they being perceiv'd in that bigness by those parts of the *Soul of the World* that are at a convenient nearness to them.

. . . .

CHAP. XVII.

1. *That the Authour having safely conducted the Soul into her* Aëreal *condition through the dangers of Death, might well be excused from attending her any further.* 2. *What reasons urge him to consider what fates may befall her afterwards.* 3. *Three hazzards the Soul runs after this life, whereby she may again become obnoxious to death, according to the opinion of some.* 4. *That the Aëreal* Genii *are mortal, confirmed by three testimonies.* 5. *The one from the Vision of*

CHAP. XVIII.

by a special act of Omnipotency. 9. *The third,* That they lye senseless in an eternal Death. 10. *The fourth,* That they are in a perpetual furious and painful Dream. 11. *The fifth and last,* That they will revive again, and that the Earth and Aire will be inhabited by them. 12. *That this last seems to be fram'd from the fictitiou*s παλιγγενεσία *of the* Stoicks, *who were very sorry* Metaphysicians, *and as ill* Naturalists. 13. *An Animadversion upon a self contradicting sentence of* Seneca. 14. *The unintelligibleness of the state of the Souls of the Wicked after the* Conflagration. 15. *That the* Æthereal Inhabitants *will be safe. And what will then become of* Good Men *and* Daemons *on the Earth and in the Aire. And how they cannot be delivered but by a supernatural power.*

CHAP. XIX.

1. *That the* Extinction of the Sun *is no* Panick *feare, but may be rationally suspected from the Records of History and grounds of Natural* Philosophy. 2. *The sad Influence of this Extinction upon Man and Beast, and all the Aëreal* Daemons *imprison'd within their several* Atmospheres *in our* Vortex. 3. *That it will doe little or no damage to the* Æthereal Inhabitants *in reference to heat or warmth.* 4. *Nor will they find much want of his light.* 5. *And if they did, they may pass out of one* Vortex *into another, by the Priviledge of their* Æthereal Vehicles; 6. *And that without any labour or toile, and as maturely as they please.* 7. *The vast incomprehensibleness of the tracts and compasses of the waies of Providence.* 8. *A short Recapitulation of the whole Discourse.* 9. *An Explication of the* Persians *two Principles of* Light *and* Darkness, *which they called* Θεὸς *and* Δαίμων, *and when and where the Principle of* Light *gets the full victory.* 10. *That Philosophy, or something more sacred then Philosophy, is the onely Guide to a true* 'Αποθέωσις.

AN
APPENDAGE

To this first PART

Concerning the

POSSIBILITY
OF
APPARITIONS
AND
WITCHCRAFT,

Containing

The easie, true and genuine NOTION,
and consistent EXPLICATION of
the NATURE

OF A
SPIRIT

Whereby

The POSSIBILITY of the EXISTENCE
of SPIRITS, APPARITIONS, and
WITCHCRAFT is farther Confirmed.

London: Printed MDCC.

ADVERTISEMENT

Hitherto reacheth the Author's ingenious *Considerations about Witchcraft*. But understanding by his Letters and Papers, that he intended something farther to enlarge this first part of his *Saducimus Triumphatus*, which concerns the *Possibility* of the Existence of *Spirits, Apparitions* and *Witches*, but that he has done nothing therein, being prevented by Death, I thought it might prove not an unuseful Supplement, to Translate most of the two last Chapters of Dr. *H. M.* his *Enchiridon Metaphysicum* into *English*, and add it to this first part, as a suitable Appendage thereto. Which is as follows

THE

Easie, True, and Genuine

N O T I O N ,

And consistent

E X P L I C A T I O N

Of the NATURE of a

S P I R I T .

SECT. I.

The Opinions of the NULLIBISTS *and* HOLENMERIANS *proposed.*

That we may explicate the *Essence* or *Notion* of *Incorporeal Beings* or *Spirits,* with the greater Satisfaction and Success, we are first to remove two vast Mounds of Darkness, wherewith the Ignorance of some hath encumbred and obscured their Nature.

And the first is of those, who tho' they readily acknowledge there are such things as *Incorporeal Beings* or *Spirits,* yet do very peremptorily contend, that they are *no where* in the whole World, which Opinion tho' at the very sight it appears very ridiculous, yet it is stiffly held by the maintainers of it, and that not without some Fastuosity and Superciliousness, or at least some more sly and tacite Contempt of such Philosophers as hold the contrary, as of Men less Intellectual, and too too much indulging to their *Imagination.* Those other therefore because they so boldly affirm that a Spirit is *Nullibi,* that is to say, *no where,* have deservedly purchased to themselves the Name or Title of *Nullibists.* (60)

The other Mound of Darkness laid upon the Nature of a Spirit, is by those who willingly indeed acknowledge that Spirits are *somewhere;* but add farther, That they are not only entirely or totally in their whole *Ubi* or *Place,* (in the most general sense of the Word) but are totally in every part or point thereof, and describe the peculiar Nature of a Spirit to be such, that it must be *Totus in toto & totus in qualibet sui parte.* Which therefore the *Greeks* would fitly and briefly call οὐσίαν ϱλενμερῆ, *an Essence that is all of it in each part,* and this propriety thereof (τῶν ἀσωμάτων οὐσιῶν τὴν ὁλενμέρειαν) the *Holenmerism* of *Incorporeal Beings.* Whence also these other Philosophers diametrically opposite to the former, may most significantly and compendiously be called *Holenmerians.* (61)

SECT. II.

That Cartesius *is the Prince of the* Nullibists, *and wherein chiefly consists the force of their Opinion.*

The Opinions of both which kind of Philosophers having sufficiently Explained, we will now propose and confute the Reasons of each of them; and first of the *Nullibists,* of whom the chief Author and Leader seems to have been that pleasant Wit *Renatus des Cartes,* who by his jocular *Metaphysical Meditations,* has so luxated and distorted the rational Faculties of some otherwise sober and quick-witted Persons, but in this point by reason of their over-great admiration of *Des Cartes* not sufficiently cautious, that deceived partly by his counterfeit and prestigious Subtilty, and partly by his Authority, have persuaded themselves that such things were most *true* and *clear* to them; which had they not been blinded with these Prejudices, they could never have thought to have been so much as possible, and so they having been so industriously taught, and diligently instructed by him, how they might not be imposed upon, no not by the most powerful and most ill-minded fallacious Deity, have heedlessly by not sufficiently standing upon their Guard, being deceived and deluded by a meer Man, but of a pleasant and abundantly cunning and abstruse Genius; as shall clearly appear after we have searched and examined the reasons of this opinion of the *Nullibists* to the very bottom.

The whole force whereof is comprised in these three Axioms, the first, *That whatsoever thinks is Immaterial,* and so on the

contrary. The second, *That whatever is extended is Material.*
The third, *That what ever is unextended is no where.* To which
Third I shall add this Fourth, as a necessary and manifest consectary thereof, *viz. That whatsoever is somewhere is extended.*
Which the *Nullibists* of themselves will easily grant me to be
most true, otherwise they could not seriously contend for their
Opinion, whereby they affirm Spirits to be *no where,* but would
be found to do it only by way of an oblique and close derision
of their Existence, saying indeed they *exist,* but then again
hiddenly and cunningly denying it, by affirming they are *no
where.* Wherefore doubtless they affirm them to be *no where,*
if they are in good earnest, for this reason only; for fear they
granting them to be *some where,* it would be presently extorted
from them, even according to their own Principles, that they are
extended, as whatever is extended is Material, according to their
second Axiom, It is therefore manifest, that we both agree in
this, that whatever real Being there is that is *somewhere,* is
also *extended.*

SECT. III.

The Sophistical weakness of that reasoning of the Nullibists,
*who, because we can conceive Cogitation without conceiving
in the mean while Matter, conclude, That whatsoever thinks
is Immaterial.*

With which Truth notwithstanding we being furnished and
supported, I doubt not but we shall with ease quite overthrow
and utterly root out this Opinion of the *Nullibists.* But that
their levity and credulity may more manifestly appear, lets
examine the Principles of this Opinion by part, and consider
how well they make good each Member.

The first is, *Whatever thinks is immaterial,* and on the contrary. The conversion of this Axiom I will not examine, because
it makes little to the present purpose, I will only note by the by,
that I doubt not but it may be false, altho' I easily grant the
Axiom it self to be true, but it is this new Method of demonstrating it I call into question, which from hence, that we can
conceive *Cogitation,* in the mean time not conceiving *Matter,*

concludes that *Whatever thinks is Immaterial.* Now that we can conceive *Cogitation* without conceiving *Matter,* they say is manifest from hence, that altho' one should suppose there were no Body in the Universe, and should not flinch from that Position, yet notwithstanding he would not cease to be certain, that there was *Res cogitans,* a *thinking Being,* in the World, he finding himself to be such, but I farther add, tho' he should suppose there was no *Immaterial* Being in Nature, (nor indeed *Material*) and should not flinch from that Position, yet he would not cease to be certain that there was a *thinking Being,* (no not if he should suppose himself not to be a thinking Being) because he can *suppose* nothing without *Cogitation.* Which I thought worth the while to note by the by, that the great levity of the *Nullibists* might hence more clearly appear.

But yet I add farther, that such is the Nature of the Mind of Man, that is like the Eye, better fitted to Contemplate other things than it self; and that therefore it is no wonder that thinking nothing of its own Essence, it does fixedly enough and intently consider in the mean time and Contemplate all other things, yea, those very things with which she has the nearest affinity, and yet without any reflection that her self is of the like Nature. Whence it may easily come to pass, when she is so wholly taken up in Contemplating other things without any reflection upon her self, that either carelessly she may consider herself in general as a *meer thinking Being,* without any other attribute, or else by resolvedness afterwards, and by a force on purpose offered to her own Faculties. But that this Reasoning is wonderfully weak and trifling as to the proving of the Mind of Man to be nothing else; that is to say, to have no other attributes but meer Cogitation, there is none that does not discern.

SECT. IV.

The true Method that ought to be taken for the proving that Matter *cannot think.*

Lastly, if *Cartesius* with his *Nullibists,* would have dealt *bona fide,* they ought to have omitted all those ambagious Windings and Meanders of feigned Abstraction, and with a direct stroke

to have fallen upon the thing it self, and so to have sifted *Matter,*
and searched the Nature of *Cogitation,* that they might thence
have evidently demonstrated that there was some inseparable
Attribute in *Matter,* that is repugnant to the *Cogitative Faculty,*
or in *Cogitation* that is repugnant to *Matter.* But out of the
meer diversity of Ideas or Notions of any Attributes, to collect
their separability or *real* distinction, yea, their contrariety and
repugnancy, is most foully to violate the indispensable Laws of
Logick, and to confound *Diversa* with *Opposita,* and make them
all one. Which Mistake to them that understand *Logick,* must
needs appear very course and absurd.

But that the weakness and vacillancy of this Method may yet
more clearly appear, let us suppose that which yet Philosophers
of no mean Name, seriously stand for and assert, *viz.* That
Cogitative substance is either *Material* or *Immaterial;* does it
not apparently follow thence, that a thinking Substance may be
precisely conceived without the conception of *Matter,* as *Matter*
without the conception of *Cogitation,* when notwithstanding in
one of the Members of this distribution they are joyned sufficiently close together?

How can therefore this new fangled Method of *Cartesius*
convince us that this Supposition is false, and that the distribution is illegitimate? Can it from thence, that *Matter* may be conceived without *Cogitation,* and *Cogitation* without *Matter?* The
first all grant, and the other the distribution it self supposes;
and yet continues sufficiently firm and sure, therefore it is very
evident, that there is a necessity of our having recourse to the
known and ratified Laws of *Logick,* which many Ages before this
new upstart Method of *des Cartes* appeared, were established
and approved by the common suffrage of Mankind; which
teach us that in every legitimate distribution the parts ought
consentire cum toto, & dissentire inter se, to agree with the
whole, but disagree one with another. Now in this distribution
that they do sufficiently disagree, it is very manifest. It remains
only to be proved, that one of the parts, namely that which
supposes that a *Cogitative* Substance may be *Material,* is repugnant to the Nature of the whole. This is that clear, solid, and
manifest way or Method according to the known Laws of *Logick;* but that new way, a kind of Sophistry and pleasant Mode
of trifling and prevaricating.

SECT. V.

That all things are in some sort extended, demonstrated out of the Corollary of the third Principle of the Nullibists.

As for the second Axiom or Principle, *viz. That whatsoever is extended is Material;* for the evincing the falsity thereof, there want no new Arguments, if one have but recourse to the Sixth, Seventh, and Eighth Chapters of *Enchiridium Metaphysicum,* where, by unanswerable reasonings it is demonstrated. That there is a certain Immaterial and Immoveable *Extensum* distinct from Moveable Matter. But however, out of the Consectary of their third Principle, we shall prove at once, that all Spirits are Extended as being somewhere, against the wild and ridiculous Opinion of the *Nullibists.* (62)

Whose third Principle, and out of which immediately and precisely they conclude Spirits to be no where, is, *Whatsoever is unextended, is no where.* Which I very willingly grant; but on this condition, that they on the other side concede (and I doubt not but they will) That *whatsoever is somewhere is also extended;* from which Consectary I will evince with Mathematical certainty, That God and our Soul, and all other Immaterial Beings, are in some sort extended: For the *Nullibists* themselves acknowledge and assert, that the Operations wherewith the Soul acts on the Body, are in the Body; and that Power or Divine Vertue wherewith God acts on the matter and moves it, is present in every part of the Matter. Whence it is easily gathered, That the operation of the Soul and the moving Power of God is somewhere, *viz.* in the *Body,* and in the *Matter.* But the Operation of the *Soul* wherewith it acts on the *Body* and the *Soul it self,* and the Divine Power wherewith *God* moves the *Matter* and *God himself,* are together, nor can so much as be imagined separate one from the other; namely, the *Operation* from the *Soul,* and the *Power* from *God,* Wherefore if the Operation of the Soul is somewhere, the Soul is somewhere, *viz.* there where the Operation is. And if the Power of God be somewhere, God is somewhere, namely, there where the Divine Power is; *He* in every part of the *Matter,* the *Soul* in the humane *Body.* Whosoever can deny this, by the, same reason he may deny that common Notion in Mathematicks, Quantities that are singly equal to one third, are equal to. one another.

SECT. VI.

The apert confession of the Nullibists *that the* ESSENCE *of a Spirit is where its* OPERATION *is ; and how they contradict themselves, and are forced to acknowledge a Spirit extended.*

And verily that which we contend for, the *Nullibists* seem apertly to assert, even in their own express words, as it is evident in *Lambertus Velthusius* in his *De Initiis Primae Philosophiae* in the Chapter *De Ubi.* Who though he does manifestly affirm that God and the Mind of Man by their Operations are in every part or some one part of the Matter; and that in that sence, namely, in respect of their *Operations,* the *Soul* may be truly said to be *somewhere, God every-where;* as if that were the only mode of their presence: yet he does expresly grant that the *Essence* is no where seperate from *that* whereby God or a Created Spirit is said to be, the one *every-where,* the other *somewhere ;* that no Man may conceit the *Essence* of God to be where the rest of his *Attributes* are not. That the *Essence* of God is in Heaven, but that his *Vertue* diffuses it self beyond Heaven. No, by no means, saith he, Wheresoever *God's* Power or *Operation* is, there is the *Nature* of *God ;* forasmuch as God is a Substance devoid of all composition. Thus far *Velthusius.* Whence I assume, But the Power or *Operation* of *God* is in or present to the *Matter ;* Therefore the *Essence* of *God* is in or present to the *Matter,* and is there where the Matter is, and therefore *somewhere.* Can there be any deduction or illation more close and coherent with the Premises? (63)

And yet that other most devoted follower of the *Cartesian* Philosophy, *Ludovicus De la Forge,* cannot abstain from the offering us the same advantage of arguing, or rather from the inferring the same conclusion with us in his Treatise *De mente Humana, Chap.* 12. where occur these words: Lastly, when I say that *God* is present to all things by his *Omnipotency,* (and consequently to all the parts of the Matter) I do not deny but that also by his *Essence* or *Substance* he is present to them: For all those things in God are one and the same. (64)

Dost thou hear, my *Nullibists,* what one of the chiefest of thy Condisciples and most religious Symmysts of that stupendous secret of *Nullibism* plainly professes, namely, that *God,* is present to all the parts of *Matter* by his *Essence* also, or *Substance?* And yet you in the mean while blush not to assert, that neither God, nor any created Spirit is any where; than which nothing more contradictious can be spoke or thought, or more abhorring from all reason. Wherefore when as the *Nullibists* come so near to the truth, it seems impossible they should, so all of a sudden, start from it, unless they were blinded with a superstitious admiration of *Des Cartes,* his Metaphysicks. and were deluded, effascinated and befooled with his jocular Subtilty and prestigious Abstractions there: For who in his right wits can acknowledge that a *Spirit* by its *Essence* may be present to Matter, and yet be *no where,* unless the Matter were nowhere also? And that a Spirit may penetrate, possess, and actuate some determinate Body, and yet not be in that Body? In which, if it be, it is plainly necessary it be somewhere.

And yet the same *Ludovicus De la Forge* does manifestly assert, that the Body is thus possest and actuated by the Soul, in his Preface to his Treatise *de Mente Humana,* while he declares the Opinion of *Marsilius Ficinus* concerning the manner how the Soul actuates the Body in *Marfilius* his own words, and does of his own accord assent to his Opinion. What therefore do these *Forms* to the Body when they communicate to it their *Esse?* They throughly penetrate it with their *Essence,* they bequeath the *Vertue* of their *Essence* to it. But now whereas the *Esse* is deduced from the *Essence,* and the *Operation* flows from the *Vertue,* by conjoyning the *Essence* they impart the *Esse,* by bequeathing the *Vertue* they communicate the *Operations;* so that out of the congress of Soul and Body, there is made one *Animal Esse,* one *Operation.* Thus he. The Soul with her Essence penetrates and pervades the whole Body, and yet is not where the Body is, but no where in the Universe!

With what manifest repugnancy therefore to their other *Assertions* the *Nullibists* hold this ridiculous Conclusion, we have sufficiently seen, and how weak their chiefest prop is, That *whatever is Extended is Material;* which is not only confuted by irrefragable Arguments, *Chap.* 6, 7. and 8. *Enchyrid. Mataphy,* but we have here also, by so clearly proving that all *Spirits* are *somewhere,* utterly subverted it, even from that very Concession or Opinion of the *Nullibists* themselves, who concede or aver that *whatsoever is somewhere is extended.* Which *Spirits* are and yet are not *Material.*

SECT. VII.

The more light reasonings of the Nullibists *whereby they would confirm their Opinion. The first of which is, That the Soul thinks of those things which are nowhere.*

But we shall not pass by their more slight reasonings in so great a matter, or rather so monstrous. Of which the first is, That the Mind of Man thinks of such things as are *no where,* nor have any relation to place, no not so much as to *Logical* place or *Ubi.* Of which sort are many truths as well *Moral* as *Theological* and *Logical,* which being of such a nature that they are *no where,* the Mind of Man which conceives them is necessarily *no where* also. But how crazily and inconsequently they collect that the humane Soul is *nowhere,* for that it thinks of those things that are *no where,* may be apparent to any one from hence, and especially to the *Nullibists* themselves; because from the same reason it would follow that the *Mind* of Man is *somewhere,* because sometimes, if not always in a manner, it thinks of those things which are *somewhere,* as all *Material* things are Which yet they dare not grant, because it would plainly follow from thence, according to their Doctrine, that the Mind or Soul of Man *were extended,* and so would become *corporeal* and devoid of all *Cogitation.* But besides, These things which they say are *no where,* namely, certain *Moral, Logical,* and *Theological* Truths, are really *somewhere,* viz. in the *Soul* it self which conceives them; but the Soul is in the Body, as we proved above. Whence it is manifest that the Soul and those Truths which she conceives are as well *somewhere* as the Body it self. I grant that some Truths as they are *Representations,* neither respect

Time nor *Place* in whatever sence. But as they are *Operations,* and therefore *Modes of some Subject or Substance,* they cannot be otherwise conceived than in some substance. And forasmuch as there is no substance which has not some amplitude, they are in a substance which is in some sort extended; and so by reason of their *Subject* they are necessarily conceived to be somewhere, because a *Mode* is inseparable from a *Subject.*

Nor am I at all moved with that giddy and rash tergiversation which some betake themselves to here, who say we do not well in distinguishing betwixt *Cogitation* (such as are all conceived verities) and the *Substance* of the *Soul cogitating:* For *cogitation* it self is the very *Substance* of the *Soul,* as *Extension* is of *Matter;* and that therefore the *Soul* is as well *nowhere* as any *Cogitation,* which respects neither time nor place, would be, if it were found in no *Subject.* (65) But here the *Nullibists,* who would thus escape, do not observe that while they acknowledge the *Substance* of the Soul to be *Cogitation,* they therewithal acknowledge the Soul to have a Substance, whence it is necessary it have some amplitude. And besides, This Assertion whereby they assert Cogitation to be the very substance of the Soul, is manifestly false. For many Operations of the Soul, are, as they speak, *specifically* different; Which therefore succeeding one after another, will be so many Substances *specifically* different. And so the Soul of *Socrates* will not always be the same *specifical* Soul, and much less the same *numerical;* Than which what can be imagined more delirant, and more remote from common sense?

To which you may add, That the *Soul* of Man is a *permanent* Being, but her *Cogitations* in a *flux* or *succession;* How then can the very Substance of the Soul be its successive Operations? And when the Substance of the Soul does so perpetually cease or perish, what I beseech you will become of Memory? From whence it is manifestly evident, that there is a certain *permanent* Substance of the Soul, as much distinct or different from her succeeding *Cogitations,* as the *Matter* it self is from its successive *figures* and *motions.*

SECT. VIII.

The second reason of the Nullibists, *viz. That* COGITATION *is easily conceived without* EXTENSION.

The second Reason is some what co-incident with some of those we have already examined; but it is briefly proposed by them thus; There can be no conception, no not of a *Logical Place,* or *Ubi,* without *Extension.* But *Cogitation* is easily conceived without conceiving any *Extension:* Wherefore the Mind cogitating, exempt from all *Extension,* is exempt also from all *Locality* whether *Physical* or *Logical;* and is so loosened from it, that it has no *relation* nor *applicability* thereto; as if those things had no relation nor applicability to other certain things without which they might be conceived. (66)

The weakness of this argumentation is easily deprehended from hence, That the *Intensness* of heat or motion is considered without any respect to its *extension,* and yet it is referred to an extended Subject, *viz.* To a Bullet shot, or red hot Iron. And though in intent and defixed thoughts upon some either difficult or pleasing Object, we do not at all observe how the time passeth, nor take the slightest notice of it, nothing hinders notwithstanding but those Cogitations may be applied to time, and it be rightly said, that about six a clock, suppose, in the Morning they began, and continued till eleven; and in like manner the place may be defined where they were conceived, *viz.* within the Walls of such an ones Study; although perhaps all that time this so fixt Contemplator did not take notice whether he was in his *Study,* or in the *Fields.*

And to speak out the matter at once, From the *precision* of our thoughts to infer the *real* precision or *seperation* of the things themselves, is a very putid and puerile Sophism; and still the more enormous and wild, to collect also thence, that they have no relation or applicability one to another. For we may have a clear and distinct *apprehension* of a thing which may be connected with another by an *essential* Tye, that Tye being not taken notice of, (and much more when they are connected only with a *circumstantial* one) but not a full and adequate *apprehension,* and such as sees through and penetrates all the degrees

of its Essence with their properties; Which unless a man reach
to, he cannot rightly judge of the real separability of any nature
from other natures.

From whence it appears how foully *Cartesius* has imposed,
if not upon himself, at least upon others, when from this mental
precision of *Cogitation* from *Extension,* he defined a Spirit (such
as the humane Soul) by *Cogitation* only, *Matter* by *Extension,*
and divided all *Substance* into *Cogitant* and *Extended,* as into
their first species or kinds. Which distribution notwithstanding
is as absonous and absurd, as if he had distributed *Animal* into
Sensitive and *Rational.* Whenas all *Substance* is *extended* as
well as all *Animals sensitive.* But he fixed his Animadversion
upon the *specifick* nature of the humane Soul; the *Generical*
nature thereof, either on purpose or by inadvertency, being not
considered nor taken notice of by him, as hath been noted in
Enchiridion Ethicum, lib. 3. cap. 4. sect. 3. (67)

SECT. IX.

The third and last Reason of the Nullibists, *viz. That the Mind
is conscious to her self, that she is no where, unless she is
disturbed or jogged by the Body.*

The third and last Reason, which is the most ingenious of
them all, occurs in *Lambertus Velthusius,* viz. That it is a truth
which God has infused into the Mind it self, That she is no
where, because we know by experience that we cannot tell from
our spiritual Operations where the Mind is. And for that we
know her to be in our Body, that we only perceive from the
Operations of *Sense* and *Imagination* which without the Body
or the motion of the Body the Mind cannot perform. (68) The
sence whereof, if I guess right, is this; That the Mind by a certain internal sense is conscious to her self that she is *no where,* unless she be now and then disturbed by the motions and joggings of
the Body; which is, as I said, an ingenious presage, but not
true: For it is one thing to perceive her self to be no where,
another not to perceive her self to be some where. For she may
not perceive her self to be somewhere, though she be somewhere,

as she may not take notice of her own *Individuality* or *numerical Distinction,* from all other minds, although she be one *Numerical* or *Individual* mind distinct from the rest : For, as I intimated above, such is the nature of the mind of Man, that like the eye, it is better fitted for the contemplating all other things, than for contemplating it self. And that indeed which is made for the clearly and sincerely seeing other things, ought to have nothing of it self actually perceptible in it, which it might mingle with the perception of those other things. From whence the Mind of Man is not to have any stable and fixt sense of its own Essence ; and such as it cannot easily lay aside upon occasion : And therefore it is no wonder, when as the Mind of Man can put off the sense and consciousness to it self of its own *Essence* and *Individuality,* that it can put off also therewith the sense of its being *somewhere,* or not perceive it ; when as it does not perceive its own *Essence* and *Individuality,* (of which *Hic & Nunc* are the known Characters :) And the chief Objects of the Mind are Universals.

But as the mind, although it perceives not its *Individuality,* yet can by reason prove to her self that she is some one *Numerical* or *Individual* Mind, so she can by the same means, although she by inward sense perceives not where she is, evince notwithstanding that she is somewhere, from the general account of things, which have that of their own nature, that they are *extended, singular,* and *somewhere.* And besides, *Velthusius* himself does plainly grant, that from the Operations of Sense and Imagination, we know our Mind to be in our Body. How then can we be ignorant that she is *somewhere,* unless the Body it self be *no where.*

SECT. X.

An Appeal to the internal sense of the Mind, if she be not environed with a certain infinite Extension; together with an excitation of the Nullibist *out of his Dream, by the sound of Trumpeters surrounding him.*

The Reasons of the *Nullibists* whereby they endeavour to maintain their Opinion, are sufficiently enervated and subverted. Nor have we need of any Arguments to establish the contrary

Doctrine. I will only desire by the by, that he that thinks his *Mind* is *no where,* would make trial of his faculty of Thinking; and when he has abstracted himself from all thought or sense of his *Body,* and fixed his *Mind* only on an Idea of an indefinite or *infinite Extension,* and also perceives himself to 'be some *particular cogitant Being,* let him make trial, I say, whether he can any way avoid it, but he must at the same time perceive that he is *somewhere,* namely, within this *immense Extension,* and that he is environ'd round about with it. Verily, I must ingenuously confess, I cannot conceive otherwise, and that I cannot but conceive an Idea of a certain *Extension infinite* and *immoveable,* and of *necessary* and *actual Existence:* Which I most clearly deprehend, not to have been drawn in by the outward sense, but to be innate and essentially inherent in the Mind it self; and so to be the genuine *object* not of *Imagination,* but of *Intellect;* and that it is but perversly and without all judgment determined by the *Nullibists,* or *Cartesians,* that whatever is extended, is also φανταστόν τι or the *Object of Imagination;* (69) When notwithstanding there is nothing *imaginable,* or the Object of Imagination, which is not *sensible:* For all Phantasms are drawn from the Senses. But this *infinite Extension* has no more to do with things that are *sensible* and fall under *Imagination,* than that which is most *Incorporeal.* But of this haply it will be more opportune to speak elsewhere.

In the mean time I will subjoin only one Argument, whereby I may manifestly evince that the Mind of Man is somewhere, and then I will betake my self to the discussing of the Opinion of the *Holenmerians.* Briefly therefore let us suppose some one environed with a Ring of Trumpeters, and that they all at the same time sound their Trumpets. Let us now see if the circumsonant clangor of those surrounding Trumpets sounding from all sides will awake these *Nullibists* out of their Lethargick Dream. And let us suppose, which they will willingly concede, that *Conarion* or *Glandula Pinalis, A,* is the seat of the common sense, to which at length all the motions from external Objects arrive. Nor is it any matter whether it be this *Conarion,* or some part of the Brain, or of what is contained in the Brain: But let the *Conarion,* at least for this bout, supply the place of that matter which is the common *Sensorium* of the Soul.

And whenas it is supposed to be surrounded with Eight Trumpeters, let there be Eight Lines drawn from them namely, from
B, C, D, E, F, G, H, I; I say that the clangour or sound of every
Trumpet is carried from the Ring of the Trumpeters to the
extream part of every one of those Lines, and all those sounds
are heard as coming from the Ring B, C, D, E, F, G, H, I, and
perceived in the *Conarion* A; and that the perception is in that

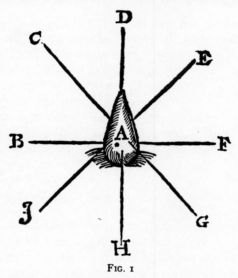

FIG. 1

part to which all the Lines of motion, as to a common Centre,
do concur; and therefore the extream parts of them, and the
perceptions of the Clangours or Sounds, are in the middle of the
Ring of Trumpeters, *viz.* where the Conarion is: Wherefore the
Precipient it self, namely the Soul, is in the midst of this Ring,
as well as the *Conarion,* and therefore is *some where.* Assuredly
he that denies that he conceives the force of this Demonstration,
and acknowledges that the *Perception* indeed is at the extreme
parts of the said Lines, and in the middle of the Ring of Trumpeters, but contends in the mean time that the Mind her self is not
there, forasmuch as she is *no where;* this Man certainly is either
Delirant and Crazed, or else Plays Tricks, and slimly and
obliquely insinuates that the *perception* which is made in the
Conarion, is to be attributed to the *Conarion* it self; and that

the *Mind,* so far as it is conceived to be an *incorporeal Substance,* is to be exterminated out of the Universe, as an useless Figment and Chimæra.

SECT. XI.

The Explication of the Opinion of the Holenmerians, *together with their two Reasons thereof proposed.*

And thus much of the opinion of the *Nullibists.* Let us now examine the Opinion of the *Holenmerians,* whose Explication is

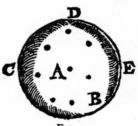

FIG. 2.

thus: Let there be what Body you please, suppose, C, D, E, which the Soul or a Spirit may possess and penetrate. The *Holenmerians* affirm, that the whole Soul or Spirit does occupy and possess the whole Body C, D, E, by its Essence; and that it is also wholly or all of it in every part or point of the said Body C, D, E, as in A, for Example, and in B, and the rest of the least parts or points of it. This is a brief and clear Explication of their Opinion.

But the reasons that induce them to embrace it, and so stifly to maintain it, are these two only, or at least chiefly, as much as respects the *Holenmerism* of Spirits. The first is, that whereas they grant that the whole Soul does pervade and possess the whole Body, they thought it would thence follow, that the Soul would be divisible, unless they should correct again this Assertion of theirs, by saying, that it was yet so in the whole Body, that it was totally in the mean time in every part thereof; for thus they thought themselves sure, that the Soul could not thence be argued in any sort divisible, or corporeal, but still remaining purely Spiritual. (70)

The other Reason is, That from hence it might be easily understood, how the Soul being in the whole Body, C, D, E, whatever happens to it in C, or B, it presently perceives it in A, because the whole Soul being perfectly and entirely as well in C, or B, as in A, it is necessary that after what fashion soever C or B is affected, A should be affected after the same manner; forasmuch as it is entirely and perfectly one and the same thing, *viz.* the

whole Soul, as well in C or B as in A. And from hence is that
vulgar Saying in the Schools, *That if the Eye were in the Foot,
the Soul would see in the Foot.*

SECT. XII.

The Examination of the Opinion of the Holenmerians.

But now, according to our custom, let us weigh and examine
all these things in a free and just Balance. In this therefore that
they assert, that the whole Soul is in the whole Body, and is all
of it penetrated of the Soul by her Essence, and therefore seem
willing to acknowledge a certain essential amplitude of the Soul;
in this I say, they come near to us, who contend there is a certain
Metaphysical and *essential extension* in all Spirits, but such as
is ἀμεγέθης καὶ ἀμερὴς, *devoid of bulk or parts,* as *Aristotle*
defines of his separate substances. For there is no magnitude
or bulk which may not be Physically divided, nor any parts
properly where there is no such division. Whence the *Metaphysical extension* of Spirits, is rightly understood not to be
capable of either bulk or parts, and in that sense it has no parts,
it cannot justly be said to be a whole. In that therefore we
plainly agree with the *Holenmerians,* that a Soul or Spirit may
be said by its Essence to penetrate and possess the whole Body
C, D, E, but in this again we differ from them, that we dare not
affirm that the whole Spirit or whole Soul does penetrate and
possess the said Body, because that which has not parts cannot
properly be called a whole; tho' I will not over stifly contend,
but that we may use that Word for a more easie Explication of
our Mind, according to that old trite Proverb, Ἀμαθέστερόν πως
εἰπὲ καὶ σαφέστερον λέγε, *Speak a little more unlearnedly, that
thou mayest speak more intelligibly or plainly.* But then we
are to remember that we do not speak *properly,* tho' more ac-
commodately to the vulgar apprehension, but *improperly.* (71)

But now when the *Holenmerians* add farther, That the whole
Soul is in every part or physical point of the Body D, C, E,* in
the point A and B, and all the rest of the points of which the
Body D, C, E, does consist, that seems an harsh Expression to
me, and such as may justly be deemed next door to an open

* *See* Fig. 2. Sect. 11.

repugnancy and contradiction; for when they say the whole
Soul is in the whole Body D, C, E, if they understand the Essence
of the Soul to be commensurate, and as it were equal to the
Body D, C, E, and yet at the same time, the Soul to be contained within the point A or B, it is manifest that they make
one and the same thing many Thousand times greater or less
than it self at the same time; which is impossible. But if they
will affirm, that the *essential Amplitude* of the Soul is no bigger
than what is contained within the physical Point A or B, but
that the *essential Presence* of the Soul is diffused through the
whole Body D, C, E, the thing will succeed not a jot the better,
for while they plainly profess that the whole Soul is in the
Point A, it is manifest that there remains nothing of the Soul
which may be in the Point B, which is distant from A, for it is
as if one should say, that there is nothing of the Soul which is
not included within A; and yet in the same moment of time,
that not only something of the Soul, (which perhaps might be
a more gentle repugnancy) but that the whole Soul is in B, as
if the whole Soul were totally and entirely out of it self; which
surely is impossible in any singular or individual thing, and as
for universals, they are not things, but Notions we use in contemplating them.

Again, if the *essential Amplitude* of the Soul is no greater
than what may be contained within the limits of a physical
Point, it cannot extend or exhibit its *essential Presence* through
the whole Body, unless we imagine in it a stupendious velocity,
such as it may be carried within one moment into all the parts
of the Body, and so be present to them: Which when it is so
hard to conceive in this scant *compages* of an humane Body, and
in the Soul occupying in one moment every part thereof, what an
outragious thing is it, and utterly impossible to apprehend touching that Spirit which perpetually exhibits his *essential Presence*
to the whole World, and what ever is beyond the World?

To which, lastly, you may add that this Hypothesis of the
Holenmerians, does necessarily make all *Spirits* the most *minute*
things that can be conceived: For if the whole Spirit be in every
physical Point, it is plain that the *essential Amplitude* it self
of the Spirit (which the two former Objections supposed) is not
bigger than that physical Point in which it is, (which you may

call, if you will, a *Physical Monad*) than which nothing is or can be smaller in universal Nature; which if you refer to any *created Spirit*, it cannot but seem very ridiculous; but if to the *Majesty* and *Amplitude* of the *Divine Numen*, intolerable, that I may not say plainly Reproachful and Blasphemous.

SECT. XIII.

A Confutation of the First Reason of the Holenmerians.

But now for the Reasons for which the *Holenmerians* adhere to so absurd an Opinion; verily they are such as can no way compensate those huge Difficulties and Repugnancies the Opinion it self labours under. For, for the first, which so solicitously provides for the *Indivisibility* of *Spirits*, it seems to me to undertake a Charge either *Superfluous* or *Ineffectual*. *Superfluous,* if *extension* can be without *divisibility*, as it is clearly demonstrated it can, in that infinite immovable Extension distinct from the moveable Matter, *Enchrid. Metaphys.* cap. 6, 7, 8. But *Ineffectual,* if all *Extension* be *divisible,* and the *essential Presence* of a *Spirit* which pervades and is extended through the whole Body C D E, may for that very Reason be *divided;* for so the whole *Essence* which occupies the whole Body C D E, will be divided into *Parts*. No by no means will you say, forasmuch as it is wholly in every part of the Body.

Therefore it will be divided, if I may so speak, into so many Totalities. But what Logical Ear can bear a saying so absurd and abhorrent from all Reason, that a whole should not be divided into parts, but into wholes? But you will say at least, we shall have this granted us, that an *essential Presence* may be distributed or divided according to so many distinctly sited *Totalities* which occupy at once the whole Body C D E; yes verily, this shall be granted you, after you have demonstrated that a *Spirit* not bigger than a *Physical Monad* can occupy in the same instant all the Parts of the Body C D E, but upon this condition, that you acknowledge not sundry *Totalities,* but one only *total Essence,* tho' the least that can be imagined, can occupy that whole space, and when there is need, occupy in an instant, an infinite one; which the *Holen-*

merians must of necessity hold touching the *Divine Essence,* because, according to their Opinion taken in the second Sense, (which pinches the whole Essence of a Spirit into the smallest point) the Divine Essence it self is not bigger than any *Physical Monad.* From whence it is apparent the three Objections which we brought in the beginning do again recur here, and utterly overwhelm the first Reason of the *Holenmerians:* So that the Remedy is far more intolerable than the Disease.

SECT. XIV.

A Confutation of the second Reason of the Holenmerians.

And truly the other Reason which from this *Holenmerism* of Spirits pretends a more easie way of conceiving how it comes to pass that the Soul, suppose in A, can perceive what happens

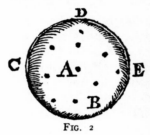

FIG. 2

to it in C, or B, and altogether in the same circumstances as if it self were perfectly and entirely in C, or B, when yet it is in A; altho' at first shew this seems very plausible, yet if we look thoroughly into it, we shall find it far enough from performing what it so fairly promises. For besides that nothing is more difficult or rather impossible to conceive, than that an Essence not bigger than a Physical point should occupy and possess the whole Body of a Man at the same instant, this Hypothesis is moreover plainly contrary and repugnant to the very Laws of the Souls perceptions: For Physicians and Anatomists with one consent profess, that they have found by very solid Experiments, that the Soul perceives only within the Head, and that without the Head there is no perception: Which could by no means be, if the Soul her self were wholly in the Point A, and the very self same Soul again wholly in the Point B, and C, nor any where as to *essential Amplitude* bigger than a *Physical Monad:* For hence it would follow, that one and the same thing would both perceive and not perceive at once; that it would perceive this or that Object, and yet perceive nothing at all; which is a perfect contradiction.

And from hence the falsity of that common Saying is detected, *That if the Eye was in the Foot, the Soul would see in the Foot;* when as it does not so much as see in those Eyes which it already hath, but somewhere within the Brain, nor would the Soul by an Eye in the Foot see, unless by fitting Nerves, not unlike the Optick ones, continued from the Foot to the Head and Brain, where the Soul so far as *perceptive,* inhabiteth. In the other parts of the Body the functions thereof are only *vital.*

Again such is the Nature of some perceptions of the Soul, that they are fitted for the moving of the Body; so that it is manifest that the very self same thing which perceives, has the power of Moving and Guiding of it; which seems impossible to be done by this Soul, which according to the Opinion of the *Holenmerians,* exceeds not the Amplitude of a small Physical Point, as it may appear at the first sight to any whose Reason is not blinded with Prejudice.

And lastly, If it be lawful for the Mind of Man to give her conjectures touching the immortal *Genii,* (whether they be in Vehicles, or destitute of Vehicles) and touching their *Perceptions* and *essential Presences* whether invisible or those in which they are said sometimes to appear to mortal Men, there is none surely that can admit that any of these things are compatible to such a Spirit as the *Holenmerians* describe. For how can a *Metaphysical Monad,* that is to say, a Spiritual substance not exceeding a Physical Monad in Amplitude, fill out an *essential Presence* bigger than a Physical Monad, unless it be by a very swift vibration of it self towards all Parts; as Boys by a very swift moving of a Fire-stick, make a fiery Circle in the Air by that quick Motion. But that Spirits destitute of Vehicles, should have no greater *essential Presence* than what is occupied of a naked and unmoved *Metaphysical Monad,* or exhibited thereby, seems so absonous and ridiculous a Spectacle to the Mind of Man, that unless he be deprived of all Sagacity and Sensibility of Spirit, he cannot but abhor so idle an Opinion.

And as for those *essential Presences,* according to which they sometimes appear to Men, at least equalizing humane Stature, how can a solitary *Metaphysical Monad* form so great a part of Air or Æther into humane Shape, or govern it being so formed?

Or how can it perceive any external Object in this swift Motion of it self, and quick vibration, whereby this *Metaphysical Monad* is understood of the *Holenmerians,* to be present in all the parts of its Vehicle at once? For there can be no perception of the external Object, unless the Object that is to be perceived, act with some stay upon that which perceiveth. Nor if it could be perceived by this *Metaphysical Monad* thus swiftly moved and vibrated towards all parts at once, would it be seen in one Place, but in many Places at once, and those, as it may happen very distant.

SECT. XV.

The egregious falsity of the Opinions of the Holenmerians *and* Nullibists, *as also their uselessness for any Philosophical ends.*

But verily, I am ashamed to waste so much time in refuting such meer Trifles and Dotages which indeed are such, (that I mean of the *Nullibists,* as well as this other of the *Holenmerians*) that we may very well wonder how such distorted and strained Conceits could ever enter into the Minds of Men, or by what artifice they have so spread themselves in the World; but that the Prejudices and Enchantments of Superstition, and stupid admiration of Mens Persons are so strong, that they may utterly blind the Minds of Men, and charm them into Dotage. But if any one, all Prejudice and Parts-taking being laid aside, will attentively consider the thing as it is, he shall clearly perceive and acknowledge, unless all belief is to be denied to the humane Faculties, that the Opinions of the *Nullibists* and *Holenmerians,* touching *Incorporeal Beings,* are miserably *false,* and not that only, but as to any Philosophical purpose altogether *useless.* Forasmuch as out of neither Hypothesis there does appear any greater facility of conceiving how the *Mind of Man,* or any other *Spirit,* performs those Functions of *Perception* and of *Moving* of *Bodies,* from their being supposed *no where,* than from their being supposed *some where;* or from supposing them *wholly in every part* of a Body, than from supposing them only to occupy the whole Body by an *Essential* or *Metaphysical extension;* but on the contrary, that both the Hypotheses do entangle and involve the Doctrine of *Incorporeal Beings* with greater Difficulties and Repugnancies.

Wherefore there being neither *Truth* nor *Usefulness* in the Opinions of the *Holenmerians* and *Nullibists,* I hope it will offend no Man if we send them quite packing from our Philosophations touching an *Incorporeal Being* or *Spirit,* in our delivering the true Idea or Notion thereof.

SECT. XVI.

That those that contend that the Notion of a Spirit *is so difficult and imperscrutable, do not this because they are of a more sharp and piercing Judgment than others, but of a Genius more Rude and Plebeian.*

Now I have so successfully removed and dissipated those two vast Mounds of Night and Mistiness, that lay upon the Nature of *Incorporeal Beings,* and obscured it with such gross Darkness; it remains that we open and illustrate the true and genuine Nature of them in general, and propose such a definition of a *Spirit,* as will exhibit no difficulty to a Mind rightly prepared and freed from Prejudice. For the *Nature* of a *Spirit* is very easily understood, provided one rightly and skillfully shew the way to the Learner, and form to him true Notions of the thing, insomuch that I have often wondred at the superstitious consternation of Mind in those Men (or the profaneness of their Tempers and innate aversion from the Contemplation of Divine things) who if by chance they hear any one professing that he can with sufficient clearness and distinctness conceive the Nature of a Spirit, and communicate the Notion to others, they are presently startled and amazed at the saying, and straitway accuse the Man of intolerable Levity or Arrogancy, as thinking him to assume so much to himself and to promise to others, as no humane Wit furnished with never so much Knowledge can ever perform. And this I understand even of such Men who yet readily acknowledge the *Existence* of *Spirits.*

But as for those that deny their *Existence,* whoever professes this skill to them, verily he cannot but appear a Man above all measure vain and doating, no Man more unskilful and ignorant, than he that ésteems the clear Notion of a Spirit so hopeless and desperate an attempt; and that I shall plainly detect, that this high and boastful Profession of their Ignorance in these things does not proceed from hence, that they have any more a sharp or discerning Judgment than other Mortals, but that they have more gross and weak parts, and a shallower Wit, and such as comes nearest to the superstition and stupidity of the rude Vulgar, who easilier fall into admiration and astonishment, than pierce into the Reasons and Notices of any difficult Matter.

SECT. XVII.

The Definition of Body *in general, with so clear an Explication thereof, that even they that complain of the obscurity of a* Spirit, *cannot but confess they perfectly understand the Nature of* Body.

But now for those who do thus despair of any true Knowledge of the Nature of a *Spirit,* I would entreat them to try the Abilities of their Wit in recognizing and throughly considering the Nature of *Body* in general, and let them ingenuously tell me whether they cannot but acknowledge this to be a clear and perspicuous Definition thereof, *viz. That* Body *is substance Material of it self, altogether destitute of all Perception, Life, and Motions.* Or thus, *Body is a substance Material, coalescent or accruing together into one, by virtue of some other thing, from whence that one by coalition, has or may have Life also, Perception and Motion.*

I doubt not but they will readily answer, that they understand all this (as to the Terms) clearly and perfectly; nor would they doubt of the Truth thereof, but that we deprive *Body* of all *Motion from it self,* as also of *Union, Life* and *Perception.* But that it is *Substance,* that is, a Being subsistent by it self, not a *mode* of some Being, they cannot but very willingly admit, and that also it is a *material* Substance compounded of *physical Monads,* or at least of most *minute Particles* of Matter, into

which it is divisible; and because of their *Impenetrability,*
impenetrable by any other Body, so that the Essential and
Positive difference of a *Body* is, that it be *impenetrable,* and
physically divisible into Parts: But that it is *extended,* that
immediately belongs to it as it is a *Being.* Nor is there any
reason why they should doubt of the other part of the *Dif-
ferentia,* when as it is solidly and fully proved in Philosophy,
That *Matter* of its own nature, or in it self, is endued with no
Perception, Life nor *Motion.* And besides, we are to remember
that we here do not treat of the *Existence* of things, but of their
intellible *Notion* and *Essence.*

SECT. XVIII.

*The perfect Definition of a Spirit, with a full Explication of its
Nature through all Degrees.*

And if the *Notion* or Essence is so easily understood in nature
Corporeal or *Body,* I do not see but in the *Species* immediately
opposite to *Body, viz. Spirit,* there may be found the same
facility of being understood. Let us try therefore, and from
the Law of *Opposites* let us define a *Spirit,* an *Immaterial substance intrinsecally endued with Life and the faculty of Motion.*
This slender and brief Definition that thus easily flows without
any noise, does comprehend in general the whole nature of a
Spirit; Which lest by reason of its exility and brevity it may
prove less perceptible to the Understanding, as a Spirit is to the
sight, I will subjoin a more full Explication, that it may appear
to all, that this Definition of a *Spirit* is nothing inferiour to the
Definition of a *Body* as to clearness and perspicuity. And that
by this method which we now fall upon, a ful and perfect
knowledge and understanding of the nature of a *Spirit* may be
attained to.

Go to therefore, let us take notice through all the degrees of
the *Definitum,* or *Thing, defined,* what precise and immediate
properties each of them contain, from whence at length a most
distinct and perfect knowledge of the whole *Definitum* will discover it self. Let us begin then from the top of all, and first

let us take notice that a Spirit is *Ens,* or a *Being,* and from this very same that it is a *Being;* that it is also *One,* that it is *True,* and that it is *Good;* which are the three acknowledged Properties of *Ens* in *Metaphysicks,* that it exists *sometime,* and *somewhere,* and is in some sort *extended,* as is shewn *Enchirid. Metaphys.* cap. 2. sect. 10. which three latter terms are plain of themselves. (72) And as for the three former, that *One* signifies undistinguished or undivided in and from it self, but divided or distinguished from all other, and that *True* denotes the answerableness of the *thing* to its own proper *Idea,* and implies right *Matter* and *Form* duely conjoyned, and that lastly *Good* respects the fitness for the end in a large sence, so that it will take in that saying of Theologers, That God is his own End, are things vulgarly known to *Logicians* and *Metaphysicians.* That these Six are the immediate affections of Being as Being, is made apparent in the above-cited *Enchiridion Metaphysicum;* nor is it requisite to repeat the same things here. Now every *Being* is either *Substance* or the *Mode* of Substance, which some call *Accident:* But that a *Spirit* is not an *Accident* or *Mode* of Substance, all in a manner profess and it is demonstrable from manifold Arguments, that there are *Spirits* which are no such *Accidents* or *Modes;* which is made good in the said *Enchiridion* and other Treatises of Doctor *H. M.*

Wherefore the second Essential degree of a Spirit is, that it is *Substance.* From whence it is understood to subsist by it self, nor to want any other thing as a *Subject* (in which it may inhere, or of which it may be the *Mode* or *Accident*) for its subsisting or existing.

The third and last Essential degree is, that it is *Immaterial,* according to which it immediately belongs to it, that it be a *Being* not only *One,* but *one by it self,* or of its own intimate nature; and not by another; that is, That, though as it is a *Being* it is in some sort extended, yet it is utterly *Indivisible* and *Indiscerpible* into real Physical parts. And moreover, That it can *penetrate* the *Matter,* and (which the *Matter* cannot do) penetrate things of its own kind; that is pass through Spiritual Substances. In which two Essential Attributes (as it ought to be in every perfect and legitimate Distribution of any Genius) it is fully and accurately contrary to its opposite *Species,* namely, to *Body.* As also in those immediate Properties whereby it is understood to have *Life* intrinsically in *it self,* and the faculty of *moving;* which in some sense is true in all Spirits whatsoever, forasmuch as *Life* is either *Vegetative, Sensitive,* or *Intellectual.* One whereof at least every Spiritual Substance hath: as also the *faculty* of *moving;* insomuch that every Spirit either moves it self by it self, or the Matter, or both, or at least the Matter either mediately or immediately; or lastly, both ways. For so all things moved are moved by God, he being the Fountain of all Life and Motion.

SECT. XIX.

That from hence that the Definition of a Body *is perspicuous, the Definition of a* Spirit *is also necessarily perspicuous.*

Wherefore I dare here appeal to the Judgment and Conscience of any one that is not altogether illiterate and of a dull and obtruse Wit, whether this *Notion* or Definition of a *Spirit* in general, is not as intelligible and perspicuous, is not as clear and every way distinct as the Idea or *Notion* of a *Body,* or of any thing else whatsoever which the mind of Man can contemplate in the whole compass of Nature. And whether he cannot as easily or rather with the same pains apprehend the nature of a *Spirit* as of *Body,* forasmuch as they both agree in the immediate Genus to them, to wit *Substance.* And the *Differentiae* do illustrate one another by their mutual opposition; insomuch that it is impossible that one should understand what is *Material* Substance, but he must therewith presently understand what *Immaterial* Substance is, or what it is *not* to have *Life* and *Motion* of it self, but he must straitway perceive what it is *to have both in it self,* or to be able to communicate them to others.

SECT. XX.

Four Objections which from the perspicuity of the terms of the Definitions of a S P I R I T *infer the Repugnancy of them one to another.*

Nor can I divine what may be here opposed, unless haply they may alledge such things as these, That although they cannot deny but that all the *terms* of the *Definition* and *Explication* of them, are sufficiently intelligible, if they be considered single, yet if they be compared one with another they will mutually destroy one another. For this *Extension* which is mingled with, or inserted into the nature of a *Spirit,* seems to take away the *Penetrability* and *Indivisibility* thereof, as also its *faculty* of *thinking,* as its *Penetrability* likewise takes away its power of *moving any Bodies.*

I. First, *Extension* takes away *Penetrability;* because if one Extension penetrate another, of necessity either one of them is destroyed, or two equal Amplitudes entirely penetrating one another, are no bigger than either one of them taken single, because they are closed within the same limits.

II. Secondly, It takes away *Indivisibility;* because whatsoever is *extended* has *partes extra partes,* one part out of another, and therefore is Divisible: For neither would it have parts, unless it could be divided into them. To which you may further add, that forasmuch as the parts are *substantial,* nor depend one of another, it is clearly manifest that at least by the Divine Power they may be separate, and subsist separate one from another.

III. Thirdly, *Extension* deprives a *Spirit* of the faculty of *thinking,* as depressing it down into the same order that Bodies are. And that there is no reason why an *extended Spirit* should be more capable of *Perception* than *Matter* that is *extended.*

IV. Lastly, *Penetrability* renders a *Spirit* unable to *move Matter;* because, whenas by reason of this *Penetrability* it so easily slides thorough the Matter, it cannot conveniently be united with the Matter whereby it may move the same: For without some union or inherency (a *Spirit* being destitute of all *Impenetrability*) 'tis impossible it should protrude the Matter towards any place.

The sum of which Four difficulties tends to this, that we may understand, that though this Idea or *Notion* of a *Spirit* which we have exhibited be sufficiently plain and explicate, and may be easily understood; yet from the very perspicuity of the thing it self, it abundantly appears, that it is not the Idea of any *possible* thing, and much less of a thing *really existing*, whenas the parts thereof are so manifestly repugnant one to another.

SECT. XXI.

An Answer to the first of the Four Objections.

I. But against as well the *Nullibists* as the *Hobbians*, who both of them contend that *Extension* and *Matter* is one and the same thing, we will prove that the Notion or Idea of a *Spirit* which we have produced, is a Notion of a thing *possible*. And as for the *Nullibists*, who think we so much indulge to corporeal Imagination in this our Opinion of the *Extension* of Spirits, I hope on the contrary, that I shall shew that it is only from hence, that the *Hobbians* and *Nullibists* have taken all *Amplitude* from *Spirits*, because their Imagination is not sufficiently defecated and depurated from the filth and unclean tinctures of *Corpority*, or rather that they have their Mind over-much addicted and enslaved to *Material* things, and so disordered, that she knows not how to expedite her self from gross Corporeal Phantasms.

From which Fountain have sprung all those difficulties whereby they endeavour to overwhelm this our *Notion* of a *Spirit;* as we shall manifestly demonstrate by going through them all, and carefully perpending each of them. For it is to be imputed to their gross Imagination, That from hence that two equal Amplitudes penetrate one another throughout, they conclude that either one of them must therewith perish, or that they being both conjoyned together, are no bigger than either one of them taken single. For this comes from hence, that their mind is so illaqueated or lime-twigged, as it were, with the Idea's and Properties of Corporeal things, that they cannot but infect those things also which have nothing corporeal in them with this material Tincture and Contagion, and so altogether confound this *Metaphysical* Extension with that Extension which is *Physical.* I say, from this *disease* it is that the sight of their mind is become so dull and obtruse, that they are not able to divide that common Attribute of a being, I mean *Entension Metaphysical* from *special* Extension and *Material,* and assign to *Spirits* their proper Extension, and leave to *Matter* hers. Nor according to that known method, whether Logical or Metaphysical, by intellectual Abstraction prescind the *Generical* nature of *Extension* from the abovesaid *Species* or kinds thereof. Nor lastly, (which is another sign of their obtuseness and dulness) is their Mind able to *penetrate* with that *Spiritual* Extension into the Extension *Material;* but like a stupid Beast stands lowing without, as if the Mind it self were become wholly corporeal; and if any thing enter they believe it perishes rather and is annihilated, than that two things can at the same time co-exist together in the same *Ubi.* Which are Symptoms of a Mind desperately sick of this Corporeal Malady of *Imagination,* and not sufficiently accustomed or exercised in the free Operations of the Intellectual Powers.

And that also proceeds from the same Source, that supposing two Extensions penetrating one another, and adequately occupying the same *Ubi,* they thus conjoyned are conceived not to be greater than either one of them taken by it self. For the reason of this Mistake is, that the *Mind* incrassated and swayed down by the *Imagination,* cannot together with the *Spiritual* Extension penetrate into the *Material,* and follow it throughout, but only places it self hard by, and stands without like a gross stupid thing, and altogether Corporeal, for if she could but with the *Spiritual* Extension, insinuate her self into the *Material,* and so conceive them both together as two really distinct Extensions, it is impossible but that she should therewith conceive them so conjoyned into one *Ubi,* to be notwithstanding not a jot less than when they are separated and occupy an *Ubi* as big again; for the *Extension* in neither of them is diminished, but their *Situation* only changed, as it also sometimes comes to pass in one and the same Extension of some particular Spirits which can dilate and contract their Amplitude into a greater or lesser *Ubi* without any Augmentation or Diminution of their Extension, but only by the expansion and contraction of it into another *site.*

SECT. XXII.

That besides those THREE *Dimensions which belong to all extended things, a* FOURTH *also is to be admitted, which belongs properly to* SPIRITS.

And that I may not dissemble or conceal any thing, altho' all *Material* things, consider'd in themselves, have *three* Dimensions only; yet there must be admitted in Nature a *Fourth,* which fitly enough, I think, may be called *Essential Spissitude;* which tho' it most properly appertains to those Spirits which can contract their Extension into a less *Ubi,* yet by a less Analogie it may be referred also to Spirits penetrating as well the *Matter* as mutually *one another,* so that wherever there are more Essences than one, or more of the same Essence in the same *Ubi* than is adequate to the Amplitude thereof, there this *Fourth* Dimension is to be acknowledged, which we call *Essential Spissitude.*

Which assuredly involves no greater repugnancy than what may seem at first view, to him that considers the thing less attentively, to be in the other *three* Dimensions, namely, unless one would conceive that a piece of Wax stretched out, suppose to the length of an Ell, and afterwards rolled together into the form of a Globe, loses something of its former Extension, by this its conglobation, he must confess that a Spirit, neither by the contraction of it self into a less space has lost any thing of its Extension or Essence, but as in the above-said Wax, the dimunition of its Longitude is compensated with the augmentation of its Latitude and Profundity; so in a Spirit contracting it self, that in like maner its Longitude, Latitude, and Profundity being lessened, are compensated by *Essential Spissitude,* which the Spirit acquires by this contraction of it self.

And in both cases we are to remember that the *Site* is only changed, but that the *Essence* and *Extension* are not at all impaired.

Verily these things by me are so perfectly every way perceived, so certain and tried, that I dare appeal to the Mind of any one which is free from the moral Prejudices of *Imagination,* and challenge him to try the strength of his Intellectuals, whether he does not clearly perceive the thing to be so as I have defined, and that *two* equal Extensions, adequately occupying the very same *Ubi,* be not *twice* as great as either of them alone, and that they are not closed with the same Terms as the *Imagination* falsely suggests, but only with equal.

Nor is there any need to heap up more Words for the solving this first Difficulty; whenas what has been briefly said already abundantly sufficeth for the penetrating their understanding who are pre-possest with no Prejudice; but for the piercing of theirs who are blinded with Prejudices, infinite will not suffice.

SECT. XXIII.

An Answer to the second Objection, where the fundamental Error of the Nullibists, *viz. That whatsoever is extended is the Object of Imagination is taken notice of.*

II. Let us now try if we can dispatch the second Difficulty with the like success, and see if it be not wholly to be ascribed to *Imagination,* that an *Indiscerpible extension* seems to involve in it any contradiction, as if there could be no Extension which has not parts real and properly so called into which it may be actually divided, *viz.* for this reason, that only is *extended* which has *partes extra partes,* which being *substantial,* may be separated one from another, and thus separate subsist; this is the summary Account of this difficulty, which nothing but corrupt *Imagination* supporteth.

Now the first Source or Fountain of this Errour of the *Nullibists* is this, that they make every thing that is *extended* the Object of the *Imagination,* and every Object of the *Imagination corporeal.* The latter whereof undoubtedly is true, if it be taken in a right Sense, namely, if they understand such a perception as is either simply and adequately drawn from external Objects; or by increasing, diminishing, transposing, or transforming of parts (as in *Chimæra's* and *Hippocentaur's*) is composed of the same. I acknowledge all these Ideas, as they were sometime some way Objects of *Sensation,* so to be the genuine Objects of *Imagination,* and the perception of these to be rightly termed the Operation of Fancy, and that all these things that are thus represented, necessarily are to be looked upon as *Corporeal*, and consequently as *actually divisible*.

But that all *perception* of *Extension* is such *Imagination*, that I confidently deny, forasmuch as there is an Idea of *infinite Extension* drawn or taken in from no external Sense, but is natural and essential to the very Faculty of perceiving; which the Mind can by no means pluck out of her self, nor cast it away from her; but if she will rouse her self up, and by earnest and attentive thinking, fix her animadversion thereon, she will be constrained, whether she will or no, to acknowledge, that altho' the whole matter of the World were exterminated out of the Universe, there would notwithstanding remain a certain subtile and immaterial extension which has no agreement with that other Material one, in any thing, saving that it is extended, as being such that it neither falls under sense, nor is impenetrable, nor can be moved, nor discerped into parts; and that this Idea is not only possible, but necessary, and such as we do not at our pleasure feign and invent, but do find it to be so innate and ingrafted in our Mind, that we cannot by any force or Artifice remove it thence, which is a most certain demonstration that all *Perception* of *Extension* is not *Imagination* properly so called.

Which in my Opinion ought to be esteemed one of the chiefest and most fundamental Errors of the *Nullibists,* and to which especially this Difficulty is to be referred touching an *Indiscerpible Extension.* For we see they confess their own Guilt, namely that their Mind is so corrupted by their Imagination, and so immersed into it, that they can use no other Faculty in the Contemplation of any extended thing, and therefore when they make use of their Imagination instead of their Intellect in Contemplating of it, they necessarily look upon it as an Object of *Imagination;* that is, as a corporeal thing, and *discerpible* into parts, for as I noted above, the sight of their Mind by reason of this *Morbus* ὑλοειδής, this *materious Disease,* if I may so speak, is made so heavy and dull, that it cannot distinguish any *Extension* from that of *Matter,* as allowing it to appertain to another kind, nor by *Logical* or *Metaphysical* Abstraction prescind it from either.

SECT. XXIV.

That Extension as such includes in it neither Divisibility nor Impenetrability, neither Indivisibility nor Penetrability, but is indifferent to either two of those Properties.

And from hence it is that because a thing is *extended*, they presently imagine that it has *partes extra partes*, and is not *Ens unum per se & non per aliud*, a Being one by it self, and not by vertue of another, but so framed from the juxtaposition of parts, when as the Idea of *Extension* precisely consider'd in it self, includes no such thing, but only a *trinal* Distance, or *solid* Amplitude, that is to say, not *linear* only and *superficiary* (if we may here use those Terms which properly belong to magnitude Mathematical) but every way running out and reaching towards every part. This Amplitude surely, and nothing beside, does this bare and simple *Extension* include, not *Penetrability* nor *Impenetrability*, nor *Divisibility*, nor yet *Indivisibility*, but to either Affections or Properties, or if you will essential Differences, namely, to *Divisibility* and *Impenetrability,* or to *Penetrability* and *Indivisibility,* if considered in it self, is it altogether indifferent, and may be determined to either two of them.

Wherefore, whenas we acknowledge that there is a certain. *Extension,* namely, *Material,* which is endued with so stout and invincible an 'Αητιτυπία or *Impenetrabilty,* that it necessarily and by an insuperable Renitency expels and excludes all other Matter that occurs and attempts to penetrate it, nor suffers it at all to enter, altho' in the simple Idea of *Extension,* this marvelous Vertue of it is not contained, but plainly omitted, as not at all belonging thereto immediately and of it self; why may we not as easily conceive that another *Extension,* namely, an Immaterial one, though *Extension* in it self include no such thing, is of such a Nature, that it cannot by any other thing whether Material or Immaterial be discerped into Parts; but by an indissoluble necessary and essential Tie be so united and held together with it self, that although it can penetrate all things and be penetrated by all things, yet nothing can so insinuate it self into it, as to disjoyn any thing of its Essence any where, or perforate it or make any Hole or Pore in it? That is, that I may speak briefly, What hinders but that there may be a *Being* that is immediately *One* of its own Nature, and held together into one by virtue of some other, either *Quality* or *Substance?* Altho' every Being as a Being is *Extended,* because *Extension* in its precise Notion does not include any *Physical Division,* but the Mind infected with *corporeal Imagination,* does falsely and unskilfully feign it to be necessarily there.

SECT. XXV.

That every thing that is extended has not Parts Physically discerpible, though Logically or Intellectually divisible.

For it is nothing which the *Nullibists* here allege, while they say, That all Extension inferreth Parts, and all Parts Division. For besides that the first is false, forasmuch as *Ens unum per se,* a Being, one of it self, or of its own immediate Nature, although *extended,* yet includes no *Parts* in its Idea, but is conceived according to its proper Essence, as a thing as simple as may be, and therefore compounded of no *Parts.* We Answer moreover, That it is not at all prejudicial to our Cause, though we should grant that this *Metaphysical Extension* of Spirits is also divisible, but *Logically* only, not *Physically;* that is to say, is not *discerpible.* But that one should adjoyn a *Physical divisibility* to such an Extension, surely that must necessarily proceed from the impotency of his *Imagination,* which his Mind cannot curb nor separate her self from the dregs and corporeal Foulness thereof; and hence it is that she tinctures and infects this Pure and Spiritual Extension with Corporeal Properties. But that an extended thing may be divided *Logically* or *Intellectually,* when in the mean time it can by no means be discerped, it sufficiently appears from hence, That a *Physical Monad* which has some Amplitude, though the least that possibly can be, is conceived thus to be divided in a *Line* consisting of any uneven number of Monads, which notwithstanding the Intellect divides into two equal Parts. And verily in a *Metaphyical Monad,* such as the *Holenmerians* conceit the Mind of Man to be, and to possess in the mean time and occupy the whole *Body*, there may be here again made a *Logical* Distribution, suppose, *è subjectis*, as they call it, so far forth as this *Metaphysical Monad*, or *Soul* of the *Holenmerians* is conceived to possess the Head, Trunk, or Limbs of the Body, and yet no Man is so delirant as to think that it follows from thence, that such a Soul may be *discerped* into so many Parts, and that the Parts so discerped may subsist by themselves.

SECT. XXVI.

An Answer to the latter part of the second Objection, which inferreth the separability of the Parts of a substantial Extensium, *from the said Parts being* Substantial *and Independent one of another.*

From which a sufficiently fit and accommodate Answer may be fetched to the latter part of this Difficulty, namely, to that which because the parts of substance are *Substantial* and *Independent* one of another, and *subsisting by themselves* (as being *Substances*) would infer that they can be *discerped,* at least by the Divine Power, and disjoyned, and being so disjoyned, subsist by themselves. Which I confess to be the chief Edge or Sting of the whole Difficulty, and yet such as I hope I shall with ease File off or Blunt. For first, I deny that in a thing that is *absolutely One* and *Simple* as a Spirit is, there are any *Physical* parts, or parts properly so called, but that they are only falsely feigned and fancied in it, by the impure Imagination. But that the Mind it self being sufficiently defecated and purged from the impure Dregs of Fancy, although from some extrinsical respect she may consider a Spirit as having Parts, yet at the very same time does she in her self, with close attention, observe and note, that such an *Extension* of it self has none; and therefore whenas it has no Parts, it is plain it has no *substantial* parts, nor *independent* one of another, nor subsistent of themselves.

And then as much as concerns those Parts which the stupid and Impotent *Imagination* fancieth in a Spirit, it does not follow from thence, because they are *Substantial,* that they may *sub-sist separate* by themselves; for a thing to *subsist by it self,* only signifies so to subsist, that it wants not the Prop of some other *Subject* in which it may inhere as *Accidents* do, so that the parts of a *Spirit* may be said to subsist by themselves tho' they cannot subsist separate, and so be Substance still.

SECT. XXVII.

That the mutual Independency *of the Parts of an extended Substance may be understood in a* two-fold Sense; *with an Answer thereto, taken in the first Sense thereof.*

But what they mean by that *mutual Independency* of Parts, I do not fully understand, but I sufficiently conceive that one of these two things must be hinted thereby, *viz.* Either that they are not *mutual* and effectual *Causes* to one another of their *Existing,* or that their Existence is understood to be connected by *no necessary condition at all.*

And as for the former Sense, I willingly confess those Parts which they fancy in a Spirit are not mutual Causes of one anothers Existence; but so, that in the mean time I do most firmly deny, that it will thence follow that they may be dis-cerped, and thus discerpt, be separately conserved, no more than the intelligible Parts of a *Physical Monad* which is divided into two by our Reason or Intellect; which surely are no mutual Causes of one anothers Existence, or the Members of the Dis-tribution of a *Metaphysical Monad* according to the Doctrine of the *Holenmerians* (*viz.* The Soul totally being in every part of the Body) which no Man in his Wits can ever hope that they may be discerped, although the said Members of the division are not the mutual Causes of one anothers Existence, for they are but one and the same Soul which is not the cause of it self, but was wholly and entirely caused by God.

But you will say that there is here manifestly a reason extant and apparent why these Members of the Distribution cannot be discerped, and discerpt seperately conversed, because one and the same indivisible Monad occurs in every Member of the Distribution, which therefore since it is a single one, it is impossible it should be discerped from it self. To which I on the other side answer, That it is as manifestly extant and apparent how frivolously therefore ineptly Arguments are drawn from *Logical* or Intellectual Divisions, for the concluding a real separability of parts. And I add further, That as that fictitious *Metaphysical Monad* cannot be discerped or pluckt in pieces from itself, no more can any real Spirit, because it is a thing *most simple* and *most absolutely One,* and which a *pure Mind* darken'd and possessed with no prejudices of *Imagination* does acknowledge no *real* parts at all to be in. For so it would *ipso facto* be a *compound* Thing.

SECT. XXVIII.

An Answer to the Independency of parts taken in the second sence.

From whence an easie entrance is made to the answering this difficulty understood in the second sence of the *mutual Independency* of the parts of a Spirit, whereby their coexistence and union are understood to be connected by *no necessary* Law or Condition. For that this is false, I do most constantly affirm without all demur: For the coexistences of the parts, as they call them, of a Spirit, are connected by a Law or Condition *absolutely necessary* and plainly *essential;* Forasmuch as a Spirit is a *most simple* Being, or a Being *unum per se & non per aliud;* that is, *one of it self or of its own nature immediately so,* and not by another either *Substance* or *Quality.* For none of those parts, as the *Nullibists* call them, can exist but upon this condition, that all jointly and unitedly exist together; which Condition or Law is contained in the very Idea, or nature of every *Spirit.* Whence it cannot be created or any way produced unless upon this condition, that all its parts be inseperably and indiscerpibly one; as neither a Rectangle Triangle, unless upon this condition that the powers of the *Cathetus* and *Basis,* be equal to the power of the *Hypotenusa.* Whence the *Indiscerpibility* of a *Spirit* cannot be removed from it, no not *virtute Divina,* as the Schoolmen speak, no more than the above-said Property disjoyned from a Rectangle Triangle. Out of all which I hope it is at length abundantly clear, that the *Extension* of a Spirit does not at all hinder the *Indiscerpibility thereof.*

SECT. XXIX.

An Answer to the third Objection touching the Imperceptivity *of an extended Substance,* viz. That whatever is, is extended, *and that the* NUILIBISTS *and* HOLENMERIANS *themselves cannot give a Reason of the* perceptive *Faculty in Spirits, from their Hypotheses.*

III. Nor is it any let (which is the third thing) to the faculty of *Perceiving* and *Thinking* in *Spirits:* For we do not thrust down a *Spirit* by attributing *Extension* to it, into the rank of *Corporeal Beings,* forasmuch as there is nothing in all Nature which is not in some sense *extended.* For whatever of Essence there is in anything, it either is or may be actually present to some part of the matter, and therefore it must either be *extended* or be contracted to the narrowness of a *point,* and be a meer *nothing.* For as for the *Nulibists* and *Holenmerians,* the opinions of them both are above utterly routed by me, and quite subverted and overturned from the very root, that no man may seek subterfuges and lurking holes there. Wherefore there is a necessity that some thing that is *extended* have *Cogitation* and *Perception* in it, or else there will be nothing left that has.

But for that which this Objection further urges, that there occurs no reason why an *extended Spirit* should be more capable of Perception than *extended Matter,* it is verily, in my judgment, a very unlearned and unskillful argutation. For we do not take all this pains of demonstrating the *Extension* of a *Spirit,* that thence we might fetch out a reason or account of its faculty of perceiving; but that it may be conceived to be some real Being and true Substance, and not a vain Figment, such as is every thing that has no Amplitude and is in no sort *extended.*

But those that so stickle and sweat for the proving their Opinion, that a Spirit is *no where,* or is *totally* in every part of that *Ubi* it occupies, they are plainly engaged of all right, clearly and distinctly to render a reason out of their *Hypothesis* of the *Perceptive faculty* that is acknowledged in *Spirits,* Namely that they plainly and precisely deduce from hence, because a thing is *nowhere* or *totally* in every part of the *Ubi* it occupies, that it is necessarily endued with a faculty of *perceiving* and *thinking ;* so that the reason of the conjunction of *properties* with the *Subject,* may be clearly thence understood.

Which not withstanding I am very confident, they can never perform; And that *Perception* and *Cogitation* are the *immediate* Attributes of some Substance; and that therefore, as that Rule of Prudence, *Enchirid. Ethic.* lib. 3. cap. 4. sect. 3. declares, no Physical reason thereof ought to be required, nor can be given, why they are in the Subject wherein they are found. (73)

SECT. XXX.

That from the Generical *nature of any* Species, *no reason is to be fetcht of the conjunction of the* Essential Difference *with it,* it being immediate.

But so we are to conclude, that as *Substance* is immediately divided into *Material* and *Immaterial,* or into *Body* and *Spirit,* where no reason can be rendered from the Substance in *Spirit,* as it is Substance, why it should be *Spirit* rather than *Body ;* nor from Substance in a *Body,* as it is Substance, why it should be *Body* rather than *Spirit,* But these *Essential Differences* are immediately in the Subject in which they are found : So the case stands in the subdivision of *Spirit* into meerly *Plastical* and *Perceptive,* supposing there are Spirits that are meerly Plastical ; and then of a *Perceptive Spirit* into meerly *Sensitive* and *Intellectual.* For there can be no reason rendred touching a *Spirit* as a Spirit in a Spirit meerly *Plastical,* why it is a Spirit meerly *Plastical* rather than *Perceptive :* Nor in a *Perceptive Spirit,* why it is a *Perceptive* Spirit rather than *meerly Plastical.* And lastly, in a Perceptive Spirit *Intellectual,* why it is *Intellectual* rather than meerly *Sensitive ;* and in the *meerly Sensitive* Spirit, why it is such rather than *Intellectual.* But these *Essential Differences* are immediately in the *Subjects* in which they are found, and any Physical and intrinsical reason ought not to be asked, nor can be given why they are in those Subjects, as I noted a little above out of the said *Enchiridion Ethicum.*

SECT. XXXI.

That although the Holenmerians *and* Nullibists *can give no reason, why that which perceives should be* TOTALLY *in every part, or should be* NO WHERE *rather than be in any sort* extended *or* somewhere, *yet there are reasons obvious enough why an extended Spirit, rather should perceive than extended Matter.*

But however, though we cannot render a reason why this or that *Substance* as Substance, be a *Spirit* rather than *Body,* or why this or that *Spirit* be *Perceptive* rather than meerly *Plastical;* yet as the reason is sufficiently plain, why *Matter* or *Body* is a *Substance* rather than *Accident,* so it is manifest enough why that which *Perceives,* or is *Plastical,* should be a *Spirit* rather than *Matter* or *Body;* which surely is much more than either the *Holenmerians* or *Nullibists* can vaunt of. For they can offer no reason why that which perceives should rather be *nowhere* than somewhere; or *totally* in each part of the *Ubi* it does occupy, than otherwise, as may be understood from what we have said above.

But now since the *Matter* or *Body* which is *discerpible* and *Impenetrable* is destitute of itself of all Life and Motion, certainly it is consonant to reason, that the *Species* opposite to *Body,* and which is conceived to be *Penetrable* and *Indiscerpible,* should be intrinsically endued with Life in general and Motion. And whenas *Matter* is nothing else than a certain stupid and loose *congeries of Physical Monads,* that the first and most immediate opposite degree in this *indiscerpible* and *penetrable* Substance, which is called *Spirit,* should be the faculty of Union, Motion, and Life, in which all the *Sympathies* and *Synenergies* which are found in the world may be conceived to consist. From whence it ought not to seem strange, that that which is *Plastical* should be a Spirit.

And now as for *Perception* itself, undoubtedly all Mortals have either a certain confused presage, or more precise and determinate Notion, that as that, whatever it is in which the abovesaid *Sympathies* and *Synenergies* immediately are, so more especially that to which belongs the faculty of *Perceiving* and *Thinking* is a thing of all things the most *subtile* and most *One* that may be.

Wherefore I appeal here to the Mind and Judgment of any one, whether he can truly conceive any thing more *Subtile* or more *One* than the *Essence* or Notion of a *Spirit*, as it is immediately distinguished from *Matter*, opposed thereto. For can there be any thing more *One* than what has no parts, into which it may be discerped? or more *Subtile* than what does not only penetrate *Matter*, but itself, or at least other Substances of its own kind? For a Spirit can penetrate a Spirit, though Matter cannot penetrate Matter.

There is therefore in the very *Essence* of a *Spirit*, although it be *Metaphysically* extended, no obscure reason why all the *Sympathies* and *Synenergies*, why all *Perceptions* and all manner of *Cogitations* should be referred rather to it, by reason of the *Unity* and *Subtilty* of its nature, than to *Matter*, which is so crass, that it is *impenetrable;* and is so far from *unity* of *Essence*, that it consists of *juxtaposited* parts. But I hope by this I have abundantly satisfied this third difficulty.

SECT. XXXII.

An Answer to the fourth Objection as much as respects the HOLENMERIANS *and* NULLIBISTS, *and all those that acknowledge that the* Matter *is created of God.*

IV. Let us go on therefore to the Fourth and last, which from the *Penetrability* of a *Spirit* concludes its unfitness for moving of Matter. For it cannot move Matter, but by impelling it; nor can it impel it, because it does so easily, without all resistence, *penetrate* it. Here therefore again, *Imagination* plays her tricks, and measures the nature of a *Spirit* by the Laws of Matter, fancying a *Spirit* like some *Body* passing through an over-large or wide hole, where it cannot stick by the reason of the laxness of the passage.

But in the mean time, it is to be noted, that neither the *Holenmerians* nor *Nullibists* can of right object this difficulty to us, whenas it is much more incredible that either a *Metaphysical Monad,* or any *Essence* that is *no where,* should be more fit for the moving Matter, than that which has some Amplitude, and is present also to the Matter that is to be moved. Wherefore we have now only to do with such Philosophers as contend that the whole Universe consists of Bodies only: For as for those that acknowledge there is a God and that Matter was created by him it is not hard for them to conceive, that there may be a certain faculty in the Soul, which in some manner, though very shadowishly, answers to that Power in God of creating Matter; Namely, that as God, though the most pure of all Spirits, yet creates Matter the most gross of all things; so created Spirits themselves may emit a certain *Material Vertue,* either spontaneously or naturally, by which they may intimately inhere in the Subject Matter, and be sufficiently close united therewith. Which faculty of Spirits the *Appendix to the Antidote against Atheism,* is called ὑλοπάθεια, the *Hylopathy* of *Spirits,* or a Power of affecting or being affected by the Matter. But I confess that Answer is less fitly used when we have to do with those who deny the Creating of Matter, and much more when with those that deny there is a God.

SECT. XXXIII.

An Answer to those that think there is nothing in the Universe but Matter *or* Body.

Wherefore, whenas we have to do with such infense Adversaries, and so much estranged from all knowledge and acknowledgment of *Incorporeal Things,* verily we ought to behave our selves very cautiously and circumspectly, and something more precisely to consider the Title of the Question, which is not, Whether we can accurately discern and declare the mode or way that a Spirit moves Matter, but whether its *Penetrability* is repugnant with this faculty of *moving* Matter. But now it is manifest, if a Spirit could be united and as it were cohere with the Matter, that it might easily move Matter; forasmuch as if there be at all any such thing as a Spirit, it is according to the common Opinion of all men to be acknowledged the true Principle and Fountain of all Life and Motion. Wherefore the hinge of the whole controversie turns upon this one Pin, Whether it be repugnant that any *Spirit* should be *united* and as it were *cohere* with *Matter*, or by whatever firmness or fastening. (whether permanent or momentaneous) be joyned therewith.

Now that it is not repugnant, I hope I shall clearly demonstrate from hence, that the *unition* of *Spirit* with *Matter*, is as intelligible as the *unition* of one *part* of *Matter* with *another*. For that ought in reason to be held and Axiom firm and sure, *That that is possible to be, in which there is found no greater* (nor to say less) *difficulty of so being, than in that which we really find to be.* But we see one part of Matter really and actually united with another, and that in some Bodies with a firmness almost invincible, as in some Stones and Metals, which are held to be the hardest of all Bodies. But we will for the more fully understanding the business, suppose a *Body* absolutely and perfectly *hard*, constituted of no Particles, but the very *Physical Monads* themselves, and without all Pores.

I ask therefore here, By what vertue, or by what manner of way do the parts of so perfect a *Solid* cohere? Undoubtedly they can alledge nothing here besides immediate *contract* and *rest:* For if they fly to any other affections which are allied to Life and Sense, they are more rightly and more easily understood to be in a *Spirit* than in *Matter;* and we will presently pronounce that a *Spirit* may adhere to *Matter* by the same vertues.

But that the *Parts* of *Matter* cohere by bare, tho' immediate contract, seems as difficult, if not more difficult, than that a *Spirit* penetrating *Matter* should cleave together into one with it: For the contract of the parts of *Matter* is every where only superficial, but one and the same *indiscerpible Spirit* penetrates and possesses the whole *Matter* at once.

Nor need we fear at all, that it will not inhere because it can so easily slide in, and therefore as it may seem, slide thro' and pass away.

For in a Body perfectly solid, suppose *A*, in which we will conceive some particular Superficies, suppose E, A, C; this Superficies E, A, C, is assuredly so glib and smooth, that there can be nothing imagined more smooth and glib, wherefore why does not the upper part of this solid Cube C, D, E, by any the slightest impulse slide upon the inferiour part of the Cube E, F, C, especially if the inferiour part E, F, C, be held fast, while the superior is impelled or thrust forward, surely this easiness of the sliding of Bodies perfectly smooth and glib,

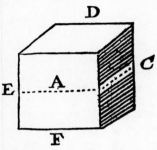

which touch immediately one another, their easiness I say, of sliding one upon another, does seem at least as necessary to our *Imagination,* as the proclivity of the passing of a Spirit through the Bodies it penetrates. Wherefore if two parts of *Matter,* suppose E, D, C, and E, F, C, which our Imagination doth most urgently suggest to us that they will always with the least impulse slide one upon another, do yet notwithstanding adhere to one another with a most firm and almost invincible Union, why may not then a Spirit, which our *Imagination* suspects will so easily pass through any Body, be united to a Body with equal firmness? whenas this is not more difficult than the other, yea rather much more easie if one would consider the thing as it is, laying aside all Prejudice. But now since the *Penetrability* of a Spirit is not repugnant with its *Union* with *Matter* it is manifest that its Faculty of moving Body is not at all repugnant with its *Penetrability.* Which is the thing that was to be demonstrated.

But it half repents me that I have with so great Preparation and Pomp attacked so small a Difficulty, and have striven so long with meer Elusions and prestigious Juggles of the *Imagination,* (which casts such a Mist of fictitious Repugnancies on the true Idea of a Spirit) as with so many Phantomes and Spectres of an unquiet Night. But in the mean time I have made it abundantly manifest, that there are no other Contradictions or Repugnancies in this our Notion of a Spirit, than what the Minds of our Adversaries polluted with the impure Dregs of *Imagination,* and unable to abstract *Metaphysical Extension* from *Cor-*

poreal Affections, do foully and slovenly clart upon it, and that this Idea lookt upon in it self does clearly appear to be a Notion at least of a thing *possible;* which is all that we drive at in this Place.

SECT. XXXIV.

How far the Notion of a Spirit *here defended is countenanced and confirmed by the common suffrage of all Adversaries.*

And that it may appear more plausible, we will not omit in the last place to take notice, how far it is countenanced and confirmed by the common suffrage of our Adversaries; For the *Hobbians,* and whatever other Philosophers else of the same Stamp, do plainly assent to us in this, That whatsoever really is, is of necessity *extended.* But that they hence infer that there is nothing in Nature but what is *Corporeal,* that truly they do very unskillfully and inconsequently collect, they by some weakness or morbidness of Mind tumbling into so foul an Error. For it is impossible that the Mind of Man, unless it were laden and polluted with the Dregs and Dross of *Corporeal Imagination,* should suffer it self to sink into such a gross and dirty Opinion.

But that every thing that is, is extended, the *Nullibists* also themselves seem to me to be near the very point of acknowledging it for true and certain, for they do not dissemble it, but that if a *Spirit* be *somewhere,* it necessarily follows that it is also *extended.* And they moreover grant, that by its *Operation* it is present to or in the *Matter,* and that the *Essence* of a *Spirit* is not *separated* from its *Operations.*

But that a thing should be, and yet not be any where in the whole Universe, is so wild and mad a Vote, and so absonous and abhorrent from all reason, that it cannot be said by any Man in his Wits, unless by way of Sport, or some slim Jest, as I have intimated above; whence their case is the more to be pittied, who captivated and blinded with admiration of the chief Author of so absurd an Opinion, do so solemnly and seriously embrace, and diligently endeavour to polish the same.

And lastly, as for the *Holenmerians,* those of them who are more cautious and considerate, do so explain their Opinion, that it scarce seems to differ an hairs breadth from ours. For they affirm that the Soul is in every part, yet they say they understand it not of the *Quantity* or *Extension* of the Soul, whereby it occupies the whole Body, but of the *perfection* of its *Essence* and *Vertue*, which however true it may be of the *Soul*, it is most undoubtedly true of the *Divine Numen*, whose Life and Essence is most perfect and most full every where, as being such as every where contains *infinite Goodness, Wisdom,* and *Power.*

Thus we see that this Idea or Notion of a Spirit which is here exhibited to the World, is not only *possible* in itself, but very *plausible* and *unexceptionable,* and such as all *Parties,* if they be rightly understood, will be found whether they will or no to contribute to the discovery of the Truth and Solidity thereof, and therefore is such as will not unusefully nor seasonably conclude this first Part of *Saducismus Triumphatus,* which treats of the *Possibility* of *Apparitions* and *Witchcraft,* but make the way more easie to the acknowledgment of the force of the Arguments of the Second Part, *viz.* The many *Relations* that are produced to prove the *Actual Existence* of Spirits and Apparitions.

APPENDIX

BIBLIOGRAPHY.
OUTLINE SUMMARY.
NOTES.

A. CRITICAL AND HISTORICAL, FOLLOWING THE ORDER OF THE OUTLINE.

B. EXPLANATORY AND BIBLIOGRAPHICAL, ON THE TEXT AS HERE REPRINTED.

BIBLIOGRAPHY

BIBLIOGRAPHY

In cases where books given in this bibliography are not directly known to the editor the authority on which they are included is indicated. The edition given is the one referred to in the introduction or in the notes. Where more than one edition is listed the one used for references is marked *. When it has seemed advisable for the convenience of the reader the date of the original publication has been given, in square brackets, as well as that of the edition to which reference is made. It has not always been possible to identify the edition used in references in More's text, but the references as given in the reprinted text have been verified unless a statement to the contrary is made in the notes.

I. The Works of Henry More.

This bibliography of More's writings has been compiled by Margaret W. Landes, sometime Hallowell Fellow at Wellesley College. Miss Landes has also contributed to Parts II and IV of the bibliography. The effort has been made to include all the editions of all books and essays written by More, but it is possible that on account of the abundance of his published works some of the slighter and more occasional writings may have escaped unnoted. The initials following the place and date of each book listed indicate certain libraries in which the book may be found. This list is not intended to be exhaustive, but is given for the possible convenience of the reader. It includes the libraries of Harvard University (Harv.), Yale University (Y.U.), University of Toronto (T.), Columbia University (C.), and Wellesley College (W.), the Public Library (B.P.L.) and the Athenaeum Library (Athen.) of Boston, Mass., the Public Library of New York City (N.Y.P.), and the British Museum Catalogue (B.M.).

BIBLIOGRAPHY

HENRY MORE, 1614–1687.

1642. ψυχωδια Platonica; or, a platonicall song of the soul, consisting of foure severall poems; viz. ψυχωξωια. ψυχαθανασια. 'Αντεψυχαπαννυχια. 'Αντιμονοψυχια. Hereto is added a paraphrasticall interpretation of the answer of Apollo, consulted by Amelius, about Plotinus soul departed this life. By H[enry] M[ore], Master of Arts, &c. 3 pt. Cambridge, 1642. B.M. Harv. C. Contents: Psychozoia. Psychothanasia. Antipsychothanasia. Antimonopsychia.

1646. Democritus Platonissans; or, an essay upon the infinity of worlds out of Platonick principles. Hereunto is annexed Cupid's Conflict, together with the Philosopher's Devotion. [In verse.] Cambridge, 1646. B.M.

1647. Philosophical Poems, etc. [An addition of some few smaller poems, etc.] Cambridge, R. Daniel, 1647. 436pp. B.M. B.P.L. Harv. C. N.Y.P.

—— Second edition. Cambridge, Printed by Roger Daniel, printer to the University, 1647. [28], 436pp. Y.U. N.Y.P. Contents: A Platonick Song of the Soul, Cambridge, 1647. Democritus Platonissans, Cambridge, 1647. The Praeexistence of the Soul, Cambridge, 1647. An addition of some few smaller poems, Cambridge, 1647. [The pagination is continuous, but each work has a separate title-page.]

—— [Second edition] The Complete Poems of Dr. H. More, now for the first time collected and edited . . . By . . . A. B. Grosart. xlvii, 244pp. (In Grosart, A. B. The Chertsey Worthies' Library, [Blackburn?] 1876.) B.M. B.P.L. C.

*—— [Same. Edinburgh] 1878. xlvii, 224pp. (In Grosart, A. B. The Chertsey Worthies' Library. [Edinburgh] Printed for private circulation, 1878.) Athen. Y.U. W. T. Contents: Same as for second edition, 1647, given above.

1650. Observations upon Anthroposophia Theomagica and Anima Magica abscondita [by Eugenius Philalethes, i.e., T. Vaughan]. By Alazonomastix Philalethes, [i.e., Henry More] O. Pullen: Parrhesia [London], 1650. 94pp. B.M. Harv.

—— [Another edition] (In his Enthusiasmus Triumphatus. London, 1656. pp.63-148) [Has separate title-page: London, 1655.] B.M. Harv.

1651. The Second Lash of Alazonomastix; conteining a solid and serious reply to a very uncivill answer to certain Observations upon Anthroposophia Theomagica, and Anima Magica Abscondita. Printed by the Printers to the University of Cambridge: [Cambridge,] 1651. 208pp. B.M. Harv.

—— [Another edition] (*In his* Enthusiasmus Triumphatus. London, 1656. pp.149–298) [Has separate title-page: London, 1655.] B.M. Harv.

1652. An Antidote against Atheisme, or an Appeal to the Natural Faculties of the Minde of Man, whether there be not a God. London, 1652. Harv.

—— [Same] London, 1653. B.M.

—— Second edition, corrected and enlarged; with an appendix thereunto annexed. London, 1655. B.M. C.

* —— The third edition, corrected and enlarged: with an Appendix thereunto annexed. . . . London, 1662. (*In his* Collection of Several Philosophical Writings, second edition. London, Printed by James Flesher, for William Morden, Book-seller in Cambridge, 1662.) B.M. Harv. W. Y.U.

—— [Another edition] Londini, 1679. (*In his* Opera Omnia, 3v. Londini, 1675–79. v.3) Athen. B.M. B.P.L. Y.U.

—— The fourth edition, corrected and enlarged: with an Appendix thereunto annexed, London, 1712. (*In his* Collection of Several Philosophical Writings, fourth edition, corrected. London, 1712) B.M. Harv. Y.U. N.Y.P.

1653. Conjectura Cabbalistica: or, a conjectural essay of interpreting the minde of Moses according to a threefold Cabbala, *viz.*, literal, philosophical, mystical or, divinely moral. (The defence of the threefold Cabbala) [Dedicated to Dr. Ralph Cudworth.] London, J. Flesher, 1653. 251pp. B.M. Harv. C.

* —— [Another edition] London, 1662. (*In his* Collection of Several Philosophical Writings, second edition. London, 1662) B.M. Harv. W. Y.U.

—— [Another edition] Londini, 1679. (*In his* Opera Omnia, 3 vol. Londini, 1675–79. v.3) Athen. B.M. Y.U.

—— [Another edition] London, 1713. (*In his* Collection of Several Philosophical Writings, fourth edition, corrected. London, 1712) B.M. Harv. Y.U.

1656. Enthusiasmus triumphatus; or, A discourse of the nature, causes, kinds and cure of enthusiasme; written by Philophilus Parresiastes [*pseud., i.e.*, Henry More], and prefixed to Alazonomastix his Observations and reply. London, 1656. B.M. Harv.

* —— [Another edition] London, 1662. (*In his* Collection of Several Philosophical Writings, second edition. London, 1662) B.M. Harv. W. Y.U. N.Y.P.

—— [Another edition] Londini, 1679. (*In his* Opera Omnia, 3 vol. Londini, 1675–79. v.3) Athen. B.M. Y.U.

—— [Another edition] London, 1712. (*In his* Collection of

Several Philosophical Writings, fourth edition, corrected. London, 1712) B.M. Harv. Y.U.

1659. The Immortality of the Soul, so farre forth as it is demonstrable from the knowledge of nature and the light of reason. London, 1659. B.M.

* —— [Another edition] London, 1662. (*In his* Collection of Several Philosophical Writings, second edition. London, 1662) B.M. Harv. W. Y.U. N.Y.P.

—— [Another edition] Londini, 1679. (*In his* Opera Omnia, 3 vol. Londini, 1675–79. v.3) Athen. B.M. Y.U.

—— [Another edition] London, 1712. (*In his* Collection of Several Philosophical Writings, fourth edition, corrected. London, 1712) B.M. Harv. Y.U.

1660. An Explanation of the grand Mystery of Godliness; or, a true and faithfull representation of the Everlasting Gospel of our Lord and Saviour Jesus Christ the onely begotten Son of God and Sovereign over Men and Angels. . . . London, Printed by J. Flesher, for W. Morden, Bookseller in Cambridge, 1660. xxx, 546, [28]pp. B.M. Y.U.

* —— [Another edition] Londini, 1674. (*In his* Opera Omnia, 3 vol. Londini, 1675–79. v.1) Athen. B.M. Y.U.

—— Tetractys Anti-Astrologica; or, the four chapters in the explanation of the Grand Mystery of Godliness, which contain a . . . confutation of Judiciary Astrology. With annotations . . . wherein the wondrous weaknesses of John Butler his answer, called A Vindication of Astrology, *etc.*, are laid open, *etc.* London, 1681. Note: This is a reprint of Bk. VII, ch. XIV–XVII of "An Explanation of the Grand Mystery of Godliness." B.M.

—— [Another edition] (*In his* Theological Works. . . . London, 1708) B.M. Y.U.

1660. Free-Parliament proposed to tender consciences; and published for the use of the members now elected. By Alazonomastix Philalethes, [*i.e.*, Henry More]. [London] 1660. B.M.

1662. * A Collection of several philosophical writings of Dr. Henry More, Fellow of Christ's Colledge in Cambridge, as namely, his Antidote against Atheism. Appendix to the said Antidote. Enthusiasmus Triumphatus. Letters to Des-Cartes, &c. Immortality of the Soul. Conjectura Cabbalistica. The second edition more correct and much enlarged. . . . London, Printed by James Flesher, for William Morden, Bookseller in Cambridge, 1662. Note: Each work is paged separately. B.M. W. Y.U. T. N.Y.P.

—— The fourth edition, corrected, and much enlarged. . . . London, Printed by Joseph Downing in Bartholemew-Close near West Smithfield, 1712. Note: Each work has separate title-page

and pagination. The date of the last two works is 1713. B.M.
Y.U. C. N.Y.P.

1662. * Henrici Mori Epistolae quatuor ad Renatum Des-Cartes: cum
Responsis Clarissimi Philosophi ad duas priores, cumque aliis
aliquot Epistolis, quarum Occasiones, Argumenta, Ordinem versa
pagina tibi commonstrabit. Londini, 1662. (*In his* Collection
of Several Philosophical Writings, second edition. London, 1662)
B.M. Harv. W. Y.U. N.Y.P.

—— [Another edition] Londini, 1679. (*In his* Opera Omnia,
3 vol. Londini, 1675–79. v.3) Athen. B.M. Y.U.

—— [Another edition] Londini, 1712. (*In his* Collection of
Several Philosophical Writings, fourth edition, corrected. London,
1712) B.M. Harv. Y.U. N.Y.P.

1662. Epistola H. Mori ad V. C. [William Coward] quae apologiam
complectitur pro Cartesis, quaeque introductionis loco esse
poterit ad universam philosophiam Cartesianam. (*In his* Collection of Several Philosophical Writings. London, 1662.)

—— [Another edition]. (*In his* Enchiridion Ethicum. Editio
secunda. 2pt. Londini, 1669) Athen. B.M.

—— [Another edition] Londini, 1679. (*In his* Opera Omnia, 3
vol. Londini, 1675–79. v.2) Athen. B.M. B.P.L. Y.U.

—— [Another edition]. (*In his* Enchiridion Ethicum. Editio
nova. Amstelodami, apud Jacobum de Zetter, 1679, pp.215–264)
B.M. B.P.L. Y.U.

—— [Another edition] (*In his* Enchiridion Ethicum. Editio
nova. Amstelodami, 1695, pp.261–321) B.M. B.P.L. Harv.

—— [Another edition] (*In his* Enchiridion Ethicum. Editio
quarta. Londini, J. Downing, 1711) Athen. B.P.L. Harv.

1664. * A modest Enquiry into the Mystery of Iniquity, *etc.* (The
Apology of Dr. H. More. Wherein is contained . . . a more
general account of the manner and scope of his writings, *etc.*
2 pt. London, 1664.) B.M. B.P.L. Harv. W. N.Y.P.

—— [Another edition] Londini, 1674. (*In his* Opera Omnia,
3 vol. Londini, 1675–79. v.1) Athen. B.M. Y.U.

—— [Another edition] (*In his* Theological Works. . . . London,
1708) B.M. Y.U.

1667. Enchiridion Ethicum, praecipua Moralis Philosophiae Rudimenta
complectens, illustrata ut plurimum Veterum Monumentis, et ad
Probitatem Vitae perpetuo accomodata. London [?] 1667.
Athen.

—— [Another edition] Londini, Excudebat J. Flesher, venale
autem habetur apud Guilielmum Morden Bibliopolam Canta
brigiensem, 1668. [14], 229pp. Y.U. C.

—— Editio secunda; cui accessit autoris epistola ad V.C. (quae
apologiam complectitur pro Cartesio, *etc.*) 2pt. Londini, 1669.
Athen. B.M. C.

—— Editio tertia: cui accessit Autoris Epistola ad V.C. Londini, 1679. (*In his* Opera Omnia, 3 vol. Londini, 1675–79. v.2) Athen. B.M. B.P.L. Y.U.

——Editio nova: cui accessit auctoris epistola ad V.C. Amstelodami, apud Jacobum de Zetter, 1679. B.M. B.P.L. Y.U.

—— Editio nova. Amstelaedami, 1695. B.M. B.P.L. Harv. C.

—— [Another edition?] 1696. (Dictionary of National Biography)

—— Editio quarta: cui accesserunt Scholia, una cum autoris epistola ad V.C. Londini, J. Downing, 1711. Athen. B.P.L. Harv.

1668. *Divine Dialogues, containing sundry disquisitions & instructions concerning the attributes of God and his providence in the World. Collected and compiled by . . . Franciscus Palaeopolitanus. [By Henry More. The Epistle is signed, Fr. Euistor] 2 pt. London, 1668. Athen. B.M. Harv. W.

—— [Another edition] Londini, 1679. (*In his* Opera Omnia, 3 vol. Londini, 1675–79. v.2, 3) Athen. B.M. B.P.L. Y.U.

—— [Second edition] Whereunto is annexed a brief discourse of the true grounds of the certainty of faith in points of religion. . . . The second edition . . . London, Printed and sold by Joseph Downing in Bartholemew-Close near West Smithfield, 1713. xxxii, 621pp. The address of "the Publisher to the Reader" is signed: G.C. B.M. B.P.L. Harv. Y.U.

—— [Another edition] 3 vol. Glasgow, 1743. Note: The pagination is continuous throughout the three volumes. B.M. B.P.L.

1668. A brief discourse of the true grounds of the certainty of faith in points of religion. (*Appended to his* Divine Dialogues, *etc.* London, 1668. II.) Athen. B.M. Harv. W.

—— [Another edition] Londini, 1674. (*In his* Opera Omnia, 3v. Londini, 1675–79. v.1) Athen. B.M. Y.U.

—— [Another edition] (*In his* Theological Works . . . London, 1708) B.M. Y.U.

—— [Another edition?] (*Appended to his* Divine Dialogues, *etc.* Second edition. London, 1713) B.M.

1669. An Exposition of the Seven Epistles to the Seven Churches; together with a brief discourse of idolatry, with application to the Church of Rome. London, 1669. B.M. N.Y.P.

—— [Another edition] Londini, 1674. (*In his* Opera Omnia, 3 vol. Londini, 1675–79. v.1) Athen. B.M. Y.U.

—— [Another edition] (*In his* Theological Works . . . London, 1708) B.M. Y.U.

1670. Philosophiae Teutonicae Censura. 1670.

*——[Another edition] Londini, 1679. (*In his* Opera Omnia, 3 vol. Londini, 1675–79. v.2) Athen. B.M. B.P.L. Y.U.

1671. * Enchiridion metaphysicum: sive, De Rebus Incorporeis Succincta & luculenta Dissertatio. Pars Prima: De Existentia & Natura Rerum Incorporearum in Genere. In qua quamplurima Mundi Phaenomena ad Leges *Cartesii* Mechanicas obiter expenduntur, illiúsque Philosophiae, & aliorum omnino omnium qui Mundana Phaenomena in Causas purè Mechanicas solvi posse supponunt, Vanitas Falsitasque detegitur. Per H.M. Cantabrigiensem . . . Londini, typis E. Flesher; prostat apud Guilielmum Morden, 1671. Athen. Harv. W. C.

——[Another edition] Londini, 1679. (*In his* Opera Omnia, 3 vol. Londini, 1675–79. v.2) Athen. B.M. B.P.L. Y.U.

1672. A brief Reply to a late Answer to . . . H. More his Antidote against Idolatry. [Together with the text of the "Antidote."] Shewing that there is nothing in the said Answer that does any ways weaken his proofs of idolatry against the Church of Rome, *etc.* (An Appendix to the late Antidote against Idolatry, *etc.*) London, 1672, 73. Athen. B.M.

—— [Another edition] Londini, 1674. (*In his* Opera Omnia, 3 vol. Londini, 1675–79. v.1) Athen. B.M. Y.U.

1674. Antidotus adversus Idolatriam: sive Dissertatio brevis multa complectens Theoremata ad dignoscendum quid sit haberive debeat Idolatria apud Christianos apprime utilia. Cum applicatione ad Doctrinam Concilii Tridentini ad sistendam, quantum fieri potest, Contagionem Romanam. . . . Londini, typis J. Macock. . . . 1674. (*In his* Opera Omnia, 3v. Londini, 1675–79. v.1) Athen. B.M. Y.U.

—— [Another edition] An Antidote against Idolatry: or, A brief discourse containing sundry considerations & conclusions tending to the discovery of what is or ought to be held to be Idolatry amongst Christians. With application to the doctrine of the Council of Trent, and for the putting a stop as much as may be to the Romish infection . . . n.p., n.d. (*In his* Theological Works, London, 1708) B.M. Y.U.

1675. De Anima ejusque Facultatibus. London, 1675. B.M.

—— [Another edition] Roter., 1677. Note: The same was also previously published in English. A refutation of the Cartesian hypothesis. B.M.

1675. * H. Mori Cantabrigiensis Opera Omnia, tum quae Latine, tum quae Anglice scripta sunt; nunc vero Latinitate donata. 3 vol. Londini, Typis J. Macock, imprensis J. Martyn & Gualt. Kettilby, 1675–79. fol. B.M. Athen. B.P.L. Y.U.

The following note appears in the British Museum catalogue: " The title given above is from the title-page of vol 2. That of vol. 1 runs thus: 'H. Mori . . . Opera Theologica,' that of vol. 3: 'H. Mori . . . Scriptorum Philosophicorum Tomus alter.'" The "contents" as given below are taken from the Yale University Library copy. The volume numbering of this set as it appears in the table of contents for the three volumes in vol. 2, and on the binding of the three volumes, does not correspond to that used by the British Museum, which follows the chronological order, regarding the volume of the theological works (1675) as vol. 1 of the set, instead of vol. 3 as indicated in the table of contents in vol. 2. The British Museum order is adopted in listing the contents below. What is apparently a reprint of the volume of theological works appeared in 1700. This, however, may have been merely a re-issue of the original sheets with a new general title-page.

Contents: V.I. Visionum Apocalypticarum . . . Londini, 1674. Magni Mysterii Pietatis Explanatio. Londini, 1674. Modesta Inquisitio in Mysterium Iniquitatis, Pars prior. Londini, 1674. Synopsis Prophetica: sive Inquisitionis in Mysterium Iniquitatis, Pars posterior . . . Londini, 1674. Expositio Prophetica Septem Epistolarum ad Septem Ecclesias Asiaticas. Londini, 1674. De Veris Rationibus sive Fundamentis Certitudinis Fidei in Rebus religionis. Londini, 1674. Antidotus adversus Idolatriam. Londini, 1674. Nuperi Antidoti adversus Idolatriam, Appendix. Londini, 1674. Divinorum Hymnorum Heptachordon. Londini, 1674. Carmina quædam in scriptis & Philosophicis Anglicè occurrentia et hîc per Autorem Latinè reddita. [n.p., n.d.] V.2. Enchiridion Ethicum, editio tertia. Londini, 1679. Epistolae H. Mori ad V.C. quae apologiam complectitur pro Cartesio, quaeque introductionis loco esse poterit ad universam philosophiam cartesiam. . . . Ed. quarta, omnium correctissima. Londini, 1679. Enchiridion Metaphysicum. . . . Pars prima: De Existentia & Natura. Londini, 1679. Philosophematum eruditi Authoris Difficilium Nugarum. Londini, 1679. Adnotamenta in duas ingeniosas Dissertationes: alteram, tentamen de Gravitatione et non-gravitatione corporum fluidorum. . . . Londini, 1679. Trium Tabularum Cabbalisticarum. . . . Londini, 1679. Quaestiones et Considerationes paucae brevésque in Tractatum Primum Libri Druschim. Londini, 1679. Visionis Ezechielis. . . . Londini, 1679. Catechismus Cabbalisticus. Londini, 1679. Fundamenta Philosophiae. . . . Londini, 1679. Philosophiae Teutonicae Censura. Londini, 1679. Ad V. C. Epistola Altera. Londini, 1679. Demonstrationis duarum Praepositionum . . . quae praecipuae apud Spinozium Atheismi sunt Columnae, brevis solidáque Confutatio. [n.p., n.d.] Dialogi Divini . . . Tres Primi Dialogi, qui de Attributis Dei tractant ejúsque Providentia in Genere. Londini, 1679. V.3. Antidotus adversus Atheismum. Londini, 1679. Antecedentis Antidoti adversus Atheismum, Appendix. Londini, 1679. Enthusiasmus Triumphatus. Londini, 1679. . . . Epistolae quatuor ad Renatum Des-Cartes. Londini, 1679. Immortalitas Animae. Londini, 1679. Conjectura Cabbalistica. Londini, 1679. Ad Defensionem Cabbalæ Philosophicæ Appendix [n.p., n.d.] Dialogorum Divinorum, postremi duo . . . qui tractant de Regno Dei. Londini, 1679.

1676. Remarks upon two late ingenious Discourses [by Sir Matthew Hale]; the one, an Essay, touching the Gravitation and non-Gravitation of Fluid Bodies; the other, touching the Torricellian experiment, so far forth as they may concern any passages in his "Enchiridion Metaphysicum." London, 1676. B.M.
—— [Another edition] Londini, 1679. (*In his* Opera Omnia, 3 vol. Londini, 1675–79. v.2) Athen. B.M. B.P.L. Y.U.

1677. Ad clarissimum . . . virum N.N. De rebus in amica sua responsione contentis ulterior disquisitio. (*In* Kabbala denudata seu doctrina Hebraeorum transcendentalis et metaphysica atque theologica. Opus antiquissimae philosophiae barbaricae variis speciminibus refertissimum, *etc.* [Edited by C. Knorr de Rosenroth] 2 tom. Sulzbaci, Francofurti, 1677, 84. Tom. 1, pt. 2, 1677, *etc.*) B.M.

1677. Aditus tentatus rationem reddendi nominum et ordinis decem Sephirotharum in duabus Tabulis Cabbalisticis ex Scriptura, Platonismo, rationeque libra. (*In* Kabbala denudata . . . 2 tom. Sulzbaci, Francofurti, 1677, 84. Tom. 1, pt. 2, 1677, *etc.*) B.M.

1677. Fundamenta philosophiae, sive Cabbalae Aëto-paedomelissaeae, *etc.* (*In* Kabbala denudata . . . 2 tom. Sulzbaci, Francofurti, 1677, 84. Tom. 1, pt. 2, 1677, *etc.*) B.M.
—— [Another edition] Londini, 1679. (*In his* Opera Omnia, 3 vol. Londini, 1675–79. v. 2) Athen. B.M. B.P.L. Y.U.

1677. Quaestiones et considerationes paucae brevésque in Tractatum primum libri Druschim. (*In* Kabbala denudata. . . 2 tom. Sulzbaci, Francofurti, 1677, 84. Tom. 1, pt. 2, 1677, *etc.*) B.M.
—— [Another edition] Londini, 1679. (*In his* Opera Omnia, 3 vol. Londini, 1675–79. v. 2) Athen. B.M. B.P.L. Y.U.

1677. Visionis Ezechieliticae, sive Mercavae expositio. (*In* Kabbala denudata. . . . 2 tom. Sulzbaci, Francofurti, 1677, 84. Tom. 1, pt. 2, 1677, *etc.*) B.M.
—— [Another edition] Londini, 1679. (*In his* Opera Omnia, 3 vol. Londini, 1675–79. v. 2) Athen. B.M. B.P.L. Y.U.

1680. Apocalypsis Apocalypseos; or the Revelation of St. John the Divine unveiled. Containing a brief but perspicuous and continued exposition from chapter to chapter, and from verse to verse, of the whole Book of the Apocalypse. By Henry More. [With the text] Printed by J. M., for J. Martyn and W. Kettilby, London, 1680. xxxi, 358 pp. Athen. B.M.

1681. An Answer to a letter of a learned psychopyrist concerning the true notion of a spirit. (*In* Glanvill, J. Saducismus triumphatus. London, 1681) B.M. Harv. W. Y.U. C. N.Y.P.
—— [Another edition] (*In* Glanvill, J. Saducismus triumphatus. London, 1682) Harv.
—— [Another edition] (*In* Glanvill, J. Saducismus triumphatus. London, 1689.) B.M. Harv.

—— * [Another edition] (*In* Glanvill, J. Saducismus triumphatus, London, 1700) W.

—— [Another edition] (*In* Glanvill, J. Saducismus triumphatus. London, 1726) B.M. B.P.L. Harv. N.Y.P.

1681. A continuation of [Joseph Glanvill's] collection: or, An addition of some few more stories of apparitions and witchcraft. (*In* Glanvill, J. Saducismus triumphatus. London, 1681) B.M. Harv. W. Y.U. C. N.Y.P.

—— [Another edition] (*In* Glanvill, J. Saducismus triumphatus. London, 1682) Harv.

—— [Another edition] (*In* Glanvill, J. Saducismus triumphatus. London, 1726) B.M. B.P.L. Harv. N.Y.P.

1681. The easie, true and genuine notion and explication of the nature of a spirit. [Translated from the Enchiridion Metaphysicum, Bk. I, ch. 27 & 28] (*In* Glanvill, J. Saducismus triumphatus. London, 1681. I, 97–180) B.M. Harv. Y.U. C. N.Y.P.

—— [Another edition] (*In* Glanvill, J. Saducismus triumphatus. London, 1682) Harv.

—— [Another edition] (*In* Glanvill, J. Saducismus triumphatus. London, 1689) B.M. Harv.

—— * The third edition with additions. (*In* Glanvill, J. Saducismus triumphatus. London, 1700) W.

—— [Another edition] (*In* Glanvill, J. Saducismus triumphatus. London, 1726) B.M. B.P.L. Harv. N.Y.P.

1681. A Plain and continued Exposition of the several Prophecies or Divine Visions of the Prophet Daniel, which have or may concern the People of God, whether Jew or Christians. London, 1681. Athen. N.Y.P.

1682. Two choice and useful treatises: the one Lux Orientalis, or an Enquiry into the opinion of the Eastern Sages concerning the praeexistence of souls . . . (by Joseph Glanvill) The other a Discourse of Truth by . . . Dr Rust . . . With annotations on them both [by H. More] 2 pt. London, Printed for James Collins and Sam. Lowndes over against Exeter Exchange in the Strand, 1682. [42], 195, [5] pp. [Annotations by More: 276pp.] C. N.Y.P.

1684. Answer to " Remarks upon his Expositions of the Apocalypse and Daniel, *etc.,* by S. E. Mennonite "; annexed, Arithmetica apocalyptica, and Appendicula apocalyptica. London, 1684. Athen.

1685. An Illustration of those two abstruse books . . . the Book of Daniel, and the Revelation of S. John, [with the text,] by continued. . . notes. . . with. . . arguments prefixed to each Chapter; framed out of the Expositions of Dr. H. More. London, 1685. Athen. B.M.

1685. Paralipomena Prophetica; containing several supplements and defences of Dr. H. More; his Expositions of the Prophet Daniel and the Apocalypse. . . . Whereunto is also added, Philicrines upon R[ichard] B[axter] his Notes on the Revelation of St. John. 2 pt. London, 1685. Athen. B.M.

1686. A brief Discourse of the Real Presence of the Body and Blood of Christ in the celebration of the Holy Eucharist: wherein the witty artifices of the Bishop of Meaux and of Monsieur Maimbourg are obviated, whereby they would draw in the Protestants to imbrace the doctrine of Transubstantiation, [By H. More] London, 1686. B.M. N.Y.P.

—— Second edition. London, 1686. xi, 86pp. B.M. Harv. Y.U.

1688. Letters philosophical and moral between [John Norris] and Dr. H. More. (*In* Norris, John. The theory and regulation of love. A moral essay. In two parts. To which are added letters philosophical and moral between the author and Dr. H. More. Oxford, 1688) B.M.

—— [Same] (*In* Norris, John. The theory and regulation of love . . . Second edition. London, 1694, pp.121–201.) C. B.M.

1690. An account of virtue: or, Dr. Henry More's abridgment of morals, put into English [by Edward Southwell] London, Tooke, 1690. [16], 268pp. B.M. B.P.L.

1692. Discourses on several texts of Scripture. By the late . . . H. More [Edited by J. Worthington] London, 1692. Athen. B.M.

1694. Letters on several subjects. With several other letters. To which is added, by the publisher, two letters . . . and . . . other discourses. Publish'd by . . . E. Elys. London, 1694. B.M.

1704. A Collection of Aphorisms, in two parts. London, 1704. B.M. N.Y.P.

1706. Divine Hymns. Upon the Nativity, Passion, Resurrection, and Ascension of our Lord . . . Jesus Christ. London, 1706. B.M.

1708. The Theological Works of the most pious and learned Henry More, D.D. Sometimes Fellow of Christ's College in Cambridge. . . . According to the author's improvements in his Latin edition. London, Printed and sold by Joseph Downing in Bartholemew-Close near West Smithfield, 1708. xiv, 856pp. B.M. Y.U. Contents: An Explanation of the Grand Mystery of Godliness. An Enquiry into the Mystery of Iniquity. In two parts. A Prophetical Exposition of the Epistles to the Seven Churches in Asia. A Discourse of the Grounds of Faith in Points of Religion. An Antidote against Idolatry. To which are adjoin'd, some Divine Hymns.

1710. Select letters written upon several occasions. (*In* Ward, Richard. Life of More. London, 1710) B.M. Harv. Y.U. C.

1819. Select sermons. (*In* Wesley, John. A Christian Library, consisting of Extracts from the Abridgements of the choicest pieces of Practical Divinity which have been publish'd in the English Tongue. 30 v. London, 1819–27. v. 23, 1819, *etc.*) B.M.

1819. Specimen. (*In* Campbell, T. Specimens of British poets, v. 4, 1819) Athen.

1837. Extracts from letters of More in Thomas Birch's "Account of the Life and Writings of " R. Cudworth. (*In* Cudworth, Ralph. The true Intellectual System of the Universe. . . . First American edition: with . . . an account of the life and writings of the author, by Thomas Birch. Andover, 1837–38. 2v. v. 1, 1837) Y.U.

—— [Another edition] (*In* Cudworth, R. True Intellectual System of the Universe. London, 1845. 3v. v. 1, 1845) Y.U.

1847. Letters from More to Dr. Worthington. (*In* Worthington, John, The Diary and Correspondence of Dr. John Worthington, [Manchester] 1847–1886. 2v. in 3. [Chetham Society, v. 13, 36, 114.] Athen. B.M. B.P.L. Harv. Y.U.

II. RELATED CONTEMPORARIES.

This list is intended to include (1) the philosophical writings of the latter part of the seventeenth century with which it is reasonable to suppose that More was familiar, (2) those in which definite reference is made to More's own works, and (3) those to which reference is made in the introduction or notes of this volume. It is doubtless incomplete since the field is wide and indefinite in its boundaries. For a bibliography of the period, more complete in some directions than the one given here, the reader is referred to Sorley's *History of English Philosophy,* 1921.

A. *The Cambridge Platonists.*

The term "Cambridge Platonists " is slightly misleading since some of the men included in the group were of Oxford, some of no University, and some of those frequently included cannot be accurately classed as Platonic philosophers. The traditional expression has, however, a picturesque and suggestive value which is lost in a more accurate term. It serves moreover to indicate, even though with some degree of over-emphasis, the fact that the leading spirits among these English Platonists were fellows and masters at Cambridge. They found in Plato and Plotinus and in the Platonists of the Italian Renaissance the food for mind and spirit which they could not find in the arid and exhausted scholasticism of their time, in the harsh Calvinistic doctrine, or in the over-emphasized ritualism of Laud and his followers. For many of them the common ground is less that of agreement in philosophical conviction than that of a broad tolerance and a certain mellow kindliness of religion. For this reason, though some were Puritans or Calvinists, and some clung to the church party, they were at first called "Latitude Men " as a term of reproach for their laxity in matters of religious dogma.

On the authority of Bishop Burnet the English Platonism of the seventeenth century is usually attributed to Whichcote, who [says Burnet] " set young students much on reading the ancient philosophers, chiefly Plato, Tully, and Plotin." Birch, in the life of Cudworth contained in the second edition of the *True Intellectual System,* quotes this remark from Burnet but applies it inadvertently to More instead of to Whichcote. J. Bass Mullinger in the *Cambridge History of English Literature* claims the honor of introducing Platonism into English thought, for John Sherman's *A Greek in the Temple.* It seems hardly necessary, however, to trace the seventeenth century Platonism to the influence of any particular writer. This northern Renaissance, later and less luxuriant than the flowering in Italy, followed the same paths and partook of the same enthusiasms. Platonism had never entirely faded out of western thought, but had endured in many of the church doctrines and in the thought of the mystics through the centuries. The revival of Platonism in England which resulted from the labours of the Italian humanists is rather a conscious and reverent recognition of the source of the tradition and a keen sense of its opposition to the prevailing tendencies of thought than a distinctly new development.

Benjamin Whichcote is to be considered the founder of the Cambridge Platonist movement less by reason of his teaching any particular metaphysical doctrine than because of the wise and far-seeing religious tolerance which he introduced into the minds of many of his followers in that age of .fanaticism and bigotry. By the influence of a fine personality and a clear and unwavering sense of spiritual values he gathered about himself some of the finest spirits in the younger men of the University and turned their minds with his own from the controversies of the day to the consideration of the essential matters of truth and faith. John Smith developed the metaphysical implications of his leader's thought on the basis of Neo-Platonic conceptions. He differs from Cudworth and More mainly in that he asserts in calm unquestioned assurance those doctrines of the reality of the soul and its ability to find truth within itself which for the other two, writing in conscious opposition to Hobbes, are imminent issues to be argued with all the force and subtlety at their command.

The characteristic Platonic or Neo-Platonic doctrines which Smith and Cudworth and More held in common, and which are touched at one point or another by the other Cambridge Platonists, the doctrines of the world-soul, the reality of innate knowledge, the substantiality and immortality of the human soul, while forming the basis on which they were called Platonists, are less important, as bonds of connection between them, than their common feeling for the unity of the natural and the spiritual world and their sense of the intimate nearness of the spirit of God to the mind of man. Their aim was to combine the new knowledge of the Renaissance with the teachings of the Church Fathers and the wisdom of the Greeks, to reconstruct theology on a basis of reason, to separate scientific fact from materialistic implication, and to show forth a unity of faith and reason which should be indeed a "candle of the Lord." The wisdom which they sought was no cold and barren thing. It was that Platonic wisdom which is one with beauty and true holiness, the vision of the eternal.

For comparison in specific points of doctrine between More and some of the other Cambridge Platonists consult the index under Cudworth, Culverwell, Cumberland, Smith, and Whichcote. For biographical detail see the articles under the separate names in the *Dictionary of National Biography*, Tulloch, *Rational Theology*, Vol. II, Bishop Burnet, *History of His Own Times*, Worthington's *Diary*; for discussion of the philosophical background and of individual philosophical doctrines, see Tulloch, *op. cit.*, Lecky, *Rise and Influence of Rationalism in Europe*, Remusat, *Histoire de la philosophie en Angleterre depuis Bacon jusqu'a Locke*, Sorley, *History of English Philosophy*, E. A. George, *Seventeenth Century Men of Latitude*.

CAMPAGNAC, E. T. The Cambridge Platonists, being selections from the writings of Benjamin Whichcote, John Smith, and Nathanael Culverwell, with Introduction by E. T. Campagnac, Oxford, 1901.

CUDWORTH, RALPH. * The True Intellectual System of the Universe, The First Part. London, 1678.
The same, The Second Edition, with Account of the Life and Writings of the Author. By Thomas Birch. London, 1743.
A Treatise Concerning Eternal and Immutable Morality, 1731.

CULVERWELL, NATHANAEL. An Elegant and Learned Discourse of the Light of Nature. Oxford, 1669 [1652].

CUMBERLAND, RICHARD. De Legibus Naturae, Disquisitione Philosophica, 1672.

GALE, THEOPHILUS. The Court of the Gentiles, A Discourse touching the Original of Human Literature both Philologic and Philosophic. From the Scriptures and Jewish Church. Oxford, 1672. [1669] Philosophia Generalis, 1676. (Sorley, Hist. English Philosophy)

GALE, THOMAS. Opuscula Mythologica, Physica et Ethica. Amsterdam, 1688. [1671]

GLANVILL, JOSEPH. Lux Orientalis. London, 1661.
The Vanity of Dogmatizing: or Confidence in Opinions. London, 1661.
Scepsis Scientifica. 1665.
Essays on Several Important Subjects in Philosophy and Religion. London, 1676.
Saducismus Triumphatus: or full and plain evidence concerning witches and apparitions. With a letter of Dr. H. More. London, 1681. (Other editions, 1682, 1689, 1700, 1726).
A Whip for the Droll. In Saducismus Triumphatus, London, 1700.
Cf. Ferris Greenslet, Joseph Glanvill, New York, 1900.

Howe, John. The Living Temple. 1675.

Mede, Joseph. The Works of the Pious and Profoundly-Learned Joseph Mede, B.D. Sometime Fellow of Christ's College in Cambridge. Edited by John Worthington. London, 1672.

Patrick, Simon. A Brief Account of the new Sect of Latitude-Men. By S. P. 1662.
A Friendly Debate between a Conformist and a Non-conformist. London, 1669.
Advice to a Friend. by Symon Patrick, D.D. London. Printed in the year 1673. Reprinted for William Pickering, 1847.

Pordage, John. Theologia Mystica, or the Mystic Divinitie of the Aeternal Indivisible. By a Person of Qualitie. J.P.M.D. London. 1683.

Rust, George. A Discourse of the Use of Reason in Matters of Religion. Written in Latin by George Rust (1677) and Translated by H. Hallywell. With Dedication to Henry More. London, 1683.
A Discourse of Truth. 1682. With Annotations by H. More. Bound with Glanvill, Lux Orientalis.

Sherman, John. A Greek in the Temple. Some Commonplaces delivered in Trinity College Chappell. Cambridge, 1641.

Smith, John. Select Discourses. London, 1660.

Whichcote, Benjamin. Select Sermons. Edinburgh, 1742. [1698.]
Moral and Religious Aphorisms, collected from the manuscript papers of the Reverend and Learned Doctor Whichcote. Republished by Samuel Salter. London, 1753.

Worthington, John. Select Discourses. 1673.
Diary and Correspondence. Published for the Chetham Society, Manchester, 1847–1886.

B. *Descartes and the Cartesians.*

More's attitude toward Descartes and the Cartesian philosophy changes in the course of his writings from enthusiastic, almost reverential, admiration to absolute opposition and disdain. The first letter to Descartes, written in 1648, expresses unbounded enthusiasm both for Descartes himself and for his philosophical theories. "Omnes quotquot existiterunt, aut etiamnum existunt, Arcanorum Naturae Antistites, si ad magnificam tuam indolem comparentur, Pumilos plané videri ac Pygmeos." In the *Conjectura Cabbalistica* More still expresses his admiration for the "transcendent mechanical inventions" of Descartes, and argues that the Cartesian philosophy is "in a manner" the same as that of Democritus, and that it contains in itself the thoughts of Pythagoras and of Moses and the Egyptians. But even in the flush of his first enthusiasm for Descartes More had found some points in which he could not agree with him, although he insists that these are minor matters which do not affect the fundamental principles of Cartesianism.

In the later letters to Descartes, in the letter to Clerselier, and in the letter to V.C. on the Cartesian philosophy, More emphasizes more strongly these differences between his thought and that of Descartes, but still retains in large measure his early enthusiasm. In spite of the inability of the Cartesian philosophy to explain all the phenomena of nature he considers that it is of the greatest value both in the explanation of the laws of mathematics and physics and in the demonstration of the reality of spirit and the existence of God. In the Preface to the *Immortality of the Soul*, 1659, More writes that in his opinion " it is the most sober and faithful advice that can be offered to the Christian World, that they would encourage the reading of Des Cartes in all publick Schools and Universities, that the Students of Philosophy may be thoroughly exercised in the just extent of the Mechanical powers of Nature, how farre they will reach, and where they fall short." The Preface to the Collected Philosophical Writings, 1662, is the last of More's writings which retains any of the old enthusiasm for Descartes. In it he refers to the " interweaving of Platonism and Cartesianism " which characterizes his writings and apparently considers the two points of view as perfectly consistent with each other. He insists, however, on Descartes' failure to explain all the facts of nature by mechanical principles. In the *Divine Dialogue*, published six years later, not only is this opposition to the mechanical interpretation of nature more pronounced, but the tone of the reference to Descartes is changed. More here belittles his own previous admiration and suggests that all that is of value in Descartes's thought had been borrowed from the ancients, while its attempted explanations of nature on a basis of pure mechanism are " erroneously and ridiculously false." The *Enchiridion Metaphysicum*, 1671, is essentially an attempt to discredit the Cartesian explanation of natural phenomena and to refute the Cartesian identification of matter and space, with the purpose of establishing firmly the conception of the universe as informed and actuated throughout by spiritual force.

The introduction of Cartesian doctrines into England is attributed by Erdmann (*History of Philosophy*, II, 268) to Anthony Legrand, a Franciscan of Douai and a member of the Catholic mission to England. The *Institutiones Philosophiae* of Legrand, however, appeared in 1675, and the principles of Descartes's philosophy must have been well known, at least in the universities, before this time. More's Letter to V.C. containing an outline of the Cartesian philosophy, was published in 1669 in the *Enchiridion Ethicum*, one of his most popular works, and even in his *Philosophical Poems*, first published in 1642, there are frequent references to the opinions of " Monsieur des Chartes." James Bass Mullinger, in his History of Cambridge University (III, p. 606), ascribes the introduction of Descartes's ideas into England to John Allsopp, senior fellow of Christ's College, " who made the acquaintance of Descartes when abroad in the earlier years of the century." Mullinger gives as his authority Dr. Peile's *History of Christ's College*.

DESCARTES, RENÉ. Oeuvres de Descartes. Publieés par Charles Adam & Paul Tannery. Paris, 1897–1910.
The Philosophical Works of Descartes. Rendered into English by Elizabeth Haldane and G. T. Ross. Cambridge, 1911–1913.
Discourse on Method, Meditations and Selections from the Principles. Translated by J. Veitch. Everyman's Library.

DE LA FORGE, LOUIS. Traitté de L'Esprit de L'Homme. Suivant les Principes de René Descartes. Amsterdam, chez Abraham Wolfgang. (No date given.)

LEGRAND, ANTHONY. An Entire Body of Philosophy according to the Principles of the Famous Renate DesCartes. Written in Latin [1675], now carefully translated by Richard Blome. London, 1694.

MALEBRANCHE, N. De La Recherche de La Verité. Paris, Garnier Frères, 1675.
Entretiens sur la Métaphysique et sur la Religion, 1688.

REGIUS, HENRICUS. Henrici Regii Ultrajectini, Philosophia Naturalis. Amsterdam, apud Ludovicum Elzevirum, 1654.

VELTHUSIUS, LAMBERTUS. Tractatus de Initiis Primae Philosophiae. In Renati Des Cartes Meditationes de Prima Philosophia. Londini, 1664.

C. *Other contemporaries of More, including those to whom reference is made either in the text or in the notes and those in whose writings there is a large amount of direct reference to More.*

BAXTER, RICHARD. Of the Immortality of Man's Soul and the nature of it and other spirits; two discourses: one in a letter to an unknown doubter, the other in a reply to H. More's animadversions on a private letter to him; which he published in his Second edition of Mr. Joseph Glanvil's Saducismus Triumphatus, etc. London, 1682. (British Museum Catalogue.)

BEAUMONT, JOSEPH. Some Observations upon the Apologie of H. More for his Mystery of Godliness. Cambridge, 1665. [Sorley.]

BERKELEY, GEORGE. Collected Works. Edited by Alexander Campbell Fraser. Oxford, 1871.

BOYLE, ROBERT. Philosophical Works. 1725.
Tracts containing new Experiments touching the relation betwixt Flame and Air, and about Explosions. An hydrostatical discourse occasion'd by some objections of Dr. H. More in his Enchiridion Metaphysicum. London, 1672.

BURNET, GILBERT. History of his own Time. [1660–1713.] Oxford, 1833.

BURTHOGGE, RICHARD. An Essay upon Reason and the Nature of Spirits. London, 1694.
Organum Vetus & Novum. Or a Discourse of Reason and Truth. London, 1678.

Of the Soul of the World; and of Particular Souls. London, 1699.

* The Philosophical Writings of Richard Burthogge. Edited by Margaret W. Landes. Chicago, 1921.

BUTLER, JOHN. Ἀγιαστρολογια; or the most sacred and divine science of Astrology. I. Asserted, in three Propositions. II. Vindicated, against the calumnies of the Revd. Dr. More, in his Explanation of the Grand Mystery of Godliness. III. Excused, concerning pacts with evil spirits, as not guilty. London, 1680.

COLLIER, ARTHUR. Clavis Universalis. Edited by Ethel Bowman. Chicago, 1909. [1713.]

CONWAY, ANNE, COUNTESS OF. The Principles of the most Ancient and Modern Philosophy. London, 1692. (Ward, Life of More.)

COWARD, WILLIAM. The Grand Essay. Or a Vindication of Reason and Religion. By W. C. London, 1704.
The Just Scrutiny. Or a Serious Enquiry into Modern Notions of the Soul. By W. C. London, 1706.

DIGBY, SIR KENELM. Two Treatises: In the one of which The Nature of Bodies, In the other The Nature of Man's Soul, is looked into. London, 1658 [1644].

GASSENDI, PIERRE. Opera Omnia. Ed. Averano. Florence, 1727 [1658]. (*Cf.* G. S. Brett, The Philosophy of Gassendi. London, 1908.)

GLISSON, FRANCIS. Tractatus de Natura Substantia energetica. 1672. (Sorley.)

HERBERT, EDWARD, OF CHERBURY. De Veritate . . . Cui Operi additi sunt Duo alii tractatus: Primus, De Causis Errorum; Alter De Religione Laici. Londini, 1645.
Autobiography. London, 1670.
Cf. W. R. Sorley, The Philosophy of Lord Herbert of Cherbury, Mind, 1894.

HOBBES, THOMAS. The English Works of Thomas Hobbes of Malmesbury, collected and edited by Sir William Molesworth. London, 1839. [Humane Nature 1650, Leviathan 1651, De Corpore 1655, Opera Philosophica 1668]

LEIBNIZ, GOTTFRIED WILHELM. Die Philosophischen Schriften. Herausgegeben, von C. J. Gerhardt. Berlin, 1875–1890.
The Philosophical Works. Translated by George Martin Duncan. New Haven, 1890.
New Essays Concerning Human Understanding. Translated by Alfred G. Langley. New York, 1896.
A Collection of Papers that passed between the late learned Mr. Leibnitz and Dr. Clarke. London, 1717.

LOCKE, JOHN. An Essay Concerning Human Understanding. Edited by Alexander Campbell Fraser. Oxford, 1894 [1690].
Lettres inedites de Locke. H. Ollion. La Haye, 1912.

NEWTON, ISAAC. The Mathematical Principles of Natural Philosophy.

Translated into English by Andrew Motte. London, 1729. [1687].

NORRIS, JOHN. The Theory and Regulation of Love. To which are added letters philosophical and moral between the author and Dr. Henry More. 1688.

Theory of the Ideal or Intelligible World. London, 1701, 1704.

The Poems of John Norris of Bemerton, collected and edited by the Rev. Alexander Grosart. 1871. (Containing an ode to Dr. More.)

Cf. F. I. MacKinnon, The Philosophy of John Norris of Bemerton. Phil. Monographs, Vol. I, No. 2, Baltimore, 1910.

PARKER, SAMUEL. A Free and Impartial Censure of the Platonick Philosophie. Oxford, 1667. [1666.]

PHILALETHES, EUGENIUS [*pseud.* Thomas Vaughan]. The Man-Mouse taken in a Trap, and tortur'd to death for gnawing the margins of Eugenius Philalethes. [A Satire on Henry More.] London, 1650. B.M.

Anthroposophia Theomagica; or a discourse of the nature of man and his state after death, etc. London, 1650.

The Second Wash; or the Moore scour'd once more, being a charitable cure for the distractions of Alazonomastix. By Eugenius Philalethes. London, 1651.

SPINOZA, BENEDICT DE. Opera, ed. van Vloten and Land. Amsterdam, 1882, 1883.

Chief Works of Benedict de Spinoza, Translated by R. H. M. Elwes. London, 1906.

[Opera Posthuma, 1677]

SPRAT, THOMAS. The History of the Royal Society of London. London, 1667.

STUBBE, HENRY. A Censure upon certaine passages contained in the History of the Royal Society . . . as being destructive to the Established Religion and Church of England. Oxford, 1670. B.M.

The Same, Second edition, Whereunto is added the letter of a Virtuoso in opposition to the censure, a reply unto the letter aforesaid, and a reply unto the . . . answer of E. Glanvill . . . also an answer to the letter of Dr. H. More, containing a reply to the untruthes he hath publish'd. Oxford, 1671. B.M.

VAN HELMONT, F. M. Paradoxal Discourses concerning the Macrocosm and Microcosm. London, 1685.

WEBSTER, JOHN. The Displaying of supposed Witchcraft. London, 1677.

WHARTON, THOMAS. Adenographia: Sive Glandularum totius corporis. Descriptio. London, 1656.

WILLIS, THOMAS. The Anatomy of the Brain. In a Medical-Philosophical Discourse of Fermentation. Translated by S. Pordage. London, 1681.

Two Discourses concerning the Soul of Brutes, which is that of the Vital and Sensitive of Man. London, 1683.

III. Sources of More's Philosophy.

This bibliography of the sources of More's thought as found in the writings of earlier thinkers includes only those works to which reference is made either in the text as here reprinted or in the notes.

Agrippa, Cornelius. Henrici Cor. Agrippae ab Nettesheym. De Occulta Philosophia. Lugdini, 1550.
(*Cf.* Henry Morley, Life of Henry Cornelius Agrippa, London, 1856.)

Anselm. Opera Omnia. J. P. Migne, Paris, 1863.
Proslogium, Monologium; An Appendix, In Behalf of the Fool; and Cur Deus Homo. Translated by Sidney Norton Deane. Chicago, 1910.

Aristotle. Opera Omnia. Lipsiae, 1831-32.
Aristotle's Psychology. Translated by W. A. Hammond, London, 1902.
De Anima. With Translation, Introduction and Notes by R. D. Hicks. Cambridge, 1907.
The Works of Aristotle Translated into English. Edited by J. A. Smith and W. D. Ross. Vol. VIII. Metaphysica. Oxford, 1908.
De Sensu and De Memoria. Text and Translation. G. R. T. Ross. Cambridge, 1906.

Augustine. Sancti Aurelii Augustini. Opera Omnia. J. P. Migne, Paris, 1841.
Works of Augustine. New Translation. Edited by Marcus Dods. Edinburgh, 1872-1908.

Boethius. The Theological Tractates. The Consolation of Philosophy. H. F. Stewart and E. K. Rand. Loeb Classical Library, 1918.

Bruno, Giordano. Opera Latine Conscripta. Recensebat F. Fiorentino. Neapoli, 1884.
(*Cf.* J. Lewis McIntyre, Giordano Bruno. London, 1903.)

Cabbala. Kabbala denudata seu doctrina Hebraeorum transcendentalis et metaphysica atque theologica. Edited by C. Knorr von Rosenroth. Sulzbaci, Francofurti, 1677-84 B.M.
Kabbala denudata, The Kabbala Unveiled. Translated into English by S. L. M. Mathers. London, 1677.
(*Cf.* J. Abelson, Jewish Mysticism, London, 1914; Johann Buddeus, Introductio ad Historiam Ebraeorum, Halae, 1702; S. Munk, Mélanges de Philosophie Juive et Arabe, Paris, 1859; Isaac Myer, Quabbala, Philadelphia, 1888; Maurice Fluegel, Philosophy, Quabala and Vedànta, Baltimore, 1902.)

Cicero. De Natura Deorum. With Introduction and Commentary by J. B. Mayor. Cambridge, 1880.

Clement of Alexandria. In the Ante-Nicene Christian Library, Vol. 4.

Diogenes Laertius. De clar. philos. vitis. Didot. 1862.

Lives of the Philosophers. Translated by C. D. Yonge. Bohn's Classical Library. 1853.

DIONYSIUS. Dionysius the Areopagite. On the Divine Names, and the Mystical Theology. Translated by C. E. Rolt. 1920.

EPISCOPIUS. Opera Theologica. Amsterdam, 1665.

ERIGENA, JOHN SCOTUS. De Divisione Naturae. Münsten, 1838.
   (*Cf.* Alice Gardner, Studies in John the Scot. London, 1900.)

FICINUS, MARSILIUS. τον θειογ ΠΛΑΤΩΝΟΣ ΑΠΑΝΤΑ ΤΑ ΣΩΖΟΜΕΝΑ Marsilio Ficino Interprete. Lugdini, 1590.

GALEN, CLAUDIUS. De Placitis Hippocrates et Platonis. Lipsiae, 1874.

IAMBLICHUS. De Vita Pythagore, In Diogenes Laertius.
   On the Mysteries of the Egyptians. Translated by Thomas Taylor. 1821.

JOSEPHUS. Antiquities of the Jews. The Wars of the Jews. Translated by William Whiston. London, 1822.

LAURENTIUS, ANDREA. Historia Anatomica. Francofurti, [1600].

LUCRETIUS. De rerum natura. Recognovit Guilelmus Augustus Merrill, Berkleiae, 1918.
   On the Nature of Things. Translated by Cyril Bailey. Oxford, 1910.

MERCURIUS TRISMEGISTUS. Translations in G. R. S. Mead, Thrice Greatest Hermes. London, 1906.

ORIGEN. In the Ante-Nicene Christian Library, Vol. 10.

PARACELSUS. The Hermetic and Alchemical Writings of Aureolus Philippus Theophrastus Bombast of Hohenheim, called Paracelsus the Great. Translated by Arthur Edward Waite. London, 1894.
   (*Cf.* Franz Hartmann, The Life of Philippus Theophilus Bombast of Hohenheim and the Substance of his Teachings. London, 1887. A. E. Waite, Lives of the Alchemistical Philosophers. London, 1888.)

PHILOSTRATUS. The Life of Appolonius of Tyana. With an English Translation by C. Conybeare. Loeb Classical Library, 1912.

PLATO. Platonis . . . scripta Graece Omnia. . . . Recensuit Immanuel Bekker. Londini: 1826.
   The Dialogues of Plato. Translated by B. Jowett. New York, 1905.

PLOTINUS. Plotini. Opera Omnia. Ed. F. Creuzer, 1835. Complete Works. Translated by Kenneth Sylvan Guthrie. London, 1918.

PROCLUS. Elements of Theology. Translated by Thomas Taylor, in Commentaries of Proclus on Euclid. London, 1792.
   Platonic Theology. Translated by Thomas Taylor. London, 1820.

TERTULLIAN. In the Ante-Nicene Christian Library, Vol. 10.

THOMAS AQUINAS. Opera Omnia. Vives, Paris, 1895.
   The Summa Theologia of St. Thomas Aquinas. Literally translated by Fathers of the English Dominican Province. 1920.

VANINI, J. C. Oeuvres Philosophique. Traduites par M.X. Rousselot. Paris, 1842.

IV. BIOGRAPHY, CRITICISM, AND COMMENT.

It would be neither possible nor desirable to include in this bibliography all references to More in later literature. In selecting this list an effort has been made to include those books which are important as the sources of later comment and those which have in themselves historical or literary value.

BAILLET, ADRIEN. La Vie de Monsieur Descartes. Paris, 1691.

BAUMGARTEN, S. J. Nachrichten von Merkwürigen Büchern. Vol. III, pp. 316–330. 1753.

BRÜCKER, JACOB. Historia Critica Philosophia. Lipsiae, 1766. Vol. IV, pt. I, ch. 4, " De Restaurationibus Philosophiae Pythagoreo-Platonico-Cabbalisticae."

BENSON, ARTHUR. Essays. New York, 1896.

BRITANNICUS (*pseud.*). A vindication of the Quakers. To which is added a more full and perfect account of the Quakers, occasioned by Dr. H. More's opinion of them. London, 1732. N.Y.P.

COLERIDGE, S. T. Notes on English Divines. London, 1853. Vol. I.

DOLSON, G. N. The Ethical System of Henry More. Philosophical Review, 1897, pp. 593–607.

GEORGE, E. A. Seventeenth Century Men of Latitude. New York, 1908.

GIBSON, JAMES. Locke's Theory of Knowledge and its Historical Relations. Cambridge, 1917.

GRANGER'S Biographical History of England. 1824. Vol. V, p. 46.

GREENSLET, FERRIS. Joseph Glanvill. New York, 1900.

HARRISON, J. S. Platonism in English Poetry of the Sixteenth and Seventeenth Centuries. New York, 1903.

VON HERTLING, GEORGE. John Locke und die Schule von Cambridge. Freiburg, 1892.

JAEGER, JOHANN W. Examen Theologiae mysticae veteris et novae, in quo . . . Archiepiscopi . . . Fenelonis de Salignac, Cardinalis Patrucii, P. Poireti, et M. de Molinos placita sub modestam censuram revocantur. (Dissertatio de Enthusiasmo. De J. Boehmio judicum H. Mori, . . . cum judicio in utrumque J. W. J., etc.) Francofurti et Lipsiae, 1709. B.M.

JOHNSON, SAMUEL. (Vicar of Great Torrington.) An Explanation of Scripture Prophecies, both typical and literal . . . To which are prefixed . . . Remarks on Dr. H. More's Exposition of the Seven Epistles to the Seven Churches, and brief observations on . . . Mr. Mede's Clavis Apocalyptica, etc. Reading, 1742. B.M.

JONES, R. M. Spiritual Reformers in the Sixteenth and Seventeenth Centuries. New York, 1914.

LECHLER, G. V. Geschichte des Englischen Deismus. 1841.

LOVEJOY, A. O. Kant and the English Platonists. In Essays Philosophical and Psychological in Honour of William James. New York, 1908.

LYON, GEORGES. L'Idealisme en Angleterre au XVIIIᵉ siècle. Paris, 1888.

MAYOR, J. E. B. Henry More. In Notes and Queries, Second Series, vol. 7. London, 1859.

MASTERMAN, J. B. H. The Age of Milton. London, 1897 Ch. XI.

MULLINGER, J. BASS. Platonists and Latitudinarians, In The Cambridge History of English Literature. Cambridge, 1912. Vol. VIII. History of the University of Cambridge. London, 1888. Cambridge, 1911.

NICHOLSON, MARJORIE. More's Psychozoia. In Modern Language Notes, 1922.

OSMOND, PERCY M. The Mystical Poets of the English Church. London, 1919.

PARKER, THEODORE. Dr. Henry More. In the Christian Examiner. Boston, 1839.

RÉMUSAT, C. F. M. de. Histoire de la philosophe en Angleterre depuis Bacon jusquà Locke. Paris, 1878.

REDGROVE, H. STANLEY. Bygone Beliefs. London, 1920. Ch. XII. The Cambridge Platonists.

SETH, JAMES. English Philosophers and Schools of Philosophy. London, 1912.

SHORTHOUSE, J. H. John Inglesant, A Romance. London, 1909.

SORLEY, W. R. A History of English Philosophy. New York, 1921.

STREET, BENJAMIN. Historical Notes on Grantham and Grantham Church. Grantham, 1857.

STREET, REV. B. Memorial Introduction to the Poems of Henry More. Chertsey Worthies Library, 1778.

TULLOCH, JOHN. Rational Theology and Christian Philosophy in England in the Seventeenth Century. Vol. II. The Cambridge Platonists. Edinburgh and London, 1874.

WARD, RICHARD. The Life of the Learned and Pious Dr. Henry More, Late Fellow of Christ's College in Cambridge. To which is annex'd divers of his useful and excellent letters. London, 1710.

WHEWELL, WILLIAM. Lectures on the History of Moral Philosophy in England. London, 1852.

WILLMOT, R. E. A. Henry More. In his Lives of Sacred Poets. London, 1834.

ZIMMERMAN, R. Henry More und die vierte Dimension des Raumes. In Kaiserliche Akademie der Wissenschaften. Philosophischehistorische Classe. Sitzsungberichte. Wien, 1881. Band 98, pp. 403–448.

OUTLINE SUMMARY OF MORE'S
PHILOSOPHICAL THEORY

ABBREVIATIONS USED IN THE FOLLOWING OUTLINE

Ant. Ath.	*Antidote against Atheism.*
Conj. Cab.	*Conjectura Cabbalistica.*
Enthus. Triumph.	*Enthusiasmus Triumphatus.*
Imm.	*The Immortality of the Soul.*
Pref. Gen.	*Preface General to the Philosophical Writings.*

As printed in *A Collection of several philosophical writings*, London, 1662.

D.D.	*Divine Dialogues.*
Ench. Eth.	*Enchiridion Ethicum.*
Ench. Met.	*Enchiridion Metaphysicum.*
True Not.	*The True Notion of a Spirit*, being chapters XXVII through XXVIII, section 30 of *Enchiridion Metaphysicum* as translated in Joseph Glanvil's *Saducismus Triumphatus.*

The quotations from the parts of *Enchiridion Metaphysicum* not included in the *True Notion* are from a manuscript translation by Professor Mary Whiton Calkins of Wellesley College.

Farther Defence.	*A Farther Defence of the True Notion of a Spirit: An Answer to a Letter of a Learned Psychopyrist.*
Mys. God.	*An Explanation of the Grand Mystery of Godliness.*

OUTLINE SUMMARY OF MORE'S PHILOSOPHICAL THEORY

I. DOCTRINE OF KNOWLEDGE.

A. SOURCES OF KNOWLEDGE

1. INNATE IDEAS OR COMMON NOTIONS

a. *Meaning of Innate Ideas*

" I do not mean that there is a certain number of ideas flaring and shining to the animadversive faculty like so many torches or starres in the firmament to our outward sight, . . . but I understand thereby an active sagacity in the soul, whereby some small business being hinted to her, she runs out presently into a more clear and larger conception." Ant. Ath. I: V: 2; *Cf.* Imm. I: II: 4, Ench. Met. XXV: 7.

b. *Argument for Innate Ideas*

Certain factors in knowledge cannot be attributed to sense or to experience of the external world, and must, therefore, be due to the activity of the mind itself. These are:

(1) Mathematical conceptions.

Mathematical demonstrations are based on perfect figures. " But this accuracy either in the circle or the triangle cannot be set out in any material subject: therefore it remains that she [the soul] hath a more full and exquisite knowledge of things in herself then the matter can lay open before her." Ant. Ath. I: VI: 1; *Cf. Ibid.* Appendix: II: 4.

(2) " Relative Notions or Ideas.

" Those that are commonly called by the name of Secundae Notiones . . . never came in by the senses, they being no impresses of corporeal motion." Imm. II: II: 9.

" Cause, effect, whole and part, like and unlike and the rest . . . equality and inequality . . . proportion and analogy, symmetry and asymmetry and such like [are] no material impresses from without upon the soul, but her own active conception proceeding from herself whilst she takes notice of external objects." Ant. Ath. I: VI: 3; *Cf. Ibid.* Appendix: II: 4–6. Imm. II:II:9–11, Ench. Met. XXV: 7.

259

(3) Necessary Truths.

"It is manifest, besides these single ideas I have proved to be in the mind, that there are also several complex notions in the same, such as are these, The whole is bigger than the part; . . . every number is either even or odd; which are true to the soul at the very first proposal, as any one that is in his wits does plainly perceive." Ant. Ath. I: VI: 6.

"To all sensitive objects the soul is an abrasa tabula, but for moral and intellectual principles, their ideas or notions are essential to the soul." Annotations to Lux Orientalis: ch. 3.

2. SENSE

"Such as hearing, seeing, feeling, &c. all which include perception in an unresistible necessity thereof, the object being present before us." Imm. II: X: 4; *Cf.* Ench. Eth. I: VI: 6.

"Sense is ever caused by some outward corporeal motion upon our organs." Imm. I: XIV: 6.

"From externall sense I exclude not memory, as it is a faithfull register thereof." Imm. I: II: 4.

3. REASON

"Reason is . . . a power or faculty of the soul, whereby either from her innate ideas or common notions, or else from the assurance of her own senses, or upon the relation or tradition of another, she unravels a further clew of knowledge, enlarging her sphere of intellectual light by laying open to herself the close connexion and cohesion of the conceptions she has of things." Mys. God. II: 11. *Cf.* Imm. I: II: 4, and II: X: 5.

B. LIMITATIONS OF KNOWLEDGE

1. THE OBJECTS OF KNOWLEDGE ARE NOT ESSENCES OR SUBSTANCES IN THEMSELVES, BUT THE ATTRIBUTES OF SUBSTANCE.

"The subject, or naked essence or substance of a thing, is utterly unconceivable to any one of our faculties." Imm. I: II: 8; *Cf.* Ant. Ath. I: IV: 3, Ench. Eth. III: IV: 3.

2. THE OBJECT OF KNOWLEDGE MUST BEAR A CERTAIN RELATION TO OUR FACULTIES.

"Whatever things are in themselves, they are nothing to us, but so far forth as they become known to our faculties or cognitive powers. . . . As nothing can concern the visive faculty but so far forth as it is visible; so there is nothing that can challenge any stroke to so much as touching, much less determining, our cognitive powers in generall, but so far forth as it is cognoscible." Imm. I: II: 1 and 2.

II. DOCTRINE OF SUBSTANCE.

A. SUBSTANCE IN GENERAL

1. DEFINITION OF SUBSTANCE

" Substance is a being subsistent by itself, not a mode of some being." Ench. Met. XXVIII: 2 (True Notion: XVIII).

" For a thing to subsist by it self, only signifies so to subsist, that it wants not the prop of some other subject in which it may inhere as accidents do." Ench. Met. XXVIII: 2 (True Notion: XXVI).

2. PROPERTIES COMMON TO ALL SUBSTANCES.

a. *Individuality*

" Every Substance is of itself an individual substance, and universals but a logical notion arising from our comparing of substances of like nature together." Mys. God. IX: II: 5; *Cf.* Preface General: 12.

b. *Activity*

" In the precise notion of substance . . . is comprised . . . Activity either connate or communicated. For matter itself once moved can move other matter." Imm. I: III: 2.

c. *Extension*

" It being of the very essence of whatsoever is, to have parts or extension in some measure or other. For to take away all extension is to reduce a thing onely to a mathematical point, which is nothing else but pure negation or non-entity." Imm. Preface: 3; *Cf.* D. D. I: XXIV: 26, Preface General: 12, Ench. Met. XXVIII: 20 (True Not. XXXIV).

(1) Meaning of extension as characterizing all substance. "Infinite, unchanging extension is not the particular shapes and sizes of moveable matter, but is rather a universal and necessary idea of the mind, the object of intellect and not of sense." Ench. Met. VI.

" By extension I here understand not actual magnitude which is really divisible, as comports with Matter . . . but simply a certain amplitude, which is one and simple in such wise that it is inherently impossible for it to be torn into parts." Ench. Met. VIII: 14; *Cf. Ibid.* XXVIII: 7 (True Not. XXII), ff., Preface General: 12, Letter to Descartes I, Imm. I: II, 12, *Ibid.* I: X: 8.

(2) Arguments for extension as a character of all substance.

(a) *Space is not material*

" For though it be wittily supported by him [Descartes] for a ground of more certain and mathematical after-deductions in his philosophy; yet it is not at all proved, that matter and extension are reciprocally the same, as well every extended thing matter as all matter extended. This is but an up-start conceit of the present age." D. D. I: XXIV.

"This infinite space because of its infinity is distinct from matter." Ench. Met. VIII: 9.

Space is "incorporeal because it penetrates matter." Ench. Met. VIII: 12; *Cf.* Letter to Descartes I; Ant. Ath. Appendix: VII: 1, 2.

"Distance is no real or physical property of a thing; but onely notional; because more or less of it may accrue to a thing . . . and parts and degrees and such like notions are not real things themselves anywhere but our mode of conceiving them. . . . Distance is nothing else but the privation of tactual union." Ant. Ath. Appendix: VII: 4 and 5.

(b) Spirit must be extended since it acts on body.

"The operations wherewith the soul acts on the body are in the body. . . . But the operation of the soul . . . and the soul itself are together. Wherefore if the operation of the soul is somewhere the soul is somewhere. . . . And if the power of God be somewhere, God is somewhere. . . . He in every part of the matter, the soul in the humane body." Ench. Met. XXVII: 5 (True Not. V).

3. CLASSES OF SUBSTANCE

    a. *Material substance, or body*

    b. *Spiritual substance, spirits or souls*

B. MATERIAL SUBSTANCE

  1. PROPERTIES DISTINCTIVE OF MATERIAL SUBSTANCE

    a. *Divisibility*

"An essential and positive difference of a body is that it be . . . physically divisible into parts." Ench. Met. XXVIII: 2 (True. Not. XVII).

"Disunity is the natural property of matter." D. D. I: VIII.

"By actual divisibility I understand discerpibility, gross tearing or cutting one part from another." Imm. I: II: 10.

"Primal matter can be clearly enough described thus, to wit, A homogeneous congeries of physical monads." Ench. Met. IX: 1; *Cf.* Imm. Preface: 3, *Ibid.* I: III: 1, I: VI: 5, Further Defence: XVII.

    b. *Impenetrability*

"These monads . . . do not or cannot penetrate each other even when they have coalesced in some body." Ench. Met. IX: 6.

"That it [matter] does so certainly and irresistibly keep one part of it self from penetrating another, it is so, we know not why." Imm. I: II: 11; *Cf.* Letter to Descartes, I, Ench. Met. XXVIII: 2 (True. Not. XVII).

Matter is, however, penetrable by spirit.

" The closest matter [is] easily penetrable and pervious to an incorporeal substance." Imm. I: VII: 5.

"Spirits can penetrate matter . . . else God could not be essentially present in all parts of the corporeal universe." Annotations in Discourse on Truth.

c. *Inactivity, inability to initiate motion*

"To attribute spontaneous motion to matter would be extremely silly since it is so clearly opposed to sense and experience. For no bodies except those which are animate and provided with organs are moved with spontaneous motion. If the contrary were true we should observe innumerable corpuscles, pebbles, hairs, stalks and things of that sort moving and twisting themselves without any external mover." Ench. Met. IX: 15; *Cf. Ibid.* IX: 8, Imm. I. XI: 2, D. D. I.

d. *Unconsciousness*

" All material or corporeal particles are so endowed that no thought or perception of any kind could in any wise belong to them." Ench. Met. XXV, 2 and 5; *Cf. Ibid.* XXVIII: 2 (True Not. XVII), Imm. II: II: 1, Mys. God. VI: IV: 1. (See also arguments for existence of spirit, below, C: 2: b).

2. EXISTENCE AND ORIGIN OF MATTER

" All agree that matter exists." Ench. Met. IX: 10.

" Matter is not of the class of things which can have their efficacy in themselves . . . for matter does not necessarily exist . . . and that which does not necessarily exist does not exist of itself." Ench. Met. IX: 10, 11. *Cf.* Ant. Ath. I: VIII: 11.

" From the highest life, viz. the Deity, there does result that which has no life or sense at all, to wit, the stupid matter." Imm. II: XI: 10; *Cf.* Ant. Ath. I: VIII: 7, Ench. Met. X: 16, Letter VI, in Ward's Life of More.

C. SPIRITUAL SUBSTANCE

1. PROPERTIES DISTINCTIVE OF SPIRIT

a. *Unity and Indivisibility*

"Spirit is utterly indivisible and indiscerpible into real physical parts." Ench. Met. XXVIII: 3 (True Not. XVIII), *Cf.* Imm. I: III: 1, I: V: 2, Ant. Ath. I: IV: 3, *Ibid.* Appendix: 3 and 10.

" I understand a spirit to be immediately one, and to want no other vinculum to hold the parts together but its own essence and existence; whence it is own nature indiscerpible."

D. D. I; *Cf.* Ench. Met. XXVIII: 3 (True Not. XVIII). Preface Gen. 12, Imm. III: XVI: 2, Annot. Lux Orientalis: 3. " That a spirit is one . . . signifies [that it is] undistinguished or undivided in and from it self, but divided or distinguished from all other." Ench. Met. XXVIII: 3 (True Not. XVIII).

   b. *Power of penetration*
      (1) Penetrating matter and other spirits
         " Spirits can both penetrate matter and penetrate one an-other." Annot. Disc. on Truth: Digression; *Cf.* Ench. Met. XXVIII: 3 (True Not. XVIII), Farther Defence: II.
      (2) Self-penetration
         " It is plain that such a spirit as we define, having the power of motion upon the whole extent of its essence, if it determine the motion of the exteriour parts inward, they will return inward toward the centre of essential power." Imm. I: VII: 2.
         " The Parts, as I may so call them, of the same spirit may, in the contraction of it self penetrate one another, so that there may be a reduplication of essence through the whole spirit." Farther Defence: IX.

   c. *Self-activity, or self-motion*
      By self-activity, " I understand an active power in a spirit, whereby it either modifies it self according to its own nature, or moves the matter regularly according to some certain modifications it impresses upon it." D. D. II: 30; *Cf.* Ant. Ath. I: IV: 3, Ench. Met. XVII: 1 and 8. Imm. I: VII: 1 and 5.

2. ARGUMENTS FOR THE EXISTENCE OF SPIRITUAL SUBSTANCE
   a. *Criticism of the materialistic position of Hobbes as being assumed and not proved.* Imm. I: IX and X
   b. *Argument from the operations or faculties of the soul and their incompatibility with matter*
      " The mundane material particles of animals are not in any way capable of the operations and functions of knowledge such as we experience in ourselves." Ench. Met. XXV: 1; *Cf.* Imm. II: I: 1, Ant. Ath. I: XI, Mys. God. II: III: 2.
      (1) Sense
         " If any matter have sense, it will follow that upon re-action all shall have the like, and that a bell when it is ringing, and a bow when it is bent . . . shall be sensitive creatures. A thing so foolish and frivolous that the mere recital of the opinion may well be thought confutation enough." Imm. II: II: 1; *Cf.* Ench. Met. XXV: 2 and 5, Ant. Ath. I: XI.

(2) Common-percipiency

"To be one more than matter is one (which is one only by juxta-position of parts) is a necessary requisite of that which is capable of the function of common-percipiency." Pref. Gen. 12; *Cf.* Ant. Ath. I: XI: 5.

"For we clearly discern that we receive the whole object; since if individual parts of the perceiver perceived merely individual parts of the object, nothing would remain which perceived the whole object and made a judgment about it: any more than three men singing a canticle of three parts, each one hearing only his own part, could judge of the whole." Ench. Met. XXV: V; *Cf.* Imm. II: II: 2 and III: XVI: V, Mys. God. II: VIII: 4, Ant. Ath. Appendix: X: 2.

(3) Memory and Imagination

"It is as impossible to conceive memory competible to such a subject [matter] as it is how to write characters in the water or in the wind." Ant. Ath. I: XI: 3; *Cf. Ibid.* Appendix: X: 3, Imm. II: V: 7 and II: VI: 7, Phil. Poems: Psychathanasia: II: 2: 25.

"For if it is fluid, the images will suddenly disappear . . . if the matter is hard or viscid, the vibration will cease suddenly and memory will immediately perish." Ench. Met. XXV: 6.

"For those imaginations or representations that are of no one object that we ever see, but made up of several, . . . how can the conarion join these together?" This would be original motion not "conveighed by any corporeal impress from another body." Imm. II: V: 8; *Cf.* Ant. Ath. Appendix: X: 4, Ench. Met. XXV: 6.

(4) Mathematical and logical conceptions

"Those notions popularly called second notions (such as many logical and mathematical conceptions) are not modifications of any bodily or mechanical reactions . . . and cannot therefore be modes of matter, but . . . must [be modes of] incorporeal substance of some sort." Ench. Met. XXV: 7; *Cf.* Imm. II: II: 9, Ant. Ath. I: VI: 3 and Appendix: X: 5, Phil. Poems: Psyathanasia: II: 3.

(5) Consciousness of Freedom

"To all this you may add that that αὐτεξούσιον of which we are conscious in ourselves is a sufficiently clear argument to prove that there is something incorporeal in nature." Ench. Met. XXV: 7; *Cf.* Imm. II: II: 11.

c. *Argument from the nature of space*

"We are unable not to conceive that a certain immobile extension, pervading all things to infinity, has always existed and will exist to eternity . . . and that this is really distinct from mobile matter. It is therefore necessary that there be some real subject basal to this extension since it is a real attribute." Ench. Met. VIII: 6.

d. *Argument from the "Phenomena of Nature."*

(1) Spirit necessary as the principle of unity in nature
"There is no vinculum imaginable in nature to hold the parts together. For you know they are impenetrable, and therefore touch one another as it were in the smooth superficies. How therefore can they hold together? what is the principle of their union?" D. D. I: XXIX; Ench. Met. IX: 4, 6 and 12.

(2) Spirit necessary as the source of motion in nature
"Motion which, since it is not substance in it self, must be derived from some substance, . . . cannot be derived from matter. It remains, therefore, that it be derived from other substance which is not material but incorporeal." Ench. Met. IX: 9–13; *Cf.* Imm. I. XI: 2, D. D. I, Farther Defence: VI.

(3) Spirit necessary to account for the orderly arrangement of the world.
"Be the matter moved how it will, the appearances of things are such as do manifestly intimate that they are either appointed all of them, or at least approved, by an universal principle of wisdom and counsel." Ant. Ath. II: I: 6; *Cf.* Farther Defence: I, D. D. I, Imm. I: XII: 1.
(See also argument for the soul of the world, below, 3, b, (1), (b).)

e. *Argument from supernatural occurrences*
"The third and last ground which I would make use of, for evincing the existence of incorporeal substances, is such extraordinary effects as we cannot well imagine any natural, but must needs conceive some free or spontaneous agent to be the cause thereof." Imm. I: XIII: 1.
"Such are the beating of men by some hand invisible on a clear day; and the impact of this hand on the body so heavily that the impress of it . . . later appears distinctly and darkly colored; . . . the carrying of sages and other men through the higher air at midday with many spectators, . . . the apparently voluntary uprising of sandals, even wooden ones, from the pavement and their flying against the bystanders, . . . the conversations of magi and sages with demons. . . . From these . . . it is manifest that the universe contains substances other than bodies." Ench. Met. XXVI: 2–4; *Cf.* Ant. Ath. Bk. III and Appendix: XII, ff., D. D. I: 13.

3. CLASSES OF SPIRITS

   a. *God*

      (1) Nature of God

         (a) *Spirit, not matter*

         " It is plain that a spirit is a notion of more perfection than a body, and therefore the more fit to be an attribute of what is absolutely perfect then a body is." Ant. Ath. I: IV: 3; *Cf.* Mys. God. I: 3–7, II: 1–2, Imm. I: IV: 2.

         (b) *Eternal and Infinite*

         Ant. Ath. I: IV: 4, Mys. God. II: I: 3, Ench. Met. X, D. D. I.

         (c) *Omnipresent*

         D. D. I: 33, Letter to Descartes, II, Annotations in Discourse on Truth: Digression.

         (d) *Wise, Good, and Powerful*

         Mys. God. II: II: 3, Ant. Ath. I: IV: 5, D. D. II: 3, Imm. III: XV: 9, Conj. Cab. Preface.

      (2) Arguments for the existence of God

         (a) *From the innate idea of God*

      (1') Ontological.

      " There is in man an idea of a being absolutely perfect. . . . If it signifies to us that the notion and nature of God implies in it necessary existence, as we have shown it does, . . . we are without any further scruple to acknowledge that God does exist." Ant. Ath. I: III: 3, I: VIII: 1, and Appendix: IV, D. D. I: 13.

      (2') Causal

      " To what purpose is this indeleble image or idea of God in us, if there be no such thing as God existent in the world? or who seal'd so deep an impression of that character upon our minds? " Ant. Ath. I: IX: 5.

         (b) *From the nature of man*

      (1') From conscience

      " Wherefore I conclude from natural conscience in a man . . . that there is an intelligible principle over universall nature that takes notice of the actions of men, that is, that there is a God; for else this natural faculty would be false and vain." Ant. Ath. I: X: 4; *Cf. Ibid.* Appendix: IX.

      (2') From universal worship

      " For there are no natural faculties in things that have not their object in the world; as there is meat as well as mouths, sounds as well as hearing, colours as well as sight, dangers as well as fear, and the like. So there ought in like manner to be a God as well as a natural propension in men to religious worship, God alone being the proper object thereof." Ant. Ath. I: X: 9; *Cf. Ibid.* II: XII, D. D. I: 13.

(c) *From the evidences of design in the world*
"Wherefore the whole creation and every part thereof being so ordered as if the most exquisite reason and knowledge had contrived them, it is . . . natural to conclude that all this is the work of a wise God." Ant. Ath. II: XII; *Cf. Ibid.* Bk. II as a whole, D. D. I: 5.

b. *Created spirits*
"That there are particular spirits or immaterial substances, God acting according to his nature, we cannot doubt but that he has created innumerable companies of spirits to enjoy themselves and their creator." Mys. God. II: III: 1.

(1) Plastical spirits
(a) *Particular plastical spirits, seminal forms, or archei*
"A seminal form is a created spirit organizing duly prepared matter into life and vegetation. . . . This is the first degree of particular life in the world, if there be any purely of this degree particular." Imm. I: VIII: 3.
"To the last puzzle propounded, whether these archei be so many sprigs of the common soul of the world, or particular subsistences of themselves; there is no great inconvenience in acknowledging that it may be either way." Ant. Ath. Appendix: XI: 9; *Cf.* Preface General: 13.

(b) *Soul of the World, or Spirit of Nature.*
(1') Nature of the soul of the world.
"The spirit of nature is . . . a substance incorporeal but without sense and animadversion, pervading the whole matter of the universe, and exercising a plastical power therein . . . raising such phenomena in the world . . . as cannot be resolved into mere mechanical powers." Imm. III: XII: 1.

(2') Argument for the existence of the soul of the world. It is impossible to explain by purely mechanical causes such phenomena as "vibrations of strings tuned unisons," sympathetic cures, magnetism and gravity, "working of wine when the vine is in flower," structure of plants and animals, instinctive actions of animals, pre-natal influences, the transmitting of souls to their appropriate matter. Ench. Met. XI–XXIV, Imm. III: XII, ff., Letter to V. C., Letter to Descartes, III.

(2) Perceptive spirits.

(a) *Sensitive spirits, or souls of beasts. Imm. I:
VIII: 4.*

We cannot, however, be absolutely certain that
animals have conscious souls since " we cannot here
demonstrate the presence of spirit from its operations as we can concerning men." Ant. Ath. Appendix: X: 7.

(b) *Intellectual spirits, souls, or selves.*

(1') Additional characters attributed to intellectual spirits.

(a') *Self-consciousness.*

" I do most intimately and distinctly perceive my
own soul or mind to be and that I am it." D. D.
I: 34.

" A man's self . . . is that in him which is properly
called soul: But not its operations . . . because
they perceive nothing, but the soul perceives them
in exerting them; nor the faculties, for they perceive
not one anothers operations; but that which is a
man's self perceives them all." Imm. III: XVI: 5.

(b') *Permanence and Immortality.*

" The soul of Man is a permanent being, but her
cogitations are in a flux or succession." Ench. Met.
XXVII: 7 (True. Not. VII).

The immortality of the soul is argued from:
History. Imm. II: XV: 7
Nature of the soul. II: XVII: 2
Universal belief. Imm. II: XVII: 10.
Nature of God. Imm. II: XVIII: 3 and 4.

(2') Powers of faculties of intellectual spirits.

(a') *Plastic power, by which the soul forms the body
and sustains the bodily functions.*

" In these plastical operations . . . a man differs
little from a plant." Enthus. Triumph. IV; *Cf.*
Ench. Eth. I: VI: 6, Imm. II: X: 3, Ench. Met.
(True Not. XVIII).

(b') *Conscious faculties.*

Sensation. Imm. II: X: 4, Ench. Eth. I: VI: 6.
Imagination. Imm. II: X: 5, Ench. Eth. I: VI: 6.
Will. Imm. II: X: 5,
Reason. Imm. II: X: 5.

(3') Grades of Intellectual spirits.

(a') *Men or Humane souls.*

" A created spirit endued with sense and reason, and
a power of organizing terrestrial matter into humane
shape by vital union therewith." Imm. I: VIII: 5;
Cf. Mys. God. II: III: 1.

(b') *Angelical souls.*
Aerial spirits.
Aethereal spirits.
"An angelical soul . . . is a created spirit, endued
with reason, sensation, and a power of being vitally
united with and actuating a body of aire or aether."
Imm. I: VIII: 7; *Cf.* Mys. God. II: III.
"These have no settled form but what they please
to give themselves upon occasion." Ant. Ath. III:
XIV: 4;*Cf.* Ench. Met. XXVI: 9, Mys. God. V:
III: 2.

D. RELATION BETWEEN SPIRIT AND BODY.

1. SPIRIT DISTINCT AND SEPARABLE FROM BODY.
See argument for existence of spirit, above, C: 2.

2. SPIRIT INTIMATELY CONNECTED WITH BODY.
"To be in such a separate state as to be where no matter is, is
to be out of the world." Imm. II: XV: 1.

a. *By "vital congruity."*
The union of the soul with matter "does not arise from any
gross mechanical way as when two bodies stick one in another . . . but from a congruity of another nature, which I
know not better how to term than vital: which vital congruity
is chiefly in the soul it self . . . but is also in the matter."
Imm. II: XIV: 8; *Cf.* Phil. Poems: Psychathanasia: Preface,
Mys. God. VI: V: 2, Moral Cabbala: II: 23.
"Vital congruity" is of three kinds: terrestrial, by which
the soul is united to the earthly body, aerial which unites the
soul of man at death to a body of air and makes her one of
"the order of genii," and aethereal, which belongs to celestial
beings, and is found also in the soul of man fitting it to unite
at last with a heavenly body. Imm. II: XV: 3, III: I: 1, ff.

b. *By the action of the soul on matter.*
(1) In creating particular bodies.
"I think it most reasonable to conclude the soul herself
to be the more particular architect . . . of the frame of
the body." Imm. II: X: 2.
(2) In moving matter.
"Spirit is to be acknowledged the true principle and
fountain of all life and motion." Ench. Met. XXVIII:
(True. Not. XXXIII).
"The actuating of the matter being the most proper and
essential operation of a soul." Moral Cabbala: II: 23.

c. *By the animal spirits.*
"The immediate instruments of the soul are those tenuious
and aereal particles which they ordinarily call the spirits. . . .

These are they by which the soul hears, sees, feels, imagines, remembers, reasons, and by moving which, or at least directing their motion, she moves likewise the body; and by using them or some subtile matter like them, she either completes, or at least contributes to, the bodie's organization." Imm. II: XVII: 3; *Cf. Ibid.* II: chs. VII and XIV, Mys. God. II: IV: 5.

NOTES

NOTES

A. Critical and Historical Comments on Various Points of More's Thought, Following the Order of the Outline.

Sources of Knowledge. (Outline I, A.)

More's characteristic tendency toward inclusiveness rather than discrimination in his philosophical thinking is nowhere more clearly shown than in his description of the sources of knowledge. The innate principles of the Platonic and Stoic traditions, the deductive reasoning emphasized by the Cartesians, the sense-knowledge brought into prominence by the growing interest in science, the historic revelation of theology, and the immediate insight of mystic religion, all have for him approximately equal value and validity. In his inclusion of sense-perception among the sources of knowledge More differs both from the masters whom for the most part he delighted to follow and from many of his closest contemporary associates. From the point of view both of the Cartesians and of the Platonists the senses are the source of confusion and error rather than of knowledge. Descartes, in spite of his interest in physics and in scientific experiment, when analyzing the sources of knowledge explicitly rules out all sense-perception as fluctuating and unreliable. " We shall here take note of all those mental operations by which we are able to arrive at the knowledge of things. Now I admit only two, viz. intuition and induction . . . the conceptions which an unclouded and attentive mind gives us so readily that we are wholly freed from doubt about that which we understand, . . . and all necessary inference from facts that are known with certainty." [1] John Smith, the Platonist, though differing from Descartes in many respects, is at one with him in this depreciation of sense-knowledge. From Plato and Plotinus he inherits the conviction that to gain true knowledge " we must shut the eyes of sense, and open that brighter eye of our understanding, that other eye of the soul, as the philosopher calls our intellectual faculty." [2]

More and Culverwell at this point follow rather the lead of the scholastic thinkers, for whom the requisites of knowledge of the natural world were the sense image and the response of the intellect, " phantasmata ex sensibilibus accepta, et lumen naturale intelligibile." [3]

---

[1] *Regulae*, III.
[2] *Discourses*, p. 16, On Attaining to Divine Knowledge.
[3] Thomas Aquinas, *Summa Theol.* I, Qu. 12, Art. 13 ; *De Prin. Ind.* Cap. I.

" Many sparks and appearances," writes Culverwell, " fly from variety of objects to the understanding, the mind, that catches them all, and cherishes them, and blows upon them; and thus the candle of knowledge is lighted." [4]

For More and Cudworth, for Smith and Whichcote, the power of reason in man is something more than a purely psychological fact. It is the " candle of the Lord," which, though sometimes immersed in affairs of time and sense, never fails to reflect the eternal realities. In the Preface to the *Conjectura Cabbalistica* More writes of the human reason as " participating in the divine reason," and in the Preface General to the *Philosophical Writings* he quotes that sentence from Clement of Alexandria which may serve as epitome and symbol not only of the thought of the Alexandrian Platonists from which it comes but also of that of the Cambridge Platonists of a later century: " The image of God is the royal and divine Logos, the image of this image is the human intellect."

Innate Ideas. (Outline I, A, 1.)

The most distinctive and characteristic part of More's doctrine of knowledge is his conception of innate knowledge. " Innate ideas," " common notions," " secundae notiones," " active or actual knowledge," [5] are the different terms that he uses in his attempt to define that element in knowledge which is contributed by the mind itself as contrasted with that which is received from external objects.

The problem which finds its solution in the doctrine of innate ideas is only in part that of a disinterested analysis of the processes of knowledge. For More and for many of his contemporaries it is far more urgently that of finding an assured basis for religious faith. The failure of churchly authority which came with the Reformation, and the new emphasis on the individual as the center of responsibility led to many groping attempts to find a starting point for religious certainty in the mind itself. Most of these efforts show a mingling, without clear discrimination, of the principles of common consent, self-evidence, innateness of origin, and mental activity, with emphasis on one or the other according to the nature of the problem in question.

The principle of universal consent as the basis of certainty is closely connected with the Stoic conception of the universal reason. Those things in which all men agree by the very necessity of their nature must be held for truth.[6] From this assertion that these common notions are valid because of the participation of all men in a common nature it was

[4] *Light of Nature*, XI.

[5] *Antidote against Atheism:* Appendix, *Immortality of the Soul:* I: II: 4, *Ibid.* II: II: 9, *Enchiridion Metaphysicum:* XXV: 7, *Antidote against Atheism:* I: V: 2.

[6] " De quo autem omnium natura consentit, id verum esse necesse est." Cicero, *De Natura Deorum:* I: 17.

a short step to the assertion that they have real existence in the mind of the individual before there is any conscious recognition of them. Thus this conception merged for later thinkers with the Platonic doctrine of reminiscence to form the doctrine of principles and ideas inborn in every man, to which everyone gives inevitable and unquestioning assent. This form of innate knowledge is illustrated in Origen's "common notions of morality, innate, and written in divine letters." [7] It is accepted by Augustine,[8] and forms an integral element in much of the thought of the middle ages and the Renaissance. According to Herbert of Cherbury, Locke's predecessor in the investigation of the nature of knowledge, the "common notions," based on natural instincts, are principles which can be neither questioned nor denied. The other forms of knowledge, those of external sense, of internal sense, and of reason, depend for their validity on the common notions which are distinguished by their priority, independence, universality, certainty, necessity, and immediacy.[9]

Self-evidence is the character of innate ideas which is most emphasized by the Cambridge Platonists. Even Culverwell, who strongly opposes the Platonic doctrine of inborn principles or ideas, assents to the belief in "some clear and indelible principles" which are immediately recognized as truth.[10] "Things of natural knowledge," writes Whichcote, "or of first inscription in the heart of man by God, these are known to be true as soon as ever they are proposed." [11] For Descartes self-evident truths are those which cannot be denied without self-contradiction; but in the thought of the Cambridge Platonists the logical principle of contradiction is far less important as a test of truth than the feeling of immediate certainty. And Descartes, it is true, did not always maintain in practice his own distinction between "natural light" and "natural impulse."

These three principles, Platonic reminiscence, universal consent, and self-evidence or immediate certainty, are interwoven and partially fused in that conception of innate ideas which after long persistence in the minds of men was in the seventeenth century approaching its end. John Smith still urges that there are "radical principles of knowledge . . . deeply sunk into the souls of men," and Glanvil, a younger follower of the same tradition, argues for the reality of "some congenite implicit principles," [12] but the spirit of the age no longer accepts without question these uncriticised assurances.

It is this form of the doctrine of innate ideas, whether found in the writings of Descartes, of Herbert of Cherbury, or among the Cambridge Platonists, that is attacked by Nathanael Culverwell and later by Locke

[7] *Adv. Celsum:* I: 4.
[8] *De Trin.* VIII: 6, et alia.
[9] *De Veritate:* Pp. 47, 60, 61.
[10] *Light of Nature:* chap. VII.
[11] *Evidence of Divine Truth,* I, Campagnac, *The Cambridge Platonists,* p. 5.
[12] Smith, *On Attaining to Divine Knowledge:* II, *Discourses,* p. 13. Glanvil, *Lux Orientalis,* I.

and by Burthogge. " Do but analyze your own thoughts," insists Culverwell, " do but consult with your own breasts. . . . Had you such notions as these when you first peep'd into being? . . . Had you these connate species in the cradle? and were they rock'd asleep with you? " [13] Richard Cumberland also, who is sometimes classed with the Cambridge Platonists, remarks on what he calls the easy method of the Platonists of avoiding difficulties by means of innate ideas, and regrets ironically that it is not open to him.[14]

Interwoven with this conception of innate ideas as " characters stamp'd upon the mind of man which the soul brings into the world with it," [15] is the other principle of the activity of the mind in building up its own object. Having its source in Aristotle's doctrine of the active reason,[16] this principle appears in mediaeval thought as the solution of some of the difficulties in the theory of perception. It is not reasonable to suppose, according to Augustine, that any impression could be made on the soul by external bodies. The image that is beheld by the soul must then be the result of the soul's own activity in response to the outer stimulus.[17]

Although Descartes in many places seems to make use of innate ideas as principles found ready and waiting in the mind, in his reply to Regius he denies that he ever " wrote or concluded that the mind required innate ideas that were . . . different from its faculty of thinking." [18] Cudworth insists on the reality of those " intelligible ideas exerted from the mind itself," and describes knowledge as an " inward and active energy of the mind, . . . the displaying of its own innate vigour from within." [19] Culverwell in his discussion of the doctrine of Lord Herbert of Cherbury urges that the latter means by innate knowledge, not " connate ideas and representations of things . . . [but] powers and faculties of the soul." [20] Other suggestions of this conception of knowledge can be found in writings of the sixteenth and seventeenth centuries. More, however, seems to be the first among these to state clearly that " relative notions " are the modes of activity of the mind, assimilating and ordering its impressions from the outside world. In spite of his clear statements More does not succeed in using this principle consistently but falls occasionally into the other way of speaking of innate ideas as inborn principles of knowledge and morality.

[13] *Light of Nature:* chap. XI, p. 76.

[14] " Verum mihi certe non obvenit tanta foelicitas, ut tanto compendio ad Legum Naturalium notitiam pervenirem." *De Legibus Naturae:* Intro. V; *Cf.* Locke, *Essay:* I: I; Richard Burthogge, *Organum Vetus et Novum*, sec. 74.

[15] Locke, *loc. cit.*

[16] *De Anima:* 430.

[17] " Nec sane putandum est facere aliquid corpus in spiritu, . . . eandem eius imaginem non corpus in spiritu, sed ipse spiritus in seipse facit." *De Gen. ad litt.* Bk. XII, cap. 16: 33; *Cf.* Thomas Aquinas, *Summa Theol.* " On Man ": Quaest. 84: Art. 6.

[18] Reply to Regius, sec. XIII, Haldane and Ross translation, Vol. I, p. 442.

[19] *True Intellectual System:* p. 731, *Eternal and Immutable Morality:* IV: 1.

[20] *Light of Nature:* XI.

The conception of the notions of " substance, accident, . . . whole and part, . . . and the like," as " entities of reason conceived within the mind " is upheld by Richard Burthogge, in his *Essay on Reason*, 1694, and forms part of Locke's doctrine of knowledge in the fourth book of the *Essay*. For though Locke vehemently attacks the doctrine of " connate species," of inborn ideas whether simple or complex, he admits the truth of self-evident propositions, and insists that the " natural faculties " contribute a necessary factor to the knowledge of the world. Leibniz, like Descartes and More, combines with the conception of the activity of the mind in forming its object a lingering demand for those " characters impressed upon the soul " which had been rejected and attacked by Culverwell, Burthogge, and Locke.[21] It remained for Kant to disentangle the doctrine of the mind's active contribution to the object of its knowledge from the traditions and prejudices in which it had been shrouded, and to set forth the distinction and mutual dependence of sense-experience and the subjective categories under which it must be known.[22]

In the development of English philosophy More's thought is continued in that of Reid and, with the addition of the influence of Kant, in that of Sir William Hamilton. The " Common-sense " of the Scottish school, like the " common notions " of More and Burthogge, provides the primary condition of intelligence, and is determined in form by " the constitution of our faculties." [23]

Limitations of Knowledge. (Outline I, B.)

In his delimitation of the possibility of knowledge More agrees closely with many of his contemporaries and immediate successors. His doctrine of the phenomenal character of all knowledge, while it seems inconsistent with certain other parts of his own thought, finds acceptance and amplification in many seventeenth century writings. Herbert of Cherbury had emphasized the same inability of our minds to attain to knowledge of things as they are in themselves." Cum facultates nostrae ad analogiam propriam terminatae, quidditates rerum intimas non penetrent; id ea quid res naturalis in seipsa sit . . . sciri non potest." [24] This limitation is strongly asserted by Locke: "Nor indeed can we rank and sort things . . . by their real essences; because ẁe know them not. Our faculties carry us no further towards the knowledge and distinction of substance than a collection of those sensible ideas which we observe." [25] For

[21] *New Essays:* I: 1: 5, II: 15: 3, IV: 2: 1, IV: 10: 1.

[22] *Transcendental Analytic*, Bk. I. For discussions of the relation between Kant and his English predecessors see A. O. Lovejoy, " Kant and the English Platonists," in *Essays Philosophical and Pychological in Honor of William James*.

[23] Reid, *Intellectual Powers*, Essay VI: chap. VI; *Cf.* Hamilton, Lectures XX, XXXVIII.

[24] *De Veritate*, p. 165.

[25] *Essay:* III: 6: 9; *Cf. Ibid.* Sections 2, 3, 6.

Richard Burthogge the immediate objects of knowledge are "*entia cogitationes*, all phenomena; appearances that do no more exist without our faculties in the things themselves than the images that are seen in water, or behind a glass, do really exist in those places where they seem to be." [26]

The resemblance between these expressions and Kant's doctrine of the phenomenal character of knowledge illustrates once more the close connection between Kant and the seventeenth century English thinkers. The doctrine of Herbert, of More and of Burthogge is that of the *Transcendental Aesthetic:* "All our intuition is nothing but the representation of phenomena; . . . Things cannot, as phenomena, exist by themselves, but in us only. It remains completely unknown to us what objects may be by themselves and apart from the receptivity of our senses." [27]

These "unknown essences" seem to strike a somewhat alien note in More's philosophy. The conception is out of harmony with his doctrine of the power of spirits to penetrate matter and spirit; and his reason for holding it is not at all clear. He does not share either the distrust of sense-knowledge of the pure rationlist, or the exclusive reliance upon it that leads the empiricist to deny all knowledge of substance. He is, however, unable to avoid the traditional distinction between substance and accident, exaggerated by the scholastic interpreters of Aristotle almost to the height of a distinction between substances. This distinction combined with his inheritance from the mystics of the doctrine of the unknowableness of God, is perhaps the basis for his inclusion of essences which, while they are unknown and for all practical purposes quite negligible, yet must be held to exist.

In his assertion that knowledge necessitates a certain adaptation of the object to our faculties as well as of the faculties to the object, More and Burthogge seem to be following again in the path of Herbert of Cherbury. Herbert rejected the belief that truth consists simply in the conformity of mental conceptions to external facts, and held rather that it is the mutual harmony between the object and its appropriate faculty. "Veritas est conformitas quaedam conditionalis . . . inter objectum quodvis apparentiam, conceptum, & intellectum . . . quando objecta per conditiones istas, cum facultatibus cognatis conformantur." [28] Somewhat the same thought had been suggested by Benjamin Whichcote in his discourse "On the Evidence of Divine Truth": "I cannot distinguish truth itself; but in way of descent to us." [29] Burthogge's expression of this doctrine resembles that of More rather closely. "To us men, things are nothing but as they stand in our analogie; that is, are nothing to us but as they are known by us; and they are not known by us but as they are in the sense, imagination or mind." [30]

[26] *Essay upon Reason*, 1678, p. 60, *Philosophical Writings*, 1921, p. 77.
[27] *Transcendental Aesthetic:* General Observations (Trans. M. Muller).
[28] *De Veritate:* p. 204; *Cf.* W. R. Sorley, "The Philosophy of Lord Herbert of Cherbury," *Mind*, 1894. [29] Campagnac, *Cambridge Platonists*, p. 4.
[30] *Organum Vetus et Novum*, 1678, p. 12, 1921, p. 12.

Substance. (Outline II.)

i. *Meaning of Substance.* (Outline II, A, 1.)

Of the meanings given by Aristotle to the term οὐσία, two were included by the writers of the seventeenth century in the word " substance." It meant either that which has independent existence or that which is the subject of attributes and is not in turn to be predicated of something else. In use the two meanings shade into each other without accurate discrimination because of their common contrast to that which includes necessary reference to something other than itself. Descartes defines substance as that " which exists in such a way as to stand in need of nothing beyond itself for its existence "; [31] but in the distinction which he draws between complete and incomplete substance he implies that a substance is not necessarily a separate and independent existent.[32] For Hobbes substance is that which is " subject to accidents." [33] Locke means by substance the " foundation of properties," [34] but leaves unresolved the ambiguity of the word " foundation," combining in his treatment of substance the two notions of subject and substratum. In Spinoza's definition the two concepts of independent self-existence and of absolute subject are explicitly combined: " Substance is that which is in itself and is conceived by means of itself." [35] Fundamental to all these definitions is the notion of independence, logical or existential or both. Burthogge includes substance in his list of the categories which are notional rather than real entities, but in his treatment substance remains for him as for the others not simply a way of thinking reality, but independent reality itself. When this independence is interpreted, as it almost invariably was by the seventeenth century thinkers, to mean separate existence, it becomes impossible to give any logical explanation of the relation between substances, and results in the denial either of the reality of relations or of the plurality of substances. More protests against this inclusion of the notion of separateness in that of substance. In his doctrine of the penetrability of spiritual substance he implies that individual substances may be distinct and yet closely connected; and in replying to certain objections he explicitly rejects the doctrine that substantiality implies separate and independent existence. " It does not follow from thence, because they are substantial, that they may exist separate by themselves; for a thing to subsist by itself, only signifies so to subsist that it wants not the prop of some other subject in which it

[31] *Principles:* I: 51; Reply to Objection IV: pt. 1.

[32] " L'esprit et le corps sont des substances incomplètes, lorsqu'ils sont rapportés à l'homme qu'ils composent; mais, étant considérés séparément, ils sont des substances complètes." Reply to Objection IV: pt. 2. *Cf.* Reply to Objection II: Def. V.

[33] *Leviathan:* III: 34.

[34] *Essay:* II: 23: 2.

[35] *Ethics:* I: Of God: Def. 3.

may inhere as accidents do." [36]   On the basis of this conception of substantiality as being perfectly compatible with necessary connection of substances More refuses the seventeenth century dilemma of substance. He denies both that the definition of substance involves the all-inclusiveness of one substance and that the assertion of the reality of individual substances involves the denial of their inter-relation.

ii.   *Activity of Substance.*

More's doctrine of the activity of all substance differentiates his thought both from Cartesianism, with its mechanistic interpretation of nature, and from the epistemological development of the English thought of his time, and connects it with the Platonism of the Rennaissance and with the dynamic idealism of Leibniz.   More's insistence that the " primordials of the world are not mechanical but vital," and that the source of natural phenomena lies in "some universal principle of inward life and motion" is closely parallelled by Leibniz's description of substance as "un être capable d'action." [37]   This connection between More and Leibniz is suggested by Höffding in his *History of Modern Philosophy*,[38] by Ludwig Stein in his *Leibniz und Spinoza*,[39] and by H. Fischer, in *Leibniz*.[40]   That Leibniz was acquainted with the works of More is clear from the many references in his writings to the English philosopher.[41]

Stein argues convincingly [42] that the term "monad" as a name for the imperishable spiritual elements of the universe was suggested to Leibniz, not by the writings of Giordano Bruno as has been frequently asserted, but by F. M. Van Helmont with whom Leibniz corresponded during the year 1696 when the term first appears in his writings.   Van Helmont was a close friend of More, and the meaning of monad in the writings of Leibniz corresponds to the meaning given it by More and Cudworth more closely than to that of Bruno.   The conception of substance as essentially active, both in the thought of the Cambridge Platonists and in that of Leibniz, must be attributed in part, however, to the influence of the nature-philosophers of the Renaissance of whom Bruno was one of the most important.   It is to be traced rather to the Platonic

[36] *True Notion:* XXVI.

[37] More, *Divine Dialogues:* I: X; Leibniz, *Principes de la Nature et de la Grâce.*

[38] " More differs from Descartes not only in his view that all substances possess extension, but also in including activity . . . in the concept of substance.   Thus he, like Hobbes and Gassendi, prepared the way for Leibniz's natural philosophy." *Hist. Mod. Phil.* Vol. I, Trans. B. E. Meyer, 1900, p. 289.

[39] " Sicherlich hat Leibniz auch von englishen Naturmystikern, wie von Henry More . . . und Cudworth gewisse anregungen empfangen." *Leibniz und Spinozan* 1890, p. 132.

[40] P. 83.

[41] *Letter to Th. Burnett*, Gerhardt: III: 217, *New Essays:* I: 1, II: 27: 14, III: 10: 14, Gerhardt: V: 64, 222, 324, *Antibarbarus Physicus pro Philosophi Reali*, Gerhardt: VII: 339.   [42] *Op. cit.* p. 210.

than to the Aristotelian factor in mediaeval thought, because of the predominant influence and importance of the *Timaeus* on the one hand, and the almost exclusively logical interpretation of Aristotle on the other. More shows no trace of the Aristotelian doctrine of ἐνέργεια ; his references to Aristotle are concerned with logical distinctions, and show formal knowledge rather than real understanding.

iii. *Extension of Substance.*

More's doctrine that all substance is extended is, in his characteristic manner, a combination of elements from various sources not thoroughly assimilated. It partakes of the older Greek idea of space as an objective reality; it includes the accepted popular doctrine of extension as an attribute of things, while refusing to limit the application of this quality to material reality; and it holds something of the more modern notion of space as a form of relation between sense-perceptions. The attempt to combine the Platonic description of space as eternal, indestructible, and changeless [43] with the assertion that distance is "notional and not real" results in a certain confusion between the notion of space as an attribute of things and that of real things as existing in space.

More's refusal to accept Descartes's identification of extension and matter has its source partly in his reaction against the Cartesian dualism and partly in the influence on his thought of Neo-Platonic and Jewish writers. For the Neo-Platonists space is an expression, or emanation, of the world-soul, not identical with matter but given to it by soul. More agrees thoroughly with Descartes that every material object is extended, but disputes the further proposition that all extended objects are necessarily material. Descartes unequivocally identifies the two concepts of space and matter. "Space, or internal place, and the corporeal substance which is comprised in it, are not different in reality, but merely in the mode in which they are wont to be conceived by us. For, in truth, the same extension in length, breadth, and depth, which constitutes space, constitutes body." [44] More insists that this is merely assumed to be true by Descartes and cannot be proved. He argues that the description and explanation of movement requires the hypothesis of space which is not identical with the bodies moved, and that space, or "internal place" necessarily includes "certain notions, such as immobility and penetrability which are inconsistent with matter." [45]

Locke and Leibniz, a little later, dispute Descartes's assertion of the identity of space and body on somewhat the same grounds as those urged by More. "Body then and extension," writes Locke, "it is evident, are two distinct ideas. For, first, extension includes no solidity, no resistance to the motion of body, as body does. Secondly, the parts of body are inseparable one from the other. . . . Thirdly, the parts of pure space

[43] *Timaeus:* 52.

[44] *Principles:* II: 10, Trans. Veitch: *Cf. Ibid.* I: 53.

[45] *Enchiridion Metaphysicum:* VI–VIII; Letter to Descartes, March, 1649.

are immoveable." [46] The objection urged by Leibniz is again that of the "inertia" or "antitypia" which is involved in the conception of body but does not form a necessary part of the notion of extension in itself.[47]

This "infinite, unchanging extension, . . . the object of intellect and not of sense," is an echo in More's thought of that mediaeval realism which in regard to all other universals he strongly repudiates. More closely allied to the realism of Anselm of Canterbury and William of Champeaux is the theory set forth by Malebranche and by John Norris of Bemerton of the ideal existence of all reality in the mind of God. Norris confesses himself quite unable to explain the relation between the "spiritual extension" and the extension of physical bodies, but insists that God, while he contains the "intelligible perfection" of extension is not to be considered as extended in the same manner as are material things.[48] More vehemently opposes the identification of intelligible extension with material bodies but he is less definite in answer to the question of the nature of that intelligible extension itself. Sometimes he seems to imply a belief in its independent existence, sometimes he treats it as one of the attributes of God, and again he argues that distance is not a real being but our mode of conceiving bodies.[49] Locke also suggests these different conceptions of the nature of extension. Which of these is correct, he adds, he "will leave every one to consider." [50]

The argument by which More urges that spiritual as well as material substance must be extended bears a close resemblance to the Aristotelian arguments against attributing motion to the soul. "If it is not indirectly that it moves, motion will be a natural attribute of the soul; and if this be so, it will also have position in space, since all the aforesaid species of motion are in space." [51] More accepts the conclusion, rejected by Aristotle, of spiritual extension primarily because of its harmony with his doctrine of the activity of spirit. An additional reason may be found in his desire to confute the assertion of Hobbes that since spirit is not extended it is nowhere, and consequently nothing.[52]

More does not stand quite alone in the seventeenth century in his doctrine of extended spirit. His fellow Platonist, John Smith, in his discourse "On the Immortality of the Soul," suggests that it will not do to deprive "everything that is not grossly corporeal of all kind of extension." [53]

[46] *Essay:* II: 13: 11–14.
[47] Letter on the Question Whether the Essence of Body Consists in Extension, 1691, Trans. Duncan, p. 41.
[48] Norris, *Theory of the Ideal or Intelligible World:* I, 1701, p. 294 ff. *Cf.* Malebranche, *Entretiens sur la Metaphysique:* I, F. I. MacKinnon: *The Philosophy of John Norris of Bemerton:* p. 51.
[49] *Ench. Met.* VIII: 12, *Ibid.* VIII: 6, *Ant. Ath.* Appendix: 7; *Cf.* Note on Argument for the Existence of Spirit from the Nature of Space, below p. 297.
[50] *Essay:* II: 13: 27.
[51] De Anima: 406a, (Trans. Hicks.).
[52] *Human Nature:* 11: 4.   [53] *Select Discourses,* p. 68.

Locke's term "expansion," which, he insists, does not necessarily refer to body, seems to have the same meaning as More's "metaphysical extension." Although Locke does not definitely attribute extension to spirits he does consider that they are in space. "Finding that spirits, as well as bodies, cannot operate but where they are," he holds it· necessary to "attribute change of place to finite spirits."[54] Limborch, Locke's friend, had some correspondence with More and agrees with him in the doctrine of the extension of spirits.[55] He was the nephew of Episcopius, the Dutch theologian, banished in 1619 for his unorthodox opinions, and would have been welcomed as a correspondent by More on that account, for Burnet reports of the Cambridge Platonists that "they read Episcopius much."[56] And in the writings of Episcopius they would find the assertion that extension must be attributed to spirit, though not in the sense of the divisible extension of material bodies.[57] After giving the matter due consideration Cudworth does not feel it necessary to decide either for or against the doctrine of extended spirit. He gives at length the arguments of Plotinus to show that if one accept the hypothesis that "whatsoever is extended is body," it is necessary to conclude that "there is some other substance besides body." " But," he continues, "there are other learned asserters of incorporeal substance, who, lest God and spirits, being thus made unextended, should quite vanish into nothing, answer that atheistic argumentation after a different manner; by granting to these atheists that proposition, that whatever is is extended, and whatever is unextended is nothing; but then denying that other of theirs, that whatever is extended is body: They asserting another extension, specifically different from that of bodies. . . . Now it is not our part here to oppose theists, but atheists; wherefore we shall leave these two sorts of Incorporealists to dispute it out friendly amongst themselves; and indeed therefore with the more moderation, equanimity, and toleration of dissent mutually, because it seemeth that some are in a manner fatally inclined to think one way in this controversie and some another."[58]

Contemporary criticism of the conception of spiritual extension is found in the *Essay upon Reason* of Richard Burthogge. In attacking More's doctrine of extension as an attribute of God, Burthogge repeats Descartes's identification of space and matter with the additional comment that if space be not matter it must be a vacuum or nothing. To More's argument from the omnipresence of God Burthogge replies that no argument can be based on this because we have no clear conception either of the essence or of the presence of God.[59]

[54] *Essay:* II: 15: 8, II: 23: 19.
[55] H. Ollion, *Lettres inedites de Locke,* p. 156.
[56] *History of His Own Times:* I: 339.
[57] "Quantitate extensione sua, licet ad modum materiae non divisibili, praedita est, per consequens certo spatio & loco definita . . . est." *Opera Theologia:* II: 2, 1665, p. 417: *Cf.* H. Ollion, *loc. cit.*
[58] *True Intellectual System,* Chap. V, 1678, p. 833.
[59] *Essay upon Reason:* 1694, pp. 119–123, 1921, pp. 115–117.

Material Substance. (Outline II, B.)

More's description of matter as that which is divisible and impenetrable is very like the account of body given by Plotinus. "There are beings which are quite divisible and naturally separable, no one part of them is identical with any other part or with the whole. . . . Such are sense-magnitudes or physical masses, of which each occupies a place apart, without being able to be in several places simultaneously." [60] The divisibility of matter is the character on which the seventeenth century writers are generally agreed. Under the influence of the new mathematics the conception of material reality as made up of homogeneous particles was gradually freed during the seventeenth and eighteenth centuries from the occult qualities and "forms" of scholastic thought to become one of the most fruitful conceptions of modern science. More's thought wavers between the conception of matter as a real entity possessing real qualities and the interpretation of it as the given facts of experience in contrast with the categories of thought. Although defined as a substance co-ordinate with spirit, in actual treatment matter is allowed to fade away into a shadowy background for spirit. The divisibility which is one of the main characters distinguishing matter from spirit is not an absolute distinction since matter is ultimately made up of particles which are not physically divisible. Impenetrability, which is the other distinguishing character of matter according to More, is emphasized also by Cudworth, Locke, and Leibniz. For Cudworth the character of matter is "resisting or antitypous extension"; Locke interprets the primary quality of solidity as meaning resistance or impenetrability; Leibniz defines matter as "that which consists in antitypia, or that which resists penetration." [61] For More, however, matter is through and through penetrated by spirit. Impenetrability, therefore, applies only to the relation between bodies, and indicates, on the one hand, simply the sense-quality of hardness, and, on the other, the mutual exclusiveness of different parts of space.

Spiritual Substance. (Outline II, C.)

i. *Spirit as Substance.*

The doctrine of the individual spirit or soul as a separate, or at least separable, immaterial substance, independent of the body, dominated orthodox theology and philosophy from the days of Augustine down to modern times. It held the ground through the middle ages and the Renaissance both against attempted revivals of the Aristotelian doctrine of the soul as the "form" of the body, and against the Arabian conception of the individual soul as an evanescent modification of the universal intelligence. Descartes, in reaction against the scholastic doctrine of

[60] *Enneads:* IV: 2 (Trans. Guthrie.). *Cf. Ibid.* II: 7: 1, IV: 7: 1, IV: 7: 5.
[61] Cudworth, *True Intellectual System:* III: 16; Locke, *Essay:* II: 4: 1; Leibniz, Letter to Bierling, 1711 (Gerhardt, VII: 501).

forms and in search of clear definitions, repudiated that part of the Thomistic conception which interpreted the soul as actuating and informing the body, and emphasized the separateness of spirit from matter to the extent of rendering the relation between them inexplicable. He revived the Augustinian criterion of self-consciousness, which he treats both as the argument for the reality of spiritual substance and as the characteristic attribute by which spirit is to be defined. More likewise insists on the substantial reality of immaterial substance, but he returns to the scholastic doctrine in his refusal to consider spirit as completely separable from body in finite creatures. He refuses, however, to define the relation between them as that of form and matter, either in the original Aristotelian sense or in the modified scholastic doctrine of separable forms.[62] His term for this relation is the somewhat vague and undefined expression "vital congruity," by which he endeavors to combine the two conceptions of the substantial reality of the soul and the intimate connection between the soul and the matter in which it is embodied.

More, while in complete agreement with Descartes as far as the substantiality of the soul is concerned, breaks with Cartesianism in his description of the essential attributes of spiritual substance. For Descartes the distinguishing attribute of spirit is thought, consciousness.[63] More, on the contrary, holds that spirit is essentially self-activity, the source of motion and change. Consciousness is to a large extent our criterion of the presence of spirit, since only through consciousness, either experienced or inferred, can we be sure of self-activity. But consciousness belongs as attribute only to sensitive and perceptive spirits. The others are blind, plastic activities, working and striving for they know not what. More argues that Descartes has illegitimately defined all spirits by the characteristic which belongs only to some.[64]

Contemporary criticism of More's doctrine of spirit is found in the *Essay upon Reason* of Richard Burthogge. "It is not conceivable," writes Burthogge, "that a spirit should be only a penetrable extension, since . . . extension has but little to do with mind or thought, which is essential to a spirit, and without which a spirit cannot be a spirit, and penetrability and impenetrability has all as little." [65]

ii. *Unity and Indivisibility of Spirit.*

More does not distinguish consistently between the different meanings of unity: oneness as opposed to plurality, indivisibility as contrasted with the divisibility of matter, and individuality in the sense of particular numerical identity. The soul, he holds, is a unity in all of these senses.

[62] *Cf.* Aquinas, *Summa Theol.* I: 3; Quaest. 71.
[63] *Meditations:* II, *Principles:* I: VIII, LXIII.
[64] *Letters to Descartes,* I and II; *Ench. Eth.* III: IV: 3; *Immortality:* I: X: IV.
[65] *Essay upon Reason,* 1694, p. 100, 1921, p. 100.

Each man has a particular soul of his own; this soul cannot be identified with that of any other person; the soul of each man is one soul, not many, and it is not divisible into parts. The last point he emphasizes particularly in criticising the " distraction and obscurity " which Hobbes brings into the discussion of free-will by " talking of faculties and operations as separable from the essence they belong to." [66]

The question of the unity or multiplicity of the soul of man had formed one of the problems of mediaeval philosophy. Its source lay in the conflicting elements which went to make up the conception of spiritual substance. The attempt to combine the thought of the soul as an immortal, immaterial substance, partaking of the nature of absolute reason, with the thought of the soul as informing and vitalizing a physical body led in many cases to the conception of a hierarchy of souls of different grades of perfection. Added to this combination of concepts was the contempt for the body and the bodily functions which characterized Platonism and formed a large element in early Christianity. This widening gulf between these functions of the soul which are concerned with the body and the higher functions of reason and will tended, on the one hand, toward a purely mechanical interpretation of bodily activities and, on the other, toward a separation of the soul into lower and higher natures. Though opposed by orthodox scholasticism on the authority of Aristotle, Augustine, and Aquinas,[67] the tradition of intermediate souls lingered on in popular philosophy in many forms. It is set forth quite uncompromisingly, for instance, by John Webster in his *Displaying of Supposed Witchcraft*, written in 1677 in opposition to the doctrine of witches as held by More and Glanvill. " The soul," Webster writes, " which is a spiritual and pure, immaterial and incorporeal substance, cannot be united to the body, which is a most gross, thick and corporeal substance, without the intervention of some middle nature . . . which is this sensitive and corporeal soul or astral spirit . . . the vinculum and nexus of the immaterial soul and the more gross body."

iii. *Penetrability of Spirit.* (Outline: II: C: 1: b.)

More's doctrine of the penetrability of spirit is a protest against that conception of the separateness of finite spirits which was vaguely implied in much scholastic discussion and attained definitive statement in Leibniz's *Monadology*. More's opposition to this conception is not very effectively stated, but it is interesting from the singular combination it shows of the notion of distinct individuality with that of intimate con-

---

[66] *Imm.* II: III: 8; *Cf.* Locke, *Essay:* II: XXI: 6, where Locke in like manner criticises the " ordinary way of speaking " of the understanding and will as two faculties. While the word is " proper enough " if rightly understood, Locke suspects that its use " has led many into a confused notion of so many distinct agents in us."

[67] Aristotle, *De Anima:* II: V: 24; Augustine, *On the Trinity:* X: XI: 18, *Sermon 63 on St. John;* Aquinas, *Summa:* I: 76: 3.

nectedness. He is opposed both to a pluralism of disconnected spirits and to any conception of the inclusion of all spirits in one.

The seventeenth century had accepted from its scholastic teachers the traditional alternative that everything that exists must exist either in itself or in another. The interpretation of the meaning of existence in another had wavered between that of inclusion in another and that of dependence on another. Spinoza boldly included the two meanings and on that basis argued his doctrine of absolute substance. Leibniz from the same logical basis argued that real existence must exclude all existence in another, either as inclusion or as dependence. More's doctrine of penetrability is an attempt, tentative and inconclusive though it may be, to avoid the two difficulties of the destruction of individuality, on the one hand, and the denial of causal relation, on the other, by holding to one of these elements in the conception of finite existence while denying the other. He does not refuse the alternative of existence in self or existence in another, but he holds that, while existence in self in the sense of self-identity is incompatible with inclusion in another, it is not incompatible with dependence on another.

Arguments for the Existence of Spirit. (Outline: II: C: 2.)

i. *Criticism of Hobbes.* (Outline: II: C: 2: a.)

More's criticism of Hobbes hardly requires detailed critical treatment. The doctrine of Hobbes that all the universe consists of body or matter in motion involved in More's mind the denial of all validity to religion and morality. Accepting as he did the Cartesian conception of metaphysics as aiming at demonstrative certainty, More fails to appreciate the attempt of Hobbes to provide an adequate interpretation of experienced reality for which the standard of judgment should be the completeness of the interpretation rather than its proof by argument. More in his criticism of Hobbes seizes upon passages which in their proper context are meant not as argument but as psychological analysis or as explanation of terms. These, he easily shows, offer no proof for the materialistic hypothesis. The casual admission that " we take notice also some way or other of our conceptions,"[68] which would seem to provide a basis on which More could have met Hobbes on his own ground and from which he might have demonstrated the incompleteness of this conception of reality was apparently overlooked by More in his insistence upon argumentation. The difference in method and spirit between Hobbes and More is greater than the difference between their respective conceptions of the nature of reality. According to Hobbes, that which has dimensions and quality is body, of which some forms are heavy and coarse while others are fine and subtle; according to More, that which has dimensions and quality is substance, of which corporeal substance is impenetrable and passive while spiritual substance is per-

[68] Hobbes, *Human Nature:* III: 6.

vasive and active. They agree, in common difference from Descartes, that all that exists is in some sense extended, and that reality cannot be divided into unrelated parts but must be sufficiently all of a kind to allow for inter-relation. This agreement was apparently recognized by Hobbes, though not by More, for in Ward's life of More Hobbes is reported to have said that the philosophy of Henry More was the one he would choose if compelled to give up his own.[69] The important difference between them lies in the fact that the realities of consciousness which were of fundamental value for More have interest for Hobbes only as the means of obtaining objective knowledge.

ii. *Argument for the Existence of Spirit from the "Operations of the Soul."*

More's argument from the nature of consciousness is a combination of the assertion of immediate consciousness as the foundation of knowledge with the traditional argument from the incompatibility of consciousness with matter. The basis of the whole argument is that immediate intuition of self-consciousness which has its first clear expression in the writings of Augustine. "We both are, and know that we are, and delight in our being, and in our knowledge of it. . . . In respect of these truths I am not at all afraid of the arguments of the Academicians who say, What if you are deceived? For if I am deceived I am." [70] Never completely dropping out of the thought of the intervening centuries, this insight finds, however, only occasional expression until Descartes once more makes it the rock on which to found a positive philosophy. " But I had the persuasion that there was absolutely nothing in the world, that there was no sky and no earth, neither minds nor bodies; was I not therefore, at the same time persuaded that I did not exist? Far from it; I assuredly existed since I was persuaded." [71] More does not, apparently, recognize this assertion as the underlying basis of his own argument, for passing over it with only occasional reference [72] he devotes himself to proving that this immediately known reality is not matter but spirit. He interprets Descartes's doctrine, on the basis of its expression in *Principles:* XI, as an argument from the necessary relation of substance and attribute, and questions the validity of the inference. It is this form of the argument which appears in Cudworth's *True Intellectual System* as part of his refutation of "Hylopathic Atheism." He argues that spirit is "no accident, or mode, of matter" because "life and cogitation may be clearly apprehended without body." It is necessary to conclude, therefore, that "cogitation is . . . a mode or attribute of another substance, really distinct from matter or incorporeal." [73] John Smith, more direct in his

[69] Ward, p. 80.
[70] *City of God:* XI: 26, Trans. Dods.
[71] *Meditations:* II, Trans. Veitch.
[72] *D. D.* I: 34, *Imm.* III: XVI.   [73] P. 760.

thought ·as well as more clear in his writing than Cudworth, has kept closer to the Augustinian assertion of self-consciousness. He bases the knowledge of the reality of spirit on a man's "own sense of himself," and considers it "no hard matter to convince anyone . . . who hath ever well meditated the powers and operations of his own soul, that it is immaterial and immortal." [74]

The argument from sensation, the assertion that if sense were an attribute of matter then all matter would be sensitive, is simply a further application of the statement of Thomas Aquinas that if the "principle of life" were in the body "then everything corporeal would be a living thing." [75] More's conviction of the complete effectiveness of this argument is fully shared by Cudworth and John Smith, each of whom makes use of it in approximately the same form. [76]

Like the argument from the insensibility of material things, the argument for the existence of spirit from the unity of perception was a common and familiar possession of the group of Cambridge Platonists. Cudworth argues that if matter were the only real substance and the body the subject of perception, then it would follow, since matter is made up of divisible parts, "that no man is one single percipient or person but there are innumerable distinct percipients or persons in every man," each corresponding to a single point of the object perceived. "Whereas it is plain by our internal sense, that it is one and the same thing in us that perceives both the parts and the whole." [77]

The term "common sense," or "common percipiency," which More uses to indicate this reference of sensations to a common center, was used by the Peripatetics to denote the united activity of all the senses. This unifying power is attributed by Plato to the soul itself in distinction from the sense organs. [78] Aristotle holds that this common perception cannot be by means of a separate faculty of inner sense, for this would again need another to perceive the union of outer and inner. It is rather the common power of unitary perception inherent in all

[74] *Select Discourses,* 1660, p. 65.

[75] *Summa:* On Man: 75: 1.

[76] Smith, *Select Discourses,* p. 72, 73: "Yet cannot the power itself of sensation arise from them [material atoms] no more than vision can rise out of a glass, whereby it should be able to perceive those *idola* that paint themselves upon it."

Cudworth, *True Intellectual System,* p. 850: "Sense itself is not a mere passion, or reception of the motion from bodies, for if it were then would a looking-glass and other dead things see." *Cf. ibid.* p. 731.

[77] *Op cit.* pp. 825, 826; *Cf.* Glanvil, *Lux Orientalis:* I: "If the soul be matter 'tis impossible it should have the sense of anything, for either the whole image of the object must be received in one point of this sensitive matter; a thing absurd at first view . . . or the whole image is imprest upon every point, and then there would be as many objects as there are points in the matter. . . . This argument is excellently well managed by the great Dr. H. More, in whose writings this fond hypothesis is fully triumpht over and defeated." [78] *Theaetetus:* 185.

the senses when they are directed toward a common object.[79] Plotinus revives the distinction between outer and inner sense and draws a definite argument for the immateriality of the soul from the need for some central principle to unify the impressions of the various senses. " The subject that perceives a sense-object must itself be single, and grasp this object in its totality by one and the same power. This happens when by several organs we perceive several qualities of a single object, or when, by a single organ, we embrace a single complex object in its totality. . . . Doubtless we do receive a sense-impression by the eyes and another by the ears, but both of them must end in some single principle. . . . The subject that perceives must then be entirely one, . . . the principle that feels must everywhere be identical with itself; and among all beings, the body is that which is least suitable to this identity." [80]

More's argument from memory also follows closely that of Plotinus: " If the principle which feels were corporeal, it could feel only so long as exterior objects produced in the blood or in the air some impression similar to that of a seal on wax. If they impressed their images on wet substances, as is no doubt supposed, these impressions would become confused as images in water, and memory would not occur. If, however, these impressions persisted, they would either form an obstacle to subsequent ones, and no further sensation would occur; or they would be effaced by the new ones, which would destroy memory. If then the soul is capable of recalling earlier sensations and having new ones, to which the former would form no obstacle, it is because she is not corporeal." [81] The argument came down through the centuries in substantially the same form with occasional new turns of thought and expression. John Smith in his re-phrasing of it urges picturesquely that it is as vain to consider matter capable of memory as to imagine " this dull and heavy earth we tread upon to know how long it hath dwelt in this part of the universe that now it doth, and what variety of creatures have in all past ages sprung forth from it." [82]

John Smith's discourses contain also the argument for the existence of spirit from the consciousness of freedom in a form very similar to that in which it is given by More. " We evidently find . . . an ἐπάυξούσιον, a liberty of will within ourselves, maugre the stubborn malice of all second causes. . . . Whatsoever essence finds this freedom within itself, whereby it is absolved from the rigid laws of matter, may know itself also to be immaterial." [83]

The argument for the reality of spirit from its possession of knowledge which is independent of perception is emphasized by many of the Cambridge Platonists. It is closely bound up with their doctrine of innate ideas, and, like that conception, has its origin, at least in part,

---

[79] *De Anima:* 425.
[80] *Enneads:* IV: 7, Trans. K. S. Guthrie.
[81] *Loc. cit.*

[82] *Select Discourses:* p. 83.
[83] *Op. cit.* pp. 89, 91.

in the Phaedo of Plato. With the development of the doctrine of the soul as an immaterial substance the Platonic argument for ideal forms is transformed into an argument for the independence of spirit from body. Plotinus urges the existence in us of a thinking principle independent of the body on the basis of our knowledge of intelligible entities which cannot be found in matter.[84] Augustine uses the reality and necessity of the truths of geometrical science as a part of his proof of the existence of God and of the immortality of the soul.[85]

This connection between the knowledge of mathematical and logical truths and the immateriality of the soul reappears in the reviving English Platonism of the seventeenth century. Sir Kenelm Digby in his treatise on *Man's Soul,* 1664, argues the incorporeality of the soul from sense, from innate notions of being and relation, from the soul's understanding of identity and difference, and from its possession of eternal truths.[86] John Smith urges more explicitly that " equality, proportion, symmetry, and asymmetry of magnitudes . . . and many such like things, every ingenuous son of that art [mathematics] cannot but acknowledge to be the true characters of some immaterial being, seeing they were never buried in matter nor yet extracted out of it." [87]

iii. *Argument for the Existence of Spirit from the Nature of Space*

More's argument for the reality of spirit from the nature of space is based on his assertion, in opposition to Descartes, that space is not necessarily correlative with matter.[88] Space is, however, a real attribute and must therefore be the attribute of a real subject. This must hold true even if distance be considered as no real physical thing but relative or notional, for the basis of this relation must be real. Moreover this " immobile extension pervading all things to infinity which has existed always and will exist to eternity " is no figment of the imagination but a necessary and inescapable idea.[89] There must therefore exist a real immaterial being, an infinite spirit, as subject of this infinite and eternal extension. For confirmation of this doctrine of the connection of space with God, More refers to the Cabbalists as quoted by Cornelius Agrippa.[90] The reference is to chapter XI of Book III of Agrippa's *De Occulta Philosophia,* where place (locum) is enumerated among the attributes of God as given by the Cabbalists. This is borne out by various references to God as the " space of the world " in the literature of Jewish mysticism, and by the often quoted analogy: " Just as the soul fills the body so God fills the world." [91]

[84] *Enneads:* IV: 7.
[85] *De Libero Arbitrio:* II: 12, 15; *De Quantitate Anima.*
[86] Chapters 5 and 6.
[87] *Select Discourses:* pp. 93, 94; *Cf.* Cudworth, *op. cit.* p. 732.
[88] *Cf.* Note on Extension of Substance, p. 287.
[89] *Ench. Met.* VIII.   [90] *Loc. cit.* Sections 8 and 15.
[91] *Cf.* J. Abelson, *Jewish Mysticism:* p. 156; S. Schlechter, *Some Aspects of Rabbinic Theology,* p. 27.

An interesting parallel to this argument that spirit must exist as the subject of space is found in the doctrine of space and time set forth by Pierre Gassendi in the second book of the first part of his *Physics.* Gassendi divides all reality into the two classes of substances, those things which exist by or in themselves and are corporeal, and attributes, those which have their being in another. Space and time, however, are real things which exist in themselves and yet are not corporeal; they are "*generali entis, seu rei in substantiam & accidens divisione non comprehendi.*" [92]

Locke, Sir Isaac Newton, and Samuel Clarke follow More in thus conceiving space as one of the attributes of God. Locke somewhat hesitatingly and without complete assurance argues that it is possible "to imagine spaces where there are no bodies," and that "if it be a necessity to suppose a being there it must be God." [93] In other connections, however, Locke definitely attributes space to God. It is "that infinite expansion" which in its "full extent" can "belong only to Deity." [94] Newton refers to space as "the boundless, uniform sensorium of God." [95] "Since every particle of space is always," he writes in the *Principia Mathematica,* "and every indivisible moment of duration is everywhere, certainly the maker and Lord of all things cannot be never and nowhere. . . . He is omnipresent, not virtually only, but also substantially; for virtue cannot subsist without substance." [96] For Samuel Clarke also the conception of space as an attribute of God is based on the conviction of the omnipresence of God. Space, he urges, is not itself a being, but it is necessarily conceived as a property of some real being. Space is one and indivisible, infinite and eternal, and is therefore a property of the infinite and eternal being. [97]

The likeness in this conception of the nature of space between More's doctrine and that of Spinoza is clearly evident. In the *Enchiridion Metaphysicum* More argues that infinite space is "not merely real but divine," that it is characterized by the attributes of God, "one, eternal, complete, all-pervasive," and is, therefore, an attribute of God, a "representation of the essential divine presence." [98] This is closely parallel to Spinoza's description of extended substance as "one of the infinite attributes of God." [99] Spinoza, like More, insists that extended substance, in so far as it is substance, is "not measurable and cannot be composed of finite parts," that it is infinite, one and indivisible." More's differentiation of physical from metaphysical extension is similar to the

[92] *Physicae,* Sectio I; Liber II: Caput I.
[93] Essay on Space, Miscellaneous papers, 1677, King's *Life and Letters of John Locke:* p. 338.
[94] *Essay:* II: 15: 8.
[95] *Optics:* Question 20.
[96] *Principia:* III: 42: General Scholium (2nd edition).
[97] *Collection of Papers,* Clarke to Leibniz, 3rd paper.
[98] Chap. VIII.
[99] *Ethics:* Part I: Prop. XV: Scholia.

distinction drawn by Spinoza between quantity "in the abstract and superficially, as we imagine it" and quantity, as substance, "as we conceive it solely by the intellect." More apparently did not recognize the resemblance. In his treatise against Spinoza he concludes that the one universal substance which Spinoza calls God is really matter and accordingly classes Spinoza with Hobbes as materialist and atheist.[100]

Cudworth, while refusing the Cartesian identification of space with matter, does not, on the other hand, accept the conclusion that space is an attribute of God. This conclusion is based on the conception of space as infinite and eternal, and, Cudworth continues, "there appeareth no sufficient ground for this positive infinity of space, we being certain of no more than this, that be the world, or any figurate body, never so great, it is never impossible but that it might be still greater and greater, without end. Which indefinite encreasableness of body and space seems to be mistaken for a positive infinity thereof."[101]

Leibniz attacks the doctrine of real space, which, he says, "is an idol of some modern Englishmen," on the ground of the divisibility of all extension. "Since space," he writes to Samuel Clarke, "consists of parts, it is not a thing which can belong to God."[102] His doctrine of representation, however, the insistence that souls, though indivisible unities, do represent the multiplicity of the universe, seems not very remote either from the conception of archetypal extension as set forth by Malebranche and John Norris or from extension as intellectually conceived by More and Spinoza. The identification of space with God is criticised by Berkeley from his general position of opposition to abstract ideas. "The doctrine of real, absolute, external space," he writes in *Siris*, "induced some modern philosophers to conclude it was a part or attribute of God . . . inasmuch as incommunicable attributes of the Deity appeared to agree thereto, such as infinity, immutability, indivisibility, incorporeity, being uncreated, passive, without beginning or end, not considering that all these negative properties may belong to nothing."[103]

iv. *Argument for the Reality of Spirit " from the phenomena of nature."*

More's argument for the existence of spirit from the facts of nature is an expression of the characteristically Platonic contempt for matter. Based on ethical and aesthetic demands, the argument denies ultimate reality to matter because of its lack of unity, of self-activity, and of

---

[100] " Apud Spinozium . . . unicam supponit in universo substantiam, eandémque, quod necesse est, . . . esse Materiam." *Demonstrationes Duarum Propositium . . . quae praecipue apud Spinozium sunt Columnae, brevis solidaque confutatio. Opera Omnia*, 1678, p. 615.

[101] *True Intellectual System*, 1678, p. 766.

[102] *Collection of Papers*, Leibniz to Clarke, 3rd paper: *Cf. New System:* XI, Letters to Arnauld, XVII.

[103] *Siris:* 270.

intelligent purpose. Since these are involved in the ideal of perfection, which, from this point of view, sets the standard for reality, the failure to find them in the common conception of matter constitutes for the followers of this tradition a proof of the existence of immaterial substance.

The doctrine of the soul as the self-moved in contrast with body which must receive its motion from another is from the Phaedrus, and re-appears whenever the influence of Plato is dominant in the thought of an individual or of an age. " The self-moving is the beginning of motion . . . and self-motion . . . is the very idea and essence of the soul. For the body which is moved from without is soulless, but that which is moved from within has a soul, for such is the nature of the soul." [104]

For all the Cambridge Platonists activity is the most essential and most general attribute of spirit. Whichcote revises Descartes's " Cogito ergo sum," to read " I act, therefore I am "; [105] More and Cudworth hold that all spirit is of its own nature active but only certain grades of spirit are possessed of consciousness. " From the principle acknowledged by the Democratick atheists themselves, That no body can move itself," it necessarily and undeniably follows, Cudworth urges, " that there is some other substance besides body, something incorporeal which is self-moving and self-active." [106] More argues the existence of spirit from the necessity of a cause for the motion in the world, but he also suggests the conception, later developed by Leibniz, that motion itself is not altogether real, that the reality is not the observed motion but the " vis agitans " which underlies the appearance.[107] John Smith in his discourse " Of the Immortality of the Soul " argues the existence of spirit from the divisibility of matter, from the inactivity of matter, since the power of producing motion or rest " is altogether inconsistent with the nature of body," and from the nature of consciousness. His statement of the argument is very like that given by More though somewhat less elaborate in detail.

v. *Argument for the existence of spirit from apparitions, witchcraft, etc.*

Witchcraft, a term since fallen into disrepute, included in the seventeenth century all those occurrences which now form the subject matter of spiritualism and psychical research. In his investigation of such matters More was particularly associated with Joseph Glanvill,[108] from whose book comes the tale of the Scholar Gipsy of Oxford. For Glanvill and More, as for many of their contemporaries, the belief in the reality of spiritual appearances, of apparitions, of rappings and mysterious movements, of miraculous cures and the evil eye, was intimately bound up

[104] *Phaedrus:* 245, 246, Jowett's translation: *Cf. Timaeus:* 89, *Laws:* 896: Plotinus, *Enneads:* IV: 7: 9, III: 13.
[105] *Sermons:* III.   [106] *True Intellectual System:* p. 844.
[107] *Divine Dialogues,* 1668, p. 98; Leibniz, *Discourse on Metaphysics:* XVIII.
[108] *Cf.* Note on Glanvil, p. 331.

with philosophical and religious convictions of the reality of the soul and the spiritual meaning of life. Witchcraft, in the minds of many sincere thinkers, could not be denied without involving the denial of the truth of the Bible, of human immortality, and of the existence and power of God. The fact that Hobbes, almost the only distinguished man of the time to express absolute disbelief in witchcraft, was also for many minds the protagonist of atheism and materialism tended to strengthen this connection between the belief in apparitions and spiritual religion. Added to this in the mind of More was the influence of the doctrine common to Platonism and Cabbalism of intermediate spirits between God and the world. As Glanvil explains in the Epistle Dedicatory of his *Saducismus Triumphatus,* there is sufficient evidence of the reality and immortality of the soul in a consideration of the nature of God and of the soul itself, but because men are "best convinced by the truths that come nearest the sense," he adds these further evidences concerning witches and apparitions.

For his stories of witchcraft More relies mainly on the books of Jean Bodin, whose tales of the supernatural form such a contrast to his clear and progressive thought in political economy, and the *De Praestigiis Daemonum* of the German physician Johann Weier, with additional references to Cardan, Scaliger, Remigius, Van Helmont, Agrippa, and Paul Grillandus. He includes also many "modern relations" of which he has learned either through correspondence or by interviews with persons interested in the occurrences.

Arguments for the Existence of God.   (Outline: II, C, 3, a, 2.)

i. *Ontological Argument.*

The ontological argument for the existence of God, first formulated by Anselm, Archbishop of Canterbury in the latter part of the eleventh century, is the epitome and the finest expression of mediaeval realism. The statement of Anselm combines the logic of argument with the devotion and fervour of prayer. "Assuredly that, than which nothing greater can be conceived, cannot exist in the understanding alone. For, suppose it exists in the understanding alone: then it can be conceived to exist in reality, which is greater. . . . There is, then, so truly a being than which nothing greater can be conceived to exist, that it cannot even be conceived not to exist; and this being art thou, O Lord, our God. . . . Whatever else there is, except thee alone, can be conceived not to exist. To thee alone, therefore, it belongs to exist more truly than all other beings, and hence in a higher degree than all others." [109]   Anselm's identification of this ultimate reality, than which nothing greater can be thought, with the God of religion is based on the inclusion of ethical predicates in the perfection of the "supreme Good." "What art thou, then, Lord God," he continues in the *Proslogium,* after asserting the necessary existence of God, "what art thou except that which, as the highest of all

[109] *Proslogium:* II and III, trans. S. N. Deane.

beings, alone exists through itself, and creates all other things from nothing? For whatever is not this is less than a thing that can be conceived of. . . . Assuredly thou art life, thou art wisdom, thou art truth, thou art goodness, thou art blessedness, thou art eternity, and thou art every true good." [110]

The argument was never accepted as valid by orthodox scholasticism. It was attacked by Anselm's contemporary, the monk Gaunilio,[111] and was rejected by Thomas Aquinas.[112] Its reappearance in the seventeenth century suggests an interesting affinity between eleventh century realism and Cartesian rationalism. The various forms in which the ontological argument appears in seventeenth century theory differ one from the other mainly in that each emphasizes by argument and repetition a different element of Anselm's statement. The distinctive feature of Descartes's formulation is the emphasis on the inclusion of necessary existence in the idea of God. "When I think of it with more attention I clearly see that existence can no more be separated from the essence of God than can its having three angles equal to two right angles be separated from the essence of a right triangle, or the idea of a mountain from the idea of a valley, and so there is not any less repugnance to our conceiving a God (that is a being supremely perfect) to whom existence is lacking . . . than to conceive of a mountain which has no valley." [113] Cudworth and Leibniz argue that, since the idea of God involves no contradictions, it is, therefore, the idea of a possible reality. "And," continues Leibniz, "as nothing is able to prevent the possibility of that which involves no bounds, no negation, and consequently no contradictions, this alone is able to establish *a priori* his existence." [114] Cudworth and More attempt to show that the idea of God, not having been received through the senses, is a necessary and inevitable idea not dependent upon experience. These later thinkers, however, refuse to grant the assertion, which is the foundation of Anselm's argument, that the qualities, through which objects are what they are, are more real than the objects themselves. In the treatment of the argument by Spinoza it returns much more nearly to its original form. The definition of God as the absolute substance, the essence which involves its own existence, which is in itself and is conceived through itself, is identical with Anselm's conception of the most real being, the "Nature, or Substance, or Essence, which is through itself . . . what it is; and through which exists whatever has any existence at all." [115]

[110] *Proslogium:* V and XVIII.

[111] In his *Pro Insipiente.*

[112] *Summa. Theol.* Pt. I: Quaest. 2: Article 1; *Contra Gentiles:* Bk. I: chap. 11.

[113] *Meditations:* V, trans. Haldane and Ross.

[114] *Monadology:* 45, *New Essays:* IV: 10: 7; *Cf.* Cudworth, *True Intellectual System:* V, 1678, p. 723.

[115] *Monologium:* IV; Spinoza, *Ethics:* Pt. I: Def. 1 and Prop. XI, Letter to De Vries.

In spite of these differences in the statement of the argument, in its fundamental elements it remains the same. Upon analysis it is found to consist in the three assertions: that reality is as we are compelled to think it, that we are compelled to think the idea of God, an absolutely perfect being, and that complete thought or conception involves the existence of its object. The first assertion is taken for granted by Anselm and by his seventeenth century followers. It receives from More only the somewhat casual remark that he has no mind to argue with absolute sceptics or such as will not trust their own faculties.[116]

The inevitability of the idea of the perfect or absolute being is based by Anslem, in the *Monologium,* on the Platonic argument for the Good, the supreme universal, including all qualities. For the seventeenth century writers the necessity of the idea of God has a psychological rather than a logical basis. It is an "innate idea," inescapable and invariable, if not inborn. The third member of the argument, the assertion that perfection involves existence, arises from the quantitative conception of perfection, by which the degree of perfection and hence of reality of anything comes to depend on the number of its assignable attributes. The more attributes a thing has, the more reality belongs to it, and that which has more attributes than anything else and consequently is the most real of all realities cannot be non-existent. For Anselm this conception of grades of reality ascending from particulars of sense through universals to God, "*quo majus cogitare non potest,*" is a part of his accepted realistic doctrine. Descartes and More, however, from their nominalistic background, reach this conception only by an arbitrary identification of the notion of moral perfection with that of perfection as the sum of all attributes. It is only by dogmatic assertion that the idea of God as the object of worship implied in all religious rites and beliefs can be identified with the idea of absolute reality as a necessity of thought. Whatever validity the argument has on the realistic basis is for the most part sacrificed, therefore, by the change to a nominalistic standpoint.

For More and Cudworth, as noted above, the foundation of the ontological argument is the innate idea of God. This idea is for More the meeting point of the theory of knowledge and the doctrine of reality. It might almost be said that his theory of knowledge has value in his eyes only as a means of establishing the possibility of this idea. In the discussion of the ontological argument More emphasizes the innateness of the idea of God not as inborn but as necessary, inescapable, and universal. Descartes, though less insistent on the innateness of the idea of God, does none the less assert the priority of that idea over all others. The notion of the infinite, he holds, precedes that of the finite; the notion of God is prior to that of myself.[117] John Smith similarly insists on the knowledge of God as the necessary pre-requisite of all lesser knowledge. "There is a natural sense of God that lodges in the

[116] *Antidote against Atheism:* Preface.   [117] *Meditations:* III.

minds of the lowest and dullest sort of vulgar men, which is always roving after him, catching at him, though it cannot lay any sure hold on him; which works like a natural instinct antecedent to any sure knowledge, as being indeed the first principle of it." [118]

More does not work out in detail or with emphasis Descartes's argument for the existence of God as the cause of the idea of God. His somewhat metaphorical statement of it [119] bears less resemblance to the Cartesian argument than to the frequent appeals in the sermons of Smith and Whichcote to the "image of God in us."

ii. *Argument from Universal Worship.*

The argument for the existence of God from the universal prevalence of religious worship is one that held a peculiar appeal for the Cambridge Platonists. It is partly an argument for the innateness of the idea of God, and partly an independent argument based on the postulate that a fundamental human instinct implies the necessary object of its own satisfaction. More's argument that God is the only proper object of worship and hence that God necessarily exists as the real object of that worship resembles the statement of Benjamin Whichcote: "Were it not for light we should not know we had such a sense as sight. Were it not for God we should not know the powers of our souls which have an appropriation to God." [120]

The argument that since the worship of God is universal God must exist as the object of this worship is closely connected with the Stoic doctrine of common consent as the test of truth. John Smith feels the force of the obvious criticism of the argument from common consent but holds that this argument, while not absolutely or universally valid, is nevertheless effective for "prime notions" such as the idea of God. [121] This argument necessarily involves that interpretation of pagan religions as intimations of the true religion which has formed a part of Christian apologetics from early times. It finds effective expression in the *De Testimonia Animae* of Tertullian. "Even with the garland of Ceres on thy brow, wrapped in the purple cloak of Saturn, wearing the white robes of the goddess Isis, thou invokest God as judge. Standing under the shadow of Aesculapius, adorning the brazen image of Juno, arraying the helmet of Minerva with dusky figures, thou never thinkest of appealing to any of these deities. In thine own forum . . . thou proclaimest God." [122] The argument is worked out with great elaboration of detail and digression by Cudworth in the fourth book of *The True Intellectual System,* where he endeavors to show that the gods of the ancient mythologies concealed but suggested the true God.

[118] *Discourses:* pp. 49, 50, "Of Atheism."
[119] *Ant. Ath.* I: IX: 5.
[120] *Aphorisms:* 861.
[121] *Discourses:* p. 64, "On the Immortality of the Soul."
[122] *Ante-Nicene Christian Library,* Vol. XI.

This interpretation of other religions either as undeveloped and immature or as debased forms of Christianity is closely connected with the attempt, characteristic of the Cambridge Platonists though by no means confined to them, to connect Christian philosophy with the older philosophies of Greece and Egypt. In the *Mystery of Godliness* More argues the identity of the Christian trinity with the Platonic trinity of the Good, the Intellect and the Soul, and with the three forms of the Neo-Platonic One.[123] Before the time of the Greeks, he concludes, this truth, committed by God to the earliest men, was "kept warm" and "polished by those heathens that knew not the use thereof." It was delivered by them "to ancient patriarchs, prophets, or holy sages of old in either Egypt or Judea, from whence Pythagoras and Plato had it . . . and prepared those parts of the world . . . to an easy reception of Christianity."[124]

iii. *Argument from Design.*

More's argument for the existence of God from the evidences of purpose and plan in nature is given in the second book of the Antidote, not here reprinted. His statement is essentially that of the theology of his time. The argument is summarized by John Smith in the assertion that even if the atoms could move themselves this would not explain "how these movable and rambling atoms come to place themselves so orderly in the universe."[125] Cudworth's statement of the argument is given with his usual discursiveness and with innumerable quotations from earlier writers in the fourth chapter of his *True Intellectual System of the Universe.*[126]

The argument itself is, of course, much older than Christianity. For Socrates[127] and for Plato[128] the order and beauty of the earth, the sun and the stars, the arrangement of the seasons, the whole harmonious system of nature, hold unquestionable evidence of the existence of the gods. Carried over into mediaeval theology by Boethius,[129] this appeal to the conception of final cause as proof of the reality of God held sway unchallenged for many centuries both in theology and in philosophy. Of the many statements of the argument the one most generally known is probably that given in the first chapter of Paley's *Natural Theology* based on the analogy of a watch. The same analogy is found in Cicero's *De Natura Deorum.* "If you understand on looking at a horologe, whether one marked out with lines, or working by means of water, that the hours are indicated by art and not by chance with what possible consistency can you suppose that the universe which contains these same products of art, and their constructors, and all things, is destitute of forethought and intelligence?"[130]

[123] Book I: chap. IV.
[124] *Op. cit.* I: V: 7.
[125] *Discourses:* p. 48, "Of Atheism."
[129] *Philosophiae Consolationis:* III: 12.
[130] *De Natura Deorum:* II: 34, trans. F. Brooks.

[126] Ed. 1678, pp. 665–692.
[127] *Memorabilia:* I: 4.
[128] *Laws:* X.

Plastical Spirits. (Outline II, C, 3, b, (1).)

i. *Archei or Seminal Forms.*

The term "archeus," was used by Paracelsus to denote the vital principle which presides over the life and growth of living beings. It is different from the intelligent soul and closely connected with the spirit of nature. The term was extended by Van Helmont to indicate not only the presiding archeus of each body but also subsidiary archei of the various parts and functions of the body. This contrast of central and subsidiary archei reappears in slightly altered form in Leibniz's theory of dominant and subordinate monads, followed in turn by the dominant and subordinate selves of recent personalistic conceptions.[131] The term "seminal forms," *rationes seminales*, comes through Augustine from the Stoic λόγοι σπερματικὸι, the active forces hidden in bodies. The conception is characteristic of the Platonic tradition, but was rejected by those who emphasized the complete discontinuity between matter and spirit. Ignored or denounced by orthodox scholasticism, it reappears in the half-magical medical theories of the Renaissance as the postulate underlying the search for the "philosopher's stone," which would heal all diseases, and in the attempts to combat the growing force of the mechanistic interpretation of nature. Compare Note on Animal Spirits, page 311.

ii. *The Soul of the World, or Spirit of Nature.*

The thought of the world of nature as a living being, one of the oldest and most pervasive of man's attempts to interpret his universe, comes into philosophical thought from early religion by many paths and in many forms. The ancient Korê, earth maiden and mother, who long held sway over the Aegean area, Cybele, the mountain-mother of Phrygia, Ishtar, Isis, and Demeter of the Olympians, these and others rise from the mists in which still earlier forms vanish unnamed. The Greek tradition in the hands of the Pythagoreans changes, or returns, to that of an immaterial and impersonal force, and in Plato's myth of the *Timaeus* it appears in the form which is definitive for later thinkers. "Now that which came into being must be material and such as can be seen and touched. . . . Thus the body of the universe was created, and he, the God, assigned to it its proper and rounded shape. . . . And God set soul in the midst thereof and spread her through all its body and even wrapped the body around with her from without. . . . And from the midst even to the ends of the heavens she was woven in everywhere and encompassed it round from without, and having her movement in herself she began a divine beginning of endless and reasonable life for ever

[131] Leibniz, *Monadology:* 70, *Principles of Nature and Grace:* 3; *Cf.* J. Ward, *Realm of Ends:* 254-259, M. W. Calkins, *Personalistic Conception of Nature.*

and evermore." [132] Although Aristotle argues against the Platonic conception of the soul of the world, his assertions of purpose in nature [133] seem to imply a certain analogy between natural forces and the soul; and in the metaphysics of the Stoics this analogy becomes a dominating principle.

In the *Enneads* of Plotinus the doctrine of the world-soul obtains definite and systematic philosophical form. The third stage in the process of emanation is the universal soul, between the rational intelligence and the dark immovable matter. It " overflows from all sides into this mass, spreading within it, penetrating into it intimately, illuminating it as the rays of the sun light and gild a dark cloud, . . . imparting to it movement, life and immortality." [134] The world-soul like the particular souls, which proceed from the single universal soul but are not included in it, partakes on the one hand of the purposeful, rational order of νοῦς from which it comes, and on the other of the blindness and unconsciousness of matter, the ultimate limit of the emanative force.[135] A later Platonist gives a more definite statement of the relation between the natural world and the spirit of nature by describing an inanimate body as one which " has not a peculiar or individual soul, but is animated by the soul of the universe." [136]

Origen speaks of the world as "some huge and immense animal, which is kept together by the power and reason of God as by one soul," [137] and in the later development of the conception the world-soul appears sometimes as the "plastic faculty" of the power of God, sometimes as an incorporeal substance, and occasionally as the third person of the Trinity. It was carried over into the thought of the middle ages by Boethius,[138] but appears in scholasticism only as an expression of extreme realism. William of Conches, for instance, the instructor and later the opponent of Abelard, writes in his commentary on Boethius: " *Anima mundi est naturalis vigor quo habent quedam res tantum moveri, quedam crescere, quedam sentire, quedam discernere. . . . Sed ut mihi videtur, ille vigor naturalis est spiritus sanctus.*" [139]

The natural philosophers of the Rennaissance revived the conception of the world-soul as a mystical and half-magical principle of production and activity. They were impelled partly by their strong sense of the unity of nature, the same impulse which later found scientific expression in the postulate of uniformity, and partly by their antagonism to the purely mechanical interpretation of observed facts. Cornelius Agrippa,

[132] *Timaeus:* 32–36, trans. Archer-Hind.
[133] *De Anima:* II: 4, *De Somno:* II, and others.
[134] *Enneads:* V: 1, trans. K. S. Guthrie.
[135] *Enneads:* III: 8, IV: 3 and 9.
[136] Hermeias, " The Immortality of the Soul," trans. Thos. Johnson.
[137] *De Prin.* II: 1, 3, trans. *Ante-Nicene Christian Library.*
[138] *Phil. Consol.* III: 2, 9.
[139] Quoted by Poole, *Illustrations of the History of Mediaeval Thought,* from Jourdain, *Notices et Extraits des Manuscrits.*

for instance, to whom More makes frequent reference, insists that the world itself has a soul and a body of like nature with those of the heavens, and that this soul is the source of many activities which cannot be otherwise explained. To confirm this belief Agrippa refers for authority to "all the greatest poets and philosophers, Manlius, Lucan, Boethius, Virgil, the Platonists and Pythagoreans, Orpheus, Trismegistus, Aristotle, Theophrastus, Avicenna, Algazales, and the Peripatetics." [140]

The upholders of this conception in the seventeenth century, More, Cudworth, Glanvil, and Burthogge, agree in their reasons and arguments in its defence, but differ somewhat in the form in which they conceive its nature. For all of them the soul of the world is a necessary hypothesis to account for many natural phenomena which seem to lie beyond the power of "mere motion of matter." Cudworth's argument, in the third chapter of his *True Intellectual System,* and that of Burthogge, in his essay *On the Soul of the World,* differ only in details from that given by More in the third book of the *Immortality of the Soul* and the second book of the *Antidote.* More and Cudworth, however, insist strongly on the distinction between the spirit of nature and God, whereas Burthogge identifies this spirit with the spirit of God. Burthogge's conception is in some ways more closely allied to that of the scholastic realists of the twelfth century than to that of More and Cudworth. For the latter it is essential to distinguish between the soul of the world and the individual souls of men, but for Burthogge this distinction is unimportant. The spirit of nature, according to Burthogge, is called "the Spirit of God because it comes from him," and is called "the spirit (or soul) of the creatures, whether these be plants, sensitives, or men," because it is "that vital principle that acts and actuates them all." [141] For More and Cudworth the relation between the soul of the world and the plastic power of human souls is that of analogy not identity. According to More the animal spirits in man correspond to the spirit of nature in the world. [142] Cudworth does not decide definitely the relation between the spirit of nature and the various activities in nature. There is a general "plastic" nature of the universe, he holds, and particular "plastic powers" in the souls of men and of animals, and "it is not impossible" that there are various other plastic natures. He does not, however, hold it "reasonable to think that every plant, herb, and pile of grass, hath a particular plastic life, or vegetative soul of its own, distinct from the mechanism of the body", nor that the whole earth is an animal endowed with a conscious soul. "There may be," he continues, "one plastic nature or life, belonging to the whole terrestrial globe, by which all plants and vegetables may be differently formed," and by which all those things may be done which are "above the power of fortuitous mechanism." [143] Joseph Glanvil also urges the necessity of

---

[140] *De Occulta Philosophiae:* II: 55, *Cf. ibid.* I: 13, I: 33.
[141] *Of the Soul of the World,* 1699, p. 22, 1921, p. 156.
[142] *Immortality:* II: X, and Preface, Sect. 11.
[143] *True Intellectual System:* III: XXXVI: 25, 1678, p. 171.

the conception of the spirit of nature as an explanation of many strange and otherwise inexplicable phenomena. These are, he insists, "not mechanical but vital, effected by the continuity of the great spirit of nature which is diffused through all things." [144] For these seventeenth century defenders of the *anima mundi* the conception of its vital power does not stand in opposition to the atomic theories of matter or to the principles of physics and physiology. It is thought of rather as a supplement to these hypotheses, as giving the explanation of various phenomena for which there can be found no adequate solution in the science of the time. The scientific explanations, it is argued, are not ultimate answers to the problems but rest in turn upon the supposition of some vital force which is the source of those activities of which science gives the description.

A contemporary criticism of the doctrine of the soul of the world as held by More and Cudworth is found in the writings of the English physicist, Robert Boyle. In his *Free Inquiry into the Vulgar Notion of Nature* he argues that the soul of the world has not been proved to exist, that it is unnecessary as an explanation of phenomena, and that it is "scarce intelligibly proposed by those who lay most stress on it." More had argued that the action of the pneumatic pump could not be mechanically accounted for, and Boyle again attempts to prove that no other than mechanical principles are needed for the explanation. "Having proved that the air we live in is not destitute of weight, I endeavored," he writes, "to explain the phenomena exhibited in our engine without recourse to a *Fuga vacui* or *Anima Mundi,* or any such unphilosophical principle." [145] Leibniz also criticised the doctrine of the soul of the world on the ground that it is an unnecessary hypothesis. Although, as he says, he admits "an active principle superior to material motion and, so to speak, vital everywhere in bodies," yet he does not "agree with Henry More and other men, distinguished for piety and genius, who so make use of a certain archeus or hylarchic principle even for the management of phenomena, as if forsooth all things cannot be explained mechanically in nature." [146]

Superhuman Spirits. (Outline: II: C: 3: b: (2): (b): 3′: b′.)

The doctrine of the hierarchy of spirits held an important place both in the theology and in the art of the middle ages. In orthodox scholasticism, in mysticism, Jewish and Christian, in magic, and in popular belief these mediating spirits play their part. The conceptions and the names and symbols that are involved in the organization of the "mys-

[144] *Of Scepticism and Certainty:* p. 60.

[145] *A Hydrostatical Discourse by way of answer to . . . Dr. More and others.*

[146] *Essay on Dynamics,* trans. A. G. Langley, in *New Essays,* Appendix, IV; *Cf. New Essays:* III: X: 14, "Considerations on the Principles of Life," "On the Doctrine of a Universal Spirit."

tical ladder " from man to God are from many and widely varied sources, from Jewish angel lore, from Neo-Platonic categories, from Oriental mysticism, and from traditional mythology. They came from the Eastern church into Western Christianity mainly through the writings long attributed to Dionysius the Areopagite. These were sent to Louis the Pious by the Byzantine emperor and later translated into Latin by John Scotus Erigena. Corresponding to the three stages of purification, illumination, and perfection, according to Dionysius, are the three groups of the " great intelligences," ascending from the angels, archangels, and principalities, which are nearest to man, through dominations, virtues, and powers to the highest group made up of seraphim, cherubim, and thrones. Through these light and life flow from the supreme source of all things outward and downward to every existing thing.[147]

Accepting the doctrine of angels left open the further question whether they were to be considered as purely spiritual beings or as composed of matter and form, body and spirit, resembling human beings. The conception of angels as physical beings possessed of bodies comes from the Rabbinic tradition of orthodox Judaism, thus giving the weight of old authority to popular tradition. Opposed to this throughout mediaeval and Renaissance theology was the conception, based on the Aristotelian doctrine of pure intelligence, of angels as incorporeal souls, spirits unconnected with any body. Thomas Aquinas discusses the question at some length, referring to Origen, Bernard, Augustine, and Gregory as upholders of the first view, and quoting Dionysius as authority for the second.[148] His own conclusion is an attempt to combine the opposing views. " Since to understand is not the act of a body," he concludes that it is not essential to the nature of any intellectual being as such to have a body united with it. But since, in his opinion, angels always do assume bodies it is permissible to consider them as embodied spirits.

Cudworth, More, and Leibniz follow Aquinas in asserting the universal connection of spirit and body in created beings, but for More and for Leibniz there is far less difference between the conception of body and that of spirit than is found in the more strictly dualistic system of the " angelic doctor." For Cudworth and More the question about the bodies of angels is intimately bound up with that of the condition of human souls after death. The grades of angelic spirits correspond to the stages of the ascent of purified souls. Leibniz also asserts his agreement with " the majority of the ancients." The doctrine of the vehicles of the soul plays an important part in the Trismegistic literature in which it is closely allied with the mystical doctrine of light. The resemblance in this respect between western theosophy and Hindoo mysticism has been emphasized by G. R. S. Mead. While the conception of the soul's vehicle is completely alien to the spirit of modern thought in science or

---

[147] *The Celestial Hierarchy:* X: 2; R. Jones, *Mystical Religion:* pp. 106 ff. *Cf.* Alice Gardner, *Studies in John the Scot.*
[148] *Summa Theologica:* I: 2: Quaest. 51.

metaphysics, it forms the philosophical basis for the widespread belief
in the possibilities of communication with the dead and of the materi-
alization of spirits.

Relation between Spirit and Body. (Outline: II: D: 2.)

i. *Vital Congruity.*

More's principle of "vital congruity" as the basis of union between
soul and body is another expression of the same conviction as that
which underlies the conception of the archei, the *rationes seminales.*
The archeus is a force embedded in bodies as the source of their activities; the principle of vital congruity is that of a natural adaptation of
matter to soul, of some turning in the matter itself toward the soul which
is to give it life, and in the soul to that part of matter which is to form
its body. Each conception involves a certain blurring of the distinction
between matter and spirit, a certain transfer to body of the activity of
spirit, an implied denial of any absolute division between the two forms
of reality.

ii. *Animal Spirits.*

The original source of the doctrine of the animal spirits is to be found
in the recognition by primitive man of a close and important connection
between life and breath. Breath, moreover, meant warm breath, and was
considered as closely allied with the natural heat of a living body. The
Heraclitean assertion of fire as the essential life of all things contains,
among many other elements, this recognition of the importance of air
and heat for organic life. Aristotle systematized the distinctions which
had been taking form in the preceding period between the nutritive, the
animal, and the intellectual aspects of life, and organized the whole conception of soul as that of an individual unity expressing itself in activities
of varying grades of complexity. The Stoics used this systematic psychology as a model by which to construct the conception of the universe.
The Pneuma which was originally the breath has now become the all-
pervading fiery air which is at once the life and the order, the soul and
the reason in the universe, and the vital force and intellectual power in
man. Later Stoics, unable to sustain the paradoxes into which they were
led by this doctrine introduced distinctions of different kinds, and the
concept of spirit in man fell apart into the two conceptions of spirit as
the higher element, the "spirit that beareth witness of the truth," and
the physiological spirit which is the life of the flesh. The discovery of
the nervous system provided, as it were, a local habitation for the activities of the bodily spirit, and in this form the conception was developed
by Galen, the second century Greek physician. According to Galen, the
blood, which is endued with nutritive properties by the liver, is carried
to the heart where some of it is mixed with air and thus becomes "vital
spirits." This arterial blood laden with the vital spirits on reaching

the brain generates the animal spirits which are carried through the nerves to perform the higher functions of sensation and will.[149]

Augustine adopted and developed the Platonic conception of the soul as immaterial and separate from body, but in so doing he found it necessary to include Galen's interpretation of the animal spirits as the intermediary between the soul and the body. In this capacity the animal spirits played their part all through mediaeval philosophy. By a mingling of Epicurean atomism with the Stoic pneuma-doctrine the spirits become, as they were for Descartes, "a certain very subtle air or wind," made up of "bodies of extreme minuteness which . . . move very quickly like the particles of a flame which issues from a torch." [150]

The animal spirits have disappeared from the terminology of modern psycho-physics. As the "airs of the body" they came to an end with the discovery that the nerves are not hollow tubes. But in the conception of nervous energy the doctrine of animal spirit continues to function in a form closely analogous to that which it had originally in the Stoic pneuma.

B. Explanatory and Bibliographical, on the Text of More's Philosophical Works as Here Reprinted.

General Note to the Texts

The portions of More's philosophical works included in this volume have been chosen with the aim of providing characteristic and representative selections, of which each should be fairly complete in itself and which taken together would cover directly or by suggestion the whole range of his thought. Chronologically the *Antidote against Atheism* represents the early years of More's philosophical activity; the *Immortality of the Soul* is from the middle period; and the *True Notion of Spirit*, translated in 1682 from the *Enchiridion Metaphysicum* of 1672, is among the last of his strictly philosophical writings. Prefaces and dedications have been omitted because, while interesting and characteristic in themselves, they contribute little or nothing to the unfolding of More's philosophical conceptions.

In reprinting the texts the original from which the reprint is made has been followed exactly even in the case of obvious misprints. Where there seems any possibility that these might prove troublesome to the reader the correct reading has been given in the notes. The only deviations from the form of the original texts are: The omission of decorative initials, the substitution of modern type for the older form of many

---

[149] Summarized from M. Foster, *Lectures on the History of Physiology*, 1901.

[150] *Passions of the Soul:* I: 7: 10, Translation Haldane and Ross.

Greek letters, and of the English s and ct, the change of More's notes in the text from marginal notes to footnotes, and the insertion of figures in parentheses referring to the editor's notes.

ANTIDOTE AGAINST ATHEISM

(1) I: II: 1, page 5, *most evidently true.* Compare Descartes, *Principles:* I: V: "Ignoramus enim, an fortè nos tales creare voluerit, ut semper fallamur, etiam in iis quae nobis quàm notissima apparent."

(2) I: II: 3, page 6, *Archimedes.* Archimedes, the Greek mathematician, of the second century B.C., was the founder of the science of hydrostatics, and is known in tradition as the author of the saying, "Give me a place to stand and I will move the earth." At the time of the capture of Syracuse by the Roman Marcellus Archimedes was slain by the soldiers while engaged in drawing mathematical figures in the sand.

(3) I: III: 4, page 9, *five regular bodies.* The five regular bodies, all of whose sides, surfaces, and angles are equal, are the tetrahedron, cube, octahedron, duodecahedron, and icosahedron.

(4) I: IV: 2, page 11, *either of indivisible points or of particles divisible in infinitum.* For reference to the use of this difficulty in the conception of matter as an argument for the existence of spirit see note on the argument for the reality of spirit from the phenomena of nature, page 299.

(5) I: IV: 3, page 13, *a spirit is a notion of more perfection than a body.* The superiority of spirit over matter is a fundamental conviction of the seventeenth century Platonists. According to Cudworth, "Nothing can be more evident than this, that mind and understanding hath a higher degree of entity or perfection in it, and is a greater reality in nature than mere senseless matter or bulky extension" (*True Intellectual System:* V: Sect. 4). For More's doctrine of the nature of spirit see *Immortality,* Bk. I, chs. III, V, and VII; *True Notion,* especially section XVIII; Outline: II: A, and II: C: 1; Notes, pp. 290 ff.

(6) I: IV: 4, page 13, *forced to acknowledge something eternal.* This assertion with its consequent alternative appears also in Locke's argument for the existence of God. "There is no truth more evident than that something must be from eternity. I never yet heard of anyone so unreasonable, or that could suppose so manifest a contradiction, as a time wherein there was perfectly nothing. . . . It is also as evident that that something must necessarily be a cogitative being." (*Essay:* IV: X: 8 and 11).

(7) I: IV: 5, page 13, *supereminently contain these.* Compare Descartes, "Reply to Objections" II: Definition IV: "The same things

are said to be formally in the objects of the ideas when they are in them such as we conceive them; and they are said to be in the objects eminently when they are not indeed such as we conceive them, but are so great that they can supply this deficiency by their excellence." The distinction, taken over by Descartes from the scholastic philosophy, forms an important element in his argument for the existence of God as the necessary cause of the idea of God.

(8) I: V: 1, page 14, *abrasa tabula.* The metaphor of the blank tablet is used by Plato (*Theat.* 191), and appears in the contrast drawn by Aristotle between the active and the passive reason (*De Anima:* III: 4, 430a). Locke likens the mind to "white paper, void of all characters" (*Essay:* II: I: 2), and continually uses the term "imprinted" to express the action of external objects on the mind. Leibniz, in criticism of the sensationalist doctrine, repeatedly refers to the metaphor of the tablet. "This *tabula rasa,* of which so much is said," he writes, in the *New Essays:* II: 1, "is in my opinion only a fiction which nature does not admit." Compare Cudworth, *Eternal and Immutable Morality:* IV: 6: 4: "The soul is not a mere Rasa Tabula, a naked and passive thing, which has no innate furniture or activity of its own nor anything at all in it but what was impressed upon it from without."

For More's doctrine of innate ideas, in opposition to the conception of the soul as a blank tablet, see *Immortality:* I: II and II: II, Outline: I: A: 1, and note on Innate Ideas, page 276.

(9) I: VII: 2, page 19, *natural light.* The term "lumen naturale" was a common expression among the scholastic thinkers who may have derived it from Aristotle's comparison of the active intellect to light (*De Anima:* III: 1, 430a). In More's usage the phrase has an indefiniteness of meaning resulting from its many-sided origin. It carries something of the Stoic sense of participation in a universal reason, and something of the Renaissance distinction between natural and theological knowledge. It has connections with the "inner light" of the Quakers and the "Friends of God," and with the "natural law" of Grotius. Descartes attempted to give the expression a definite meaning, but in his writings the sense shifts from that of a natural tendency of belief, a spontaneous certainty, as in *Principles:* I: 30, to that of self-evidence through freedom from contradiction, as in *Meditation* II. For More and for his fellow Platonists natural light is partly identical with innate knowledge. Where its meaning differs from that of innate knowledge it is expressive rather of the value of the conviction than of its source. Culverwell complains that though he finds "many authors that speak of the light of nature," he can yet "scarce find one that tells us what it is" (*Light of Nature:* III); but he does not himself succeed in avoiding the obscurity which he deplores. The analogy between knowledge and light has ever been a favorite theme of mystical philosophy. Its basis is the importance of the sense of sight, both for knowledge and

for life; its expression varies from elaborate myth to simple phrases of everyday speech.

(10) I: VIII: 1, page 21, *That God does exist.* For discussion of this argument see page 297.

(11) I: VIII: 11, page 24, *matter does not necessarily exist.* In further refutation of this possibility More writes in the Appendix to the *Antidote:* "Others there are that seem to come nearer the mark, while they alledge against the fourth posture of our argument that necessary existence is plainly involved in the idea of matter. For, say they, a man cannot possibly but imagine a space running out in infinitum every way. . . . But . . . not so much as our imagination is engaged to an appropriation of this idea of space to corporeal matter, and therefore it may as well belong to a spirit as a body. . . . There is also another way of answering this objection, which is this; That this imagination of space is not the imagination of any real thing, but onely of the large and immense capacity of the potentiality of the matter, . . . and implies no more any real essence or being then when a man recounts so many orders or kinds of the possibilities of things, the compute or number of them will infer the reality of their existence. . . . It may be answered That distance is no real or physical property of a thing but onely notional. Distance is nothing else but the privation of tactual union . . . and is measured by parts as other privations of qualities are by degrees; and that parts and degrees, and such like notions, are not real things themselves anywhere, but our mode of conceiving them." In his later works, however, More argues that space is a real attribute and as such must be the attribute of a real substance, and that this substance is necessarily God because of the infinite unity of space. See argument for the existence of spirit from the nature of space, Outline: II: C: 2: c, and note page 293.

(12) I: VIII: 12, page 24, *does not fall under sense.* Lucretius, *De Rerum Natura:* II: 312, and IV: 110:

"Omnis enim longe nostris ab sensibus infra
primorum natura iacet.

* * * * * * *

Nunc age quam tenui natura constet imago
percipe et in primis, quoniam primordia tantum
sunt infra nostros sensus tantoque minora
quam quae primum oculi coeptant non posse tueri,
nunc tamen id quoque uti confirmem, exordia rerum
cunctarum quam sint subtilia percipe paucis."

(13) I: IX: 4, page 27, *nothing in vain.* Aristotle, *De Coelo,* I: 4: 271[a31] and II: 5: 288[a2], *De Resp.* X: 476[a7]

(14) I: X: 2, page 31, *Nec fulminantis magna Jovis manus.* Horace, *Carmina:* III: 3: 6.

(15) I: X: 7, page 33, *Epicurus and Lucretius.* According to Diogenes Laertius Epicurus held that the magnitude of the sun and stars is, "as far as we are concerned, such as it appears to us to be " (Trans. Bohn's Library, 1853, p. 457). Lucretius, *De Rerum Natura:* IV: 478, 496 and V: 564:

> " Invenies primus ab sensibus esse creatam
> Notitiam veri, neque sensus posse repelli.
>
>   *   *   *   *   *   *
>
> Non possint alios alii convincere sensus.
> Nec porro poterunt ipsi reprehendere sese.
>
>   *   *   *   *   *   *
>
> Nec nimio solis maior rota nec minor ardor
> esse potest, nostris quam sensibus esse videtur."

A more elaborate discussion than that of More on this point is in John Smith's discourse " On the Immortality of the Soul."

(16) I: X: 8, page 33, *Sun that sees and hears all things. Iliad:* III: 277. For note on universal worship as an argument for the existence of God see page 300.

(17) I: XI: 2, page 36, *the conarion.* The word " conarion," or " conarium," is from the Greek diminutive for pine cone or kernel. The gland itself is the vestigial remainder of an unpaired mesial eye and its function is still incompletely determined. For further reference by More to the conarion and to the Cartesian theory of its function, see *Immortality:* II: IV: 9, and II: VII: 15. On the animal spirits see note, page 307. On the argument for the existence of spirit from the nature of consciousness see *Immortality* Bk. II, Outline: II: C: 2: b, and note on page 290.

(18) I: XI: 7, page 38, *Fontanus.* Nicholas Fontanus, or Fonteyn, was a Dutch physician of the seventeenth century, professor of anatomy at Amsterdam, author of many treatises on medical subjects, and of the *Responsionum et curationum medicinalum,* 1639, a collection of letters and commentaries containing many curious stories. The present editor has not been able to find the report to which More refers.

(19) I: XI: 8, page 39, *Spectatum admissi.* Horace, *Ars Poetica:* 5.

(20) I: XI: 12, page 40, *statue of the Deity.* Compare John Smith, *Discourses,* p. 123 f.; " Both that God is and what he is . . . we may best learn from a reflexion upon our own souls, . . . and if we would know what the impress of souls is, it is nothing but God himself."

IMMORTALITY OF THE SOUL

Book I

(21) I: II: 3, page 61, *Common notions, Externall Sense . . . and Reason.* See Outline: I: A, and note on Sources of Knowledge, page 275.

(22) I: II: 8, page 62, *naked essence or substance of a thing.* See Outline: I: B, and note on Limitations of Knowledge, page 279.

(23) I: II: 9, page 63, *immediately pertaining to a thing.* Compare Aristotle, Metaphysics: Z, 1041ᵃ 15: "Now why a thing is itself is doubtless a meaningless inquiry; for the fact or the existence of the thing must already be evident. . . . Evidently then in the case of simple terms no inquiry or teaching is possible." Aristotle's distinctions, on the one hand between substance, or being, and attribute, and, on the other, between essential attributes and accidents, were deeply imbedded in Scholastic thinking. Instead of serving, however, their original purpose as instruments of investigation, they acted rather as impediments in the way of progress, having been transformed, as it were, from signposts into stone walls.

(24) I: II: 11, page 64, *There is no Substance but it has . . . the Three Dimensions.* Compare *True Notion:* V, Outline: II: A: 2: c, and note on Extension of Substance, page 283. A conception closely resembling that of More of the extended character of mind, appears in some forms of modern realism, as in S. Alexander's *Space Time and Deity*, vol. I, page 97: "Turning to Space, we find that mind enjoys itself spatially, or is extensive, in the same sense as it is successive and endures in enjoyed time."

(25) I: II: 12, page 65, *to which it must be competible.* Compare Descartes, *Meditations:* VI: "I remark likewise certain other faculties as the power of changing place, of assuming diverse figures and the like, that . . . must belong to some corporeal or extended substance, since in their clear and distinct concepts there is contained some sort of extension, but no intellection at all (Trans. Veitch).

(26) I: II: 13, page 65, *Iamblichus, Philostratus.* Iamblichus of Chalchis, pupil of Porphyry, master of Proclus and of Julian the Apostate, endeavored to combine in one system the concepts of Neo-Platonic doctrine, the mystical and mathematical speculations of Neo-Pythagoreanism, and the divinities of popular mythology. He was called by his followers "the divine" because of his powers of divination and his mystic ecstasies.

Philostratus of Lemnos was born about 172 A.D., studied at Athens and at Rome, and wrote the life of Apollonius of Tyana at the request of the Empress Julia. Apollonius, sage, mystic, ascetic, and wonder-worker, was the subject of innumerable legends and traditions.

The account of his life by Philostratus was denounced by many Christian writers as an attempt to set up Apollonius as a rival to Christ.

(27) I: III: 2, page 66, *Definition of a spirit . . . as intelligible . . . as that of a body.* Compare *Antidote:* I: IV: 2. This argument for the reality of spiritual substance on the ground that the notion of spirit is no more difficult of comprehension than that of body reappears in Locke's *Essay:* II: 23: 31: "If this notion of immaterial spirit may have, perhaps, some difficulties in it not easy to be explained, we have therefore no more reason to deny, or doubt the existence of such spirits, than we have to deny, or doubt the existence of body because the notion of body is cumbred with some difficulties very hard, and, perhaps, impossible to be explained, or understood by us."

(28) I: V: 2, page 71, *Intentional Species.* In the scholastic theory of perception, following with some changes the Greek analysis, the intentional species are intermediate between the soul and the physical sensation. They arise from the interaction of the soul and the physical world and are the immediate object of perception. The doctrine apparently arose from an interpretation of the Aristotelian conception of the medium of sensation in terms of the images or εἴδωλα of Epicurus and Democritus.

The analogy of the soul with light is a common conception among the followers of Plato. Plotinus uses it to illustrate the relation of the world soul to the physical universe: "The soul resembles an immense light which weakens as it becomes more distant from its source, so that at the extremity of its radiation, it has become no more than an adumbration" (*Enneads:* IV: 3: 9).

More's note to I: V: 2 should read "Appendix to Antidote, 3 and 10," and in his note to I: V: 3 the reference should be 3: 2 instead of 13: 2.

(29) I: V: 3, page 72, *Scaliger.* Although no first name is given here the reference is probably to Julius Scaliger, to whom More refers on other occasions. According to his own account Julius Caesar Scaliger was a prince of Verona and spent his early life in the service of the Emperor Maximilian. Later, determining to take holy orders, he attended the University of Bologna. His writings display an enormous amount of learning and a close observation of facts, but are marred by arrogant dogmatism and self-glorification. They include numerous scientific works in the form of commentaries on Aristotle, Hippocrates, Theophrastus, and other earlier writers. Scaliger is probably best known, however, for the fierce attack which he made on the *De Subtilitate* of Cardan in his *Exercitationes* of 1557.

(30) I: VI: 2, page 74, *emanative cause.* The doctrine of emanation, or emanative causality, is common to Christian and Jewish mysticism. It is an attempt to reconcile the conception of God as absolute, infinite, and independent of all relation with the conception of God as cause of the world. It appears in various forms in Indian philosophy, is sug-

gested by the Platonic doctrine of the scale of realities culminating in the idea of the good, and is characteristic of many forms of Gnosticism. In the conception of Plotinus and of the Cabbalists the doctrine of emanation finds more complete expression. The universe of Neo-Platonism is formed by emanation from the One, through the descending stages of the intelligence, the soul, and the world, with formless matter, or unreality, as the ultimate limit of the emanative power. According to the Cabbala, God, the infinite One, who cannot be described or comprehended, cannot be said either to be or not to be, makes himself manifest through ten emanations, the ten Sephiroth. These proceed by a gradual decrease of power and perfection from the archetypes of spiritual qualities, of souls, and of blessings, to the actual world of spirits and of material things. Compare Plotinus, *Enneads:* III: 8: 10, V: 1: 6, V: 2: 1; Abelson, *Jewish Mysticism:* pp. 106 ff; Myer, *Quabbalah:* Book Zohar, pp. 135, 195, 363, 381 ff.

In these conceptions of the emanative process it appears as a timeless, eternal necessity, producing its effects as light illuminates the darkness without suffering any change in its own essence. More, however, adopts the doctrine of emanation without working out the problem of its relation to his other convictions. It does not for him conflict with the theory of historical creation or with the theory of the volitional activity of God in the production and guidance of the world. It expresses his sense of the close and intimate connection between God and the world, and his opposition to the mechanical interpretation of the causality of God which characterized most of the contemporary theology, both scholastic and Calvinistic. Emanation in this somewhat indefinite sense was a characteristic conception of the English Platonists of the seventeenth century. It finds expression in their frequent use of the analogy of light and in such phrases as "the candle of the Lord" in reference to the human spirit.

(31) I: VI: 6, page 77, Compare *Immortality:* Preface: 3: " Matter consists of parts indiscerpible, understanding by indiscerpible parts, particles that have indeed real extension, but so little that they cannot have less and be anything at all, and therefore cannot be actually divided. . . . The parts that constitute the indiscerpible particles are real, but divisible only intellectually; it being of the very essence of whatsoever is to have parts or extension in some measure or other."

(32) I: VIII: 8, page 85, *Nóes and Ĕnádes.* The Noes and Henades of the later Neo-Platonists are intermediate respectively between the Intellect and the Soul and between the One and the Intellect of the Neo-Platonic trinity. See Proclus, *Elements of Theology:* Prop. XXI: Corollary: "And to an intellectual essence it is peculiar to possess an intellectual unity and a multitude of intellects proceeding from one intellect. . . . And to the one prior to all things a multitude of unities is present and to unities themselves a return to the one. Hence, after the first one, unities subsist; intellects after the first intellect; souls after

the first soul; and natures after universal nature" (Trans. Thomas Taylor). Cudworth, in the *Intellectual System,* page 568, urges that these intermediate orders of spirits are "not the Catholick doctrine of the Platonic School, but only a private opinion of some doctors among them," and claims that they are not found in the writings of Plato or Plotinus and are rejected by Porphyry. Dr. Taylor, on the contrary, asserts that the Henades are not newly introduced into Platonic doctrine by Proclus but are simply given clearer and more explicit recognition in his treatment. He quotes the following passage from Plotinus in defense of his assertion: "It is necessary (says he) that the principle and cause of intellect, and the deity himself should be present with the soul; and that this supreme principle should be present not in any divisible manner but perfectly stable, not indeed in place, but in himself. And, in the meantime, he must be considered in each of the natures capable of receiving him as something different from their essence, just as the centre also abides in itself. But every line in the circle terminates . . . in the centre to which it tends. And by something analogous to this, which our essence contains, we also may touch, coalesce, and be conjoined with the supreme" (*Enneads:* VI: 5: 1; *Cf. Ibid.* VI: 4: 4, and Proclus, *Platonic Theology:* Book III: chapters II and XXI).

(33) I: VIII: 9, page 85, *the argument of Descartes.* Descartes, *Principles:* I: 11: "It must be remarked, as a matter that is highly manifest by the natural light, that to nothing no affections or qualities belong; and, accordingly, that where we observe certain affections, there a thing or substance to which these pertain, is necessarily found. . . . Now, it is manifest that we remark a greater number of qualities in our minds than in any other thing; for there is no occasion on which we know anything whatever when we are not at the same time led with much greater certainty to the knowledge of our own mind" (Trans. Veitch).

(34) I: X: 2, page 92, *Pomponatius, Cardan, Vaninus.* Petrus Pomponatius (Pomponazzi), 1464–1524, sometimes known as Pomponatius of Mantua, was an Aristotelian of the Renaissance, "one of the earliest of the moderns and one of the last of the schoolmen." Many of his doctrines were condemned as heretical by the Fifth Lateran Council and his book *De Immortalitate* was publicly burned at Venice. According to M. De Wulf (History of Mediaeval Philosophy, p. 471) and J. A. Symonds (*Renaissance in Italy,* Vol. V, pt. II, p. 472) Pomponazzi upheld the Aristotelianism of Alexander of Aphrodisias in opposition to that of Averroes. In partial contradiction of this view, A. H. Douglas interprets the thought of Pomponazzi as a reaction against both Alexandrists and Averroists and a return to Aristotle's direct analysis of human intelligence (*The Philosophy and Psychology of Pietro Pomponazzi,* Cambridge, 1910).

Giralamo Cardan, 1501–1576, Italian mathematician, physician and astrologer, was born in Pavia, educated at the universities of Pavia and Padua, and was successively professor of medicine at Pavia, medical advisor of Archbishop Hamilton, brother of the regent of Scotland, and professor at Bologna. He was accused of heresy and, though released from prison, was prohibited from teaching or publishing anything for the last fifteen years of his life. His most important works, *De Subtilitate*, 1551, and *De Varietate Rerum*, 1557, contain suggestions of modern scientific principles, of organic development, of the variability of species, the effect of climate, and the relation of animal instincts to race preservation, combined with those fantastic speculations of astrology and number-mysticism which were the delight of the natural philosophers of the Renaissance. In connection with Cardan's scientific and mathematical studies it is interesting to note that his father was a friend of Leonardo da Vinci. For a delightfully vivid account of Cardan's life, based on his own autobiography, *De Vita Propria*, see Henry Morley's *Jerome Cardan*, London, 1854.

Lucilio Vanini, born 1585, in a Neapolitan town, attended the University of Naples and then wandered through most of the capitals and universities of Europe, teaching, studying, and writing. He expressed unbounded admiration for Aristotle, "the father of human wisdom," for Averroes, for Pomponazzi, "into whose body Pythagoras would have sworn the soul of Averroes had passed," and for Cardan. He followed none of them blindly, however, for he had only contempt for unquestioning reliance upon authority. In the *Mystery of Godliness*, VII, 4, More describes Vanini as one who "having a great pique against incorporeal beings is desirous to lessen their number as much as he can, and seems pleased that he had found out that one only soul of the heavens will serve as effectually . . . as the Aristotelian Intelligences; and therefore establisheth this as the only intellectual or immaterial principle and highest Deity; but such as acts no otherwise than in a natural way by periodical influences of the heavenly bodies." This conception of Vanini, while quite in accord with popular opinion of him, does not seem to be entirely justified by his most important work, the *Amphitheatre*, in which he upholds the reality of God against "ancient philosophers, atheists, Epicureans, Peripatetics and Stoics." None the less his *Dialogues on Nature*, sceptical in conclusions, satirical in tone, derisive of religious dogma and of ecclesiastical authority, aroused the powers of the church against him and he was condemned to be burned at Toulouse in 1619. According to tradition he exclaimed while being led out to execution, "Let us go, let us go joyfully to die as becomes a philosopher." *Oeuvres Philosophiques de Vanini*, Traduites par M.X. Rousselot, Paris, 1842; John Owen, *The Skeptics of the Italian Renaissance*, London, 1893.

(35) I: X: 4, page 93, *Letters to Monsieur Descartes.* "You define matter or body in too general a manner as extension. For all existing realities, even God, must be conceived as extended" (Epistola Prima ad R. Cartesius, in More's *Collection of Philosophical Writings*, 1662, p. 62).

(36) I: X: 8, page 96, *divisible and indivisible substance.* Plato, *Timaeus,* 35a: " He made the soul . . . out of the following elements and on this wise; . . . of the indivisible and unchangeable essence and also the divisible and corporeal which is generated " (Trans. Jowett). Cp. Plotinus, *Enneads:* IV: 1, " Intelligence therefore remains inseparable and indivisible; but the soul, inseparable so long as she remains on high, nevertheless possesses a divisible nature. For her " dividing herself " consists in departing from the intelligible world, and uniting herself to bodies; it might therefore be reasonably said that she becomes divisible in passing into bodies. . . . In what way is she also indivisible? In that she does not separate herself entirely from the intelligible world, ever residing there by her highest part, whose nature it is to be indivisible " (Trans. K. S. Guthrie). Cp. John Smith, "Of the Immortality of the Soul ": III: " Though the soul, as Plato hath well observed, be . . . various and divisible accidentally in these sensations and motions wherein it extends and spreads itself as it were upon the body . . . yet it is indivisible, returning into itself " (*Discourses:* p. 81).

(37) I: XI: 8, page 102, *Divine Matter dispersed in the World.* Cp. Cudworth, *Intellectual System:* II: sec. 3: " There is indeed another form of atheism, which we . . . shall call Stratonicall; such as . . . would allow to the several parts of matter a certain kind of natural (though not animal) perception . . . together with a plastic power. . . . And these atheists may be also called hylozoic, because they derive all things in the whole universe from the life of matter." Cp. *Ibid.* III: sec. 4, ff.

(38) I: XII: 1, page 103, *Order . . . in the World.* See Outline: II: C: 2: d, and Notes pp. 295 and 301. More does not discriminate between the argument for some undefined spiritual force as the cause of the order of the universe and the argument for the existence of God.

(39) I: XII: 6, page 105, *Ignorance of Second Causes.* Hobbes, *Leviathan:* I: XII: " In these four things, opinion of ghosts, ignorance of second causes, devotion towards what men fear, and taking of things casual for prognostics, consisteth the natural seed of " religion." In agreement with More's opposition to Hobbes, Cudworth insists that " Philosophy and the true knowledge of causes leads to God: and . . . atheism is nothing but ignorance of causes and of philosophy " (*True Intellectual System:* V: 43). The essential harmony between science and religion in spite of all apparent divergences is a fundamental conviction of all the Cambridge Platonists. Believing firmly that a closer " acquaintance with all the events and phenomena " of the world " would contribute much to free men's minds from the slavery of dull superstition," they are convinced that the spread of scientific knowledge would also " breed a sober and amiable belief of the Deity, and . . . be as fertile with religion as the ignorance thereof in affrighted and base minds is with superstition " (John Smith, " Of Atheism," *Discourses:* p. 47).

(40) I: XIII: 5, page 107, *Aristotle and Avenroes.* Aristotle, *De Coelo:* II: XII: 2: "We must consider the agency of the stars as analogous to that of plants and animals"; Cp. Metaphysics: L, 1073^{a30}, 1973^b.

The Latin name Avenroes, or its more usual form Averroes, comes from the Arabian, Ibn-Roschd, by way of various Spanish transformations and appears in innumerable different forms. Averroes was the last of the great Arabian philosophers of the middle ages. His importance in the history of philosophy lies largely in his commentaries on Aristotle which had a wide influence both on the philosophical thinking of the Jews and on the doctrines of the Christian Schoolmen of succeeding centuries. His doctrine of the stars as a hierarchy of celestial intelligences in endless movement, contained in his *De Substantia Orbis,* is an elaborate commentary on the XIIth book of Aristotle's *Metaphysics.* See Ernst Renan, *Averroés et Averroïsme,* Paris, 1861.

(41) I: XIII: 5, page 107, *Sadducees.* See *Acts of the Apostles:* XXIII: 8: "For the Sadducees say there is no resurrection, neither angel nor spirit"; and Josephus, *Antiquities of the Jews:* I: 4: "The doctrine of the Sadducees is this, that souls die with the bodies." The Sadducees rejected the doctrines of individual spirits and individual immortality developed by the Pharisees. They retained the older Hebrew conception of the soul as expressed in Genesis: II: 7 and Ecclesiastes: XII: 7, according to which the soul, the bearer of individuality and personality, is no other than the animated quickened body, and the spirit, which gives life, is the "breath of God," immortal in that God is eternal, but without individual personality. (From R. H. Charles, *Eschatology,* 1913). For the Epicureans ghosts were the images or ἀπορροιαì given off by bodies when alive which might remain floating in the air even long after the death of the bodies from which they came. See Lucretius, *De Rerum Natura:* Bk. IV, 730, 760.

(42) I: XIV: 1, page 110, *Paracelsus.* The passage in his *Enthusiasmus Triumphatus* to which More refers attributes to Paracelsus the following explanation of divination: "A man has a sydereall body, besides this terrestriall, which is joyned with the stars; and so when this sydereall body is more free from the elements, as in sleep, this body and the stars confabulating together, the mind is informed of things to come. . . . The stars are struck with a terrour or a horrour of any man's death, whence it is that no man dies without some sign or notice from them, as the dances of dead men, some noise in the house, or the like." Compare Paracelsus: *Hermetic Astronomy:* "No man dies without portents. When a man is about to die the constellation within him loses its operations, and this loss takes place by means of a sign or great mutation. . . . From motions taking place in nature the death of every man can be prognosticated. . . . These are not the work of spectres but are natural operations . . . by means of the stars." (Trans. A. E. Waite.)

Paracelsus, whose rightful name was Theophrastus Bombast von Hohenheim, has been the subject of so many legendary tales that it is practically impossible to discriminate between fact and fiction in the account of his life. Born towards the end of the fifteenth century, he was instructed in alchemy, surgery, and medicine by his father, and after a brief sojourn at the University of Basel, he devoted himself to the study of occult science under Johann Trithemus, Abbot of Spannheim. Still in search of hidden knowledge he wandered through far lands, studied the customs of strange peoples, gained wisdom, as he said, from birds and beasts, and returned to his native country filled with the lore of the East and confirmed in his opposition to the orthodox medical theory of his time. Appointed professor of physics and medicine at Basel he began his teaching by burning the works of Galen and Avicenna in a brass pan with sulphur and nitre to show his disregard for traditional doctrine. The teaching of Paracelsus was apparently a strange medley of experimental observation and mystical nature-philosophy. He endeavored to free medical practice from the bonds of tradition and superstition, emphasized the value of pure chemicals in opposition to the customary use of complex mixtures of herbs, and insisted that the physician should learn rather from nature than from books. See A. E. Waite, *Lives of the Alchemistical Philosophers;* Franz Hartmann, *Paracelsus.*

(43) I: XIV: 7, page 112, *Alcibiades, his patrimony.* The reference is probably to the Platonic Dialogue I Alcibiades, 123.

(44) I: XIV: 7, page 112, *Lansbergius.* Lansbergius was one of the important mathematicians of the seventeenth century. Born in Zealand, he was minister to various churches in Antwerp, Goes, and Middleburg until his death in 1632. His works include *Chronologia Sacra,* 1626, *Progymnasmata Astronomiae restitutae,* 1629, *Triangulorum Geometricorum,* 1631, *Uranometriae,* 1631, *Commentationes in motum terrae diurnam et anuum,* 1630. (Bayle's Dictionary.)

(45) I: XIV: 8, page 114, *Hobbes's Conjecture.* Hobbes, *Concerning Body,* Part IV: Ch. XXV:, sec. 5.

IMMORTALITY OF THE SOUL.

Book II.

(46) II: I: 2, page 117, *the suffrage of Mr. Hobbes.* Hobbes, *Concerning Body:* Part IV: ch. 25: "Sense, therefore in the sentient, can be nothing else but motion in some of the internal parts of the sentient."

(47) II: II: 1, page 120, *competible to matter.* See Outline: II: C: 2: b, and Note on the Argument for existence of spirit from "the Operations of the Soul," page 290.

(48) II: II: 3, page 122, *Cartesius . . . colour and light.* Descartes, *Météores:* VIII: " La nature des couleurs . . . ne consiste qu'en ce que les parties de la matière subtile, qui transmet l'action de la lumière, tendent a tournoyer avec plus de force qu'a se mouvoir en ligne droit; en sorte que celles qui tendent a tourner beaucoup plus fort, causent la couleur rouge, & celles qui n'y tendent qu'un peu plus fort causent la jaune." See also Descartes's *Principles of Philosophy:* III: 55, ff; *Le Monde:* XIII and XIV.

(49) II: II: 9, page 125, *Secundae Notiones.* Compare *Antidote against Atheism:* I: VI, and Outline: A: I. B: 2. Sir William Hamilton, *Discussions,* 1861, IV: page 139: " The distinction which we owe to the Arabians of first and second notions — A first notion is the concept of a thing as it exists in itself, and independent of any operation of thought. . . . A second notion is the concept not of an object as it is in reality, but of the mode under which it is thought by the mind."

(50) II: IV: 1, page 128, *the Seat of Common Sense.* 1. " That the whole body is the Seat of Common Sense." See Plotinus, *Enneads:* IV: 3: 23, IV: 8: 8; Thomas Aquinas, *Summa Theologia:* I: 76: 8: 1: Quaest. 4. The opinion that the whole body is the " seat of the soul," the basis of unlocalized sensation and of unified perception was widely held through the middle ages. More argues against it in chapter IV: 2 and VII: 2, but his insistence, in chapter X, that the soul is not " so confined " to that part of the body which is the common sensorium " that it is essentially no where else in the body " but that it spreads out on occasion " into all the members," seems to imply a conception very like the one which he here rejects.

2. " That the orifice of the Stomach " is the seat of common sense. This opinion More refers in VII: 4 to Van Helmont, *De Sede Animae.*

3. " The Heart." See Aristotle, *The Parts of Animals:* II: 10, *The Generation of Animals:* II: 6, *On Youth and Age:* III; Hobbes, *Concerning Body:* IV: 25: 4.

4. " The Brain." Plato, *Phaedo:* 96ᵇ, *Timaeus:* 73, 74.

5. " The Membranes." This opinion is attributed to Erasistratus, the Alexandrian physician of the second century B. C. on the authority of Galen, *De Placitis:* VII: 602, XV: 360.

6. " The Septum Lucidum." Sir Kenelm Digby, *Of Bodies and Man's Soul:* Ch. XXV: " The brain . . . contains toward the middle four concavities . . . in truth one great concavity. Now, two rooms of this great concavity are divided by a little body, somewhat like a skin (though more fryable) which of itself is clear . . . but hanging a little slack it somewhat shriveleth together; and this anatomists do call Septum lucidum, or speculum. . . . This part seemeth . . . to be that and onely that in which the fancie or common sense resideth." Sir Kenelm Digby, 1603–1665, son of one of the conspirators of the Gunpowder Plot, had a varied and romantic career. A youthful prodigy in mathematics at Oxford, a member of the household of Prince Charles,

a privateer against the ships of France and Spain, Commissioner of the navy, chancellor to Queen Henrietta, envoy to the pope on behalf of the English Roman Catholics, diplomatic agent for Cromwell on the continent, imprisoned, exiled, restored, the tale of his life is that of English political life of the seventeenth century. Digby was possessed of a wide range of knowledge in which scientific fact mingled with the wildest superstitions of astrology and alchemy. Besides his philosophical writings *On Bodies* and *On the Immortality of Man's Soul,* originally published in Paris in 1644, he wrote treatises in defence of Roman Catholicism and several volumes of translations and of memoirs.

7. "Some small and perfectly-solid particle in the body." In chapter IV, section 8, below More refers this opinion to Henricus Regius, *Philosophia Naturalis:* lib. 5, cap. 1. Here Regius is arguing against the necessity of holding that the mind dies with the body. "Cum corpore subjecto dividenda . . . illa [mens] tum in minima sensorii communis atomo, sive corpusculo propter parvitatem & soliditatem suam naturaliter indivisibili posset existere." Henricus Regius, or Henri LeRoi, was originally a disciple of Descartes and the leader of the Cartesians of Utrecht. In 1640 he defended the doctrines of Descartes in public debate. Later, disowned and disavowed by Descartes because of his distortion of Cartesianism into materialism, he turned against his former master and became one of the leaders in the opposition against Cartesian doctrine. See Descartes's Letter to Regius, 1645, Letter to Elizabeth, March 15, 1647, and "Notes Directed against a Certain Programme" (Reply by Descartes to attack of Regius), Adam and Tannery edition of Descartes, Vol. XI. pp. 672–687.

8. "The Conarion." See below, IV: 9, and VII: 16, where More gives various references to Descartes's discussions of the conarion as the organ of common sense. A characteristic passage is that from the *Passions of the Soul:* I: XXXI and XXXII: "The soul is really joined to the whole body, and we cannot, properly speaking, say that it exists in any one of its parts to the exclusion of the others, because it is one and in some manner indivisible. . . . Though it be joined to the whole body there is yet in that a certain part in which it exercises its functions more particularly than in all the others. . . . In examining the matter with care it seems as though I had clearly ascertained that the part of the body in which the soul exercises its functions immediately is in no-wise the heart or the whole of the brain, but merely the most inward of all its parts, to wit, a certain very small gland which is situated in the middle of its substance. . . . The reason which persuades me that the soul cannot have any other seat in all the body than this gland wherein to exercise its functions immediately, is that I reflect that the other parts of our brain are all of them double, just as we have two eyes, two hands, two ears, and finally all of the organs of our outside senses are double; and inasmuch as we have but one solitary and simple thought of one particular thing at one and the same moment . . . there must somewhere be a place where the two impressions which pro-

ceed from a single object by means of the double organs of the senses can unite before arriving at the soul. . . . There is no other place in the body where they can be thus united unless they are so in this gland." (Trans. Haldane and Ross.) In the Appendix to his *Antidote Against Atheism* More apparently had accepted the opinion of Descartes which he here rejects, for he writes of the " conarion, or Pine-Kernell," as " the Tent or Pavilion wherein the soul is chiefly seated " (Appendix: X).

9. "The concourse of the Nerves about the fourth ventricle of the Brain." The upholder of this opinion of the seat of the soul as the " concourse of nerves " or the " spinal marrow " of the fourth ventricle of the brain More gives, in VI: 1 and VII: 18, as Thomas Wharton, 1614–1673, author of *Adenographia: Sive Glandularum totius corporis Descriptio*. Wharton was an English physician and surgeon, student at Cambridge and at Oxford, and later connected with St. Thomas's Hospital. The passage to which More gives reference is the *Adenographia*: Cap. XXIII, 1656, page 153: " Species sentiuntur potiùs ubi deferuntur; at primò deferuntur principium spinalis medullae, quae pars certè multo nobilior, majorq; hac glandula est."

10. "The Spirits in that fourth ventricle." See below VI: 2 and VII: 18. This location of the seat of the soul in the animal spirits of the fourth ventricle of the brain, which More accepts is apparently derived from Galen, the celebrated physician of the second century who was the main authority for anatomy and medicine throughout the middle ages. Galen combined with his anatomical knowledge and theories a somewhat metaphysical conception of the "pneuma," the soul, or life, and held that the fine and subtile animal spirits of the fourth ventricle of the brain either are the soul itself or are the particular part of the body in which the soul abides. Galen, *De Placitis:* V: 604, quoted in Siebeck, *Geschichte der Psychologie,* 1880, II: 269. See also Walther Sudhoff, " Die Lehre von den Hirnventrikeln in textlicher und graphischer Tradition des Altertums und Mittelalten," *Archiv für Geschichte der Medizin,* VII. The same conception is attributed to Constantio Varoli, and was set forth by Thomas Willis, professor of natural philosophy at Oxford, in his *Two Discourses concerning the Soul,* 1672.

(51) II: VII: 10, page 139, *Laurentius.* Andrew Laurens (Laurentius), died 1609, was professor of physic in the University of Montpellier and first physician to Henri IV. His most important work, *Historia Anatomica corporis & singularum eius partium multis controversis observationibus novis illustrata,* was dedicated to Henri IV and was published in Paris in Latin in 1600 and in French in 1610. More's reference is to this work, Lib. IV, Controversiae, Quaest. VII, De Ortu Nervorum: " Praeterea maior apparet continuatio nervi cum cerebro, qual cum corde; si enim ligetur nervus in medio, pars superior cerebrum versus, sentiet & movebitur, pars vero cordi vicinior insensilis erit & immobilis."

(52) II: VII: 12, page 141, *Galen. De Placitis:* VII: 611.

(53) II: VIII: 10, page 144, *Boeotum crassu-.* Horace, *Epistolae:* II: 1: 244: "Boeotum in crassu jurares aëre natum."

(54) II: X: 3, page 147, *Enthusiasmus Triumphatus, 3. 4. 5.* "We are therefore to take notice of the several degrees and natures of the faculties of the soul, the lowest whereof she exercises without so much as any perception of what she does; and these operations are fatall and necessary to her so long as she is in the body; and a man differs in them little from a plant. . . . The lowest of those faculties of whose operations we have any perception, are the outward senses, which upon the pertingencie of the object to the sensitive organ cannot fail to act. . . . From whence it is plain that the soul is of that nature, that she sometimes may awake fatally and necessarily into phantasms and perceptions without any will of her own. Which is found true also in imagination, though that facultie be freer than the former. For what are dreams but the imaginations and perceptions of one asleep?"

(55) II: X: 6, page 148, *symptomes of fear.* See Descartes, *The Passions of the Soul:* I: XXV, XXVI: "Thus, for example, if we see some animal approach us, the light reflected from its body depicts two images of it, one in each of our eyes, and these two images form two others, by means of the optic nerves, in the interior surface of the brain which faces its cavities; then from there, by means of the animal spirits with which its cavities are filled, these images so radiate towards the little gland . . . that the two images which are in the brain form but one upon the gland, which, acting immediately upon the soul, causes it to see the form of the animal. And, besides that, if this figure is very strange and frightful . . . the spirits reflected from the image thus formed on the gland, proceed thence to take their places partly in the nerves which serve to turn the back and dispose the legs for flight, and partly in those which so increase or diminish the orifices of the heart . . . that this blood . . . sends to the brain the spirits which are adapted for the maintenance and strengthening of the passion of fear" (Trans. Haldane and Ross). In the *Divine Dialogues,* "Address of the Publisher to the Reader," More refers with some scorn to Descartes's *Treatise on the Passions,* where the combat between the flesh and the spirit is at last resolved into the ridiculous noddings and joggings of a small glandulous button in the midst of the brain."

IMMORTALITY OF THE SOUL

Book III.

(56) III: XII: 1, page 169, *Spirit of Nature.* See Note on the Soul of the World or the Spirit of Nature, page 302. The conception of the spirit of nature appears in modern philosophy in Fechner's *Ueber die Seelenfrage* (summarized and quoted in James's, *A Pluralistic Universe,*

chapter IV), and plays some part in the nature poetry of the nineteenth century. Wordsworth, for instance, in the ninth book of *The Excursion,* asserts this unity of the life of nature:

" To every form of being is assigned
* * * * * *
An active principle: — howe'er removed
From sense and observation, it subsists
In all things, in all natures; in the stars
Of azure heaven, the unenduring clouds,
In flower and tree, in every pebbly stone
That paves the brooks, the stationary rocks,
The moving waters and the invisible air.
* * * * * *
Spirit that knows no insulated spot,
No chasm, no solitude, from link to link
It circulates, the Soul of all the worlds."

Cudworth like More insists that the activity of the spirit of nature is not mechanical. He seems, however, to question the possibility of an intermediate category between mechanism and consciousness. For in *The Intellectual System,* page 159, he decides that " this controversie whether the energy of the plastic nature be cogitation or no, seems to be but a . . . contention about words. For if clear and express consciousness be supposed to be included in cogitation, then it must needs be granted that cogitation doth not belong to the plastic life of nature; but if the notion of that word be enlarged so as to comprehend all action distinct from local motion, and to be of equal extent with life, then the energy of nature is cogitation."

(57) III: XII: 6, page 171, *attraction of the loadstone.* Descartes, *Principles:* IV: 133 ff.

(58) III: XII: 6, page 171. *Letter to V. C.* William Coward, the V. C. of More's letter was an English physician, born about 1657. In his *Essay* he criticises More's doctrine of spirit on the ground that immaterial substance is unthinkable. Extension is " the essence of body," he urges, " no immaterial substance has extension." and consequently immaterial substance is unreal. He derides the notion of a separate soul as a " heathenish invention," unsupported by evidence. More's letter to V. C. contains a general account of the philosophy of Descartes, defends Descartes against charges of atheism and materialism, and emphasizes his arguments for the existence of God and the reality of spirit. More insists, however, that while Descartes has given satisfactory explanations of all those facts of nature which are subject to mechanical interpretation, there are still many occurrences which are by nature incapable of such interpretation.

(59) III: XVI: 3, page 175, *in my Poems. Philosophical Poems,* " Song of the Soul, Antimonopsychism."

True Notion of Spirit

This translation of chapters 27 and 28 of More's *Enchiridion Meta-physicum* was included in the edition of Joseph Glanvil's *Saducismus Triumphatus* which was edited by More and published in 1681. The core of the *Saducismus* appeared much earlier under the title *Philosophical Considerations concerning Witchcraft*, in which Glanvil argued that the hypothesis of invisible spirits provided the only possible explanation for many undoubted facts. This treatise proved so popular that a fourth edition was brought out in 1668, entitled *A Blow at Modern Saducism*. In 1681 this was republished as *Saducismus Triumphatus* with the addition of letters, postscripts, and "advertisements" by several hands. It includes not only these chapters from the *Enchiridion* but also More's "Further Defence of the True Notion of Spirit, in Answer to a letter of a Psychopyrist" and several letters from More concerning some of the events recounted in Glanvil's "Collection of Relations."

Joseph Glanvil, 1636–1680, of Exeter and Lincoln Colleges, Oxford, was at one time chaplain to one of Cromwell's lords, and later, after the Restoration, chaplain in ordinary to Charles II. Active, versatile, interested in many things, he was a close friend of More with whom he shared particularly his interest in psychical research. Like More he was one of the founders of the Royal Society, but his interest was that of an open and questioning mind, eager for new ideas, rather than that of the worker either in science or in philosophy. His *Vanity of Dogmatizing*, which contains the story of Matthew Arnold's "Scholar Gipsy," is mainly an attack on the scholastic philosophy; the *Lux Orientalis* is a defence of the doctrine of pre-existence of souls. He published also various polemical writings on points of church doctrine and several volumes of exposition of Scripture.

(60) I, page 183, *Nullibists*. Compare *Divine Dialogues:* "Publisher to the Reader." The unusual term "nullibists" first appears, according to the *Oxford Dictionary*, in More's Preface General to the *Collection of Philosophical Writings*. It is used by Doddridge, 1763, in reference to those who "affirm that God is nowhere," by W. Taylor in the *Monthly Magazine*, 1803, as applying to the denial of actual existence in space of physical objects, but is now completely obsolete. The reference to Joseph Glanvil's *Saducismus Triumphatus* given in the *Oxford Dictionary* for the use of the term should be to chapter 27 of More's *Enchiridion Metaphysicum* included in the *Saducismus*.

(61) I, page 184, *Holenmerians*. More apparently coined the word Holenmerians to refer to those who held that the soul, being indivisible, must exist as a whole in each part of the divisible body. See Plotinus, *Enneads:* IV: 2: 1: "When you separate bodies the form within them also divides, but in such a way that it remains entire in each part. . . . The soul entirely inheres in the whole body and in each of its parts ";

and Thomas Aquinas, *Summa Theologia:* I: 76: 8: "The soul is wholly in the whole body and at the same time wholly in each part of the body." This conception of the relation of the soul to the body is historically closely connected with the similar conception of the relation of the universal to particulars.

(62) V, page 188, *Enchiridion Metaphysicum.* In these chapters of the *Enchiridion* More argues that space and matter cannot be identified (1) from the nature of motion, which he holds is inexplicable without the hypothesis of empty space, and (2) from the inconsistency of certain attributes of space, such as infinity, penetrability, and immobility, with the solidity and moveability of matter. See note, page 283, on More's doctrine of the extension of substance.

(63) VI, page 189, *Lambertus Velthusius. Tractatus De Initiis Primae Philosophiae:* "De Ubi": p. 104: "Ubicumque Dei potentia, aut operatio est, illic etiam est Dei natura, cum Deus sit substantia omnis compositionis expers." Velthusius, or Velthuysen, 1622–1685, theologian and physician, was one of the Cartesians of Utrecht, a strong advocate of religious toleration, and the author of several works on moral philosophy and religion besides the *De Initiis* to which More refers. He does not, however, accept the conclusion which More draws from the quotation, but insists that the soul is in the whole body not by virtue of a common extension but rather by immediate presence.

(64) VI, page 190, *Ludovicus de La Forge.* The *Traité de l'Esprit de l'Homme* of La Forge is intended as an exposition of purely Cartesian principles. It illustrates, however, the instability of Cartesianism and its tendency to pass over into occasionalism. Starting from Descartes's difficulty in explaining the action of mind on matter, La Forge emphasizes the dependent character of matter with the consequent dependence of bodily change on the concurrence of God, and insists that the interaction of mind and body is no more incomprehensible than the interaction of separate bodies. He rejects the conception of the extension of soul on the ground that if the soul were extended it would fall under the category of quantity and would therefore be subject to division and to the limitations of physical space. In chapter XII, in answer to some who hold that space is an attribute of all created beings, La Forge urges that when one speaks of the soul as being in a certain place one does not mean that the soul itself is extended, but rather that it is joined to one particular body rather than to another.

(65) VII, page 192, *Cogitation . . . the very substance of the soul.* Descartes, *Principles:* I: LXIII: "We may likewise consider thought and extension as constituting the natures of intelligible and corporeal substance; and then they must not otherwise be considered than as the very substances that think and are extended, *i.e.* as mind and body" (Trans. Haldane and Ross).

(66) VIII, page 193, *The Mind exempt from all extension.* Descartes, *Principles:* I: VIII: "This, then, is the best way to discover the nature of mind and the distinction between it and the body. For, in considering what we are who suppose that all things apart from ourselves (our thought) are false we observe very clearly that there is no extension, figure, local motion, or any such thing . . . which pertains to our nature, but only thought alone" (Trans. Haldane and Ross). See also Descartes's Letters to the Princess Elizabeth.

(67) VIII, page 194, *Enchiridion Ethicum:* III: IV: 3: "Ad perfectam cuiusque rei scientiam requiri ideam, sive notione, non solum claram & distinctam, sed plenam & adequatam, quae omnia attributa inseparabilia quae ei competunt complectatur. Possumus enim vel de industria vel per incuriam subjectum concipere sine aliquibus eorum attributorum quae re ipsa sunt ab ipsa inseparabilia. Quod mihi fecisse videtur Cartesius in notione Animae humanae, dum ea sola cogitatione definit."

(68) IX, page 194, *Velthusius. De Initiis:* "De Ubi," p. 105, 106.

(69) X, page 196, *Object of Imagination.* Descartes, *Meditations:* VI: "When I attentively consider what imagination is, I find it is nothing but a certain application of the faculty of knowledge to the body which is immediately present to it." *Meditations:* II: "To imagine is nothing else than to contemplate the figure . . . of a corporeal thing." Descartes does not, however, hold, as More seems to imply, that the extension itself is the object of the imagination. On the contrary he insists that extension cannot be known by imagination but only by purely intellectual knowledge.

(70) XI, page 198, *The Reasons that induce them to maintain it.* See Plotinus, *Enneads:* IV: 3: 3: "Even for organs whose functions are different, as the eyes and ears, it will not be claimed that there is one part of the soul in the eyes, and another in the ears — such a division would suit only things that have no relation with the soul. We should insist that it is the same part of the soul which animates these two different organs"; and Anselm, *Proslogion:* XIII: "For if the soul were not wholly in every organ of its body it would not be able wholly to have feeling in every member." Augustine likewise argues that it is the same soul which feels a pain in the foot, observes by the eyes, speaks with the tongue, and moves the hands, and that this would be impossible unless the soul were wholly in every part of the body (*De Immortalitate Animae:* XVI: 25). This principle is clearly suggested by Aristotle in *De Anima:* I: V: "The parts of the soul are all found in every one of the bodily divisions, and they are of like kind with each other and with the entire soul."

(71) XII, page 199, *Speak a little more unlearnedly, etc.* Aristophanes, *The Frogs,* 1, 1445. The last word of the quotation, printed as

σαρέστερον, both in the *Enchiridion Metaphysicum* of 1671 and in the *True Notion of Spirit* in the *Saducismus* of 1681, should be, not σαρέστερον, but σαφέστερον.

(72) XVIII, page 208, *Enchirid. Metaphys.* cap. 2. sect. 10. " Praeterea, quod omne Ens fit quantum, ex illius materia intelligitur; quod etiam quale, ex forma & quod alicubi, rursum ex materia. . . . Neque sane esse potest, & tamen numquam esse, hoc est, non aliquando, vel aliquandiu; quorum utrumque moram aliquam includit."

(73) XXIX, page 222, *Enchirid, Eth. III, IV, 3.* " Essentalia attributa immediate competere Subjecto nec rationem ullam physicam peti debere, darive posse, cur insint."

INDEX

This index does not include names of writers that appear only in the Bibliography. For systematic reference to various parts of More's philosophical theory the reader is referred to the Outline, pages 259–271.

331

Printed in the United States
86421LV00005B/11/A

9 781432 588472